MULTIMEDIA
MANIA

Experience the Excitement of Multimedia Computing

- ◆ Sound boards and sound recording
- ◆ Understanding CD-ROM
- ◆ Windows 3.1 and multimedia extension
- ◆ Capturing and editing pictures
- ◆ Using animation
- ◆ The world of MIDI

by Harald Frater and Dirk Paulissen

INCLUDES COMPANION CD-ROM WITH SAMPLE PROGRAMS

Abacus
A Data Becker Book

Copyright © 1993   Abacus
5370 52nd Street SE
Grand Rapids, MI 49512

Copyright © 1992   Data Becker, GmbH
Merowingerstrasse 30
4000 Duesseldorf, Germany

Managing Editor:	Scott Slaughter
Editors:	Louise Benzer, Gene Traas, Robbin Markley
Technical Editors:	Gene Traas, George Miller
Book Design:	Scott Slaughter
Cover Art:	Dick Droste

Library of Congress Cataloging-in-Publication Data

Paulissen, Dirk, 1963-
    Multimedia mania / by Dirk Paulissen, Harald Frater.
        p.   cm.
        Includes index.
        ISBN 1-55755-166-9 : $49.95
        1. Multimedia systems. I. Frater, Harald, 1953-   . II. Title.
    QA76.575.P38   1993
    006.6--dc20
                                        92-44948
                                        CIP

Printed in the U.S.A.

10 9 8 7 6 5 4 3 2

Quick Contents

Multimedia Mania

Contents

Multimedia Mania

Introduction: Read This First

About Abacus

Abacus has published software and computer books since 1978.

As a publisher of computer specialty books, Abacus has published well over three hundred titles in the past thirteen years, with many best-sellers.

We've been successful because we deliver high value, exceptional quality and moderately priced products to the end user. These products include comprehensive, information-packed books and high quality Windows software.

Abacus has sold these products through an extensive network of resellers. Many resellers have been selling Abacus products for over ten years.

We advertise widely and aggressively in many of the major PC magazines.

The Icons

Since multimedia is a new subject for most users, we'll emphasize important tips, ideas and warnings throughout the book. We've found the best way to do this is to have Merlin provide the tips and warnings to you.

Therefore, as you read through **Multimedia Mania**, make certain to notice Merlin's margin icons. These icons indicate that a nearby paragraph or paragraphs are of special interest.

Reference icon

This icon can refer you to additional information about the subject. We'll mention in the paragraph where you'll find the additional information, such as chapter or section number.

Note icon

This icon provides additional information about the current subject. It also indicates the possibility of errors or other problems. Read the highlighted paragraph carefully before continuing.

Hint icon

This icon indicates a tip and trick which will help with your multimedia application.

Companion CD-ROM icon

This icon refers to the companion CD-ROM. You'll see this icon whenever the text refers to information or programs on the companion CD-ROM.

Chapter 1

Multimedia - Smoke and Mirrors?

It informs and educates, persuades and entertains us with dazzling effects of color, animation and sound. From its humble monochrome beginnings, the PC has joined the dazzling world of entertainment and electronic information. With each passing day, we've come to expect even more spectacular sensations and effects.

> *"The most beautiful thing we can experience is the mysterious. It is the source of all true art and science. He who has never known wonder, who cannot be enchanted and captivated in astonishment and awe, is as good as dead. His eyes are closed."*
>
> Albert Einstein

According to all the computer magazines, the hottest new trend in computing is multimedia. Hardware and software developers vying for market share bombard us with new multimedia products daily.

The question we might ask is whether multimedia is really important or if manufacturers are using multimedia to help stimulate a slow hardware market.

Certainly multimedia is more than just a buzzword. But a plethora of confusing definitions may confront a potential user who finds himself (or herself) the target of energetic sales pitches coming from every direction.

Multimedia Overview

This chapter brings some order to this confusion and defines some limits as to what multimedia encompasses. Also, as an overview of its many possible applications, we'll offer some ideas to help you put this latest technological development to work for you.

1.1   What Is Multimedia?

An overwhelming flow of information, varying in style and substance, streams by us continuously in the modern world. We receive and process this information on both conscious and unconscious levels.

For example, walking through a department store, we see an assortment of attractive packages on the shelves, which offer their contents with striking visual appeal. Soft background music subtly increases our readiness to buy, while salespeople eagerly answer questions and promote their wares.

In the larger stores, which have limited personnel, videos present product demonstrations. Strategically placed VCRs and monitors hawk the advantages of a product to passing shoppers. A soothing voice, backed up by a melodious soundtrack, reads from a script designed to anticipate customers' questions.

Everyday Multimedia

Both these cases illustrate components of multimedia. The components deliver information in a variety of ways, but achieve their greatest effectiveness through their interaction. In the first case, packaging, music and sales personnel combine to convey information.

In the second case, technology provides a more effective presentation for less expense. Information, images and sounds are technically and aesthetically integrated, then focused on a single product.

Without going deeper here into the subject of product marketing, the term multimedia describes the use of different media and technologies to present information. The term first appeared in education during the 1960s and 1970s, when it described new media supporting the learning process in classroom instruction.

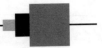

A Problem of Definition

Today the term multimedia has gained a new dimension. Unlike many other areas of computing, multimedia suffers not from the fact that few people understand it, but rather that everyone understands it differently.

The manufacturers should take responsibility for this because few standards exist between products. Any departure from traditional word processing and number crunching is immediately labeled multimedia.

Integration and Interaction

Generally the term multimedia means the integration of text, graphics, sound, animation and video to convey information. A key element of the multimedia concept is interaction.

What is interaction?

The word interaction, from its Latin origins, describes a mutual dealing between two or more people. A dictionary of sociology distinguishes different types of interaction by which communication between people or groups occur through speech, symbols and gestures. This communication results in changes of attitudes, expectations and behavior.

If we apply the same word to computers, interaction means that program execution depends on the user's input; the user can actively control program flow.

In a totally interactive multimedia concept, the user affects the path the information takes. We can apply this concept to our previous example of a shopper watching a promotional video in a store.

The customer should be able to decide which products will be described in the presentation, what details will be given about these products, and whether any of this information will be repeated.

1.2 Multimedia Requirements

Since we are considering multimedia in connection with personal computers, the PC will be the basis of our analysis. Most standard PCs can control multimedia applications, with a few added pieces of hardware.

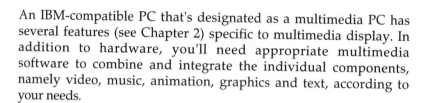

An IBM-compatible PC that's designated as a multimedia PC has several features (see Chapter 2) specific to multimedia display. In addition to hardware, you'll need appropriate multimedia software to combine and integrate the individual components, namely video, music, animation, graphics and text, according to your needs.

The Basic Idea

More important than a knowledge of the tools themselves is the "multimedia idea." Whether you want to compile a music database, create an audio-visual product presentation, or mix a video film with computer animation, the multimedia idea ultimately determines the proper use of hardware and software.

With the PC as the central controller, various devices of communications and entertainment electronics can be managed and coordinated. The type of application determines whether you will use a stereo system, video recorder or camera, or simply the PC by itself.

Integrating all the possibilities can be difficult (and costly). For example, expensive hardware is required to store video sequences in the computer or mix them with other sources. This may also require some experience in electronic image processing to get acceptable results.

However, it's relatively easy (although even here, a little technical know-how doesn't hurt) to record a sound file and place it within a text.

1.3   Uses For Multimedia

In our introduction to the concept of multimedia we've mentioned some practical uses for presenting and conveying information with this technology.

Conveying Information

Since information is distributed so intensively today, the effectiveness of multimedia components is constantly studied and reviewed. Advertisers constantly seek new techniques to appeal to the increasing appetites of potential customers.

In the introduction, we described a sales presentation that uses all the components of the MPC (Multimedia Personal Computer) strategy (although video is not yet included in the official MPC definition):

- Speech

- Sound effects and music

- Graphics

- Animation

- Video

The use of all these components results in a genuinely effective means of conveying information. Presenting and informing are the essential tasks of multimedia.

Interaction

The effectiveness of multimedia is increased even further by incorporating user interaction. Here the user is included in the process, since he or she controls the path and type of information presented. The most successful learning procedures use this type of interaction.

In this section we'll introduce to you some of multimedia's many exciting possibilities. In an armchair excursion through the world of the multimedia PC, we will explore the multimedia terminology, its current uses, and its ongoing development.

Presentation and Information

An important aspect of sales promotion is the presentation of the product. This can be done in various ways, such as direct conversation, a lecture or an advertising film. In any case, it involves the use of several multimedia components. Certainly each means of presentation has its own advantages and disadvantages.

In sales presentations made through conversation or lecture, the seller can answer customer questions and direct the presentation along different lines. However, this method requires a lot of manpower and time. And, except for door-to-door sales, the seller must wait to be approached by the buyer before he can deliver his message.

Mass Marketing

Compare this method with offering products through catalogs or advertising films. These methods are considerably less costly but also less flexible than direct personal sales. An important part of the goal here is to make the product interesting enough to attract a customer who did not himself initiate contact with the seller.

If we mix together all the advantages of the various sales methods and extract their essence, what we get in return is really multimedia:

Products presented on-site (i.e., at a place convenient to the customer), with aesthetic, methodological and educational appeal, with consideration to the user's need for interaction to control information flow.

Quite a big definition. And how does all this theory appear in practice? To answer this question, we can draw on several studies, as well as actual multimedia applications that have been developed to give presentations and convey information.

Product presentations are found almost anyplace people gather. Trade shows are a good example. Many companies specialize in promotional materials, including multimedia presentations, for leading businesses. These firms developed an interactive information terminal at which trade show attendees can view clients' products.

In this system, various information in the form of text and "films" (digitized photos and motion pictures) can be accessed from a touch-screen monitor. For example, at an auto industry trade show, users can press a button, for example, to select "*New products*" after a brief introduction about the current line of motors.

In "*Applications*" they are presented with a search tree showing typical utility vehicle categories and the motors intended for these categories. Selecting a motor type starts one of the above-mentioned films.

Another presentation designed for the trade show circuit represents multimedia in its highest form. The product is an electrical circuit breaker, represented by an animated cartoon character named Schalti (from the German word for breaker), who speaks in a voice that sounds something like TV's ALF.

In a conversation with a live moderator, Schalti explains his features and his benefits. Other components on the stage are coordinated with the dialog. Additional monitors show pictures and graphics to help Schalti illustrate his point.

Since the moderator can control the action and dialog using buttons not visible to the spectators, this state-of-the-art presentation has a delightful spontaneity and flair.

Multimedia As a Planning Aid

Three-dimensional processing techniques literally add another dimension to product presentations. In the computer-aided design of a trade show booth, for example, the client can experience the atmosphere of the proposed setup while still in the planning phase.

By changing the observer's perspective and adding typical trade show sound effects (music, background conversation, announcements, etc.), the computer creates the illusion of reality.

Virtual Reality

In virtual reality, such illusion gets yet another twist. The user takes a participative role at the center of the action, not only seeing and hearing his surroundings, but manipulating them with natural body movements.

In Chapter 12 we'll discuss how using a data glove or data suit worn by the user, converts and transfers actual movements to the simulated space of the computer screen. This allows the user to "virtually" open a door, for example.

Simulation lowers costs

Simulation is an important application of virtual reality. It is useful in medicine, air travel, military maneuvers and other situations where a safer or less expensive alternative to "actual reality" is desired.

Architecture and Landscape

Multimedia provides another form of presentation simulation in the area of city and landscape planning. Architectural proposals are visualized by overlaying landscape pictures with those of the proposed structures.

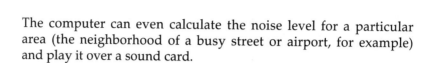

The computer can even calculate the noise level for a particular area (the neighborhood of a busy street or airport, for example) and play it over a sound card.

A customer can click on a home design and move through the rooms, adding and arranging furniture, selecting colors and patterns, and viewing the overall effect of all components to aid the decision process, like the client designing a booth in our earlier example.

Information Terminals

Presentation and information systems are located in the reception areas of many major businesses. They provide an interesting way for visitors to learn about the firm and its products when they are calling on prospective business partners.

Whether multimedia PCs or sleek futuristic terminals, these systems deliver their messages through cleverly combined multimedia components. By selecting menu items, the user can retrieve specific information, again presented using text, graphics or animation.

Many vendors think it's important that an information terminal not look like a computer. In such cases, color and design are used to overcome a fear of computer technology, which many people still have.

Touch screen monitors are helpful in these instances. This type of screen has a touch-sensitive surface that eliminates the need for conventional input devices like the mouse and keyboard. The user selects an option from the display with the press of a fingertip. Many automated teller machines have used touch screens for some time.

Multimedia Wall Systems

Another multimedia system fills an entire wall. These wall systems, which use whole arrays of monitors to maximize visual impact, offer interesting possibilities for alternating and juxtaposing multiple images.

Networking with Multimedia

Cebit '92 marked IBM's unveiling of a LAN (Local Area Network)-based multimedia application. The showcase for this concept involves company-wide distribution of IBM's employee "TV magazine" *Tele-Report* over the IBM Token-Ring Network.

Live video sequences are displayed in one window of OS/2 Presentation Manager, allowing employees to follow the news on-screen as they work. The continuous central information capability ensures quick intercommunication among divisions.

Ultimedia

IBM also offers its exclusive Ultimedia concept, employing multimedia hardware and software in a form of audio-visual communication that will eventually become publicly available through the installation of broadband networking called ISDN (Integrated Services Digital Network).

The Ultimedia systems are not guaranteed to run MPC software possibly because IBM believes that OS/2 is better suited than Windows when integrating sound and pictures (especially moving pictures).

Multimedia Databases

As a natural extension to the concept of databases, multimedia offers extraordinary power to unlock these huge storehouses of theoretical knowledge, and help the user through their almost boundless archives.

In a process called hypertext searching, a researcher can research information by following a thread that links the topic of interest with other subject areas.

Structuring through hypertext

Hypertext technique

The hypertext technique uses the multi-level structure of a database. Like cross-references to related topics in an encyclopedia entry, clicking hyperguides (specially marked key words in hypertext) provide cross-referencing.

Additional options permit scanning the entire text sequentially and re-tracing your steps with the History function.

Of course, the real impact of multimedia is achieved only when the application goes beyond text display, effectively integrating sound, animation and graphics. For example, animation can clearly demonstrate the workings of the heart and circulatory system, or complex processes in the natural sciences.

Sound gives the user an opportunity to hear the musical works of famous composers. For these purposes, animation and sound surpass the capabilities of the written word.

Microsoft Bookshelf

Several databases are available in CD-ROM format. Microsoft Bookshelf offers a full assortment of such resources, including an encyclopedia, an atlas, two books of quotations, a dictionary, a thesaurus and an almanac on one CD-ROM.

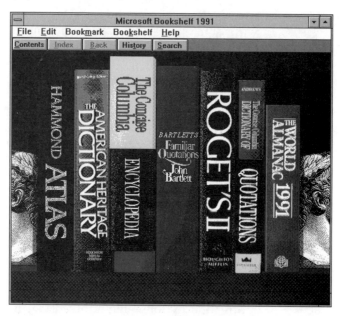

Microsoft Bookshelf

An important feature of the Bookshelf is its cross-referencing capability. When searching for a specific term, the user obtains a cross-reference of all seven books.

Compton's Family Encyclopedia

Also notable is Compton's Family Encyclopedia. It's designed help develop research skills. It features all 26 volumes of the 1991 print edition on "Compton's Encyclopedia" which includes over 8 million words and 24,000 graphs, illustrations and maps.

Tourist information

Tourists can prepare their next vacation with the help of a country database that incorporates articles, photos, native music and even foreign-language speech recordings for their country of interest.

Great Cities Of The World Volume 1

Great Cities of the World, Volume 1 from InterOptica offers information on ten major cities on six continents. The information includes descriptions of hotels, sightseeing opportunities, and typical music. A second edition, called Great Cities Of The World, Volume 2 offers information on ten more cities.

Beethoven's music

Beethoven: Symphony No. 9

A rather unusual and interesting product is the CD-ROM Beethoven: Symphony No. 9. In addition to factual accounts of the artist and his life, it includes a detailed analysis of the Ninth Symphony, using sound samples of individual passages. The symphony can also be played in its entirety, with explanatory text accompanying the music.

Beethoven:String Quartet No. 14

This CD is a comprehensive exploration of Beethoven's String Quartet No.14 and includes historical information and pictures.

A look at the advertisements in multimedia periodicals reveals the variety of offerings already available on CD-ROM. Bird guides, aircraft lexicons, medical questions and answers, terrorist group profiles, country data from the CIA, complete information on the Gulf War on the CD-ROM Desert Storm—all these incorporate multimedia in some way.

The Complete Audubon

An example is The Complete Audubon from CMC Research. It includes over 500 full-color bird lithographs, 150 lithographs of mammals, and bird songs and mammal calls.

Foreign databases

Wer Liefert Was? (Who Supplies What?)

Wer Liefert Was? (Who Supplies What?) is a worldwide trade company which has published a CD-ROM containing 118,000 companies from Germany, Austria and Switzerland. The disk contains connections between different products, services, suppliers, etc. The software searches for products, companies, postal codes, etc.

Medical Databases

The Family Doctor

The Family Doctor from CMC Research is an easy-to-understand medical reference guide. This guide contains answers to 2000 most asked questions about different diseases, injuries, infections, etc. It also contains an illustration of the human anatomy. A consumer guide to more than 1600 prescription drugs, dosages, side effects, etc. is also included.

Pediatrics MEDLINE

Pediatrics MEDLINE, edited by David G. Nathan, M.D. and Robert A. Stranahan, M.D., includes all articles by the National Library of Medicine.

These articles include clinical treatment and research of diseases, behav ioral disorders, injuries, etc. in infants and children. Also includes excerpts from several children's medical magazines and journals. There are over 260,000 reviews and clippings from the past 5 years.

Education and Multimedia

In recent years, Computer Based Training (CBT) has become a popular educational medium. Even before the multimedia blitz, many different learning systems appeared, using the components and techniques we now associate with the term multimedia.

Interaction as the crucial element

The most important aspect of a learning program, aside from the content itself, is interaction. Staged learning dictates that the student can repeat a lesson or part of a lesson at will until he or she masters that lesson.

Through interaction, the student sets his or her own pace, determining when and what to study. Chapters can be skipped, too, if desired. Many interactive programs display the answer to a question automatically after allowing the student a certain number of unsuccessful tries.

Increasing efficiency

Multimedia components, such as graphics, animation and sound, augment the learning process through visualization. As we said in the discussion of databases, animation can explain many complex subjects better than text. ·

The auto industry uses multimedia programs to show trainees how engines and transmissions operate. Constant effort is required to upgrade skills in keeping with accelerating technological development in this field.

In-house training with the help of multimedia programs helps businesses stay competitive, while avoiding costly instructors and facilities, and the rigid scheduling constraints of standard educational institutions.

Language training

Programs called vocabulary trainers can be used in the earliest stages of foreign-language instruction. Terms are displayed on the screen from a programmed dictionary as the student enters their translation. Working exclusively with text, however, such programs can only reinforce traditional classroom teaching.

The sound capabilities of multimedia can greatly enhance the effectiveness of computerized language instruction. With speech output, the student is no longer dependent on an instructor for proper pronunciation. This makes home study a viable alternative. Graphics and music can contribute additional information and enjoyment to the study of foreign lands.

Learn To Speak French

A few examples of foreign languages include Learn To Speak French from the HyperGlot Software Company. It emphasizes speaking and aural comprehension skills. The 39 lessons are read by native French speakers.

Languages of the World

Languages of the World gives you instant translations, definitions, and synonyms of 132 language combinations and more than seven million words. You can select from one of the twelve languages on the CD-ROM and search for its translation or full dictionary entry. You can also search for headwords or subheadwords.

Training through simulation

Some learning programs act as simulators, predicting results based on user input. One example is a photography training program that exists in CD-I (Compact Disk Interactive) format. By experimenting with the simulated results of different shutter speeds, lighting conditions, and so on, a student can spare the cost of expensive photographic materials, even a camera, while refining his techniques.

Application Tutorials

Every major software application today has its own tutorial, whether it be Excel, Word for Windows or Works. It acquaints the user step-by-step with the program's use and features. The Microsoft Works tutorial is a multimedia application in itself.

Tutorials for children

Many educational programs have been prepared in comic or nursery-story style for children. These object-oriented tutorials let the child choose an object to learn about by clicking it with the mouse.

Just Grandma and Me

Just Grandma and Me from Broderbund is a multimedia application that includes animation and sound in the data that runs when objects are selected.

The main character, called Little Critter, faces different adventures from riding on a wind-blown umbrella to snorkeling.

Where In The World Is Carmen Sandiego?

Another multimedia application designed for children from Broderbund is Where In The World Is Carmen Sandiego? The Deluxe Edition includes hundreds of animations, over 3200 clues, and 150 digitized traditional and folk songs.

Object-oriented learning programs can be easily created with the help of multimedia authoring systems.

Authoring Systems

Authoring systems are an important factor in creating multimedia applications. These systems allow the creation of applications without detailed programming knowledge. The developer assigns graphic objects to screen pages using an event tree or flowline. When an object is activated, the underlying function executes.

ToolBook

Multimedia authoring systems, such as ToolBook from Asymetrix, integrate text, sound, graphics, animation and video. These components can be assigned to certain objects or events. The object in this case includes a property that determines how it will behave when activated.

ToolBook implements hypertext using "hotwords", or defined areas within text which a user can click with a mouse.

You can even control a CD-ROM drive and sound card in applications created with Toolbook.

Individual training

Some professional firms go beyond providing authoring systems as program development environments, to providing a complete spectrum of services for computer users.

Every stage of system development, from the idea of forming an application, to the right choice of hardware and software to handle the client's needs, even the development of special training facilities, can be provided by these consultants.

Of course, such individual, problem-oriented solutions, while highly effective, do have their price. Major companies can decrease this expense by eliminating the need to send employees off-site for training seminars in the standard applications.

Multimedia In Standard Applications

In addition to the "pure" multimedia applications, there are many programs that can integrate some areas of multimedia. We'll discuss later in this book how Microsoft Windows applications fit into this area.

A variety of applications support the creation of particular multimedia files. Video images can be captured using overlay functions, then manipulated with the appropriate image processing software. The Windows Sound Recorder and Media Player applications provide easy methods of creating speech and music files.

A multimedia authoring system is not always necessary to integrate multimedia components. The question often arises whether linking a digitized video image in Microsoft Word for Windows can be called multimedia. Since many people use such media combinations effectively, isn't this multimedia?

Sound files can already be integrated as objects in other applications under Microsoft Windows 3.1. You can link a digitized video image in Write using the Clipboard, accompanied by an embedded sound file. When you double-click the sound file to play it, the result has a multimedia feel to it.

Video image in Write with embedded sound file

Excel and multimedia

Microsoft Excel 4 carries this one step further. While the ability to place graphics into an Excel worksheet using the Clipboard has been around for some time, the use of sound notes represents a new development in the direction of multimedia. Any worksheet cell can be assigned a Microsoft Wave format (*.WAV) sound file.

These can even be recorded from external audio sources, such as a stereo connected to your computer through a sound card. This means you could create a musical theme database, or add voice annotations to worksheet calculations.

See Section 5.8 for more information on sound notes.

Excel also offers the ability to create slideshows, in which graphic sequences can be coordinated with music and other multimedia effects.

Microsoft MDK

Since its release in the fall of 1991, the Multimedia Development Kit from Microsoft has made available on CD all the necessary tools for manipulating multimedia files, such as graphics, sound, and MIDI data. These can be captured, modified, mixed and converted.

The incorporation of the MDK tools into a programming environment such as Visual Basic, C, or Toolbook, allows the integration of multimedia components in accordance with the MPC definition. A series of manuals accompanying the MDK describe in detail the development of a multimedia application.

Games

The use of sound cards for games is becoming more and more common. They greatly increase a game's appeal with realistic sound effects and background music. The Wing Commander game is an example of successful use of this technology.

The CD-ROM format is also becoming increasingly popular for games. One that is included in many multimedia kits is Jones in the Fast Lane from Sierra On-Line. Up to four players can pursue their dreams of career, money, education and good fortune, almost as in real life.

In the game Sherlock Holmes: Consulting Detective from Icon Simulations, you sharpen and test your detective skills, as graphics, voice, music and digitized video immerse you in the role of the famous sleuth.

Sherlock Holmes: Consulting Detective

Multimedia chess

The popular Battle Chess game from Interplay is another example of game meeting multimedia. The latest version of Battle Chess, packaged on CD-ROM, features animation, CD audio and sound effects.

1.4   1984 and Multimedia's Future

As you can see from this introduction to multimedia's possibilities and present-day realities, it will play a pivotal role in the communication systems of the future.

Orwell's 1984

As television, telephone and video recording technology continue to evolve, the PC will emerge as the connecting link for all these components. Videotelephone communication via PC is feasible— all that's needed is a long-range ISDN network for fast, error-free data transmission.

ISDN implementation will take a few years. In the meantime, the rapid pace of development brings to mind George Orwell's 1984, a "future" whose communication process reveals a darker side as it draws home and hearth ever more into its grasp.

Private Video Productions

Professional advertising and marketing consultants may be hurt by the advance of multimedia. Like desktop publishing (DTP), once smugly dismissed by professional typesetters, desktop video (DTV) will tempt hobby users to profit from their video image processing skills and capabilities.

The advantages are obvious:

- Video presentation production costs will be lowered

- Many smaller businesses will invigorate supply and demand

- The entry threshold for vendors will be lowered through low-cost solutions

- There will be increasing segmentation and specialization by application type

- A more colorful video culture will emerge

Simulation

The use of multimedia simulation by scientists and researchers will continue to grow. Effective simulations can provide faster, safer, and less expensive methods of training and research than many real life situations.

The height of this technology is virtual reality, which creates an illusion of reality that includes movement and touch. The data glove, now used largely in a recreational context, will replace other types of control, such as keyboard entry, in more serious applications, such as robotics.

Who Wins With Multimedia?

Who has the most to gain from multimedia development? Does the user, who can finally use the full capabilities of his or her PC, win? Or do hardware and software vendors, who see (and perhaps create) a new market to bolster falling profits, win?

Whatever the case, multimedia represents a growth market, from which many companies can profit.

How long-isolated hardware, such as Commodore's CDTV (Commodore Dynamic Total Vision), can hold out depends entirely on the buyer. Fortunately, the computer industry is now ready and willing to face new development with clearly defined standards and cooperation among competitors.

The overlap between computer and entertainment electronics makes this issue critical. For multimedia to succeed, it must be affordable, and meet the needs of a large and varied user base.

Sound and video will likely become a more significant part of popular applications, such as word processors and spreadsheets. However we use multimedia, it's likely to become a major force in how we use our computers in the future.

Chapter 2

Multimedia Theory

Multimedia combines various technologies into a single application. Some of these technologies were originally used by professionals. Because of this, today's multimedia users are confronted with new terminology and procedures that were once limited to specialists in diverse fields.

Several features determine the audio and video performance specifications of a particular multimedia system.

What are the basics?
First we'll discuss the basics of multimedia technologies, such as audio, CD-ROM, and electronic image processing. We'll also discuss printer fundamentals. Also, we'll explain technical terms and concepts in plain English so that they are easy to understand, even for a multimedia novice.

2.1 The MPC Definition

The Multimedia PC Marketing Council, consisting of Microsoft and other leading hardware and software manufacturers, published a multimedia standard in a text called the Red Book.

This standard was intended to apply to future developments in PC multimedia. The Windows graphical user interface forms the foundation of this standard, enhanced by multimedia software components and programming tools.

MPC as a marketing symbol

Initially the Microsoft Windows Multimedia Extension provided the software interface to Windows 3.0 for multimedia products from a variety of manufacturers.

The corresponding multimedia drivers and interfaces have since been incorporated into Windows 3.1 (see Chapter 4).

Using CD-ROM drives for memory-intensive graphics and sound file processing places rigorous demands on PC hardware. Both sound cards and CD-ROMs are specified as components of the Multimedia PC (MPC) standard.

A PC configuration must include all components and meet all specifications defined in the standard to qualify for the MPC seal.

The MPC seal

Hardware manufacturers wishing to submit their products for MPC approval must apply to the Multimedia PC Marketing Council in New York. Approval certifies that the product fulfills the requirements of the MPC standard.

The MPC Standard

A personal computer system that has qualified for the MPC title has specific characteristics that make it suitable for multimedia use.

The initial standard adopted by the Multimedia PC Marketing Council was modest enough so owners of Intel 80286 based computers could enjoy the benefits of multimedia.

Although the following specifications were later upgraded, they formed the first definition of the MPC standard:

First MPC Standard

•   80286 based PC

•   Minimum 10 MHz clock speed

•   2 Meg main memory (RAM), configured as extended memory

- 30 Meg hard drive capacity

- 1.44 Meg 3.5-inch disk drive

- 101-key IBM keyboard

- Serial interface (9-pin or 25-pin), programmable up to 9600 baud, selectable without interrupts

- Parallel interface (25-pin)

- VGA card and monitor with 640 x 480 pixel resolution, 16 colors

- Mouse (2-button)

- Analog joystick port (IBM-compatible)

- MIDI port

- MPC-compatible sound card

- MPC-compatible CD-ROM drive

- System software compatible with Microsoft Windows Multimedia Extension

However, soon it was obvious that basing the multimedia specification on the Microsoft Windows platform would lead to performance problems on the system previously described.

System software   In discussing system software, it was important to consider both the user interface and compatible APIs (Application Programming Interfaces) and the related functional and performance features.

These features include those provided in the Microsoft Windows Software Development Kit (SDK), Volume I and II (Version 3.0), and in the Microsoft Multimedia Development Kit (MDK).

These interfaces and extensions helped make Windows, which is both powerful and user-friendly, a reasonable choice for the multimedia standard.

However, the minimum hardware configuration was soon upgraded to give this software the power it needed to run effectively.

Current MPC Standard

The standard now includes the following specifications:

- 386 or higher

- 80386SX based PC

- Minimum 16 MHz clock speed

- 2 Meg main memory (RAM), configured as extended memory

- 30 Meg hard drive capacity

- 1.44 Meg 3.5-inch disk drive

- 101-key IBM keyboard

- Serial interface (9-pin or 25-pin), programmable up to 9600 baud, selectable without interrupts

- Parallel interface (25-pin)

- VGA card and monitor with 640 x 480 pixel resolution, 256 colors; or 800 x 600 pixel resolution, 16 colors

- Mouse (2-button)

- Analog joystick port (IBM-compatible)

- MIDI port

- MPC-compatible sound card

- MPC-compatible CD-ROM drive

- System software compatible with Microsoft Windows Multimedia Extension

Remember that the MPC logo does not guarantee the quality of the products, only that the products have met the specifications of the MPC Council. Therefore, you should look for the MPC specifications and not necessarily the MPC logo when shopping for a multimedia system.

The general rule concerning hardware is: the faster the better. Clock speed, hardware cache, disk access and the speed of the graphics card are deciding factors in PC performance under Windows.

Even with a fast processor, system performance can be seriously hindered by a slow video card or hard drive. Microsoft states that MPC specifications describe a minimal configuration, which should be upgraded as required.

An example of a complete MPC computer is the Sensation® from Radio Shack.

The Radio Shack Sensation is a complete multimedia PC

Sensation not only includes software but also a large library of ready-to-use CD-ROMs and multimedia versions of Microsoft Bookshelf for Windows and Tandy WinMate.

Additional items include fax capability, headphones, voice mail, CD-ROM drive, clip art, microphone, FM synthesis and more.

For information on upgrading system performance under Windows, see Chapter 3.

Speakers and Microphones

Active and passive

A sound card, like a stereo system, is only as good as its speaker system. They can be either active or passive. Active speakers have their own built-in amplifiers and volume controls. These speakers boost the sound received from the sound card output.

Power supply

Active speakers require batteries or a separate power supply. We recommend using a power supply, since batteries can wear out quickly.

Passive speakers play the sound card output without further modification. Volume is controlled at the card itself. With a sound card capable of 4 watts at 4 ohms per stereo channel, ordinary passive speakers, like those used on most stereo systems, are suitable.

Car speakers also work well, since they are compact and produce high-quality sound. This also applies to speakers designed for use with a Walkman®. These are enclosed in finished cases and are affordable.

Voice input through a microphone

A sound card meeting MPC specifications has a microphone connector, which you can use to record voice or sound effects. Using the programs of the Microsoft Windows Multimedia Extension, you can create, edit and play your own sound files.

A good microphone should have the following features:

Microphone Features	
Feature	**Ideal setting**
Impedance	600 ohms
Sensitivity	74 decibels (dB) or higher

If excellent recording quality isn't a major factor, the built-in microphone of a portable stereo recorder should be sufficient.

Games and joysticks

Several games already use sound cards to create extremely realistic sound effects. In many of these games, the player moves a joystick to guide the cursor on the screen, then triggers a certain action at the desired position by pushing the fire button. Most sound cards have a joystick connector.

Normally the analog joysticks that are used with personal computers must be calibrated before you can use them. Refer to the documentation for your applications for more information on joystick calibration.

Performance features of CD-ROM drives and sound cards, along with their minimum MPC specifications, are explained in the following section.

Sound card requirements

Sound cards generate, record or play back sounds of any kind. These sounds include speech, music and sound effects. Besides recording over a microphone or stereo system connected to your sound card, you can create and record your own musical compositions on special synthesizers or keyboards attached through a MIDI interface.

Connection options

Microphone and Line-in connector

In addition to a sound card's general performance capabilities, the connections it offers to external audio sources is also important. You should be able to connect your sound card to a microphone and to a stereo system.

With these capabilities, you can make music, radio and voice recordings, and even mix microphone input with other audio signals.

As an alternative to direct microphone input, you can connect your sound card to another device (e.g., a tape player) through the Line-in connector. This allows you to record sounds at remote locations and then transfer them to your computer.

Speaker connection

Obviously, another important connection is for speakers. As we mentioned, you can use active or passive speakers, depending on your needs and your sound card's output capacity.

Software volume control

Volume is usually controlled by appropriate software. Almost all sound cards have a mixer program, which not only regulates output volume, but enables separate volume control for each input and output signal.

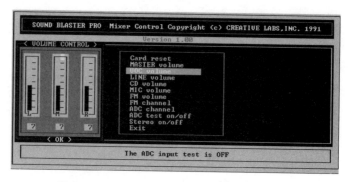

Volume control for the Sound Blaster Pro

Additional features offered by some cards are a balance control (independent settings for the left and right stereo channels) and a volume control on the back of the card.

MIDI

Another important connection, which is also part of the MPC standard, is a MIDI interface. MIDI (Music Instrument Digital Interface) is a standardized (manufacturer-independent) file format for recording and exchanging musical instrument sound data.

Besides the actual musical notes, a MIDI file contains information such as dynamics, articulations, and instrument types. When played, the music is created by a sound card's synthesizer chips or by a synthesizer connected through a MIDI interface.

MIDI interface

The MIDI interface is a special connector over which MIDI data is sent to a MIDI device (MIDI OUT), or received from a MIDI device (MIDI IN). This usually connects to the joystick port of a sound card, and may in turn contain its own joystick port.

The MIDI interface allows the use of MIDI devices, such as synthesizers for reproducing songs and keyboards for entering songs. Sequencer programs can also create MIDI files.

These programs usually display an organ-like keyboard on the screen, which can be "played" with the mouse or computer keys. You can record your own compositions and store them in MIDI format.

MIDI files can subsequently be edited by any program that processes the MIDI format.

We'll discuss this in more detail in Chapter 8.

Some sound cards permit the use of a CD-ROM drive, usually by means of an integrated AT bus on the card. In other cases, a CD-ROM drive is connected through a SCSI interface, which requires an additional controller.

It's also possible to connect a CD-ROM drive to a sound card so audio data is played over the sound card directly.

Sound reproduction

Built-in amplifier Sound reproduction in stereo is a minimum requirement for sound card selection. There are also other factors to consider when evaluating output quality and performance. Power is measured in watts, as it is for stereo systems.

Typical sound cards deliver from 1 to 6 watts per stereo channel at 4 ohms. Although this doesn't sound like much, it's actually quite sufficient. Most stereos, even the less expensive ones, are capable of at least 35 watts per channel.

However, only 1 to 2 watts are needed for normal room listening volume.

Another measure of sound reproduction capability is the number of synthesizer voices that can be produced per stereo channel. The process of frequency modulation can generate some very pleasant synthesized sounds.

In frequency modulation, the electrical oscillations that represent a sound can be adjusted, thus generating a different type of sound.

Although this process may seem complicated, it's easily accomplished with the proper software and hardware. Most sound cards offer 11 voices per stereo channel.

The special FM chips found in sound cards (e.g., Yamaha) create the familiar background for many games and other synthesizers.

MPC specification The following lists the major sound card requirements of the MPC standard:

Sound Card Requirements
External connections
Microphone
Speakers / headphones
Stereo system
MIDI devices
CD-ROM drive

Sound Card Requirements
Input and output
Built-in amplifier
Synthesizer
Stereo channels
8-bit DAC / ADC (16-bit recommended)
22.05 KHz sampling rate (44.1 KHz recommended)

CD-ROM Drive Requirements

A CD-ROM drive must meet certain performance specifications for data transfer to qualify for the MPC seal. However, the minimum transfer rate required by the MPC definition (150K/sec) produces disappointing results in animation. The motion will look jerky if your CD drive cannot keep up with the huge quantities of graphics data involved.

Audio functions According to the Red Book specifications, a CD-ROM must have audio capability, which means that it can play your conventional audio CDs.

You connect it to your sound card for output. You also need a headphone connector that taps into the audio signal. The volume of the audio output can be adjusted through a separate volume control, which is usually located on the front of the CD-ROM drive.

Access time　Mean access time cannot exceed 1 second. This seems pretty slow when you consider that large hard drives work with access times of under 20 ms. Even floppy drives are faster.

Data transfer rate　Another measure of data access speed is the data transfer rate. According to the standard, the minimum is 150K per second. Hard drive controllers operate with transfer rates of 250 - 500K/sec (the MFM process) and 600 - 900K/sec (the RLL process). Using a SCSI interface, it's possible to achieve parallel transfer rates as high as 4 Meg/sec.

The size of the data block read must be at least 16K. The execution time cannot exceed the time required to read a data block into the CD-ROM buffer.

Here a data transfer rate of 150K/sec would yield a maximum CPU efficiency of 40%. We recommend that the drive have a 64K data buffer.

Driver software　An appropriate system driver is required for the operating system to recognize the CD-ROM drive. MSCDEX.EXE Version 2.2 meets this requirement. This driver implements the extended audio functions of the API.

Alternatively, the CD-ROM XA (Extended Architecture) can be used, in which audio data is stored separately from other data. This makes it possible to read audio data and video data, for example, in parallel.

Data security　Another specification involves the data security of a CD-ROM drive. The standard requires a minimum MTBF (Mean Time Before Failure) of 10,000 hours. This means that an error can be expected to occur after an average of 10,000 hours.

Of course this is just an average, and absolute safety can never be guaranteed. You could be unlucky and have trouble after only five hours. However, generally, the higher the MTBF value, the more reliable the drive should be.

MPC specification overview　The following is a summary of the key features of a CD-ROM drive as defined by the MPC standard:

CD-ROM Drive Key Features
Features
Data transfer rate of 150 K/sec
Mean access time of 1 second or less
Headphone output
Separate volume control for headphone output
CPU access less than 40%
Audio function (CD - DA)
MTBF of 10,000 hours
MSCDEX.EXE driver support, Version 2.2

2.2 Audio Technology - Sound

As we continue to discuss sound cards, we'll use certain terms to describe the qualities or performance features of a particular card. These terms originated from the fields of acoustics and electronic music. We'll define these terms as we use them in this section.

In this section we'll present a general introduction to the subject of sound. We'll examine how sounds are made, then how a sound card generates sound. We'll use easy-to-understand language to explain specialized terminology and concepts that will appear in subsequent chapters.

Sound Basics

Any technical discussion of sound, regardless of whether the sound is music, speech, or simply noise, is based on the concept of sound waves. A sound wave is a physical disturbance, which we interpret subjectively as sound. Music, speech, thunder, and everything we hear reaches our ears as sound waves. So we'll begin our discussion of sound by studying the physical properties of sound waves.

Producing sound waves

A simple experiment demonstrates how sound waves are produced. You'll need a metal or wood ruler for this experiment. Place the ruler flat on a hard table top, perpendicular to the edge, so that about one half of the ruler extends off the table top.

Pressing one hand on the ruler, close to the edge of the table top, press and quickly release the "loose" edge of the ruler with the other hand. The ruler will vibrate. The more ruler hanging in space, the slower the vibrations, and the lower the sound.

Conversely, the less ruler hanging in space, the faster the vibrations, and the higher the sound. When the vibrations stop, so does the sound.

Tuning forks

Borrow a tuning fork from a musician friend, or buy one from a music store (ask for an inexpensive A-440 tuning fork). If you've never handled a tuning fork before, ask the friend or salesperson how to use it.

Hold the handle in your hand, and strike one of the tines of the tuning fork against your knee. It generates a tone, and you can see the tines of the tuning fork vibrate.

When the vibrations stop, so does the sound. Actually, the vibrations eventually become so slight that our ears cannot hear the sound.

Strike the tuning fork on your knee again, and place the tuning fork tines in a glass of water while holding the tuning fork handle. The vibrations cause ripples (concentric rings) in the water. In water, these vibrations move water molecules, which move adjacent water molecules.

The water shows you what happens in the air. A series of concentric sound waves moves away from the vibrating object, as air molecules alternately compress and decompress. We hear the sound when these waves reach our ears.

Cannot travel in a vacuum

Sound cannot travel through a vacuum. A medium (substance), such as air, must exist, through which vibrations can travel.

The time it takes for a sound to reach our ears depends on our distance from the sound's source and on the medium through which the sound must travel. You can hear an approaching train sooner with your ear to the rail because iron carries sound faster and farther than air.

Airspeed of sound

When we speak of the speed of sound, we refer specifically to its speed in air. This is about 1088 ft/sec (340 m/sec). Although the medium affects the speed at which a sound travels, the source of the sound does not.

When we listen to a symphony orchestra, the different instrument parts reach us at once, regardless of our distance from the stage.

For a precise description of the properties of sound, we must use a few specialized terms from the field of physics.

Visualizing sound

As we've seen, a sound travels in waves created by the vibration of molecules in a medium. These waves can be measured, recorded, and thus ultimately processed electronically.

Sound wave activity can be observed on an instrument called an oscilloscope. Sound waves appear on a screen as a curve. An oscillogram is a picture of an oscilloscope reading.

The curve on an oscilloscope representing the vibrations (oscillations) of a sound wave, possesses some specific properties.

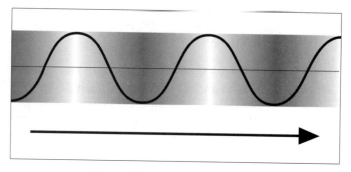

The oscillation as a sine wave

The basic oscillation of a pure tone, like many natural processes, forms a sine wave. The height of the wave from the middle line to the wave's highest (or lowest) point is called the amplitude.

Periods

One cycle is the movement described by the wave, beginning at the middle line, then proceeding through the upper and the lower extensions of the wave, to arrive at the middle line again.

The time required for this cycle to occur is called the period. The term "frequency" describes the number of cycles per unit of time, expressed in a measurement unit called Hertz (Hz):

```
1 Hz = 1 cycle / sec.
```

The following illustrates different cycles or Hertz:

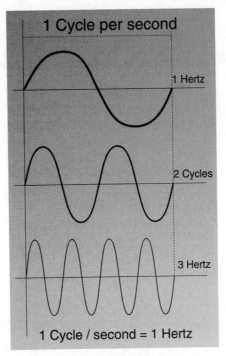

Kilohertz and megahertz

Since sound often deals with very high frequencies, you'll often see units called kilohertz and megahertz.

```
1 kilohertz (KHz) = 1,000 Hz
1 megahertz (MHz) = 1,000,000 Hz (1,000 KHz)
```

Period and frequency are reciprocal values. A frequency of 22 KHz implies a period of 1/22000 sec. (1 second / number of cycles). Conversely, a period of 1/5 sec means a frequency of 5 Hz. The relationship can be expressed as follows:

```
Frequency = 1 / period
```

So how do the properties of these oscillations affect a sound? You'll remember our experiments with a ruler and tuning fork earlier. The intensity with which you strike a tuning fork varies the amplitude (volume) of the fork—the frequency (A-440) should remain the same. Changing the ruler's position on the table changes the frequency sounded, and the intensity with which you "twang" the ruler changes the amplitude.

Thus, an increase in amplitude means an increase in volume (loudness).

If you get a tuning fork set at a different pitch (e.g., C-523.251), you can see that the period of the oscillations changes.

Relationship of oscillation to volume

The higher the frequency (or the lower the period), the higher the pitch, and vice versa.

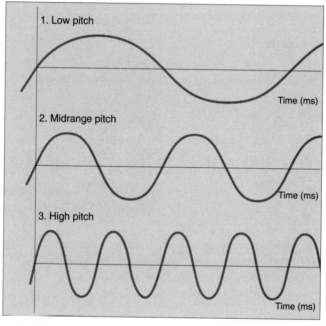

Harmonic tones This refers to a *harmonic* tone—a "pure" tone characterized by a sine wave. More complex sounds like speech and music appear as very irregular patterns on an oscilloscope. This is because the overall wave form comes from interference—several basic wave forms superimposed on one another.

These basics should give you a general understanding of the concept of sound. Now we'll discuss electronic sound recording.

Conversion to electronic oscillations

You may be wondering how an acoustical sound wave is converted to a form that can be processed by electronic devices such as sound cards. Consider how a microphone records sound. The microphone "picks up" vibrations in the air, rather than the sound itself.

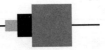

Sounds are analog information

A microphone consists of mechanical parts and electrical parts. The microphone's vibration-sensitive membrane picks up a sound. This vibration is converted by the electrical parts to an analog electronic oscillation.

Analog means that the oscillation is measured by a continuum of values, not by discrete steps. The hour hand on an analog watch constantly moves from one hour to the next and will occupy every position between the two hours as it moves. The hour readout on a digital watch jumps suddenly from one hour to the next. By itself, it can indicate only the two discrete values, nothing in between.

The analog watch expresses its measurements of time continuously by position. The digital watch expresses time in numbers, which are discrete.

How a sound card works

This brings us to a little problem with the sound card. We have an analog signal (the electronic oscillation) which we want to store and process on our computer. But computers process only digital information (information expressed numerically). This means that the sound card must convert the analog signal (oscillations) to a digital signal (numbers).

Devices called converters change a signal from analog to digital or vice versa.

ADC or DAC   A sound card contains both an Analog/Digital Converter (ADC); for recording sound and a Digital/Analog Converter (DAC); for playing it back.

Sampling sounds

Most sounds a user accesses from a sound card are sampled. We've seen that a microphone picks up a sound, and converts that sound into an electrical impulse or oscillation. To convert it to a digital signal, we must sample it (measure the sound at discrete intervals) and record these measurements in discrete numbers. In this way, we develop a digital representation of the sound.

Recording quality

The sequence of the sampled values represents the sound, whether it's music, speech, or noise. The closer together the samples are

taken, the better the resulting quality of our recording, because it is more sensitive to the finest changes in the oscillation. The frequency of sampling is called the sampling rate.

So, a sound card's sampling rate (expressed in Hertz or kiloHertz) is one indicator of its quality. Audio CDs use a sampling rate of 44.1 KHz.

Proper digitization of an analog signal requires a sampling rate of at least double the frequency of the signal itself. A factor of 4 is recommended for clean, distortion-free recording.

The highest frequencies audible to the human ear are in the range of 13 Hz to 18 KHz. The exact upper limit depends on the person, but generally decreases with age.

What is actually measured when a sound is sampled is the amplitude of the oscillation at that precise instant. The ability to sample and distinguish the amplitude of a sound signal is called resolution; and is expressed in bits. Audio CD players have 16-bit sampling capability, allowing 65536 possible conditions. Sound cards, however, use 8-bit sampling, resulting in 256 conditions.

DMA (Direct Memory Access)

Obviously, all these measurements must be recorded as they are taken. They are first placed in RAM and then written to the hard disk. The process is speeded up by the use of DMA (Direct Memory Access). DMA lets the sound card transfer data directly to memory, so that the CPU isn't overburdened with this task at the expense of all other tasks.

DMA controller

Your computer has a special chip, called the DMA controller, that controls access to RAM by the CPU and peripherals to prevent conflicts. This access takes place over DMA channels, and only one device can access RAM over a particular channel. When you install your sound card, you establish the proper DMA channel assignment for it. We'll discuss this in more detail later.

Electronic tone generation

Built-in synthesizer

So far we've discussed how a sound card digitizes and records a sound. But sound cards also have the ability to generate sounds in an infinite variety themselves. They do this electronically through a built-in FM synthesizer. This component of a sound card combines individual sounds, generated by oscillators, into a total "sound picture."

Since the sound image depends on the frequencies of an oscillation, changing the frequency changes the sound's quality. This process, called frequency modulation (FM), can instruct the sound card to imitate different musical instruments, such as organs, woodwinds, etc.

High fidelity

In entertainment electronics, the term "high fidelity" has been an indicator of true-to-life sound reproduction. It means that recorded sound is played back with the same quality as the original (i.e., it is a "faithful" reproduction).

The principle here is quite simple. Sound is characterized by its frequency. The task in reproducing sound is to convert the information in a recording (either analog or digital) to a sound that matches the original as closely as possible, by recreating all frequencies that make up the desired sound. However, there are limits to this process.

The DIN 45500 high fidelity standard calls for a minimum frequency reproduction of 40 Hz. However, some bass violins can produce tones as low as 32 Hz, and some pipe organs can play notes as low as 16 Hz. So these couldn't be played with true high fidelity on a unit that just meets the minimum standard.

Limits of audibility

The audible frequency spectrum for humans (i.e., the range of frequencies that our ears can detect) varies slightly with age, especially at its upper limit. Babies can hear sounds up to 20 KHz. For each decade of age, this upper limit tends to drop about 2 KHz.

Of course, there is also variation from person to person. The lower limit is more constant. The following figure shows the frequency ranges of some typical sound sources.

Dynamics also determines quality

The term "dynamics" is often used in the field of high fidelity technology. It expresses the difference between the highest undistorted volume and the presence of interference, such as hissing. For example, inferior dynamics indicate that even the softer passages of a musical recording will have noise. The greater the dynamics, the more true-to-life the reproduction.

This criterion is expressed as the signal-to-noise ratio. The decibel is used as the unit of measure. Because the sensitivity of the human ear to changes in volume is logarithmic rather than linear, the ratio is given on the logarithmic scale.

The following illustration shows some dB values and their corresponding signal-to-noise ratio.

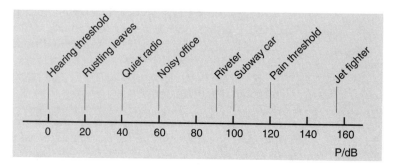

The decibel unit here is the same unit used to express the amplitude of a sound.

Harmonic distortion factor

One final measure of high fidelity is the harmonic distortion factor. Harmonic distortion is the introduction of unwanted frequencies caused by overloading electronic components.

The harmonic distortion factor is expressed as a percentage of distortion frequencies to original frequencies; the lower the factor, the higher the quality. Amplifiers with less than 1% harmonic distortion can easily be manufactured.

2.3   CD-ROM—New Mass Storage Device

A reasonably priced but powerful storage medium must be used for storing graphics, digitized video and sound files. The compact disc (CD), originally intended for audio use, now meets this need. A special CD-ROM drive allows CDs to be used with a computer.

CDs offer high storage capacity (up to 600 Meg, depending on density) and almost complete protection against data loss from electrical and magnetic damage. Unlike diskettes or hard drives, CD-ROMs cannot be deleted or overwritten by standard drives.

Still, as in the audio market, the CD-ROM serves the purpose of storing huge quantities of data (e.g., the Oxford English Dictionary).

Writeable CDs

The WORM (Write Once, Read Multiple) CD allows an initial writing from the user. WORM CDs will certainly play a major role in archiving data the user wants to save without changing later (documents, bookkeeping records, long-established recipes, etc.).

A WORM CD drive allows users to save data only once but read the data as often as necessary. The ultimate in data security and acceptable access times (50-80ms) make these disk drives attractive to users who need to create data inventories requiring no maintainance or revision but which must be permanently stored.

CD technology will be extremely useful for software manufacturers because a CD is fully copy-protected. Loading the data to a hard drive would be possible but impractical, because of its huge quantity.

Quick program installation

Loading programs to a hard drive, however, can be very practical from CD format. A single CD can replace the several installation diskettes that are sometimes required today.

Using a CD-ROM drive

Microsoft's MSCDEX.EXE driver allows access to a CD-ROM drive just like a normal hard drive or floppy disk drive. MSCDEX.EXE assigns the next available drive letter to the CD-ROM drive. For example, if you have a hard drive with partitions C: and D:, the CD-ROM drive will be assigned the letter E:.

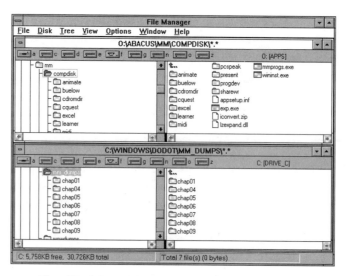

The CD-ROM drive in Windows File Manager

A CD contains normal path and file names. Data can be read and programs started from it. However, any write access will quit with an error message. Special programs also allow you to play conventional audio CDs over an installed sound card in near-perfect stereo quality.

How data is stored on the CD

Compact disks are usually 4 3/4 inches (12 cm) in diameter by about 1/16 inch (1.2 mm) thick. This is the standard size of the audio CD. For some time now, the single CD, measuring 3.5 inches (8 cm) in diameter, has also been available. This format is not widely used in electronic data processing. The laserdisk has a diameter of 12 inches (30 cm).

Although audio CDs and data CDs are similar in construction and appearance, you should never try to play a data CD in an audio CD player—this could damage your stereo system.

Data is written to a CD according to a special digital recording and encoding process. The basic unit of data is the data block. One data block is 2352 bytes. Of these 2352 bytes, only 2048 bytes are actual data.

The remaining bytes are used for synchronization, block identification and error control. To minimize the number of bit changes from 1 to 0 and vice versa, the data appears in 14-bit format. Decoding thus takes place through a process called EFM (Eight-to-Fourteen Modulation) coding.

Similar to audio CDs

The physical arrangement of the data is similar to that on an audio CD. All data blocks occur sequentially along a spiral track with a width of 0.6 mm. The track offset is 1.6 mm. With the 20,000 revolutions that fit on the standard 12 cm CD, the resulting storage density is 125,000 bits per square mm.

Data blocks are designated from the center out, in minutes, seconds and block numbers. One second contains 75 blocks; the entire CD contains about an hour. The capacity can be calculated as follows:

```
(75 blocks * 2352 bytes) / 1024 = 172.3 K/sec
(172.3K * 3600 sec) / 1024 = 605.7 Meg/CD
```

CLV recording

Constant Linear Velocity

In the CLV (Constant Linear Velocity) recording process, every data block always has the same length. So the outer track has more data blocks than the inner track because of the greater radius.

The laser beam (1.5 to 1.7 mm thick) moves between outer and inner tracks to read the data from the CD. Depending on its position, different rotation speeds are required to ensure a constant rate of movement of data past the read head. The rotation speed therefore decreases from the inner to the outer track. This constant adjusting of the rotation speed results in relatively slow access.

In the CAV (Constant Angular Velocity) process, which is used, for example, in hard drives, the medium spins at the same rate, and each concentric track contains the same amount of data. This allows for faster data transfer, but the cost is wasted disk space on the outer tracks, which can contain no more data than the innermost one.

PIT as the unit of information

The active surface of a CD consists of a thin layer of reflective aluminum. The information itself resides on this surface in the form of "pits" and "land". The pits are depressions in the land, or surface of the disk. When a CD is inserted in the drive, the laser is focused on the surface so as to achieve maximum reflection.

When it encounters a pit, the laser is defocused, and the photoreceptor detects a decrease in intensity, which is interpreted as a transition from 0 to 1.

Every transition from pit to land and from land to pit is interpreted as a bit of value 1. Everything else has a value of 0.

A stretch of land or pits thus represents a string of 0's, up to the next transition.

Since the data is represented by physical indentations, it cannot be corrupted by electrical or magnetic forces. So you should avoid scratching the disks because this could result in read errors.

Using CDs

CD-ROM drives can operate as internal or external computer components. Internal drives, which are housed in the computer like internal disk drives and are supplied by the computer with current, are more practical and less expensive.

External drives require their own housing and power supply, and are consequently more expensive.

Inserting the CD

There are two ways to insert CD's. If the drive has an ejectable CD tray, you can place the CD in it like you would in a standard audio device. Pressing an [Open/Close] button slides the tray in or out.

Other devices have a special CD caddy, into which the CD must first be inserted. Though at first this may seem more bothersome, the caddy protects the CD from any damage while inside the drive.

The caddy is marked with an arrow to indicate how it should be inserted in the drive. Pressing an [Eject] button ejects the caddy from the drive.

You may want to buy several caddies and keep your favorite CD-ROMs in them constantly. This saves time when you want to use them and offers a good way to keep them safe.

Some applications (e.g., the Microsoft Windows Media Player) let you eject tray-style CD-ROM drives from within the application.

Performance Features

A CD-ROM drive's performance is determined by its data transfer rate (data throughput) and its mean access time.

Data transfer rate

The data transfer rate describes the speed of data transfer from the CD or CD controller (often found on the sound card) to the computer. It is measured in bytes per second. Since such high speeds are now achieved by hard drives, the unit Meg/sec is often used.

The higher the transfer rate, the higher the drive performance. The MPC standard requires a minimum data transfer rate of 150K/sec. So, they are substantially slower than hard drives.

Even more pronounced is the difference in mean access time. While the maximum mean access time for a CD-ROM drive is 1 second, according to the MPC standard, almost any hard drive today delivers between 15 and 25 milliseconds (ms).

Access time

Mean access time is the average time required to locate a particular piece of information on the disk. The first generation of CD-ROM drives had access times of almost 1 second. Later models decreased the access time to 600 milliseconds (ms).

For most CD-ROM drives available today, the access time is between 150 and 350 milliseconds, which is comparable to floppy drives.

However, there is a large range of access times, from 275 milliseconds to 1500 milliseconds. Some CD-ROM drives are considerably slower than floppy drives, and their use in multimedia applications is questionable.

Controller cards

Another consideration is if the CD-ROM uses a proprietary controller card or a SCSI (pronounced "scuzzy") card. Each card has advantages and disadvantages.

Proprietary controller card

A proprietary controller card works only with the drive of one vendor. Also, most proprietary cards do not work as well as SCSI cards.

SCSI is an industry standard which allows you to use one controller to access several cards. Therefore, SCSI cards provide greater performance and are easier to expand than proprietary controller cards.

Transfer bufffer size

A large transfer buffer size is not important if you're using your CD-ROM for text-based searches or retrievals without pictures and sound.

However, when using mulitmedia applications, a 32K or higher transfer buffer size becomes very important.

Audio CD

Most CD-ROM drives include software which allows you to play audio CDs.

Internal/external

If you have empty drive bays in your system and desk space is important, consider using an internal CD-ROM drive.

Even if you have empty drive bays, you may want to use an external CD-ROM drive. External drives are portable and include output jacks to connect to an amplifier. This lets you use the amplifier to listen to audio CDs.

2.4 CD-ROM Based Technologies

With the introduction of the CD-ROM into electronic data processing, several firms announced CD-based products intended to serve as complete multimedia solutions in the area of entertainment electronics.

CD-I

Introduced by Phillips and Sony, CD-I (Compact Disc Interactive) is a CD-playing device for the consumer market that can be connected directly to a home TV set. One CD may hold up to 70 minutes of live video along with complete stereo sound.

Based on a Motorola 68000 series chip, the player evolved from the original audio CD, developed by Phillips, to provide the home user with live video and interaction.

A CD-I system has the following components:

- The CD system

- Audio system

- Video system

- Input devices such as remote control, mouse, etc.

- Non-volatile RAM

Contact with the PC

The CD-I players can also act as audio CD players and CD-ROM drives, with appropriate hardware additions. Integrated serial, Ethernet and SCSI interfaces ensure upward compatibility to protect the buyer's investment.

Many applications for CD-I already exist. Independent developers can obtain the license and technical equipment from Phillips to bring their own titles to market.

CD-TV

A similar development to Phillips' CD-I is the CD-TV (Commodore Dynamic-Total Vision) system from Commodore. Here, again, a separate device forms the basis of multimedia applications by connecting to an ordinary TV on which the CD-TV discs are played. Unlike videotape, which allows only sequential forwarding or rewinding, the CD-TV system offers direct positioning to another place on the disc.

Expanded by a keyboard, mouse, monitor and diskette drive, the CD-TV forms a complete Amiga 500 system.

Compatibility between CD-TV and CD-I

Devices called bridge discs permit exchange of CD's between CD-I and CD-TV. The effect of this capability remains to be seen.

Kodak Photo CD

In 1990 Kodak introduced a completely new process for storing and archiving photographs. In addition to normal chemical development, photos can be digitized from 35mm film by a special scanner with a resolution of 18 million pixels.

This far surpasses not only current television images, but the television of the future (HDTV) as well.

100 photos on CD The photographs are stored on CD using a proprietary data compression technique. In this format, 100 photos can be stored on a single CD.

Transferring of images from film to CD is performed by a Write-Once CD drive (e.g., PCD-Writer). This can be done by a service bureau. Since a roll of 35mm film holds a maximum of 36 pictures, subsequent films can be added to the CD at any time.

Besides showing the electronic photos on your television (using a CD-ROM XA or CD-I player), you can print them on a special high-quality thermoprinter.

Video Information System

Introduced by Radio Shack and Memorex, the Memorex MD-2500 Video Information System connects to any home television. You also have the option of connecting the system to your stereo.

VIS provides instant electronic access to reference books, learning, educational and instructional games and information.

By using the wireless hand controller, you can interact with the pictures, voice, music and animation sequences included with VIS applications.

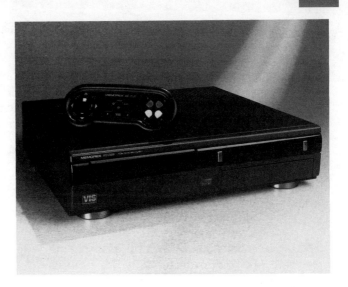

The VIS system developed by Memorex and Radio Shack

The Memorex MD-2500 includes a specially designed VIS version of the Compton's Multimedia Encyclopedia. This gives you access to thousands of colorful illustrations, animated sequences, and digital sound and speech.

2.5   Basics of Electronic Image Processing

The cliche "A picture is worth a thousand words" especially applies to computers and presentations. People will quickly become bored with a long-winded verbal description of an abstract and complicated concept unless visual images are used.

Graphic illustration of complex procedures

A photograph or graphic can bring a boring presentation to life. Computerized graphics can easily be created by using the many draw and paint programs that are currently available. Video digitization offers especially exciting illustrative possibilities. With this method, special hardware and software applications capture video images and convert them to computer graphics for display on a PC monitor.

Scanning - an alternative

Scanning technology offers another way of feeding "live" pictures into a computer. Scanners can scan all types of documents (drawings, photographs, texts, etc.) and convert these documents to computer-readable form.

This opens up an entire world of electronic image processing. The computerized image can be manipulated in various ways, from captioning or retouching, to dramatic artistic effects achieved by changing the color palette.

Special programs can create effects using an overlay technique. A chroma key function defines a screen color, onto which a video image can be superimposed. You can define red as the colorkey, for example, and run a presentation with a red background. The presentation will then appear with the video picture in the background (e.g., satellite weather maps).

Video tricks   The genlock process provides another enhancement—synchronizing and mixing multiple image sources. The result can be sent to a television or video recorder. In connection with your computer, this usually means mixing the VGA picture with a video signal. This can be accomplished by special cards designed for video processing, such as the Screen Machine from Fast. Numerous video tricks are possible with a genlock card. Titling a video film is a simple example.

With virtually unlimited possibilities available, from multimedia presentations to picture databases and visual lexicons, electronic images are an extremely important multimedia component.

In this section we'll present the basics of electronic image processing.

We'll discuss creating and manipulating electronic photos in more detail in Chapter 6. A similar discussion of live video (motion picture sequences) can be found in Chapter 11.

Video and PC

Now let's discuss the technical details of converting real-life images to computerized graphics. A (video) overlay card enables the simultaneous display of a VGA (computer) signal and a video signal on a standard computer monitor.

Although this card isn't a component of the MPC specification, it's only a matter of time (or price) before it will be. It is, after all, the buyers who ultimately determine whether a particular feature will be accepted.

Prices drop   Since video overlay cards are still quite expensive, they aren't
considerably   widely used. However, prices have dropped considerably so that basic models now cost under $500.

A video overlay card allows video signals from a variety of sources to be displayed on the computer monitor. Possible sources include the following:

• Camcorder

• Video recorder (VHS, S-Video)

• Still-video camera

• Video disk

• Television tuner

An overlay card, which is usually inserted between the VGA card and the monitor, has inputs for several external video sources. For example, a video recorder can be connected to the overlay card through its Video-out connector.

For more information on installing an overlay card, refer to Section 3.5.

The incoming video signal cannot simply overlay the VGA signal. The two signals have different scanning frequencies and resolutions.

First the overlay card scans and digitizes the video image's entire bandwidth of 5.5 MHz. The digitized image data is then output from video RAM, synchronized to the VGA monitor frequency. This process takes place in real time, so that live video is displayed on the screen.

For the video signal to show up clearly on the screen, the VGA signal must be darkened where the video signal will appear. Software and hardware accompanying the video card define an area for the video image.

The same principle is applied in the more expensive televisions, where one image is shown within another so that you can watch two programs simultaneously.

Manufacturers supply the necessary Windows software support so a video film can be shown in its own window.

Similarly, the video signal can be manipulated under DOS. However, the size of the display can be varied as needed. Regardless of the graphics card resolution, video images can be displayed in TrueColor (16.7 million colors) by using an overlay card.

Both signals are displayed independently of each other. You can demonstrate this by creating a hardcopy in Windows by pressing the Prt Sc key under Windows. A black patch replaces the video output.

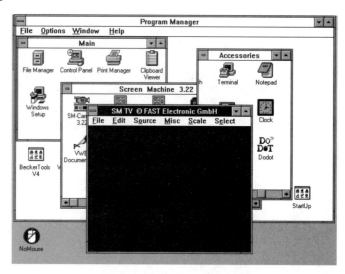

Where is the video signal?

This happens because, instead of reading the overlay card's video RAM, the Windows hardcopy function reads only the video memory of the graphics card.

Framegrabber option

By overlaying the VGA image, an overlay card displays the video signal in TrueColor on a standard PC monitor.

Framegrabber

A feature called a framegrabber captures individual images from a full-motion video sequence and stores them as computer graphics. Any overlay card, such as the Screen Machine from Fast or the VideoBlaster from Creative Labs, has this as an essential function.

As we mentioned, a video image must be digitized and read into the overlay card's video RAM before it can be mixed with the VGA signal.

To capture individual video images, all you need is software that can read the data from this RAM area and make it available to your graphics processing programs.

Unfortunately, the overlay card's video RAM is organized quite differently than that of the VGA card. Remember that the video image is in TrueColor format, while a VGA graphic has only 256 colors. Therefore, the image must be converted to a VGA graphic before your program can use it.

Processing audio signals

Some cards have two audio inputs for the left and right stereo channels, in addition to the video input. This allows you to play a film score or the sound recorded with your video camera, for example, along with the video signal.

Generally the audio signal is only temporary and cannot be stored and modified by the video overlay card. However, you can record it using a sound card.

Refer to Chapter 11 for additional information on adding sound to a video film.

Differences In VGA and Video Signals

The screen

The interface between the user and the machine, in computers as well as video, is the screen. For the most part, this is a picture tube.

Hand-held TVs and laptops usually have liquid crystal displays (LCDs), but color versions of these are still very expensive.

To create an image on a picture tube, a luminescent layer, usually consisting of a phosphor compound, is momentarily excited by an electron beam.

So we see a picture and not just a point of light; the electron beam moves across the screen surface in rows. The frequency with which the beam moves from left to right is called the horizontal deflection frequency.

As soon as the electron beam reaches the bottom of the screen, it's quickly returned to the top. The frequency with which it moves from top to bottom, making a complete image, is called the vertical deflection frequency or scanning frequency.

Both frequencies display sawtooth curves because the beam moves relatively slowly from left to right and top to bottom, and is returned quickly from right to left and bottom to top.

If a high scanning frequency is used, the perception of flickering should be eliminated. Now if the beam must create more than just an evenly illuminated surface, besides being deflected in the scanning pattern, it must itself become more or less intense. This causes the appropriate distribution of varying degrees of brightness.

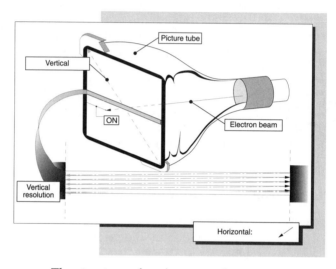

The structure of an image on the screen

Pixels are picture elements

As it moves horizontally across the screen, the beam is switched on and off to produce many individual points, called pixels (picture elements). We'll use an example to explain the frequencies that are used.

Suppose that a screen resolution of 800 by 600 pixels and a scanning frequency of 72 Hz is used. At this resolution, a maximum of 400 vertical lines can be displayed. This is because differences in color cannot be perceived unless two adjacent lines are separated by a space. So, the electron beam is switched on and off 400 times per row.

Meanwhile, it's moving 43200 (600 * 72) times per second from left to right across the screen. This produces a horizontal frequency of 43.2 KHz. The frequency with which the beam is switched on and off is 400 times per row * 600 rows * 72 images per second, or a total of 17.28 MHz, which the monitor's input amplifier must process.

When color is added, this process becomes more complicated. All colors are created by mixing the basic colors red, green and blue.

Each has its own electron beam, which excites a luminescent layer of the corresponding color.

Since the eye can easily be deceived, the three different colored points placed close enough together are seen as one. If all three are fully lit, we see white.

Each electron beam must be directed so only the appropriate color on the phosphor layer is lit. As you can see in the diagram, a mask with holes in it, called a shadow mask, is used to do this.

In color picture tubes, where a shadow mask is always used, the resolution that can be obtained is limited by the number of holes in the mask.

How VGA works The electron beam is controlled by the input signal coming from the graphics card. The monitor must meet certain technical requirements to handle this signal properly. It must support both deflection frequencies and be able to process the video signal of the appropriate frequency.

The maximum number of displayable colors depends on the graphics card's ability to control different conditions of the individual electron beams. In TrueColor, each electron beam can have 256 different conditions, represented by 8 bits. At 8 bits per color component, each colored pixel requires 3 * 8 = 24 bits.

The maximum number of colors is determined by the following calculation:

```
256 * 256 * 256 = 16.7 million
```

Currently, 16.7 million is the maximum number of colors displayable on the PC. A special graphics card is required for this, however. With this many colors, it's possible to create extremely realistic photographic images.

However, most computers usually work with far fewer colors; 256 VGA colors at a resolution of 800 x 600 pixels is common. The resolution expresses the number of pixels displayable horizontally (first figure) and vertically (second figure).

The structure of a Scanning frequencies of VGA cards are usually from 50 to 72Hz.
computer image This is sufficient to give the impression of a flicker-free picture. The higher the scanning frequency, the more stable the image. This is the basis of the SSI standard that specifies a scanning

frequency of 72 Hz. The IBM standard is 60 Hz at a resolution of 640 x 480 pixels.

There is a special reason for this. Actually, the frequency indicates where the equipment was made. The preferred frequency is that of the standard power supply because it provides a very stable oscillator. In America, standard current has a frequency of 60 Hz. So this was chosen as the standard television scanning frequency.

In Europe, the power supply and scanning frequency are both 50 Hz. Early in computer development, the same norm was adopted for graphics cards, so their signal could also be displayed on a video monitor.

The makeup of a video signal

Although the video signal (e.g., a TV picture) has a different structure than the VGA signal, they have the same basic function.

According to the television and video norm used in this country (NTSC or National Television Standards Committee), a picture consists of 525 interlaced lines (i.e., 262.5 horizontal lines).

VGA—better than television

A VGA signal offers much higher resolution than the NTSC television and video signal.

Resolution isn't the only difference between VGA and video signals. The television picture, unlike the computer image, is displayed using a process called interlacing. In this method, a complete image (frame) is actually displayed as two half images (fields). This is done by alternately drawing odd and even lines.

Although the scanning frequency of each half image is only 30 Hz, this process doubles the overall frequency to 60 Hz. This reduces flickering to acceptable levels.

Different norms

The television norm used in Europe is called PAL (Phase Alternation Line). It was developed during the 1960s by the German professor Walter Bruch. Besides displaying 625 (512 actual) lines per image, the PAL norm can correct the color fluctuation caused by phase errors in transmission. The correction is performed by reversing the reference color carrier on alternating lines.

Separate processing and amplification of the three colors, as it occurs in the VGA card and its corresponding monitor, isn't common in television and video. Processing signals separately produces higher quality, but requires more amplification and processing steps.

Since image quality is less critical with motion pictures, the video composite technology provides acceptable results while requiring relatively inexpensive transmission and receiving equipment.

NTSC, the
original norm

The NTSC norm, used in the U.S. and Japan, was the model for the PAL norm. This committee issued a set of standards for the transmission and reception of television signals.

With the development of color television, a color standard based on the YIQ model was created. In this method, the image is obtained from a black/white component (luminosity Y) and two color difference signals (chrominacity I and Q). The color information is calculated from the difference between the red component and the luminosity (I = R - Y) and the difference between the blue component and the luminosity (Q = B - Y).

Besides the different color systems, there is also another difference between the PAL and NTSC norms. The PAL standard defines 625 lines per image and the NTSC defines only 525 lines. Another difference is the vertical frequency of 60 Hz, with 30 half images displayed per second under the NTSC norm.

It's now possible to convert films from one standard to the other by using a norm converter. However, since these devices are very expensive, they're not intended for amateurs. Using a video recorder or screen that is designed for the wrong norm can cause problems.

SECAM

This refers also to the SECAM (Système Electronique Couleur Avec Mémoire) norm, which is used in France and Eastern Europe, in which the color signal is sent sequentially from line to line.

If you're using PAL, you must also use a video overlay card whose chip set supports the higher standard (e.g., Phillips). Some overlay cards are based on chip sets designed to handle only the NTSC norm. These display an ingoing PAL signal rather poorly.

Converting Video Images To Computer Graphics

Suppose that you want to take a section from a video sequence that's being displayed in real time and save it in a format the computer can understand. First a video overlay card, such as the Screen Machine or VideoBlaster, must create still images from the motion video image.

The card digitizes images and stores them in its own video memory. These digitized images are then read according to the VGA frequency and displayed on the screen. Software supplied with the overlay card can also read data from the card's video memory and convert it to the desired VGA format.

You can usually choose from various target formats. Besides the format, you can specify the color depth to which the overlay card's TrueColor data should be translated.

As we mentioned, a television image is constructed from two half images. The first half image contains all the odd-numbered lines of the image, and the next one contains all the even-numbered lines. These images are separated chronologically by exactly 1/60 second (1/50 second in Europe). This short time interval is adequate for motion pictures such as television. Here the eye will perceive smooth movement.

However, when a still image is shown as two alternating and slightly different half images, the eye can perceive the differences. The result is a noticeable flickering effect. Many overlay cards are able to use only one half image for video snapshots. Special software routines then interpolate the missing lines (rows) from those that are present to recreate a complete image. This process is called row correction.

Storage requirements of a video image

A video image can be stored in various formats. Besides the "normal" graphics formats, such as PCX and GIF, other formats, which are specially adapted to the video signal, are available for video images.

Video overlay cards work internally with the YUV color model, which is designed specifically to the human eye. The luminosity Y (brightness signal) of a video signal is digitized at full resolution. The color difference signals U and V are digitized at a reduced resolution and reside in a narrower bandwidth within the video signal. The UV signals actually contain only a fourth as much information as the Y signal.

This model uses the properties of the human eye, which has several black/white-sensitive rods but only a few color-sensitive cones. A signal in YUV format takes just half the storage space of the corresponding RGB signal, which has intensity values for each individual color.

The Screen Machine digitizes a full image under PAL with a resolution of 640 x 512 pixels. The values required by the YUV model are stored separately. To determine the storage size of an image, we need the following calculations:

The luminosity (Y) is derived from the maximum number of pixels.

Luminosity Y (640x512)	327680 bytes
Chrominacity U (1/4 Y)	81920 bytes
Chrominacity V (1/4 Y)	81920 bytes

These values total 480K.

For storage in RGB format:

640 * 512 pixels	
Red values (1 byte/pixel)	327680 bytes
Green values (1 byte/pixel)	327680 bytes
Blue values (1 byte/pixel)	327680 bytes

These values total 960K.

Depending on the target format (TIFF, PCX, BMP, etc.), header records and other format-specific data may add to the storage requirement. However, some formats (e.g., GIF) have built-in data compression techniques that can drastically reduce file size. Since all image formats use specific encoding schemes for image and color information, the file size depends mainly on image content.

Graphic format and colors

As we mentioned, the video signal is displayed on the screen in TrueColor. This means a palette of 16.7 million colors is used, which provides realistic images of photographic quality. Some graphic formats (TGA, TIFF, BMP) allow full color preservation. Such files are extremely large, however.

To use the image in other applications, a selection of 256 colors is usually sufficient. Actually, only a few applications can process a palette of even this size.

The size of the available palette depends on the color depth used:

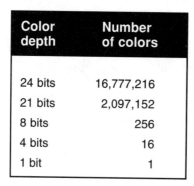

Color depth	Number of colors
24 bits	16,777,216
21 bits	2,097,152
8 bits	256
4 bits	16
1 bit	1

Some formats can convert colors to shades of gray. Usually a maximum of 256 gray scale values can be stored. This is actually far more than our eyes can distinguish. The color information of an image that's not stored in TrueColor is kept in a separate palette.

The color palette Theoretically, a VGA graphics card can also store 16.7 million colors, but it cannot display all of them simultaneously. To reduce file size and save valuable video memory, individual pixels are encoded with a reference to one of the 256 (maximum) colors of the palette. The actual red, blue, and green components of the color are defined only on the palette itself.

Color reduction Which colors are used when you store an image of 16.7 million colors as a 256-color file? The algorithms used for color reduction vary depending on the card. Basically, similar colors are grouped together and represented by a single color. A total of 256 groups can be defined, with a total of 256 displayable colors.

Problems can occur when an image has, for example, a foreground with weak contrast and a background with many different colors. Color reduction may result in complete loss of contrast in the foreground and too much contrast in the background. The algorithms test the intensity of colors on the overall surface.

Rasterizing and dithering Another method of color reduction involves rasterizing an image. This method is used mostly in connection with simple color reduction.

Again, the weakness of our visual acuity is exploited. When two different colored pixels are placed very close together, we see them as if the colors were mixed. Rasterizing uses essentially the same process as a printer that varies the density of black dots to represent shades of gray. Dithering is a special form of rasterizing in which the distribution of different colors is varied to create color blends.

Data Compression

Various authoring systems and development tools are available to construct a motion picture from a sequence of individual images. A display rate of 25-30 images per second is needed to create the illusion of fluid motion. The amount of data involved can amount to 12 Meg in uncompressed form, which far exceeds practical limits of data storage.

As a result, extravagant compression techniques and devices have been developed for reducing the storage requirements of video data. One such device is the DVI board, which is a joint product of IBM and Intel. With the help of the DVI board, video sequences recorded in real time can be compressed to manageable proportions.

The compression of both single images and film sequences requires sophisticated algorithms.

Still video compression
A still video is a single video image captured from a moving (live) video sequence by using a framegrabber. A group called the Joint Photographic Expert Group (JPEG) was created to address the problem of storing this type of image. They defined standardized methods of still video data compression.

The algorithms developed now enable storage of video images with a 50:1 compression ratio without visible loss of quality. Two factors are important in this process:

• Quality:
  The higher the compression rate, the greater the effect on picture quality, because more information is combined and therefore generalized.

• Time:
  The time it takes to write the image to a data carrier depends on the hardware used. This computation-intensive process taxes both the computer's system clock and the data transfer rate of the hard drive. The Screen Machine using a 25 MHz 386 processor compresses a complete image (480K) in about 6 seconds.

For a compressed image to be displayed again on the screen, it must first be decompressed. This reverse process is faster because,

depending on the degree of compression, corresponding less data is involved.

Live-video compression

Compared to still video, live-video storage has completely different demands. Time is the biggest problem. For the eye to perceive smooth motion, images must be displayed at a rate of about 30 per second.

In recording, each image must be saved in real time at the brief instant it's available. Successive images must be digitized, compressed, and stored all at the same fleeting speed.

This process is much more complicated than with still video. So, a separate group, called the Motion Picture Expert Group (MPEG), was created to define the appropriate standards.

DVI technology

Intel and IBM teamed up to produce a new form of technology that provided the first major breakthrough in live-video compression. Called DVI technology, it combines two circuit boards on a device named the ActionMedia II card.

At the heart of the DVI card is the i82750 chip set from Intel. There are two processor groups, designated as PB and DB.

i82750PB

The i82750PB, acting as the pixel processor, is responsible for the real-time compression of the video images. Special algorithms conforming to the MPEG norm are implemented on the chip as microcode.

This processor is supported in the compression process by extremely fast video RAM. The algorithm is designed to capture and store only the actual changes between two successive video images.

i82750DB

The second component, the i82750DB, is responsible for screen output. This processor reads the data from the video RAM, where it resides in the YUV color format, and converts it to RGB format.

The display processor achieves a maximum resolution of 1024 x 512 pixels in TrueColor mode (16.7 million colors). Another task of the DB processor is the interpolation of data during decompression to recreate missing colors.

Lower resolution

One of the current digitization and compression techniques is called Real Time Video (RTV). This process provides a maximum resolution of 128 x 120 pixels. All irrelevant information about the image is filtered out and removed by a special algorithm.

Because of their limited resolution, video sequences stored by the RTV process should be displayed only in small windows.

Production Level Video (PLV) digitization and compression provides a resolution of 256 x 240 pixels. PLV sequences can be displayed in full-screen mode without loosing any quality. However, this process requires very expensive, specialized equipment.

Scanner Basics

If you can't justify the cost of expensive video equipment, there is another way to get true-to-life images into your computer and saved in the graphics format of your choice.

Scanners let you take a photograph or other still picture on paper and convert the visual information into data a computer can understand. Any kind of image that exists on paper, whether it's a photograph, drawing, or text, can be scanned.

It's much more difficult, though not impossible, to capture images from a television or computer monitor with this technology. First you must photograph the screen.

For best results, you may first want to experiment with different exposure times. The distortion that appears around the curved edges of the picture tube can be removed later with appropriate image processing software.

A document that you want to scan with a normal gray scale scanner should have good contrast, because this type of scanner operates on the principle of lightness and darkness.

Gray scale scanner A gray scale scanner translates all colors into shades of gray. Depending on the sensitivity of the scanner, weakly contrasted details may be lost in the scanned image.

There are also color scanners that can translate color documents into color graphic images. However, the color information results in large file sizes for the scanned images.

How A Scanner Works

In the actual scanning process, a document is illuminated by a light beam and sampled by a light-sensitive unit. Differences in color or gray scales produce differences in reflectivity.

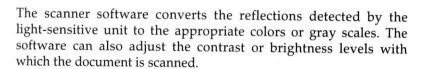

The scanner software converts the reflections detected by the light-sensitive unit to the appropriate colors or gray scales. The software can also adjust the contrast or brightness levels with which the document is scanned.

Most scanner programs have a prescan function that samples the document at a lower resolution. The user can use this function to mark the desired area, which is then scanned at full intensity.

The resulting file can be saved in various image formats, including TIFF, PCX or BMP. Many image-processing programs already have their own scanning modules (e.g., Paintbrush Plus), which allows the image to be scanned and manipulated directly.

Color Scanners

A color scanner is like three scanners in one. As in a gray scale scanner, the image is illuminated and the quantity of reflected light measured with photo-diodes. Three scanning passes are needed to scan a color document.

Since the image is illuminated with three different colors of light, the intensity levels of the three basic color components are determined separately. From these three values, the software computes the proper color for each pixel.

Selecting the right resolution

By now you're familiar with resolution as a measure of quality. Resolution as applied to scanners is expressed in dots per inch (DPI), and indicates the scanner's ability to distinguish two adjacent points.

The scanned image is divided into individual pixels, with each pixel assigned a color or gray scale value. With gray scale scanners, the resulting raster image can consist of true shades of gray (a halftone image) or it can use varying densities of black dots to create a similar impression.

For more information on scanners and scanned images, refer to Section 3.5.

Scanners usually operate with a resolution of 300-400 DPI, but higher resolutions are possible. Remember that very high resolutions are useful only when used with suitable documents and output devices.

Laser printers and 24-pin printers usually can achieve a resolution of only 300 DPI. However, professional phototypesetter devices can achieve resolutions of up to 3500 DPI.

If the scanned document will be displayed on a computer screen in a multimedia presentation, it's really a matter of overkill, since the screen resolution itself is only about 96 DPI. The number of colors that can be obtained to produce realistic images is much more important in this instance.

Using excessive resolutions to read printed documents can even impair image quality. Since printed matter consists of pixels, scanning them with a resolution much higher than was used in printing can cause a muddling effect by producing intensity values that are determined not just by the brightness of the original image, but by how many raster points are being sampled.

The problem of scanning at a resolution that's too low can cause the same problem.

Scanner Types

There are various scanner types available, depending on the application and the size of your budget.

Hand-held scanners

The hand-held scanner is an affordable choice. With this device, you perform the scanning process manually by passing the scanner over the document.

Reading a full page requires multiple scans, since the light-sensing unit is only 4-5 inches (10-12.5 cm) wide. Most of these sensors are based on LDR (Light Detect Resistor) technology.

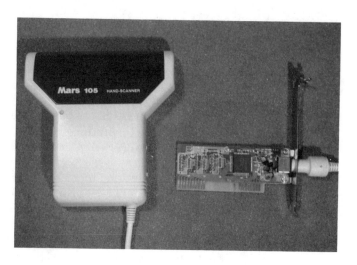

A hand-held scanner

Hand-held devices also have guides and rollers to facilitate the smooth, even movement required by the user. The scanned images are pieced together by software to draw the complete page.

Flatbed Scanners

Exact positioning is the main advantage of the flatbed scanner. The document is placed on a glass plate, similar to a photocopier.

The actual scanning unit, which consists of special lamps and the light-sensing elements driven by a motor, samples the document from below. An automatic page feed feature can easily read multiple pages.

OCR

Text documents, like other types of documents, are stored internally as graphics when they are first scanned. In a process called OCR (Optical Character Recognition), special software can then convert the scanned characters back to text files that can be read by word processing programs.

Barcode scanner

The barcode scanner is a scaled-down version of the conventional scanner. These devices scan a simple barcode, instead of detailed graphics. Most of the work involved in this process is in the interpretation of the barcode by the software.

The trick in designing the barcode itself is to ensure that it's readable in any direction that it's scanned (i.e., forward, backward or diagonally).

Because it's easy to use, the barcode is used throughout the industrialized world. Computer systems based on barcode identification can automate point-of-sale pricing, tracking of retail and warehouse product movement, inventory control and many other important business tasks.

3D scanners

In viewing three-dimensional objects, scanning technology offers a specialized solution alongside the video digitization process described in the previous section. With the 3D scanner, which is basically a fancy video camera, objects can be scanned up to a certain depth.

LogiTech Fotoman

One such product is the LogiTech Fotoman. This digital camera can immediately digitize an image "snapped" by the user. The data is converted by the scanner software and passed to the PC.

These scanners offer a promising solution for many applications. However, currently they are very expensive and have a limited resolution (75 DPI).

As you can see, there are several options for processing photographs and video images. Whatever your application and price range, you can find a way to incorporate these images to enhance your multimedia presentations.

2.6 Printer Output

Video overlay cards' ability to digitize video signals in TrueColor (16.7 million colors) is always stressed. With this enormous array of colors, the most intricate details of an image are captured with amazing realism.

However, further processing of these images in multimedia presentations, databases and desktop publishing applications can produce disappointing results. Very few graphics cards or programs support the display of TrueColor images that now exist as graphics files.

Printer Output Quality

Generally, images are reduced to 256 colors or gray scales for screen display. An image file in TrueColor format retains all the color values, but they cannot all be displayed on the screen. Although the image is still realistic, there are gaps and a certain degree of coarseness.

However, the results are worse when you try to print the image. The image comes out looking like a newspaper photograph. There is a simple explanation for this: A laser printer simply cannot print shades of gray.

For example, if the overlay-digitized image is saved in 1-bit dithered TIFF format (i.e., 1-bit means only black or white, no gray), the screen display and printout will be identical.

Resolution is also an important factor for printers. Like scanner resolutions, printer resolution is expressed in dots per inch (DPI). The printed image appears as an array of black and white dots (or rather, "black dots" and "no dots").

The same type of rastering process is used for printing newspaper photos.

Simulating Gray Scales

Gray scales are easily simulated in printing by varying the density of the black dots. The more black dots there are per unit area, the darker the overall appearance, and vice versa.

Therefore, varying the number of dots per unit area creates the impression of grayscaling.

This sort of array of black dots is called a rasterized image. The finest possible raster (i.e., the one that uses the greatest density of dots), produces the best quality image.

In referring to a raster, the unit actually used is a measure of linear density, either LPI (lines per inch) or L/cm (lines per centimeter).

The following table shows different rasters and their uses:

Raster		Intended use	Quality
LPI	L/cm		
50	20	Laser printer	Good font image, strong rastering in graphics
75	30	Newspaper	Rastering still visible, gray levels possible
114	45	Reproduction	Rastering barely visible, good graphic quality
150	>60	High-quality reproduction	Rastering not visible, standard for high-quality printing

Another way to simulate gray levels is to vary the size of the dots instead of their density. Although most laser printers don't have this ability, a little trick can help.

A logical surface is created in the form of a square that can contain a variable number of printed dots. To simulate 16 shades of gray, the surface must be able to assume 16 different conditions.

Therefore, the surface must be composed of 16 parts, which is a 4x4-pixel square. A surface of 16x16 pixels can accommodate 256 shades. Setting all pixels produces the darkest shade (black); no pixels produces the lightest shade (white).

What can a laser printer do?

Laser printers generally work with a resolution of 300 DPI. This isn't affected by any PostScript capability, which is based on the interpretation of special print commands that aren't relevant to graphics resolution.

If we want to print an image with 25 levels of gray, 5 linear pixels (in two dimensions, 5 x 5 = 25) per raster unit are needed. This leads to the following calculations, using the factor 2.54 to convert inches to centimeters (1 inch = 2.54 cm):

```
300 DPI / 5 pixels = 60 LPI

60 LPI / 2.54 = 24 L/cm
```

With 25 gray levels, we get a 24th cm raster. This is lower quality than a newspaper photo (see table above). Even at newspaper quality, with a 30th cm raster and 64 gray levels (8x8 pixels), the limitations are easily seen. Here are the calculations:

```
30 L/cm * 2.54 = 76 LPI

76 LPI * 8 pixels = 608 DPI
```

For 608 DPI representation, the normal laser printer is no longer adequate. It's capable of only 300 DPI.

Accessory cards have been available for some time (e.g., from Canon) to enable the printing of 256 gray levels (up to 1000 DPI) by ordinary 300 DPI laser printers. These cards use a technique that changes the dot size to create different shades. The amplitude of the laser is changed to produce this variation.

Printer requirements of video images

Since the makeup of a video signal is different from that of VGA, there are also some special printing considerations in these instances. Maximum quality is achieved only at a specific image size.

The ability of the overlay card to digitize the entire bandwidth of the video signal is a measure of its resolution. In this case, 640 x 512 pixels should be attained. To make this resolution available at the video output as well, the video signal must also exhibit the corresponding bandwidth. As we explained earlier, in a PAL norm video signal, 50 half images or 25 images are transmitted every second. The resulting frequency for pure image data is:

```
640/2 * 512 * 25 = 4.09 MHz
```

A video image, however, contains additional lines that are used for other information. Also, the electron beam requires a certain amount of time, however short, to be switched off and moved from right to left for each line, and from bottom to top for each half image.

This provides a video bandwidth of 5.5 MHz, from which the actual image data must then be refiltered. If the video signal itself is present in a more restricted resolution (e.g., VHS with 4.4 MHz), complete image data won't be given to the overlay card. Sharpness and contrast are reduced in this case. This means that the quality of the video signal also ultimately determines the quality of the image.

Studio cameras with three-chip technology, expensive optics and appropriate video bandwidth deliver the full resolution of 640 x 512 to 680 x 560 pixels. Simple devices are simply not capable of this. Object illumination also determines the quality of the picture.

Determining raster width and image size

The degree of rastering, number of gray levels, and size of the video image are important parameters for deciding the optimum size and rastering to use for printing.

Image size

The maximum image size is obtained from the fixed resolution of the overlay card. The print quality of a 45th cm raster is assumed. (To represent 256 gray levels with this raster, an 1800 DPI printer is needed):

```
Image width = (640 pixels x 2.54) / (114 LPI * 1.2)

Image width = 11.9 cm (4.68 inches)

Image height = (512 pixels x 2.54) / (114 LPI * 1.2)

Image height = 9.5 cm (3.75 inches)
```

The image size is thus derived from the horizontal and vertical resolution of the overlay card, as well as the appropriate rastering factor. (The figure 1.2 is a correction factor for a 45th cm raster.) So the digitized video image can be printed at a size of 4.68 x 3.75 inches (11.9 x 9.5 cm) without losing any quality.

Raster degree

The maximum degree of rastering can be calculated based on the desired picture size. For example, suppose that the picture must be produced at a width of 3.15 inches (8 cm):

Raster degree = 640 pixels / (3.15 inches x 1.2)

Raster degree = 169 LPI

Raster degree = 640 pixels / (8 cm x 1.2)

Raster degree = 67 L/cm

According to this calculation, a 3.15 x 2.52 inch (8 x 6.4 cm) image can be printed with a 67th cm raster. Various phototypesetters are available for this. Some of these phototypesetters can print 256 gray levels with this raster based on a resolution of up to 3000 DPI. The next section provides an overview of all the available printing processes.

Which printing process should be used?

Because of the limitations of conventional laser printers, which we discussed, the printouts from these printers won't have the same quality and richness of color produced by scanners and overlay cards.

Common Printers and Technologies

Now we'll discuss the most common printers and printing technologies currently being used.

Laser Printers

Standard laser printers, with a maximum resolution of 300 DPI, are useful only under certain conditions. These printers can handle text very well but they cannot produce quality detailed graphics. Although laser printers cannot print gray scales, they can simulate gray scales by varying pixel density.

An example of a laser printer is the HP LaserJet

Accessory cards can increase the number of gray scales and the resolution by modifying the electron beam.

PostScript Printers

PostScript is a page description language that describes and programs the format of the printed page. PostScript files are transferred to a phototypesetter, where a raster image processor (RIP) uses formulas and instructions to interpret the Postscript commands. Text, lines and images are composed from the pixels obtained in this process.

Commands replace pixel matrix

Instead of the matrix tables used by dot-matrix printers, PostScript printers use formulas to create letters and graphic elements. PostScript provides the same page layout on any PostScript printer.

The quality of the page proofs are limited only by the quality of the printer (i.e., a page printed using a phototypesetter will be better quality than a page printed on a standard PostScript printer).

Phototypesetter

A phototypesetter consists of multiple components: The phototypesetter itself, a raster image processor (RIP) and a developer. The document is first exposed on a light-sensitive film with the help of the raster image processor.

The RIP is a computer of sorts, which prepares the document described in the PostScript file for the phototypesetter. The PostScript commands are interpreted, and a page is constructed through this interpretation. The resulting pixel structure then passes from RIP to phototypesetter by means of a laser beam focused on the film.

This method of printing is similar to that of a PostScript laser printer, but with much greater resolution. Phototypesetters achieve resolutions of up to 3500 DPI.

Phototypesetter prices start around the $35,000 range, and are intended for professional use only.

Color copiers

Color and gray scale images can be produced on color copiers with the appropriate computer interface. By changing the amplitude of the laser beam, color copiers can vary pixel size.

Component colors are superimposed in a process called four-color separation, using the basic components of the YCM (Yellow, Cyan, Magenta and Black) model. With each of these having 256 possible intensity levels, such devices can achieve TrueColor image printing (16.7 million colors).

Image appearance is improved by the use of a separate black achieved by combining other colors.

Thermotransfer printers

The thermotransfer process is widely used in color printing. The print head of a thermotransfer printer consists of a complete printed line, containing the corresponding number of thermal elements.

Thermal printers use special heat-sensative paper. The printhead travels a short distance over the paper. A chemical reaction occurs in the paper resulting from the high temperature of the printhead. This chemical reaction causes the paper to darken and form specific characters.

Up to 12 heating elements per mm transfer the image to paper using a color ribbon composed of the four base colors. The colors are transferred sequentially, with the full width and height of the page being printed four times.

Thermal printers are quiet, relatively inexpensive and reliable. However, they do have disadvantages:

- They cannot use multipart paper.

- Cost of heat-sensitive paper is high.

- The print quality is only fair.

- The print speed is slow.

Dye sublimation printers

These printers currently produce the best printing results. The four base colors are steamed onto the paper in varying intensities. Intricate electronic control of the print head, which is heated between 98.6°F (37°C) and 102.2°F (39°C), determines the amount of wax transferred from a color foil to the paper, thus controlling the degree of color.

The 4096 nuances of each color, and the superior mixing that occurs when wax already on the paper is rewarmed by a new color cloud, result in living color (16.7 million) images of exceptional brilliance.

Video printers

A video printer provides the fastest way to transfer a video signal from monitor to paper. By pressing a button, you can obtain instant photos measuring approximately 4 x 3.15 inches (10 x 8 cm) with a resolution of 800 x 576 pixels. Image quality is also determined by the resolution of the video camera or card.

Video printers use a combination of the thermotransfer and dye sublimation processes. Therefore, they are able to produce images in 16.7 million colors. A video printer should have a computer interface that enables direct printing of images displayed using an overlay card.

Inkjet printer

The inkjet printer is another example of a non-impact printer and has recently become a serious competitor to laser printers. This is mainly because mechanical parts and reduced production costs for the inkjet printer.

The inkjet printer is a special type of dot-matrix printer. However, instead of pins, inkjet printers use jets. These jets spray a fine stream of ink onto the paper.

Chapter 3

Multimedia Workshop

Your computer needs special hardware extensions to access multimedia capabilities. You can build your multimedia PC system with many possible configurations. This chapter introduces these possibilities and helps you assemble or upgrade to the multimedia PC system that's right for you.

3.1 Essential Components

Adding to existing hardware

In Chapter 2 we defined the multimedia PC. The essential components are a PC, sound card and CD-ROM drive. There are many ways of incorporating these essentials into a solution tailored to meet your specific needs.

The solution you choose depends on the multimedia applications you intend to use, the devices you already use and, to some degree, your budget.

The more standard multimedia PC applications require relatively inexpensive equipment. However, if you want to digitize video images, you'll need a video overlay card. A slightly less expensive way to get started with electronic image processing is to buy a scanner (see Chapter 6).

The following list can help you decide how to assemble your multimedia-PC system:

Case #1   **No computer is currently available**

Solutions:

1.   Purchase a complete multimedia system (Section 3.3).

2.   Purchase a 386 PC and a multimedia upgrade kit (Section 3.2).

> Know exactly what you're getting when you compare prices. In some cases, upgrade kits include more components (microphones, speakers, etc.) than a "complete" system. The number of CDs included (these can be very expensive when purchased individually) also varies greatly. When pricing bundled systems, always compare the quality and performance specifications of the individual components.

Case #2   Computer with 80286 processor

Solutions:

1.   Upgrade computer to a 386 (replace board) and purchase a multimedia upgrade kit.

2.   Purchase a complete multimedia system.

> Upgrading from a 286 may require several new components (RAM chips, controllers, etc.). Even so, your system may still be limited by the slower performance of the remaining components (e.g., access time of an older MFM hard drive).
>
> In the long run, the cost of the individual parts may add up to more than that of a complete system, not to mention the inconvenience of doing your own assembly.

Case #3   Computer with 386 processor and sound card
**   available**

Solutions:

1.   Purchase a CD-ROM drive. If your sound card is MPC-compatible and includes a CD-ROM controller, a separate controller isn't needed.

2.   If your sound card isn't MPC-compatible, purchase a multimedia upgrade kit.

If you obtain the sound card and CD-ROM drive separately, ensure that they are compatible. The audio cable of the CD-ROM drive must fit the sound card connector. If it doesn't, however, there is still a little trick that lets you use the audio function of the CD-ROM drive (Section 3.5).

Software is the key

To complete your multimedia system according to the MPC specification, you'll need Windows. Windows 3.1 already contains all the necessary multimedia interfaces. If you have Windows 3.0, either upgrade it with the Windows Multimedia Extension 1.0, or upgrade directly to Windows 3.1.

We recommend the upgrade to Windows 3.1, which is much faster and more stable than Version 3.0 and includes all the necessary multimedia interfaces.

3.2 Multimedia Upgrade Kits

In this section we'll discuss some of the most important products that are currently available for upgrading a PC for multimedia use.

You should use at least a 486SX processor although a 386 processor will work. The extra speed provided by a 486SX processor will come in handy.

486SX processor recommended

The CD-ROM in your upgrade kit should be fast. An access time of about 300 ms is usually enough (although new "double-speed" drives can transfer 300K of data per second).

An 8-bit audio or sound card is acceptable for games and reproducing speech. A 16-bit audio or sound card is necessary for stereo for CD-quality production work.

Choosing An Upgrade Kit

Check before buying

The individual components of upgrade kits can change, so always check before you buy. We didn't include prices because they are so volatile. Contact your distributor or dealer for pricing information.

Upgrade kits usually include the following:

Sound card and MIDI interface

Sound cards must be included in all MPC upgrade kits. If you can afford it, look for a 16-bit stereo sound capability and 44.1 KHz.

CD-ROM drive

Most upgrade kits include either an internal or external CD-ROM drive.

Internal drives Make certain your PC has enough room for an internal drive. Also, make certain the cable is long enough to reach from the SCSI board to the drive.

External drive If you want an external drive, make certain the cables are long enough. Also, you may want to consider a second SCSI port for daisychaining to a second SCSI drive.

Multimedia Windows software

Many upgrade kits are bundled with software such as games and reference tools.

Sound Blaster Multimedia Upgrade Kit

The Sound Blaster Multimedia Upgrade Kit is based on the Sound Blaster Pro, which is one of the best-selling sound cards. The 8-bit card provides all the necessary connections, including microphone, Line-in, MIDI, game port and speaker output. Volume can be controlled separately on the back of the card.

Interrupt, DMA channel and I/O port must be configured on the card with jumpers if the default installation produces conflicts (see Section 3.5).

Stereo amplifier

The built-in stereo amplifier has a maximum output capacity of 4 watts per channel at 4 ohms or 2 watts per channel at 8 ohms. The microphone input is designed for 600 ohms impedance; microphone sensitivity should be at least 74 dB.

Sound generation

Frequency modulation sound generation is based on the 4-operator OPL3 FM music chip. A total of 8 different waveforms can be selected. The OPL3 chip has the following modes:

- 9 melodic instruments and 5 percussion instruments

- 6 melodic (4 operators), 3 melodic (2 operators) and 5 percussion instruments

- 15 melody (2 operators) and 5 percussion instruments

DAC transfer modes

The card also contains a stereo digitized sound channel (2 x 8-bit DAC). The following DAC transfer modes are available:

- Direct mode - direct bytewise transfer through the CPU

- DMA mode - no CPU participation required

- Compression methods:

  8-bit data, no compression

  2:1 data compression, 4-bit ADPCM, hardware decompression

  3:1 data compression, 2.6-bit ADPCM, hardware decompression

  4:1 data compression, 2-bit ADPCM, hardware decompression

Sampling rate

The Sound Blaster Pro has an 8-bit stereo analog/digital converter for sound signals. Sampling rate is variable between 4 kHz and 44.1 kHz (44.1 kHz mono, 22.05 KHz stereo).

Connector for CD-ROM drive

An advantage of the Sound Blaster Pro card is the integrated AT bus controller connecting the CD-ROM drive from Japanese electronics giant Matsushita. The drive itself has the disadvantage that CDs must be loaded into a caddy. However, this drive has a high transfer speed (176K/sec) and access time (350 ms). The drive has a headphone jack and volume control on the front panel, in accordance with MPC specifications.

Software completes the kit

Windows 3.1, multimedia drivers and an assortment of DOS and Windows software completes the kit. DOS programs include the "Talking Parrot," the VEDIT software for Sound Blaster Pro voice editing, the TEMPRA package, and a DOS-based multimedia demo. The Windows applications include a sound mixer, applications for playing WAV and MIDI files, and two multimedia authoring packages.

Depending on price level, varying numbers of CDs with multimedia applications complete the package.

Media Vision Multimedia Upgrade Kit

Media Vision's kit features a standard SCSI interface for connecting to its 380 ms Sony CD-ROM drive, and the Pro AudioSpectrum Plus or Pro Audio Spectrum 16 sound card.

The Media Vision Multimedia PC provides excellent sound capabilities. It occupies one 8-bit slot and the software includes Windows with Multimedia, a game, some sound effects and sound applications, and Compton's *Multimedia Encyclopedia* for Windows. A MIDI kit with MIDI connector is available separately.

Media Resources MKA-01

The upgrade kit from Media Resources features a 280 ms NEC CD-ROM drive and the Pro AudioSpectrum Plus sound card.

The MKA-01 kit also includes a Roland SCC-1 Sound Card. This sound card combines 24-voice stereo and MIDI workstation.

The software which accompanies the MKA-01 kit includes Windows 3.1 and its multimedia extensions, a sequencer (MIDIsoft Recording Session), a multimedia desk accessory package (*At Your Service* from Brightstar) and a screen saver (*Screen Craze* from Gold Disk).

Other Upgrade Kits

MultiSound MPC Upgrade Kit

This upgrade kit from Turtle Beach features a Toshiba 330 CD-ROM drive and the Turtle Beach MultiSound sound card.

Bundled software includes Wave for Windows, Cakewalk or Asymetrix Toolbook.

Tandy MPC Upgrade

The upgrade kit from Tandy features an internal CDR-1000CD-ROM drive and the Tandy Audio Adapter sound card.

Sample applications are bundled with the Tandy MPC Upgrade kit.

NEC Multimedia Gallery

This upgrade kit from NEC Technologies features an NEC Intersect CDR-74 CD-ROM drive and the NEC Multimedia Plus Audio Board sound card.

Several applications are bundled with this upgrade kit including Just Grandma and Me, Sherlock Holmes, Guiness Book of World Records, and more.

3.3   Starting With A Full Multimedia System

You now know that a multimedia system requires:

- A PC with enough power to handle all this visual and aural data.

- A sound card, speakers, microphones, and other audio equipment if you plan on developing your own sound effects.

- A CD-ROM drive that can also play audio CDs.

- A high-performance graphics card and suitable monitor.

- Software on diskette and CD-ROM.

Naturally, you'll also need some special software to put the new media to work. Getting up and running with all this requires a certain know-how that can be obtained only with good documentation and user-friendly interfaces.

For many users, the obvious solution is to purchase a complete multimedia system on the assumption that it has been adequately assembled by competent specialists. Of course, in addition to a dazzling performance, many advertisements claim that their products are easy to use. So, setting up and learning how to use your system is supposedly very simple.

Ease of use and learning are important considerations when buying a multimedia PC. Can we believe the advertiser's claims, or will our first encounter with the world of multimedia be an exercise in frustration?

If you're interested in starting from scratch, there are several systems on the market from such manufacturers as ALR (their Flyer 3SX/25 MPC and their Flyer 32DT 4SX/25 MPC), Ares Microdevelopment, CompuAdd and Phillips.

The first impression

All the complete systems mentioned correspond to the minimum MPC requirements. When shopping for a "dedicated" multimedia system, we recommend that you consider the list of necessities we stated earlier, and the following:

*   Processor type and clock speed:
    Is a 386SX/18 really going to be fast enough to handle multimedia?

*   CD-ROM drive:
    Is the seek time fast enough? Is the drive built according to MPC specifications (headphone jack, front-panel volume control)?

*   Sound card hardware extras:
    Does the system include amplified speakers? Microphones? A MIDI connector?

*   Software:
    Does the package include practical software, like a MIDI sequencer, sound capture software, or drawing or animation programs?

3.4 PC Fine-tuning

The performance classes specified for hardware in the MPC definition represent the minimum configuration, which is subject to limited use. However, more power can definitely be useful. In this section we'll discuss some of the limitations, and suggest ways to deal with them.

Basically, no one component of a computer system determines the system's power and speed. Instead, this is determined by the interaction of all the components.

For example, you'll get better results using a 386 processor with 4 or 8 Meg of RAM and a fast hard drive, than you will using a 486 with "only" 2 Meg of RAM and a slow drive.

Processors

Although the minimum prerequisite of an 80286 processor permits the use of an AT class computer for multimedia applications, Windows requires at least an 80386SX to achieve full performance.

Virtual memory   Here Windows operates in 386 Enhanced mode, and is capable of multitasking (running multiple tasks concurrently) and using part of the hard drive as virtual memory. Virtual memory is a storage area used for temporarily storing memory blocks.

This relieves shortages of main memory (RAM). Data not immediately needed can be swapped to virtual memory and retrieved again when required. Accessing the disk, however, is always slower than accessing RAM. Therefore, additional RAM can significantly improve performance by reducing disk access.

Clock frequency   The processor's clock frequency is also an important factor in determining performance. The minimum recommendation is 16 MHz; 25MHz is the realistic minimum.

Main Memory

Unlike DOS, Windows has complete access to extended main memory. The limit to its performance lies in exhausting the main memory capacity.

Under Windows multitasking, efficiency is affected by the number of applications in main memory. Each one requires computer time.

Even when an application is inactive, Windows must constantly check to see if it's waiting for input. In addition, each application is occupying valuable memory. If memory is full, something must be swapped out to the disk and read back in later when it's needed.

This process takes time and affects the operating speed. Therefore, adding more working memory can increase the speed of your system.

With an 80286 processor, you should have at least 2 Meg, and with an 80386 processor, you should have at least 4 Meg of main memory installed as extended memory.

Hard Drives

As re-writable mass storage, a hard drive is an important PC component. Windows applications seldom reside entirely within main memory during use. Instead, they are loaded from disk in

segments as needed. This is especially true when main memory (RAM) is full.

Access time is important

This ongoing disk access becomes noticeable with a slow hard drive. So access time as well as capacity is important in selecting a hard drive. An access time of 20 ms should be considered the minimum prerequisite.

A hard drive doubler such as DoubleDensity can be used to increase the capacity of your present drive. These programs automatically compress the data as it's written to the disk and decompress it when it's read. This is an inexpensive way to nearly double your hard drive capacity.

On a fast 386 computer, this can also speed up read access. This is possible because, in compressed form, there is less data to read, and decompression in memory is faster than reading the extra data from the disk.

The compression process also takes time, however, and affects write time even on faster systems. Therefore, you shouldn't put frequently written files on a doubled hard drive partition.

Graphics Cards

In choosing a graphics card, an important consideration is whether the card has its own intelligent graphics controller to perform graphics operations without help from the processor. Special graphics chip sets (e.g., Tseng ET4000 or Trident T8900) execute fast translation of graphics operations.

For multimedia applications that work extensively with graphics, Windows should be used with at least 256 colors for good quality display.

Graphics drivers for Windows

A high scanning frequency is needed for good results. This is the number of images drawn per second. For various resolutions in the VGA standard, this should be 72 Hz. When buying a graphics card, ensure that you also get compatible drivers for Windows 3.0 and 3.1.

Also, be aware that your monitor must support the performance features of the card, since both components work as a unit.

3.5 Complete Multimedia

In this section we'll discuss installing and using multimedia extensions, such as sound cards, CD-ROM drives, video overlay cards and scanners. You'll learn what to look for when different components interact and how to solve some of the problems that might occur.

The PC Speaker

Usually you can play sound files only if your computer has an appropriate sound card (Sound Blaster, AdLib, Pro Audio Spectrum, etc.).

Using the PC speaker

However, it's also possible, to play digitized sounds over the PC's built-in speaker. All you need is a special Windows driver that passes the sound data to the internal speaker in Microsoft WAV format. Microsoft supplied us with this driver. It can also be obtained directly over the Microsoft Hotline.

PCSPEAK.EXE is a self-unpacking file in the \WINDOWS\SPEAKER\ directory on the companion CD-ROM. This file contains additional files.

Copy the file to your hard drive, preferably into a separate directory (e.g., C:\WINDOWS\SPEAKER\), and select the directory in File Manager. Besides some text files, the directory will include the info file OEMSETUP.INF and the driver file SPEAKER.DRV.

Installing the driver

Go to the Windows Control Panel and select **Settings/Drivers....** Click the [Add...] button and select the entry "Unlisted or Updated Driver".

A dialog box asks you to insert a diskette with the OEMSETUP.INF file. Enter the directory into which you have unpacked the PCSPEAK.EXE file.

The selection list shows the entry Sound driver for PC speaker. After confirming this entry, you'll see another dialog box for controlling sound properties, such as volume and playing speed.

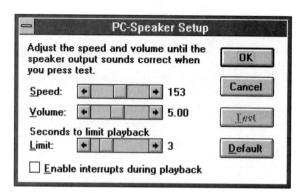

Driver settings options

You can check the effect of your settings by clicking on the [Test] button.

We recommend that you enable the "Enable interrupts during playback" check box. Otherwise, all other interrupts in the system will then be deactivated while the speaker is playing a sound file. This disables keyboard and mouse input and allows full control of the speaker during play.

For you to hear any sound, the appropriate WAV file must be read into memory and passed to the speaker in the proper form. This is very taxing on the processor, because much information must be processed in a very brief time. When a sound card is used to play the WAV file, the card itself does this processing.

PC Speaker And Sound Card

A Windows sound card driver controls the use of the sound card under Windows only. Various acoustical warning signals under DOS will still be sent to the internal speaker.

With a little skill you can change this by disconnecting the line from the main board to the speaker and rerouting it to Jumper 1 on the Sound Blaster card.

Consider whether you really want to disable the internal speaker entirely. Sometimes it's useful to have another sound source besides your sound card. Some sequencers or music recording programs, for example, output the metronome over the internal speaker to keep it separate from the synthesizer sound. Furthermore, a wrong connection can damage your sound card or even the motherboard.

If you decide to do this, be sure to disconnect the power to your computer before you start. Follow the instructions carefully and in the proper sequence. If you're not sure how to locate the right cable, it's better to have a trained technician do the job than to risk damaging your system.

Depending on how the main board feeds your computer's speaker, you need one or two lines for the connection. First disconnect the cable from the speaker. This can be very difficult, depending on the housing.

To save yourself as much soldering work as possible, you should leave a few centimeters of wire attached to the speaker and fasten it with a jumper similar to those on the Sound Blaster card. You can get these in a computer store. This will make it easier if you want to reactivate the speaker later. In this case, you must only switch the connection from the sound card to the loudspeaker.

Now let's return to the sound card. The current-carrying (+5V) line of the speaker must be connected to Pin 1 of Jumper 1. Use your instruction manual for the main board to locate the right cable. Mistakes can cause a short circuit with unpleasant results. The other line delivers the reference signal and should be connected to Pin 2. Now you can test the connection by rebooting, if your computer normally responds with a beep during the boot process. Otherwise, you must improvise an acoustic signal.

Pin	Signal	I/O
1	+5V	IN
2	SPK	IN

If you don't hear anything, check the connections again.

Installing A Sound Card

Installing a sound card should be fairly simple. In our discussion, we use one of the most popular cards, the Sound Blaster Pro, as an example. Since this card is similar to most other cards, the steps described here should be good general guidelines.

Interrupts

The Sound Blaster Pro requires an interrupt line for communicating with the processor. An interrupt is a signal that the card sends to the processor to initiate a certain function.

The processor executes the function after receiving the interrupt signal. Only certain lines are designated for carrying interrupts. Since some of them are already used by other hardware components, such as diskette drives and various interfaces, only a few possibilities are left for the sound card.

The Sound Blaster must be assigned an available interrupt line (i.e., one that isn't already being used), because conflicts can interfere with the card's operation.

Assignment of Interrupts in the AT	
IRQ0	System timer
IRQ1	Keyboard
IRQ2	Not used
IRQ3	Not used/COM2
IRQ4	COM1
IRQ5	Not used/LPT2
IRQ6	Diskette controller
IRQ7	Not used/LPT1
IRQ10	Not used

Using an interrupt

Sound Blaster is preset to use Interrupt 7. This is also used in some cases by printer spoolers. However, you won't have a problem unless you try to print and reference the sound card at the same time.

Alternatively, you could use Interrupt 5. This is usually available. However, it may also be used by a second printer connection. It's important to verify interrupt assignments when other cards, which may require their own interrupts (e.g., scanner cards), have already been installed.

How interrupts work

*Interrupt request
(IRQ)*

An interrupt request (IRQ) is a signal that a device sends over a designated line to the CPU. This signal requests that a particular function be executed.

Interrupts ensure that the CPU doesn't constantly have to check with the various devices for their needs. As soon as the status of one of the seven hardware interrupt lines changes, the CPU suspends its current task and checks to see which device requires attention.

Once the device is recognized, the CPU services the request by jumping to the appropriate address, which is usually set when the device is installed.

If two devices use the same interrupt, the CPU can jump to the wrong (inactive) device's program, possibly causing the system to "lock up."

Therefore, it's very important to ensure, when installing a scanner, sound card, mouse, video board, etc., that interrupt assignments don't overlap.

*Jumper
configuration*

If you want to reassign the Sound Blaster Pro's interrupt number, you must change a jumper on the card itself. A jumper is a small removable bridge that activates a particular line by forming a connection.

The following lists the jumpers and their functions in Sound Blaster Pro.

Functions of Sound Blaster Pro jumpers	
Jumper	**Function**
JP1	PC speaker connection
JP4	Joystick enabled/disabled
JP5	DRQ0 for DMA channel 0 (with JP15)
JP6	DRQ1 for DMA channel 1 (with JP16)
JP7	DRQ3 for DMA channel 3 (with JP17)
JP13	22x for base address I/O port 220 Hex

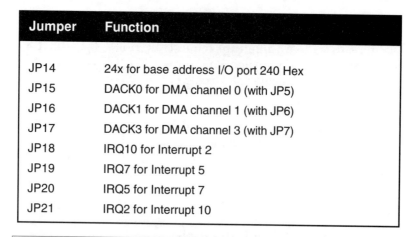

Jumper	Function
JP14	24x for base address I/O port 240 Hex
JP15	DACK0 for DMA channel 0 (with JP5)
JP16	DACK1 for DMA channel 1 (with JP6)
JP17	DACK3 for DMA channel 3 (with JP7)
JP18	IRQ10 for Interrupt 2
JP19	IRQ7 for Interrupt 5
JP20	IRQ5 for Interrupt 7
JP21	IRQ2 for Interrupt 10

If you're not sure which interrupts are still free, try the default setting. You can check later for conflicts with the test program.

If you're using a joystick from a separate game port on your computer, you should deactivate the Sound Blaster joystick connector by removing jumper J4.

You could operate your joystick from the Sound Blaster, but then you must deactivate the other game port.

Port addresses A sound card also needs a port address. With this and subsequent addresses, the sound card communicates with your computer. Every card and interface requires such a communication area. Usually only the base (beginning) address is given.

The Sound Blaster's base address is 220 Hex. The following table shows port addresses for some key components and expansion cards. As with interrupt lines, a port address can only be used by one device, since device-specific data is exchanged here.

Base address When setting the base address for your sound card, make sure you choose one that is not already in use. Conflicts can cause a system crash.

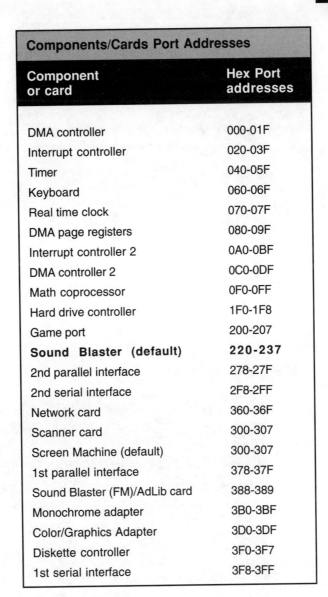

Components/Cards Port Addresses	
Component or card	**Hex Port addresses**
DMA controller	000-01F
Interrupt controller	020-03F
Timer	040-05F
Keyboard	060-06F
Real time clock	070-07F
DMA page registers	080-09F
Interrupt controller 2	0A0-0BF
DMA controller 2	0C0-0DF
Math coprocessor	0F0-0FF
Hard drive controller	1F0-1F8
Game port	200-207
Sound Blaster (default)	**220-237**
2nd parallel interface	278-27F
2nd serial interface	2F8-2FF
Network card	360-36F
Scanner card	300-307
Screen Machine (default)	300-307
1st parallel interface	378-37F
Sound Blaster (FM)/AdLib card	388-389
Monochrome adapter	3B0-3BF
Color/Graphics Adapter	3D0-3DF
Diskette controller	3F0-3F7
1st serial interface	3F8-3FF

Installing the card

For safety reasons, always unplug the power cord before opening the computer housing. Then remove the screws from the back of the housing, take off the cover, and locate a free 16-bit slot.

If possible, leave an open slot next to the sound card so its front side has room for heat to dissipate. If you're also going to connect a CD-ROM drive to the card, ensure that the data cable can reach it.

Before picking up the card, touch the computer case to discharge static electricity. The elements on the card and in your computer are so sensitive that the slightest electrical charge can ruin them.

Remove the cover plate from the back of the computer and set the screw aside carefully; you'll need it again momentarily. Press the card carefully into the slot; touch the card only by the edges. Once the card is in place, secure it by replacing the screw.

> If you're not installing additional components (e.g., a CD-ROM drive), replace the cover on your computer. Wait to see that the card works properly and is using the right jumper settings before replacing the screws.

Testing the card   On the accompanying installation diskette, you'll find a testing program that will check for interrupt, DMA channel and port address conflicts with other cards. It starts with the command:

TEST-SBP

The card's default settings are Interrupt IRQ7, DMA channel 1 and port address 220 Hex.

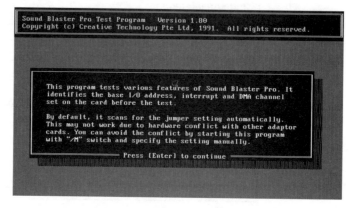

The Sound Blaster Pro testing program

If conflicts occur, an error message is displayed and you must make the appropriate changes.

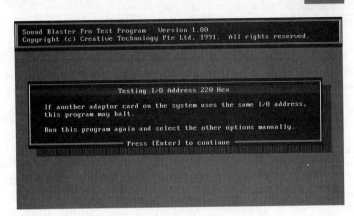

TEST-SBP also plays back FM music and digitized sound demos. Check to see that the speakers or headphones are connected properly and set the volume to the desired level.

If everything works, the hardest part is over. If not, you'll find some suggestions later on for resolving possible problems.

Installing the software

After successfully installing the card itself, you must install the software. This is also located on the Sound Blaster installation diskette. The following command starts the process:

```
INST-HD C:
```

C: represents the drive where the software should be installed.

The install program copies the Sound Blaster programs to the appropriate directories on the hard drive. The values assigned for interrupt, DMA channel and output port are again checked and entered automatically into the AUTOEXEC.BAT file. These are called environment variables and are specified as follows:

```
SET BLASTER=A220 I7 D1 T2
```

The entry A220 specifies the output port, I7 the interrupt and D1 the DMA channel. The entry T2 refers to Sound Blaster Pro. Another environment variable specifies the directory containing the Sound Blaster files:

```
SET SOUND=C:\SBPRO
```

The complete Sound Blaster software library is divided into separate subdirectories below C:\SBPRO.

Installation under Windows

Both the Sound Blaster and Windows software must be correctly configured to use the sound card under Windows. The configuration procedure depends on which version of Windows (Windows 3.1, or Windows 3.0 with Multimedia Extension 1.0) you're using.

Windows 3.0 and Sound Blaster

If you use Windows 3.0, you must copy the DLL (Dynamic Link Library) files from \SBPRO\WINDOWS to your Windows directory:

```
COPY PC:\SBPRO\WINDOWS SNDBLST.DLL C:\WINDOWS
```

Start Windows and select **File/New...** in the Program Manager. Create a program group for the programs JUKEBOX.EXE, SBMIXER.EXE and SETUP.EXE from the \SBPRO\WINDOWS directory. Then run the Sound Blaster setup program to automatically enter the following values into the Windows initialization file WIN.INI:

```
[SoundBlaster]
Port=220
Int=7
DMA=1
```

After successfully completing the installation and setup, you must perform a warm boot to activate the settings. Now you can use your sound card with the Windows applications (see Chapter 5). First, however, you should switch off your computer and finish putting everything back together.

Windows 3.1 and Sound Blaster Pro

With its multimedia capabilities, Windows 3.1 has its own Sound Blaster drivers. The drivers supplied with Windows work with Sound Blaster 1 or 2.

For Sound Blaster Pro, there are improved drivers that are either supplied with the sound card or can be obtained through Creative Labs, or through the Creative Labs BBS. Normally these will be located in the \WIN31 subdirectory under \SBPRO. Here also is a file called OEMSETUP.INF, which coordinates the installation.

The Windows 3.1 Sound Blaster drivers are installed using the **Settings/Drivers...** item on the Control Panel. After selecting this option you'll see a list of the drivers currently installed. Before adding the new drivers you should delete any older versions or drivers for other sound cards. To do this, select the driver to be deleted and click the Remove button. Don't remove the MCI driver.

When all unneeded drivers have been removed, click Add... to install the new drivers. In the "List of Drivers" list box, choose "Unlisted or Updated Driver" and click the OK button.

You'll be asked to enter the directory where the new driver can be found. Type the directory, for example

```
C:\SBPRO\WIN31
```

and click the (OK) button.

A list of the three drivers located in this directory will appear. Add each one in turn. As Windows copies the drivers, it will ask you for interrupt, DMA-channel and port-address settings, which you should answer according to your sound card setup. After each driver, Windows asks if you want to restart to activate the new settings. You don't have to do this until you're finished with the last driver.

Then, if everything goes smoothly, you'll hear the "tada" greeting on Windows startup, announcing the multimedia readiness of Windows 3.1. As a final step, you should put the SBPMIXER.EXE and MMJBOX.EXE into a program group in Program Manager.

Using the sound card connections

To put your sound card to work in a full-fledged multimedia application, you now need to make the proper connections to other components.

Connecting the speakers
Before testing the sound card, you should hook it up to your speakers or headphones over the Speaker connector. The jack fits a miniature (3.5 mm) plug. For headphones, a Walkman headset works well. You can also purchase an adapter to accommodate the older style stereo headphones equipped with a standard (6.35 mm) plug.

This also applies to connecting room speakers. If they are not already equipped with the miniature plug, first obtain the appropriate adapters. Then to hook both speakers to the single sound card connector, you will need a Y-cable with a miniature plug for the sound card and two miniature jacks for the speakers.

Connecting a stereo unit
Over most sound cards you can also play sound from external sources, such as a radio or tape deck. A Y-cable is usually included to connect the external source to the sound card's Line-in connector.

The single end of the cable has a miniature stereo plug for connecting to the sound card, and the double end has audio plugs for connecting to the sound source. You can hook up a stereo tape deck, for example, by connecting the audio plugs to the tape deck's Line-out. Then simply turn on the tape deck to listen to recorded music over the sound card as you work with your computer (see Chapter 5).

Problems With Sound Card Installation

In this section, we'll discuss the problems you might have in installing and using your sound card, their possible causes, and how to solve them.

Conflicts with other cards

Other devices in your computer system besides the sound card may access interrupts, DMA channels and I/O ports. Problems can occur if two devices are trying to use the same resource. These conflicts may be caused by scanner controllers and video overlay boards.

What exactly is an I/O port?

When the CPU accesses a peripheral device, it uses a certain address area where data and instructions for this device are stored. Usually in the case of an I/O port, only the beginning or base address is given, although a series of contiguous addresses are actually used. Sound Blaster's normal base address is 220 Hex. In this and subsequent locations, sound card data is exchanged with the processor.

A list of port addresses used is located in the previous section.

The program TEST-SBP, which is included on the Sound Blaster diskette, helps locate the cause of a conflict. To resolve the problem, you can change either the sound card's settings or those of the other card involved. If you're not sure which card that is, you can find out by removing the other cards one at a time until the problem disappears.

Experimentation is needed

You may have to experiment with different settings to resolve the conflict. Usually the problem is the interrupt line or DMA channel instead of the port address.

Possible settings are given in the following table. If the card causing the conflict has more settings available than the Sound Blaster card, you may want to try those settings first.

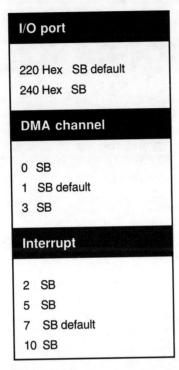

If you change the Sound Blaster's port address from 220 Hex to 240 Hex, you must also change the CD-ROM driver's port address in CONFIG.SYS to the new value, if you have installed the CD-ROM drive from CPS:

```
DEVICE=C:\DOS\SBPCD.SYS /D:MSCD001 /P:240
```

If you don't do this, the CD-ROM drive won't be recognized.

Most common error causes The interrupt and DMA channel are the most frequent cause of conflicts between cards, so be especially careful not to duplicate these settings. Different interrupts or DMA channels are selected with the jumpers on the card.

Refer to the card's documentation for the correct jumper positions. Then test the settings by running the appropriate software. For example, after changing a setting on a scanner controller, run the scanner program to perform a scanning operation. If problems persist, you must try another setting.

> Make a list of all the installed cards with their interrupt, DMA channel and port address settings. Then you'll know which ones are available the next time you add a new card.

With the Sound Blaster card, you must do more than simply change the jumper position when you select a new setting. You must also inform certain programs and files of the new setting. To ensure that it works, you should test the change using the FM music options provided in TEST-SBP.EXE. Then run the program INST-DRV.EXE to assign the new settings to the Sound Blaster DOS drivers.

Similar procedures are needed when you make changes to other cards. Consult the appropriate documentation to determine what software changes are needed and how to make them.

The Windows files WIN.INI and SYSTEM.INI must be changed to reflect your new card setup. For Windows 3.0, find the [SoundBlaster] section of WIN.INI.

```
[SoundBlaster]
int= (interrupt number)
port=(port number)
DMA= (DMA channel number)
```

For Windows 3.0 with the Multimedia Extension, the same entries are found in the SYSTEM.INI file. The section name is also the same as in WIN.INI. For Windows 3.1, the required information is specified in SYSTEM.INI in the [sndblst.drv] section:

```
[sndblst.drv] (Windows 3.1)
int= (interrupt number)
port=(port number)
dmachannel(DMA channel number)
```

Change the entries as needed to correspond to the jumper positions on the Sound Blaster card. Remember that the changes aren't activated until you restart Windows.

With Windows 3.0, you can automatically change WIN.INI by running SBSETUP.EXE. This program checks the positions of the jumpers on the card and makes the appropriate entries in WIN.INI.

First you indicate the type of Sound Blaster card you have. Then dialog boxes for the port, interrupt and DMA channel appear. You can click the appropriate selection within these boxes, or have the program make the selection for you by choosing the AutoScan option.

With Windows 3.1, you must select **Settings/Drivers...** from the Control Panel, then click the Setup button for each of the Sound Blaster drivers listed. Enter the new settings in the Setup dialog box.

Using the right driver

There are many versions of drivers for Sound Blaster Pro. Three separate drivers are needed for Windows:

- SBPAUX.DRV

- SBPFM.DRV

- SBPMID.DRV

These drivers must be present in the Windows SYSTEM directory. If the sound card doesn't work even with the correct line and address settings, the problem might be caused by outdated or incompatible drivers. Some possible sources for Sound Blaster Pro drivers are the CD Windows with Multimedia, or the Sound Blaster Pro installation diskettes.

Possible driver problems include the Windows Sound Recorder not working and a hissing noise from the sound card after leaving Windows (this can be suppressed by turning down the FM volume in SBPMIXER). If you know your card settings aren't the problem, ensure that you have the most current drivers.

If you have run the Multimedia Extension Setup (Chapter 4) since installing your sound card, you may have overwritten the new drivers with older versions. To correct this, manually copy the drivers from the Sound Blaster installation diskette or Sound Blaster directory of your hard drive into the Windows SYSTEM directory.

Sound Blaster Pro

With some versions of Sound Blaster Pro, there may be problems with the drivers supplied on the installation diskette, especially for SBP2FM.DRV. A bad version of this driver can cause a permanent hiss from the FM voices.

This problem can be alleviated by using an older version (SBPFM.DRV) with the other two current drivers. If you do this, you should then check the [drivers] section of SYSTEM.INI because multiple installations can result in multiple MIDI entries here. If this happens, set the MIDI entry as shown later and delete the others (e.g., MIDI1= and MIDI2=).

The Windows system initialization file contains all the necessary parameters for starting Windows and coordinating the various peripheral devices. If you make subsequent changes to Sound Blaster's interrupt, DMA channel or port address settings, these changes must be updated in the [SoundBlaster] or [sndblst] section, as we discussed earlier.

When new drivers are installed, however, additional entries in the [386Enh] or [drivers] section of SYSTEM.INI must also be verified or changed:

```
device=vsbpd.386
```

The name of the virtual device must be entered here in order for Sound Blaster to work in 386 Enhanced mode. Ensure that the current version has been copied into the SYSTEM directory of Windows. Also, if the previous entry is preceded by an older entry in the form of

```
device=vsbd.386
```

Sound Blaster Pro won't work. To correct the problem, simply remove this line from the SYSTEM.INI file.

```
[drivers]
timer=timer.drv
CDAudio=mcicda.drv
Joystick=ibmjoy.drv
MidiMapper=midimap.drv
MIDI=sbp2fm.drv  (sbpfm.drv for Sound Blaster Pro 2)
AUX=sbpaux.drv
Wave=sbpsnd.drv
```

This section specifies the driver files assigned to the drivers installed in Control Panel. The last three entries refer to Sound Blaster Pro. Normally the proper entries in SYSTEM.INI are made automatically as new drivers are added under Control Panel. These should be verified if you've made multiple installations or copied some of the driver files manually.

If this process becomes too confusing, you may have to start over with the following steps:

1.   Start Windows.

2. Open the Control Panel and select Drivers.

3. Remove all drivers that access a sound card.

4. Exit Windows and change to the Windows SYSTEM directory.

5. Delete the files:

   VSBPD.386   VSBD.368

   SBPFM.DRV   SBP2FM.DRV

   SBPAUX.DRV   SBPSND.DRV

   SBPMIXER.CPL

6. Change to the Windows directory and load the SYSTEM.INI file into an editor, for example by entering:

   ```
   EDIT SYSTEM.INI
   ```

7. Delete the following lines, if available

   ```
   device=vsbpd.386
   device=vsbd.386
   ```

   and resave the file.

8. Start Windows and add the new drivers as described earlier.

9. Exit Windows and restart it. The drivers should now be in order and fully functional.

Permanent volume setting

A mixer application was included with older driver versions. This was copied into the Windows SYSTEM directory and performed the same function as the program SBPMIXER.EXE. However, using it may lead to problems. You should delete this program from the Windows SYSTEM directory and use it only for volume control under Windows.

This program lets you adjust the volumes of the various sound sources individually. Once you have the settings the way you want them, click the (Save) button and SYSTEM.INI is updated with the appropriate entries.

The volume settings you select in the mixer program are saved in the [sndblst.drv] section of SYSTEM.INI in the following form (values from 0 to 15 are specified for the left and right stereo channels):

```
MasterVolume= 9, 9
FmVolume= 10, 10
CDVolume= 9, 9
LineVolume= 8, 8
MicVolume= 0, 0
VoiceVolume= 10, 10
```

Although you could also edit these yourself, using the mixer is much easier. Also, you can test the settings as you adjust them.

As you can see from the previous example or the first time you use the mixer, the microphone volume is preset to 0. This is normally done to prevent sudden feedback when the microphone is connected or switched on.

If the joystick stops working

The MPC definition specifies that a sound card must have a MIDI connector. This uses the same type of plug as a joystick connector and can actually serve a double purpose (i.e., for either a MIDI box or an ordinary IBM-compatible joystick). If you use a MIDI box here, your joystick can be connected to the box. The joystick works the same way in either position.

However, conflicts can occur if you're using a second game port from a multi-I/O card. The problem is corrected by disabling one of the two ports.

A Y-cable allows you to use two joysticks (for two players) from a single game port. However, this may not be possible on the sound card's joystick port. In this case, you should use the game port of the multi-I/O card and disable the joystick port on the sound card. This won't affect how the MIDI connector operates.

To disable the joystick port of the Sound Blaster, remove the jumper JP4 on the card.

Installing A CD-ROM Drive

Installing a CD-ROM drive is just as easy as installing a card. Locate a free drive bay, preferably under the diskette drive, and remove the cover from the front of the PC case.

No room in the PC case

If your computer is a flat desktop model and all the drive bays are already occupied, you have two options. The first one is to buy an external CD-ROM drive with its own housing. You can also consider changing to a tower case.

External CD-ROM drives are more expensive than internal models. They require that you install a card and run a cable out to the drive.

If you will be needing room for more multimedia hardware (video overlay card, scanner card, etc.), now is a good time to make the change. If you're not completely comfortable performing your own installation, take your system to a qualified technician.

Now let's discuss the installation itself. Slide the drive into the bay with the help of the plastic guides (these are also used for guiding a hard drive or floppy drive).

Before fastening the screws, install the data cable, leaving a little extra room.

Connecting the cable

Locate a free power supply connector to plug into the CD-ROM drive. The plug fits in only one direction so you can't do this incorrectly.

> Most power supplies (especially in smaller cases) don't have many extra connectors. If yours are already in use with perhaps two floppy drives and two hard drives, one can be shared with a Y-adapter. You can find these adapters at computer specialty stores.

Now connect the ribbon cable (SCSI or AT bus) with the controller, which is either on a separate card or on the sound card itself. Make sure Line 1 (marked in red on the cable and numbered on the controller connector) is properly connected. The ribbon cable should not be kinked.

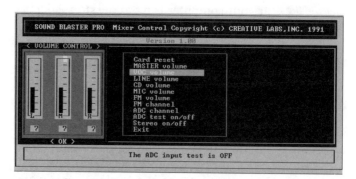

CD-ROM drive and cable configuration

Finally, connect the thin audio cable to the sound card. This allows audio CDs to be played over the sound card. If your system wasn't purchased as a complete multimedia kit, there may be compatibility problems with this connection.

If the audio cable doesn't fit, or if you don't get any sound after connecting it, you can try something else. Purchase a cable with miniature (3.5 mm) stereo plugs at both ends.

Plug one end into the headphone output of the CD-ROM drive and the other into the Line-in input of the sound card. This should give you the full audio function (Chapter 5).

Installing the driver

For DOS to reference the CD-ROM drive like a normal drive, certain programs must be included in the AUTOEXEC.BAT and CONFIG.SYS files.

The CD-ROM drive of the Sound Blaster Multimedia Upgrade Kit is installed using the following program:

```
INST-CD C:
```

This program is located on the installation diskette. If you have MS-DOS Version 5, the CONFIG.SYS file requires the following entry:

```
DEVICE=C:\DOS\SETVER.EXE
```

This prevents conflicts with the CD driver program. This entry should appear before the entry for the CD-ROM drive.

CONFIG.SYS   The installation program makes the following entry in CONFIG.SYS:

```
DEVICE=C:\SBPRO\DRV\SBPCD.SYS /D:\MSCD001 /P:220
```

This entry is needed for the interaction between the CD-ROM drive and the Sound Blaster card, which contains the controller for the Matsushita drive. The string "D:MSCD001" identifies the drive, and "P:220" identifies the output port of the Sound Blaster card.

AUTOEXEC.BAT   The final thing you must do to make the CD-ROM drive operable is to start the driver program MSCDEX.EXE Version 2.2. This program uses certain parameters that, in the case of the Sound Blaster kit, are found in the batch file CDDRIVE.BAT. The path information is also given here.

To make the CD-ROM drive always available, you should insert the corresponding commands into AUTOEXEC.BAT. For the Sound Blaster kit they appear as follows:

```
CD\SBPRO\DRV
MSCDEX /V /D:MSCD001 /M15
CD\
```

The first line indicates the path to the directory where the driver program is located. This may vary depending on the installation. The parameter /V displays a listing of memory allocation when the program starts.

The parameter D:MSCD001 provides the name by which the CD-ROM drive should be referenced. If you change it here, make sure you do the same in the CONFIG.SYS file. The parameter /M15 provides the number of read buffers.

More buffers provide faster execution because the CD is read less often. The price of this speed is memory. The driver uses about 2K of RAM per buffer.

If you want the driver to use expanded memory, you can add the parameter /E. This saves main memory. You won't be setting up any extra expanded memory, however, if you're working in Windows.

Accessing The CD-ROM Drive

When you've completed the installation procedures, restart your computer. The CD-ROM drive is then assigned the next available drive designation.

> If you have a partitioned hard drive or an added RAM disk, the Drive letter E: may be in use. In this case, you must provide a new drive designation by adding the command LASTDRIVE=Z to CONFIG.SYS.

Access under DOS and Windows

A CD-ROM drive is referenced by its assigned designation letter just like a normal disk drive. The only difference is that you can only read the data. If you try to delete a file from the CD under DOS 5.0, the following error message appears:

```
Extended Error 65
```

You can also reference the CD-ROM drive as usual in the Windows File Manager, where it has its own symbol. If you try to delete a file, Windows 3.1 assumes that this is network access, and denies access.

Otherwise a data CD is treated normally. Trying to read an audio CD will also cause an error message to appear.

Audio CDs

If you're not satisfied with the sound quality of an audio CD played over the sound card, you can also attach headphones, with a miniature plug, directly to the CD-ROM drive. The volume adjustment on the front of the drive controls the volume for the headphone output.

> If you also have speakers connected to the sound card, they'll parallel the music output of the headphones on the CD-ROM. You can silence them by setting the volume to 0 with the sound card mixer program.

Installing A Video Overlay Card

Installing a video overlay card is usually quite simple. However, most of these cards can be used only by a graphics card with an interface called a feature connector. This is a 26-pin connector located at the upper edge of the VGA card.

How an overlay card works

Superimposing video signals

An overlay card works by superimposing a video signal over a VGA signal. The VGA signals are directed over a special cable from the monitor connector of the graphics card to the overlay card.

There an area of the VGA signal is overlaid with the incoming video signal, and the composite signal is sent to the VGA monitor, which is connected to the overlay card (see diagram).

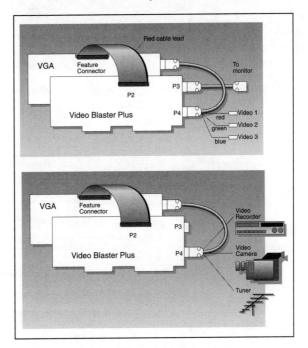

Video overlay card schematic

Besides the above-mentioned cable, a feature connector usually links the two cards together as well. The overlay card controls the graphics card over this connector.

This allows you, for example, to block out certain colors from the graphics card and replace them with the video signal (color keying).

Video overlay cards (e.g., Screen Machine, Video Blaster) usually have multiple RCA phono jacks for picking up multiple video sources. You need a special cable for connecting your video recorder or video camera.

If the source signal is S-VHS, two input jacks are used, one for luminance and the other for chrominance (Screen Machine).

Audio options

By using the tuner of a video recorder, you can easily watch television over your PC. Unfortunately, the sound is missing. Some manufacturers offer optional audio modules for their overlay cards, which you connect to the video recorder over an Audio-out cable.

> Since you already have a sound card in your PC, however, you can connect the Audio-out from the video recorder directly to the Line-in of the sound card and save some money. This way you can even record the sound.

Installation

We'll discuss only a general installation configuration. If there are no address conflicts with other cards, the following procedure should provide successful results:

1. Remove the housing and locate a free slot near the VGA card.

2. Insert the card carefully in the slot but don't fasten it tightly yet.

3. Connect the ribbon cable to the feature connector of the VGA card.

4. Remove the monitor connection from the VGA card and connect it to the VGA analog output on the overlay card.

5. Connect the output of the VGA card to the VGA analog input on the overlay card using the special cable. The RCA phono jacks for the inputs must also be on this side.

6. Connect the Video-out cable of the video source with one of the video inputs on the overlay card.

7. Install the software and run a function test.

8. Secure the card and replace the housing.

To test the system after the software is installed, call the video display program and switch on the video source. If nothing shows up, the problem may be selecting the wrong input.

You have to activate the one selected by the software. There is an option in the program for this purpose.

Address conflicts If you have the right input but there isn't a picture, the problem may be an I/O address conflict. Most overlay cards are easily compatible with other cards, since they don't access interrupts or DMA channels.

Jumpers are used to set the I/O address. Consult your card's documentation for the proper jumper placement.

Using A Video Camera

Video cameras or camcorders are used to create and process electronic images. Many amateur photographers are familiar with these devices. With the video overlay card, these devices can be used with personal computers.

The main advantage of using a video camera is its ability to capture individual images at any time. Scanner technology can also do this, but only with two-dimensional documents. With an appropriate video camera, you can assemble documents and images from anywhere and use them with your computer.

The following are some other advantages and disadvantages of using video cameras in personal computing:

Advantages

- Can be used anywhere

- Any subject, not just documents

- Captures 3-dimensional objects

- Zoom capability

- Shows different perspectives

- Relatively widely used

Disadvantages

- Relatively limited resolution

There are two types of video cameras, camcorders and still-video cameras.

Camcorder

The camcorder is loaded with a video cassette, on which the image is recorded. The VHS-C format, which has a recording length of 30 or 45 minutes, is widely used. Some camcorders have a Long play function that doubles the recording capacity of the cassette. The cassettes used are smaller than the conventional video cassette and are very portable. However, there are also devices that use 8 mm cassettes, or standard VHS cassettes.

There are two ways to view your video recordings. One way is to play the recording on a video recorder over a connecting cable. The alternative is to buy a video cassette adapter, and play the cassette in your "at home" video recorder.

Some older units use a camera and an independent video recorder. These may also require a separate monitor.

Still-video cameras

Unlike camcorders, still-video cameras record single still pictures. These images are usually recorded on a special diskette. These cameras are connected to a monitor or TV set to display the images.

A still-video camera can also be connected to a video recorder for taping. Camcorders act like still-video cameras when their recordings are played back in single-image mode. Usually the image is slightly fuzzy, however, since a camcorder normally operates with a shutter speed of 1/50 sec.

To alleviate this problem, more expensive camcorders have the ability to record with shutter speeds as short as 1/10,000 sec. Pictures recorded in this way are as sharp when shown in single-image mode as still-video pictures.

Use the same principle

Both camera types operate according to the same principle: Light entering the objective passes through a shutter to reach an electronic image sensor called a charge coupled device (CCD) sensor.

This is a small plate containing up to 480,000 phototransistors, which emit a charge when struck by light. Integrated electronics amplify and convert this to a video signal, display it in a viewer and record it on the appropriate medium. The signal is also relayed to an output jack, where it can be viewed over a monitor or overlay card.

Which is better?

Since still-video cameras are usually less expensive than camcorders, they are excellent for home use in capturing electronic images. They are convenient and simple to use. However, the camcorder, which is widely used, is much more versatile because of its ability to take motion pictures.

Right connection is crucial

The right connection is crucial for communication between camera and computer. The cable used for this purpose conveys the video data from the camera to the RCA jacks of the video overlay card.

These cables are available for any camera model. Actually, the cable is usually sold with the camera, since it is also used to connect the camera to a video recorder. Some cables may require an adapter to connect to the overlay card.

Connect up to three video sources

With most overlay cards, up to three video sources can be connected. So, a video recorder and video camera can be connected simultaneously. You use the software to switch back and forth between the sources. If a camcorder is connected directly to the overlay card, it serves the same function as a still-video camera. The still subject appears in the video window on the screen.

If you want to show images from multiple sources on the monitor simultaneously, you need multiple overlay cards in your computer. Obviously, this can be very expensive.

The incoming video signal can now be processed as discussed in the previous section.

Installing A Scanner

Requires a scanner card

To use a scanner with your computer, normally you must install an appropriate scanner card. Most hand-held scanners come with their own interface card. Flatbed scanners are controlled through an SCSI interface or bi-directional parallel interface. They also send data over this interface.

The appropriate interface card is installed like any other card. The connection between scanner and card should be over a parallel or SCSI interface because the timing of serial transfer is not well suited for this purpose.

> For the operating system to recognize your scanner, some models require a special driver and its corresponding entry in the CONFIG.SYS file.

When problems occur

Your scanner configuration can cause conflicts, usually with interrupts or DMA channels. If a sound card, video card and perhaps other cards are already installed, free interrupts may not be available.

Depending on the options available to your scanner, you must reassign its interrupt or DMA channel or those of the other card to solve the problem. Obviously, you must first know which card is responsible for the conflict. Without good documentation, you simply must experiment by removing one card at a time until the problem disappears.

Scanner software

Most scanners include their own software, which can be used for saving and editing the scanned image. Then the picture is usually loaded to a full-fledged image processing program for additional editing.

Many of these specialized image processing programs include their own scan modules (e.g., Paintbrush IV Plus, PhotoStyler). In this case, you indicate the type of scanner you have (like a printer driver). If you do this, you don't have to use the scanner software first.

Chapter 4

Windows and Multimedia

Microsoft Windows, the popular graphical user interface, is the platform of the future for multimedia. Acting as the interface between the hardware devices in this environment (sound cards, overlay boards, etc.) and the programs that address them is a key software component called the Media Control Interface (MCI).

Printer drivers provide a familiar example of the function of the Media Control Interface. MCI drivers are transferable to the hardware products of any manufacturer. The MCI concept is the cornerstone of Microsoft's multimedia foundation in Windows.

A quick glance at Windows 3.1 or the Multimedia Extension of Windows 3.0 reveals a few new multimedia enhancements, including Sound Recorder and Media Player.

In this chapter we'll introduce the multimedia applications of Windows 3.1 and Multimedia Extension 1.0. Multimedia Extension 1.0 first provided the MCI base and its new multimedia applications under Windows 3.0. In Windows 3.1, these components have for the most part been fully integrated. We'll indicate the few differences between the two systems during our discussion.

4.1   Windows 3.1

Windows 3.1 includes all the prerequisites for using and controlling multimedia components. Several new applications and options distinguish it in this respect from Version 3.0. We'll begin by introducing these applications and options.

Sound (Control Panel)

The Sound option of Control Panel allows you to replace Windows' familiar warning beep with the WAV-format sound file of your choice. You can also assign different sound files to various Windows events.

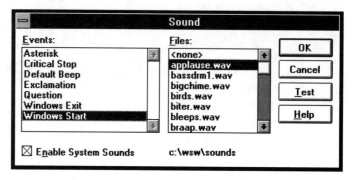

Sound file selected for Windows Start

On the left is a list of events that can be assigned a sound file. These events are:

- Asterisk
- Critical Stop
- Default Beep
- Exclamation
- Question
- Windows Exit
- Windows Start

Select an event, then choose the sound file to be assigned to the event from the list on the right. You can hear the sound by clicking the Test button.

Windows 3.0 and Multimedia Extension 1.0 offer a few other events. Other applications, such as *Wicked Sounds for Windows* (available from Abacus), add more events, and show you how to program for other events as well.

The "Enable System Sounds" check box activates the above settings, which replace the playing of a simple warning tone on the PC's internal speaker. Of course, in a multimedia environment it's assumed that you have a sound card.

Even without one, however, you can play a reasonable rendition of the system sounds over the internal speaker by installing a SPEAKER.DRV or similar driver.

By using the Sound Recorder, you can even record your own sound files for system events. This includes speech recorded over a microphone, so you can have your system say "Hello" when you switch on your computer.

MIDI Mapper (Control Panel)

The MIDI Mapper option ensures that data from an external MIDI device (keyboard or synthesizer), that's connected to your sound card's MIDI interface or your own sound card's synthesizer, is played correctly over the sound card.

MIDI Patch Map: 'SB2Pro'

1 based patches

Src Patch	Src Patch Name	Dest Patch	Volume %	Key Map Name
0	Acoustic Grand Piano	0	100	[None]
1	Bright Acoustic Piano	1	100	[None]
2	Electric Grand Piano	2	100	[None]
3	Honky-tonk Piano	3	100	[None]
4	Rhodes Piano	4	100	[None]
5	Chorused Piano	5	100	[None]
6	Harpsichord	6	100	[None]
7	Clavinet	7	100	[None]
8	Celesta	8	100	[None]
9	Glockenspiel	9	100	[None]
10	Music Box	10	100	[None]
11	Vibraphone	11	100	[None]
12	Marimba	12	100	[None]
13	Xylophone	13	100	[None]
14	Tubular Bells	14	100	[None]
15	Dulcimer	15	100	[None]

OK   Cancel   Help

Standard MIDI instrument numbering

MIDI Mapper lets you reassign instrument numbers, channels and rhythm sounds for a MIDI device that doesn't use Microsoft's standard MIDI assignments (more on this in Chapter 8).

Drivers

Before you can use a new multimedia device, you must prepare the appropriate driver to access it, as with a printer. This may be either a custom driver, such as for Sound Blaster and Pro Audio Spectrum, or one of the MCI drivers, which provides a standard interface for several devices.

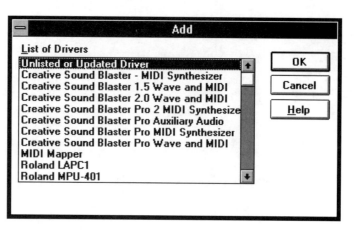

Setup for an additional driver

MCI drivers generally have a fixed set of functions. If a particular hardware component is being supported by an MCI driver, only the MCI driver functions can be used. In this case, you cannot use any additional capabilities provided by the hardware.

We'll discuss installing and setting up drivers in Section 4.3.

Sound Recorder

Sound
Recorder

Sound Recorder lets you create or mix sound files over your sound card. Sound sequences can be modified with special effects. If you have a microphone connected to the sound card, you can make voice recordings. These can be saved and edited, just like musical sound files.

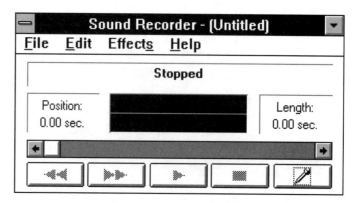

Music with the Sound Recorder

You can use Sound Recorder to make musical recordings by connecting a stereo or similar sound source to the sound card.

We'll discuss Sound Recorder basics in Section 4.4 and then present some practical applications in Chapter 5.

Media Player

Media Player is a versatile multimedia controller program. It allows access to all installed MCI drivers for playing animation, sound, video or MIDI files. A major aspect of its use is in controlling the CD-ROM drive. The Media Player screen contains a series of buttons, similar to those on a conventional audio CD player.

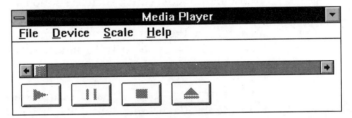

The Media Player

Media Player supports the audio function of the CD-ROM drive, allowing the playing of conventional audio CDs.

4.2 Windows Multimedia Extension

Microsoft Windows Multimedia Extension 1.0 provides the multimedia applications previously described and the MCI drivers for Windows 3.0.

With this extension, this version of Windows is fully qualified for multimedia use. Multimedia Extension comes on a CD and includes a complete set of Windows Version 3.0. The CD is sold only as part of a complete multimedia kit (Chapter 3). It cannot be obtained separately.

The Multimedia Extension shouldn't be used with Windows 3.1, because driver compatibility problems can occur. If you like the applications included with Multimedia Extension, copy these applications to their own group, install Windows 3.1 and delete the Multimedia Extension.

Hyper Guide and Music Box Multimedia Extension has two interesting applications, Hyper Guide and Music Box. In Windows 3.1, the Music Box has been replaced by the Media Player.

Multimedia Extension is sold only as part of a multimedia kit. Besides the specific hardware components included in the kit, the appropriate manufacturers' device-specific drivers and driver programs (e.g., a mixer) are also included on the Multimedia Extension CD. These are automatically installed during the setup process.

4.3 Configuring Multimedia Drivers

To use multimedia cards, such as sound cards like AdLib or Sound Blaster, and control MIDI devices, the necessary drivers must be included in the Windows environment. This applies to both manufacturer-supplied drivers and the standardized drivers found in the Media Control Interface.

Drivers

Correct driver installation and setup is a prerequisite for using both Media Player and Sound Recorder. This is done from the Drivers icon of Control Panel. Double-clicking the Drivers icon displays a dialog box that lists the multimedia drivers currently installed.

Configuring The Sound Blaster Card

When you configure a new multimedia device, you must add its driver to this list. Before you do this, the device itself should be installed in the computer. Then, to install the driver, click on Add... from the "Drivers" dialog box. A list of available drivers appears.

If you want to install a new version of an already installed driver, first remove the old version and restart Windows.

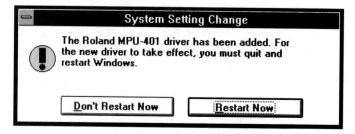

Selecting a multimedia driver

Select the driver for your device. If the appropriate driver isn't listed, you have two choices. You can either select the driver for a compatible device, if one is available, or use one supplied by the device manufacturer.

To do this, click on "Unlisted or Updated Driver". Then you must indicate the directory or drive where the new driver is located and insert the appropriate floppy diskette, if needed. The driver is copied to your Windows System directory when you click OK. A dialog box will ask you for any special settings.

The Sound Blaster driver Setup

The "Setup" dialog box varies, depending on the driver being installed. The Sound Blaster Setup requests the appropriate port, DMA and interrupt settings.

To determine whether the driver works, for example with Sound Blaster, you can use the "Sound" icon of Control Panel to assign a sound to an event. Then perform a warm boot to initialize the card, invoke the event and listen for the sound.

If problems occur (e.g., the Sound Blaster card plays a continuous tone), double-click "Drivers" to reconfigure the driver. The same dialog box will appear as when the driver was added. Most conflicts occur from overlapping assignment of interrupts.

For more information about changing the Sound Blaster interrupt and other settings, refer to Chapter 3.

4.4 Sound Recorder

Sound Recorder

Sound Recorder lets you record sound from various sources by digitizing the data and saving it as a sound file. You can also modify the structure of sound files or mix several files into one. Of course, these files can also be played using Sound Recorder.

A sound file can have a maximum length of 60 seconds.

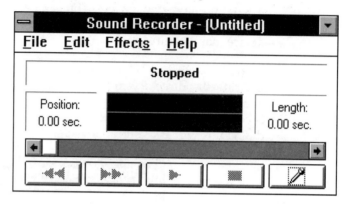

The Sound Recorder screen

Operating Sound Recorder

The Sound Recorder screen contains control buttons similar to those of a cassette recorder. The following describes each button:

The Rewind button takes you to the beginning of the sound file. The current position within the file is indicated by the position indicator and the scroll bar.

The Forward button advances to the end of the file. Again you can see your position on the scroll bar and position indicator.

The Play button plays the sound file. By playing the file, you can acoustically locate a certain position where you want to add effects or insert a new file.

Use the Stop button to stop recording or playing. The position is indicated on the scroll bar and position indicator.

The Record button starts recording from microphone input or from the output of Media Player or Music Box.

Determining the position in a file

As we mentioned, the scroll bar indicates the current position within a sound file. It's important to know your exact position when editing or mixing sounds.

The scroll bar and position indicator work together. The initial position is shown on the position indicator as 0.0 sec. The length of the entire file, in seconds, is displayed on the right.

You can move around within the file by positioning the scroll button with the mouse or by clicking the direction arrows at either end of the scroll bar.

You can also use the arrow keys on your keyboard to move in precise intervals of 0.1 sec. The wave box also shows sound activity graphically within the file.

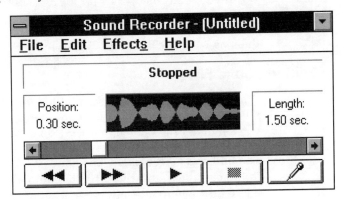

Graphic display of position

Creating Sound Files

To create a sound file, open the **File** menu and choose **New....** This isn't necessary when you first start Sound Recorder. In this case, a file hasn't been loaded yet so it's assumed that you're starting a new file. If you select **New...** while a current file is still open, you're reminded to save any changes you've made to the current file.

Only one file is actually open at a time. When you mix several files, you add new sounds in steps, saving subsequent versions under new file names.

Selecting Files

To load an existing file, select **File/Open...**. The "Open" dialog box lists all files with the .WAV extension. The WAVE format is the only sound file format compatible with Sound Recorder. The file you select is then available for editing.

After changing or manipulating the current file, you can restore it to its last saved status with **File/Revert...**. If you confirm the restoration, the changes will be permanently undone.

Recording From External Sources

Clicking the Record button records music or voice input. When recording speech over an attached microphone, you can either make a new file or mix the sound with an existing one.

Once you've set the position where you want recording to begin, press the Record button and begin speaking into the microphone. When you're finished, click on the Stop button.

With other sound sources properly connected, you can record from them as well. We'll discuss this in more detail in Chapter 5.

Editing Sound Files

When you combine or edit sound files, you'll probably want to save the result under a new file name. Once you resave a modified version under the same name, the previous version is lost.

The **Edit** and **Effects** menus provide various ways to make changes to the current sound file. **Effects** commands affect the entire file, while **Edit** commands affect a particular position within the file.

As an example of the latter, suppose that you want to insert another sound file within the current file. First position the current file indicator in the place where the new sound will be inserted. If this is at the beginning of the current file, the new file will be inserted before it.

At the end of the current file, the new file will be appended. In either case, both files will simply play in sequence, one after the other. If the file indicator is positioned anywhere within the current file when the new one is inserted, it will be interrupted with the new sound and then resumed.

You can use the insertion technique to add words to a voice recording. Suppose that you want to expand the phrase "Hello, fellow workers" to "Hello, my dear fellow workers." There are two ways to do this. Let the original recording play until just after the word "Hello," and then stop it.

Now you can record the phrase "my dear fellow workers." This will replace the original ending entirely, which in longer recordings may be a big disadvantage. The alternative is to first open a new file and record just the words that are to be inserted.

Then add this at the appropriate position in the original recording using the **Edit/Insert File...** item. Your expanded file is limited to a total of 60 seconds.

Deleting Segments

Two **Delete...** items will remove unwanted segments of a recording, such as periods of silence. To remove everything before a certain position, go to the beginning of the point you want preserved, then select **Edit/Delete Before Current Position**.

To remove everything after a certain position, move to the end of the point you want preserved, then select **Edit/Delete After Current Position**. You must confirm the deletion before it will take effect. The length of the file is reduced by the length of the deleted portion.

Mixing Files

Unlike inserting one file within another, mixing lets you superimpose multiple files. Before initiating the Mix command, position the current file where you want the mixing to begin. Then select the secondary file to be mixed.

Mixing occurs for the entire duration of the secondary file. The length of the primary file does not change, unless it must be extended to accommodate the secondary file.

Using Effects

Sound Recorder has several special effects for modifying sound files. The **Increase Volume (by 25%)** item turns up the volume by 25%. To turn the volume down by the same amount, select **Decrease Volume**.

The **Increase Speed (by 100%)** item doubles the playing speed of a sound file, while the **Decrease Speed** item halves it.

You can achieve an echo effect with the **Effects/Add Echo** item. This applies echo to the entire file (more on this in Chapter 5). The **Effects/Reverse** item reverses the direction of a sound file, so it plays "from back to front."

If you don't like the changes you've made, select **File/Revert** to restore the file as it was last saved. Doing so will destroy all other changes you have made, so you may want to save important changes by using **File/Save As...** before experimenting with effects.

4.5 Sound Files As Objects

Sound files in Windows 3.1 can be embedded as packages in other applications using Object Packager. So, text files or spreadsheets can be annotated with spoken instructions, for example.

To create a link from Sound Recorder to Object Packager, run the Sound Recorder and open the sound file you want. Now select **Edit/Copy** to copy the file to the Clipboard. The file will be transferred to the Clipboard and displayed with the Sound Recorder icon. Keep Sound Recorder running (do not exit).

Object
Packager

Open Object Packager and choose **Edit/Paste Link**. The Packager makes a link between the Sound Recorder icon and the active sound file.

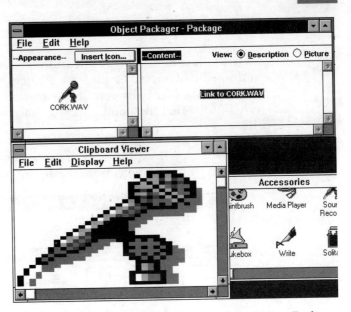

The Sound icon on the Clipboard and in Object Packager

Select **Edit/Copy Package** to copy this object package. Open another application (we used Microsoft Windows Write). Create a document and select **Edit/Paste**. This places the object package in the Write document.

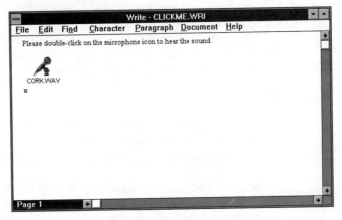

Sound objects inside documents

A double-click activates the object and plays the sound file.

4.6 Media Player

Media
Player

Media Player is an application for controlling external multimedia devices. Sequences created by these devices are played using Media Player. The sequences may be, for example, WAV files, MIDI files, audio CDs or Microsoft Multimedia Movie files.

With the proper MCI driver, you can also play other types of files produced by applications from third-party vendors.

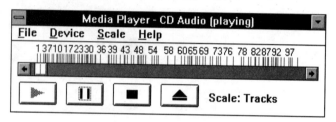

Media Player and audio CDs

Audio CDs

Media Player distinguishes two types of devices. A simple device, such as a CD-ROM drive, is controlled simply by the operating buttons on the Media Player screen. The data that's accessed is whatever is currently in the device.

So, Media Player's Play (>) button plays the CD that's currently in the CD-ROM drive. The only requirement is that the **CD Audio** item is selected from the **Device** menu.

MIDI Files

Selecting **Devices/MIDI Sequencer...** lets you access a MIDI file for playback. MIDI (Musical Instrument Digital Interface) is a specification for digital music file generation.

If you have a sound card capable of handling a MIDI connector (e.g., Sound Blaster Pro), or a dedicated MIDI interface card (i.e., a Roland MPU-401 or compatible) and a MIDI synthesizer, you can play MIDI files through the synthesizer. If you have a sound card but not a MIDI connector, and if the Windows MIDI Mapper is accessing your sound card instead of a MIDI Out port, Media Player plays the MIDI file over the sound card's integrated synthesizer.

Selecting A Device

In the previous section we discussed how the "Drivers" option of
Control Panel is used for installing various kinds of multimedia
devices. After a driver is installed, you restart Windows to
initialize the new device.

There are two types of Multimedia devices: simple and compound.
These devices appear in the **Device** menu of Media Player. When
you select a simple device (e.g., **CD Audio**), you do not open a file
for it to play. Instead, you simply activate the appropriate
operating controls.

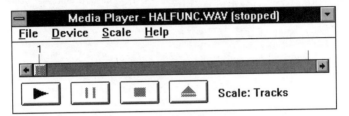

The Media Player set to play a sound

Selecting A File

When you select a single device (**CD Audio**), the Player buttons
adapt to control an audio CD. When you select a compound device
(e.g., **Sound...**), the "Open" dialog box appears. From this dialog
box you select a file to load for playing. Normally only those files
with a particular extension are displayed, depending on the type
of device selected.

For example, if you select **Device/Sound...**, only .WAV files are
displayed. When you open a compatible file, it becomes available
for play.

You cannot play a sound file in Sound Recorder while playing
a sound file in Media Player. Only one device at a time is
available for sound file output.

Controlling A Device

There are four buttons for controlling a multimedia device. A scroll
bar is available for positioning within the file. Depending on the
device, you can choose to show the position in **Time** (e.g., for sound
files) or **Tracks** (e.g., for audio CDs) from the **Scale** menu.

The Play button starts the appropriate playing process for the device.

Play can be interrupted with the Pause button. Pressing Pause again resumes play at the same position where it was interrupted.

Play ends when you press the Stop button.

The Eject button is useful only for devices that have an automatic eject feature. This doesn't include the type of drive that uses a caddy. The Eject function cannot be used during play.

4.7 Sound Card Software

SB Pro Mixer

Several drivers and programs are usually included as part of a sound card package. This software helps you control the sound card under DOS and Windows. We'll discuss only Windows programs that control the volume and mixing of separate channels.

The SBPro Mixer

The SBPro Mixer lets you control the volumes of individual audio devices, each of which has its own sound channel. Settings are effective for the entire Windows environment, and for every multimedia application that accesses the sound card.

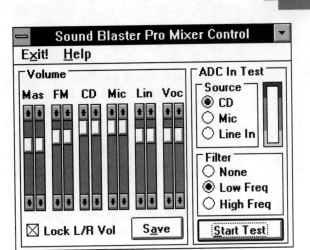

Channel settings

Both right and left channels have slider controls that work like scroll bars. The following sound sources can be controlled separately:

SB Pro Mixer Volume Settings	
Setting	**Sound source**
Mas	Master volume
FM	Synthesizer channel
CD	CD-ROM drive
Mic	Microphone input
Lin	Line-in input (e.g., stereo)
Voc	Voice source (Sound Recorder)

The "Lock L/R Vol" check box disables separate control of left and right channels and simplifies unit volume setting.

Saving settings

The SBPro Mixer has a set of default settings. To make your customized settings effective for future sessions, use the Save button to store them permanently.

Testing the input signal

The "ADC In Test" group box gives you a visual check on the level of the input signal coming from the Analog/Digital Converter (ADC). You can also select from two optional filters.

To use the "ADC In Test" group, first select the desired source in the "Source" group box. If you're playing an audio CD with the Media Player, for example, select the CD option. Start the playback on the Media Player, then click (Start Test) on the SBPro Mixer.

The "meter" in the "ADC In Test" group box shows the input levels. Selecting one of the "Filter" option buttons changes the sound level by adding or removing sound filters.

Mixing sound sources

With the simultaneous output of several sound sources, individual sounds can be emphasized or downplayed by adjusting their relative volumes.

> You can mix a CD on the Media Player with a WAV file in Sound Recorder, and even add your own singing or commentary using the microphone.

Pro Audio Spectrum applications

MediaVision's Pro Audio Spectrum card includes two applications for controlling sound channels: The Multimedia Mixer for setting volume, and the Pro Mixer for controlling stereo channels.

Chapter 5

Sound Recording Made Easy

Music, speech and various sound effects are basic elements of any multimedia presentation. Various computer tasks can be enhanced by using sound, from a personal greeting at startup to spoken help text and informational messages in numerous applications.

Even an average user with a well-equipped multimedia PC can produce professional-sounding results. In this chapter we'll discuss the various ways you can incorporate sound into your own applications. We'll focus on the following topics:

- Recording live sound via microphone

- Recording from a stereo system

- Recording from an audio CD in the CD-ROM drive

- Mixing sound from multiple sources

- Editing sound files

- Using sound files in applications

We assume that you're already familiar with the Sound Recorder and the mixer programs discussed in Chapter 4.

5.1 Requirements

First, you need a multimedia PC that's equipped with a suitable sound card. A microphone for making live recordings of voice or nature sounds is an extremely useful accessory. The quality of the microphone depends on your needs. The minimum recommendation is a sensitivity of 74 dB and 600 ohms impedance.

If you don't have a separate microphone, you can also record onto a cassette tape with a built-in microphone of an ordinary tape recorder. Then attach your tape player to the Line-in connector of the sound card to feed the recording into your computer.

Generally the highest-quality recordings can be made from a good high-fidelity stereo device directly over the Line-in input. The stereo components of such a device are much better than those of an ordinary sound card. Normally the required connection is easily made by using a cable supplied with the sound card.

Connecting Cables

Sometimes a special cable may be needed. Different types of cables are available in specialty stores or, if necessary, you can easily make one yourself. You'll find a list of the types of cables that are used at the end of this chapter.

Another source for excellent recording is an audio CD played from the CD-ROM drive. Actually many data CDs already contain sound tracks. These can be placed on any mass storage device just like other data.

Required Software

Now you need the appropriate software. Windows 3.1 (or Windows 3.0 with the Multimedia Extension) provides all the necessary software to perform the activities we listed earlier. Here Sound Recorder and Media Player are responsible for recording, editing and playing the desired sound files.

Another important program is the mixer, which is usually included with the sound card. The mixer controls the volumes of individual channels (refer to Chapter 4).

Recording and editing at the DOS level

Other programs outside the Windows environment are also available for working with sound. For example, under DOS there is Voice Editor, which enables you to record and edit sound files.

Voice Editor   Actually, Voice Editor offers better quality and more features than Windows' Sound Recorder. In the description that follows, we'll explain how to use the Windows programs and then Voice Editor and CD Player, two components of the Sound Blaster kit.

When using a DOS application to record sound, you shouldn't start it under Windows. If the sound card is installed under Windows and an application, such as the mixer, is activated to access it, the card isn't available to DOS applications.

Also, Windows requires a lot of processor time, even for background execution. This takes time away from your DOS program. The impact on sound digitization, a highly computation-intensive process, results in inferior recording quality.

5.2 Recording With A Microphone

Most sound cards have a separate microphone input. If you also have an external microphone, you're ready to record. Condenser microphones, unlike dynamic microphones, require a separate power supply (usually batteries). You should use reliable batteries, such as alkaline series.

The right connection

Stereo microphones usually have a standard (6.5 mm) phone plug. An appropriate miniature (3.5 mm) will allow you to plug the microphone into the sound card's miniature (3.5 mm) jack (see Section 5.9).

If your microphone has two plugs (for the left and right stereo channels), one of them isn't used, since the sound card's microphone input is mono only.

Don't switch on the microphone until you're ready to record. This not only saves batteries, if your microphone uses them, but also prevents the recording of unwanted noises.

If you don't have a separate microphone, simply make your own cassette tapes using a tape recorder with a built-in microphone. Then you can play them into your sound card over the Line-in input.

Although a built-in microphone usually lacks the quality of an external one, it should be sufficient for everyday use.

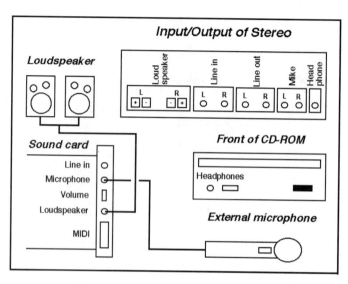

Structure for microphone recording

The same technique can be used any time you need to record "on location." You may still want to connect an external microphone to your tape recorder because of its portability and sound quality. Directionality is another important aspect of a microphone.

A directional microphone is useful for outdoor recording where background noise cannot be controlled. This type of device has a narrow angle of reception to reduce the range of sounds that will be picked up. This will help keep the sound of a passing vehicle, for example, from ruining your tape.

Recording Over Sound Recorder

Now let's return to the direct microphone input to continue our discussion of the PC recording process. With the microphone attached, start Windows and activate the Sound Recorder. Currently, the most important object is the Record button.

Start recording with a click

Here's a description of what happens. Analog signals in the form of sound waves reach the microphone and cause a membrane inside the device to vibrate.

This vibration is converted to an analog electrical oscillation, depicting the pattern of the sound waves. The signal is then digitized (sampled) by the sound card in conjunction with Sound Recorder and stored as digital data in RAM. Now you can save the data as a sound file on the disk or process it in any way.

This procedure is similar to recording with an ordinary tape recorder. The only difference is in the digitizing of the signal, since sound resides in analog format on a conventional cassette tape.

Controlling Disturbances

Take time to prepare your setting before you start to record. Close doors and windows, and try to anticipate and prevent any interruptions and distractions.

For voice recording, speak distinctly and avoid colloquialisms and slang. What sounds fine in everyday conversation may not be appropriate for a formal presentation.

Run a few test recordings using different volumes and different distances from the microphone. Depending on the instrument's sensitivity, even a small change in the source can significantly alter the result.

Creating Effects

You may even want to experiment with some special effects, such as covering the microphone with a cloth. However, you don't have to be too creative, since your computer has its own tricks for manipulating sound.

Many programs that create or edit sound files (e.g., Sound Recorder and Voice Editor) can add echo, change speed or modify the sound in various ways. These effects are explained in more detail in the appropriate sections.

Stereo Recording

To make your own live stereo recordings, you need a stereo system or portable recorder that has a stereo microphone connector or two separate microphone connectors (for right and left stereo channels). Usually each channel has its own input.

You cannot record in stereo directly by microphone to the sound card because the sound card's microphone input is monaural. Therefore, you must record on the other device and then play the recording from it to the sound card's Line-in input, which is stereo.

Limit of 60 seconds

Unfortunately, Sound Recorder has one small limitation. Your recordings must be limited to 60 seconds in length. Sound files longer than this reach unmanageable proportions in Wave format.

However, an entire minute of sound effects or informational text is actually longer than you may think.

Sound in Wave Format

Standard multimedia format

Sound Recorder creates files in Microsoft Wave format. This is a standard multimedia format that's used by many applications. The Multimedia Extension as well as diskettes and CDs from many sound card manufacturers include Wave files of various sounds. This provides a collection of sounds that can be mixed.

The DOS program Voice Editor can also create Wave files. Under DOS, for example with VEDIT2.EXE, your computer devotes itself to recording only. Windows, however, performs various management tasks that slow down processing time.

The result, especially when recording with high sampling rates on minimal computer configurations, is a noticeable background noise in your recording.

5.3   Recording From A Stereo

For your own enjoyment (not to mention impressing your friends), there's nothing like playing your favorite artist straight off the hard drive. To make the recording, an appropriate cable, which is usually supplied with the sound card, connects the card to your stereo.

One end of the cable should have a miniature (3.5 mm) plug to plug into the sound card. At the other end you need two RCA phono plugs for the left and right stereo channels of your stereo system.

In this case, component stereo systems (systems consisting of individual components) are preferable to one-piece compact stereos. Signals generated by the stereo components are amplified and sent to the speaker or headphone output. In order for the computer to record these signals, it must somehow intervene in this process.

The Line-in Connection

Sound card is the amplifier

Most sound cards, like Sound Blaster Pro, have a separate Line-in input for connecting to a stereo unit. Here the sound card takes over the role of amplifier and sends the amplified signal to the speakers that are in turn connected to it. It also gives you the opportunity to access the input signal with Sound Recorder or similar software.

Since the sound card acts as an amplifier, you can record from only a tape deck, for example, without requiring the complete stereo system. In most cases this will have two RCA phono jacks marked Line-Out (R/L). These are the jacks that are used to connect the sound card with the cable mentioned earlier.

Basically all high-level connections can be made to the sound card. A CD player or tape deck is connected directly, which uses the sound card's amplifier. Phono and microphone connections use special rectifiers that modify the signals without the amplifier.

If the supplied cable isn't long enough to reach from your stereo to the computer, you can use an extension cable.

In terms of available connectors, compact or portable units (boom boxes, radio recorders, etc.) usually have different designs. Some have several RCA phono jacks on the back of the unit. Others don't have any external connectors; all connections, except for speaker and/or headphone output, are made inside the housing.

Using the correct cable

To use such a unit for making digital recordings over your sound card, you need a connection between the sound card's Line-in input and the unit's speaker or headphone output. Since these inputs and outputs are stereo, a stereo cable should be used.

Headphone jack is easiest

Using a headphone jack is the easiest solution. A simple connecting cable with a miniature (3.5 mm) stereo plug at either end is sufficient. If your headphone jack is standard (6.35 mm), you'll also need an adapter.

If your unit doesn't have a headphone output, you must use the speaker output and perhaps some improvisation. The exact solution depends on just how the unit's speaker connections are made. Various methods are used, including direct wiring, RCA phono plugs, etc.

You need a miniature (3.5 mm) stereo plug for the left and right stereo channel and a length of speaker cable. Each speaker has two outputs (+/-), which (ideally) are marked differently. Similar markings may be on the speaker cable. The goal is to keep the positive connections separate (for the left and right channels), while joining the negative connections. If your speakers take RCA phono plugs, assume that the central portion of the plug is positive, and the outer "ring" that fits around an RCA phono jack is negative.

You use the same principle for constructing the cable. The miniature (3.5 mm) plug has three connections to which you can solder cable. Unscrew the housing (the plastic or metal cover) from the plug. Thread the cable through the housing (this is important).

The two shorter connections with "eyeholes" are the items to which you must solder the positive connections. The longer connection running along the outside is the one to which you must solder the negative connections.

Notice the two metal "wraps" at the end of the negative (or ground) connection. Once you solder the connections, bend these wraps around the cable insulation. This reduces pull on the cable, decreasing the likelihood of your accidentally pulling the wires out of the plug.

Now you can connect the free ends of the cable to your stereo. You will need to use special plugs or clamps, depending on your stereo equipment.

Sound card with Y-cable

If your unit has no headphone jack, you'll probably have to run a Y-cable from the speakers. This cable should have two plugs or jacks at one end (for the speaker outputs on the stereo unit) and a 3.5 mm stereo plug at the other (for the sound card Line-in).

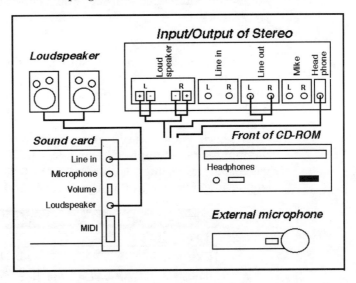

Connection diagram for recording from a stereo unit

Before testing your connection, make certain the stereo volume is turned down before switching it on. Since the output signal from this device is already amplified, the sound card may be damaged if its maximum input level is exceeded. A volume that's too high can also result in sound distortion. Turn up the volume gradually to find the best setting.

Even a Walkman® portable stereo can be used as an input device to your sound card. Simply connect the Walkman's headphone output to the sound card's Line-in input by using a cable with a miniature (3.5 mm) stereo plug at each end.

Recording Over Line-in

Now that your input unit is connected to the sound card, we can finally discuss recording with Sound Recorder. Because of its stereo capability, the sound card's Line-in connector is perfectly suitable for this.

If you don't hear anything

Don't be alarmed if you click the ⌈Record⌉ button and the Sound Recorder wave box shows no activity. In this case, turning up the volume on your stereo unit won't help either, because the cause lies elsewhere.

Before you can record from the Line-in source in Sound Recorder, you must select this as the source in the SB Pro Mixer. The available options are "Line In", "CD" and "Mic". If you don't hear anything even with the "CD" or "Lin" volume controls on high, double check the connections between components.

After selecting the desired source and volume level, you can test the input signal. Simply click the ⌈Start Test⌉ button and watch the gauge. Before starting to record, you must click the button again to stop testing. Otherwise, the signal won't reach Sound Recorder.

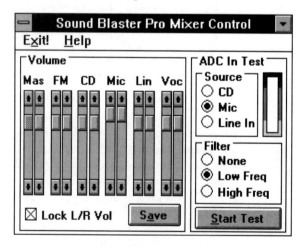

The Sound Blaster Mixer

Buttons for enabling a low-pass (Low Freq) or high-pass (High Freq) filter are located below the source selection area.

Incoming signals are shown graphically in Sound Recorder

Setting The Volume

You should always use the following sequence when adjusting volume. First turn the volume all the way down on the input device. Then adjust the "Lin" volume in Mixer. If the highest setting is still too soft, gradually increase the volume on the device.

Take 1!...

The [Record] button in Sound Recorder starts the recording. You can record up to 60 seconds of sound at a time. However, use this capability carefully. One minute of sound data takes up an enormous amount of disk space (1.3 Meg).

You cannot control the input signal from within Sound Recorder. However, other programs, such as WaveEdit from the Microsoft Multimedia Development Kit (MDK), are more versatile.

5.4 Recording From A CD-ROM Drive

Even if you don't have an audio CD player, you can play audio CDs from your computer's CD-ROM drive. You can do this under Windows using Media Player (or for Windows 3.0 users, the Music Box of Multimedia Extensions).

In Media Player you must select the **CD Audio** item from the **Device** menu. Then click the ▷ button to start the CD.

Playback With Sound Recorder

The CD is played over a separate channel on the sound card (the CD channel) and is sent directly to the attached speakers. To record with Sound Recorder, you must use the Mixer to select CD as the source channel.

Recording audio CDs over the internal CD-ROM drive is possible only with a proper internal connection between the CD-ROM drive and the sound card. A special audio cable is used for this (see Chapter 3). If your drive doesn't have this type of connection, or if the connection is defective, you can still read data. However, some extra work is needed in order to play audio CDs.

Using the correct cable

In this case, we'll use the CD-ROM drive's stereo headphone output. According to MPC specifications, this output has a volume control on the front of the drive.

By now you're familiar with the hardware for this connection. A cable with a miniature (3.5 mm) stereo plug at each end is all you need.

The trick is to connect the drive and the sound card so you can record in Sound Recorder and hear the sound through the speakers simultaneously.

Connect one end of the cable to the headphone output on the front of the CD-ROM drive and the other end to the sound card's Line-in input. In this way, the stereo signals of the headphone connection are output to the sound card and can be recorded with Sound Recorder as we described.

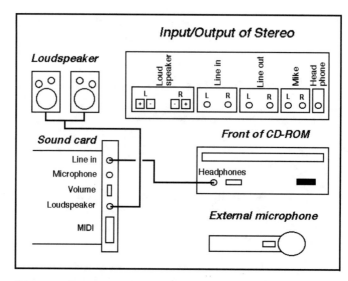

Diagram for connecting CD-ROM audio to the sound card

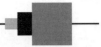

Volume adjustment for recording

The volume control on the front of the CD-ROM drive is used to adjust the volume of the outgoing signal. This is the only way to adjust the output volume, because the mixer controls only the components of the sound card. However, you can still change the output volume of the Line-in channel.

5.5   Recording Computer Sound To A Stereo

So far we've only discussed how to use a sound card to make digital computer recordings of signals coming to the card from various sources.

Suppose that you want to take one of your computerized compositions and put it on tape. You may also need to do this if you don't have an audio CD player, but want to make a cassette recording from an audio CD by using your CD-ROM drive.

The microphone input shouldn't be used

The proper connections must be made between components. You could use the tape recorder's microphone input, connecting it to the headphone output on the CD-ROM drive or to the sound card's speaker output. Usually this isn't a good solution, because the tape will pick up a lot of noise.

If there is no other alternative, experiment with different volumes first to get the best possible result.

> The best way to obtain a high-quality recording is to connect the sound card's speaker output to the tape deck's Line-in. This can be done with the same type of cable that's generally used to connect a stereo unit to the sound card. Such a connector is usually included with the card.

This connector has a miniature (3.5 mm) stereo plug at one end and two RCA phono plugs at the other. The RCA phono plugs are connected to the Line-in RCA phono jacks on the back of the tape deck. These may already be used, in which case you must switch connections temporarily to make your recording.

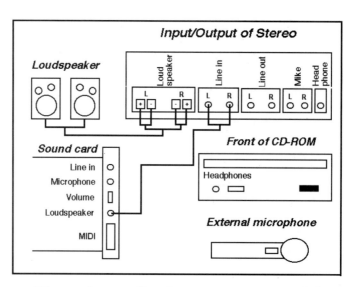

Diagram for recording from computer to tape deck

The output volume from the sound card can be adjusted using the wheel at the back of the card.

How To Record

To record from an audio CD in the CD-ROM drive to a conventional cassette tape, start Media Player and set the tape deck to Record. If you want to hear what's being recorded, you can use a headset connected to the CD-ROM drive.

To record to tape from a sound file on your hard drive, start the program and open the file. Set the tape deck to Record and activate the file. You won't be able to hear the sound directly from the sound card, because its speaker output is going straight into the tape deck.

If speakers are connected to the tape deck, however, they will play the sound. Otherwise, many such units also have a separate headphone output that allows you to listen along.

5.6 Recording From Multiple Sources

To create really interesting sound effects, combine sounds from multiple sources. For example, you can record yourself singing along to an instrumental accompaniment or mix two different noises together. These effects are possible by using a few simple tricks with your sound card and software. The recording medium can be either a cassette tape or a Sound Recorder sound file.

A sound studio isn't needed By using the sound card's capacity to process multiple input signals, you can play an audio CD from the CD-ROM drive, for example, and add microphone input simultaneously. Relative volumes of the individual sources can be controlled with the Mixer. The combined output signal can then be recorded to a cassette tape, as we described in the previous section.

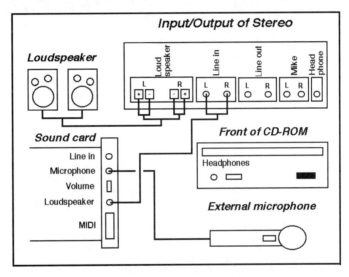

Diagram for recording music and voice to tape

With this arrangement, the audio CD is played in Media Player. This signal and the simultaneous voice input from the microphone are output together over the sound card's speaker connector. From here the sound can be conveyed by a cable to your tape deck's Line-in for recording.

Recording With Sound Recorder

Depending on your sound card, a little extra setup work may be needed to record mixed inputs to a file in Sound Recorder. Since the only recording input to this program is the microphone channel, our output file usually wouldn't include the music from the audio CD in the previous example.

We can use the Pro Audio Spectrum card, with its versatile mixing capabilities for fading in and out, cross-channel fading and combining sound sources, to solve this problem for us. In the case of

Sound Blaster and other cards, we must provide a cable to bring the audio CD signal to the card's microphone input.

Again we use the CD-ROM drive's headphone connector and its separate volume control. The single end of a Y-cable goes into the sound card's microphone input. The double end of the cable goes to the headphone output of the CD-ROM drive and to the microphone and/or a stereo component acting as an input source.

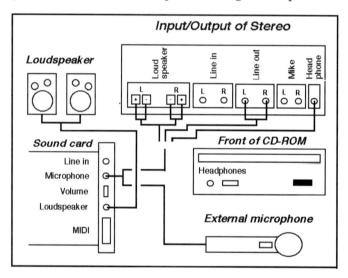

A Y-cable brings multiple signals to the microphone input

Volume is important

You may have to experiment to get the right volume relationship between voice and musical background. Usually the volume must be turned down for the music sources so they don't overpower the singing.

The microphone can no longer be separately regulated because its input already includes the other source signals. The CD-ROM drive's volume control can be used to adjust the audio CD volume. For other sources, such as a stereo tape deck, use the Output Level control on the unit itself. In this case, the connection should be made through the Line-in rather than the microphone input.

If you've connected the stereo unit to the sound card via its speaker output, the volume can be adjusted using the master volume control.

When you're ready to record, turn on the music and the microphone and click the Sound Recorder's [Record] button.

Editing   After recording your sound file, you can edit it. Delete any unwanted segments at the beginning or end, insert or mix in another sound file or use the **Effects** menu to add some interesting effects.

The **Add Echo** item gives your recording the sound of a concert-hall stage performance. With a little work, you can make this even better.

First record the sound normally. Use the **Edit/Delete Before Current Position** and **Edit/Delete After Current Position** items to delete any unwanted sound segments, periods of silence, etc. The scroll bar lets you move around within the sound file in one-second increments or, by clicking the arrows, in 1/10th second increments. Save your file when it contains only the sound you want to echo.

Then select the **Effects/Decrease Volume** item and save the new version under a different file name. Repeat this two or three times, saving each result under a different name.

Now open the original file and position the scroll bar one or two tenths of a second from the beginning. At this point, mix in the file with the next softer volume using the **Edit/Mix With File...** item. The exact time delay depends on the size of the hall you're trying to simulate; the longer the delay, the farther the "walls" are from your "stage."

With successive mixing of softer versions, the result sounds like a live performance.

As you can see, the Sound Recorder lets you create some professional-sounding recordings that are definitely better than the original sounds. Even greater enhancements are possible using DOS-level software. We'll discuss some of these programs in the following section.

5.7 Recording With DOS Programs

The procedures for creating sound files that we described in the previous sections involved using the Windows programs Sound Recorder and Media Player. This is simply because the MPC specification is based on Windows. However, it's also possible to record sound files under DOS. The same connections between the individual hardware components also apply for DOS.

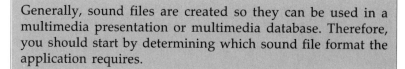

Generally, sound files are created so they can be used in a multimedia presentation or multimedia database. Therefore, you should start by determining which sound file format the application requires.

For a Windows application, such as Toolbook, you'll usually want the Wave format (*.WAV) created by Sound Recorder. The VOICE format (*.VOC), created by the Sound Blaster Voice Editor programs, can be used in DOS multimedia applications, such as SantaFe Media Manager and MMPlay.

Pure sound files of other formats can also be used in these DOS applications after a header is added by the VOC-HDR.EXE program. This program is a component of Voice Editor and is started from the DOS level with the following command:

```
VOC-HDR        <Source_file> <Target_file>
```

There are also programs that convert files between VOC and WAV format, including the Sound Blaster utilities WAV2VOC and VOC2WAV. These are very useful because recordings created under DOS usually have higher sound quality than those created under Windows.

Differences Between Windows and DOS Recordings

You're probably wondering why DOS recordings are better than Windows recordings. The reason lies in the graphical user interface and multitasking capabilities of Windows. Although the Windows environment is powerful and easy to use, managing this environment requires much of the processor's time.

Sound recording is an extremely time-critical activity, especially with a high sampling rate and limited main memory. The sound must be digitized and saved to disk instantaneously. Other tasks demanding processor time affect this process.

The result is that sound files recorded under Windows contain more noise than those recorded under DOS, where the CPU is dedicated exclusively to the recording task.

5.8 Sound Blaster Pro

Recording With Voice Editor

The VEDIT2 program is located in the VEDIT2 subdirectory in your
Sound Blaster Pro directory. Voice Editor offers options you won't
find in Sound Recorder. For example, you can remove segments not
only from the beginning and end, but from anywhere within a sound
file, and also reposition them.

Another advantage is the ability to vary the sampling rate of a
recording. However, the higher the sampling rate, the less time is
available for recording. Stereo sampling can be up to 22.05 KHz
and mono sampling up to 44.1 KHz with Sound Blaster Pro.

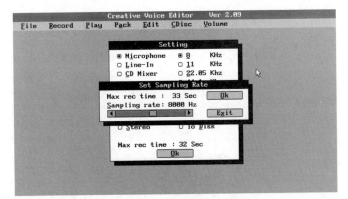

Setting the sampling rate

Besides regulating the volumes of the various inputs, Voice Editor
also has complete control of the CD-ROM drive. This means that
other programs aren't needed to record directly from a CD.

When you start the program, a screen, which is empty except for
the menu bar and information box, appears. The box disappears
when you select a menu item.

Preparation

Under the **Record** menu, you'll find all the necessary commands for
making a sound recording. Before you start, use the **Settings**
command to specify the source, sampling rate, filter selection and
destination (**To Memory** or **To Disk**). Recording to memory provides
better results but limits the recording time. The exact time limit,
which is shown at the bottom of the Settings box, depends on your
computer and the sampling rate.

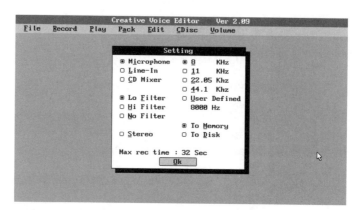

Settings in VEDIT2

Recording level

Unless you're using the microphone as the source, you should check the input level before starting to record. Select the desired source in **Settings** and choose **Scan Input** to display the sound graphically. If the display shows spikes being cut off at the top and bottom, as in the following illustration, use the **Volume** command and the sliding volume control to reduce the source volume.

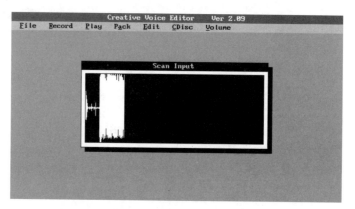

VEDIT2 with input signal too high

This is done either with the mouse or by typing "R" or "L" (right/left), followed by the cursor control keys.

Check the input signal again at the new level. An optimal setting is shown below.

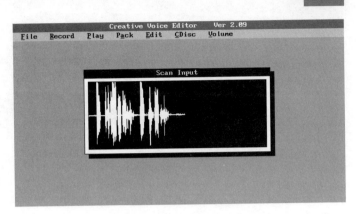

A good input signal level

Once you've selected the appropriate input level you can start to record. If you're recording to memory and haven't yet saved a previous file in memory, a warning message appears.

If you're recording to the hard drive, the entire amount of free space is available. This is reflected in the maximum recording time shown in the "Settings" box. A dialog box requests the name of the destination file before you begin to record.

When you've finished recording to a file, you must then load it to memory before it can be edited. Actually, instead of being loaded all at once, the entire file is loaded by segments called blocks. The recording process divides your file into several blocks. Editing options allow you to manipulate these in various ways. Block functions are used only by the VOC format.

Besides the actual sound sample data, a VOC file can contain indicators for block repetition, silence periods of any duration and even text. An example is found on the companion CD-ROM in the \SOUNDS\VEDIT directory.

Now let's discuss the direct manipulation of digitized sound. Selected blocks can be changed using the **Modify** command from the **Edit** menu. When you choose this command, a new screen appears.

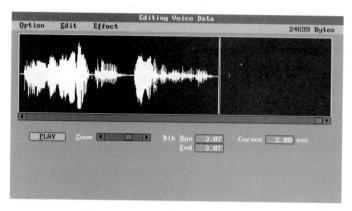

Editing sample data with VEDIT2

The **Modify/Option** menu lets you split a block at a designated position or vary the sampling rate for selected blocks from 4000 Hz to 44000 Hz, which also produces a change in pitch.

With **Edit** you can save the selected portion or cut it out of the file. Once cut, it can also be inserted at a new location. Unfortunately this can only be done once. So it isn't possible to make repeated copies of the selected area. Also, the new data can only be inserted, not superimposed in VEDIT2.

The last two items in this menu allow you to insert a value from 0 to 255 within a block and thus create a period of silence.

The **Effects** menu provides some useful sound tools. You can amplify a selected section, choosing the amplification rate to the nearest percent, unlike in Windows' Sound Recorder. The percent expresses the new output level relative to the old. So 150% increases the volume by 50%, while 80% reduces it by 20%.

You can add an echo, also with more versatility than in Sound Recorder, by selecting the volume of the echo as a percentage of the original, and the time delay in milliseconds.

Finally, there are options to fade the selected area in or out, and to do both these functions reciprocally in a stereo file, which has the effect of panning across channels.

Although Voice Editor is more powerful than Sound Recorder, it still doesn't have many of the features offered by other sound recorders.

Shareware Programs for Sound Recording

As sound cards become more popular, shareware and public domain software offers ever increasing sound card support. These programs are more numerous and in many cases better than their commercial counterparts.

Blaster Master

The Blaster Master from Gary Maddox is already in its fifth version. This program handles many sound file formats, including VOC files. For example, it can also read and write the WAV format directly.

Powerful effects   In Blaster Master, you can record, play and edit files on the screen. Sections can be cut, moved and copied. An entire file or part of one can be given special effects. This program exceeds the capabilities of Voice Editor. You can change the speed or sampling rate without affecting the pitch, or conversely change the pitch independent of the sampling rate. Also, it's easy to mix different files with the built-in mixer.

5.9   A Music Database With Excel 4

Excel provides a special feature for assigning music and sound effects to cells. These "sound notes" can consist of a spoken word, music or sound of any kind. External sound files can also be imported and assigned to cells. The only requirement is that they be in Microsoft Wave format. Such files are indicated by the .WAV extension.

A sound note contained within a cell is played by double-clicking. The companion CD-ROM includes a file called MUSIC.XLS under \EXCEL\SNDNOTES that contains a sound file. When you double-click one of the right-hand cells beneath the "Snd Note" title, the database plays back a sample of the music. If your computer doesn't have a sound card, first you must install the speaker driver as discussed below.

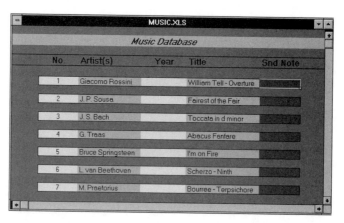

No.	Artist(s)	Year	Title	Snd Note
1	Giacomo Rossini		William Tell - Overture	
2	J. P. Sousa		Fairest of the Fair	
3	J. S. Bach		Toccata in d minor	
4	G. Traas		Abacus Fanfare	
5	Bruce Springsteen		I'm on Fire	
6	L. van Beethoven		Scherzo - Ninth	
7	M. Praetorius		Bourree - Terpsichore	

A music database with sound test

> To make your own sound recordings for use as sound notes, you need the appropriate hardware and software. This includes a sound card such as the Sound Blaster and, for voice recording, a microphone. Sound Blaster allows recording of music from various sources into Wave format using Windows software.

Playing Sound Notes Without a Sound Card

If you have Windows 3.1 or the Microsoft Windows Multimedia Extension, you can link and play Wave files in Excel without a sound card.

To do this, you must use Control Panel to install a driver that plays the sound files over the internal PC speaker. This driver is included on the companion CD-ROM (see Section 3.5 for more information).

Assigning a sound note

Assigning a sound note is quite simple. The procedure is similar to the one used for a normal text note. Sound notes are assigned using the **Formula/Note...** item.

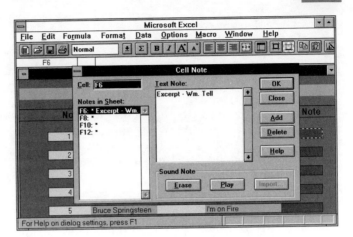

The dialog box contains the sound notes

Instead of (or in addition to) assigning a sound note, there are two options. Clicking the (Record...) button lets you record the sound directly from a sound source (this requires a sound card and the appropriate hardware connections).

Clicking the (Import...) button opens a file selection dialog box, from which you can select an external Wave file for assignment to the cell. Click (Add) to add the file to the worksheet. Clicking the (Play) button plays the file.

> When you save the worksheet, the sound notes are saved with it. The original sound file doesn't have to exist in order to play the note. Remember that sound notes can quickly increase the size of your worksheet. For example, a 20-second music file can easily occupy 200K.

Playing sound notes

Double-click the cell to play a sound note. If the cell contains only a sound note, it plays immediately and you can continue working.

If there is also a text note assigned to the cell, the text dialog box appears while the sound plays. Confirm the text note before continuing.

Deleting sound notes

There are two ways to delete a sound note from a cell. The **Edit/Clear...** item lets you remove all notes from the cell. This includes both text and sound notes.

In the other method, choose the **Formula/Note...** item. Then click the (Delete) button that appears in the "Cell Note" dialog box.

If a sound note isn't currently assigned to the cell, a (Record...) button appears instead.

Creating Your Own Sound Notes

Excel contains a record function for making your own sound notes from external audio sources. A sound note recorded in this way is linked directly to the worksheet and doesn't exist as a separate file.

You must have the appropriate hardware connected to your sound card, the same as for other recordings.

Usually this means hooking the sound card's Line-In jack to a stereo Line-Out or headphone jack, using a special cable provided with the sound card (we discussed this earlier in this chapter).

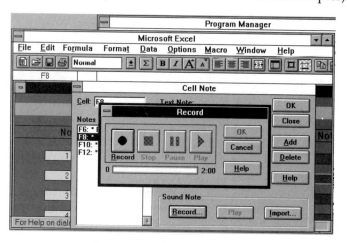

External recording can begin

Alternatively, you can use a microphone connected to the corresponding sound card input. As soon as you activate the microphone or other audio source with the mixer, Excel is ready to record sound. Select **Formula/Note...** and click the (Record...) button. The "Record" dialog box appears.

The (Record) button on the left begins the recording process. You can follow the time on the scale and click (Stop) to end recording. The (Pause) button is also useful, especially with microphone input.

Use the (Play) button to check the recorded note. At this point it can no longer be changed.

You may need to experiment with the volume. Most sound cards include a Windows application for adjusting volumes of the various input and output channels.

5.10 Sound Editors

Audio View

AudioView from Voyetra is an MPC-compatible waveform editor. It includes a CD-ROM audio player and an audio mixer controller.

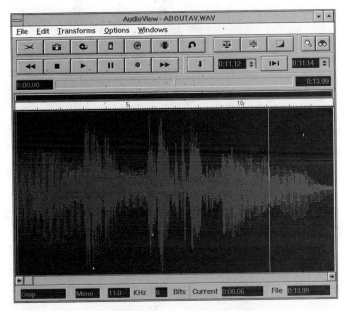

AudioView from Voyetra

The CD-ROM Audio Player is a utility which lets you play, sort, view and create your own playlists.

Audio Mixer
Controller

The Audio Mixer Controller controls record and playback volume, tone and other effects. The mixer supports several types of PC sound cards. It can automatically determine which mixer controls your sound card can support.

CD Player

This utility acts as a control panel for the audio functions on a CD-ROM drive. The CD-ROM Audio Player lets you use buttons similar to those on your home stereo to select and play a track range, name tracks, create custom play lists, check track lengths and create CD titles.

EZSound FX

EZSound FX includes four utilities for sound editing and enhancement for Windows.

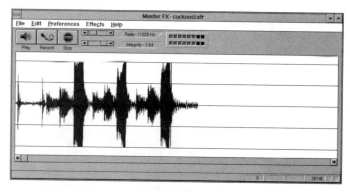

EZSound FX

Master FX

Master FX lets you record, edit and playback either your sounds or a sample sound included with the package. Also, you can import sound files from other platforms.

Digital FX and
Synth FX

The Digital FX lets you attach sampled sound effects to Windows events, for example when resizing a window. By using Synth FX, you can attach synthesized sound effects to certain Windows events.

CD FX and
Music FX

You can use CD FX to play your favorite music in the background when working in Windows. Music FX includes 100 ROL and CMF song files.

Panel FX

You can use the Panel FX utility to control the volume level and customize your sound board.

5.11 Cables Used In Sound Recordings

The following summarizes the cables used for sound recordings:

1. Stereo miniature (3.5 mm) plug and two RCA phono plugs, mono

Stereo-to-sound-card connection for recording from a stereo unit in Sound Recorder. Sound-card-to-stereo connection for recording computer sound to stereo (tape).

2. Stereo miniature (3.5 mm) plugs at both ends

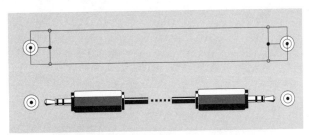

CD-ROM-to-sound-card connection
(for recording with Sound Recorder)

3. Two mono standard (6.35 mm) plugs and one mono standard (6.35 mm) jack.

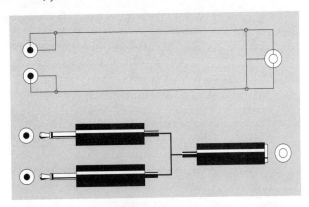

Connection of microphone to separate microphone
input for left and right stereo

4. One stereo standard (6.35 mm) phone plug and one mono miniature (3.5 mm) jack.

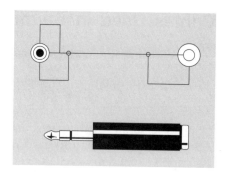

Using a standard jack for a device with a miniature plug

5. Stereo miniature (3.5 mm) plug and stereo standard (6.35 mm) jack

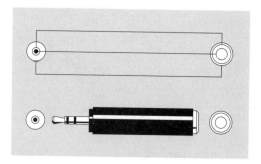

6. One stereo miniature (3.5 mm) plug and two speaker output connectors (will vary with the speaker)

Stereo-to-sound-card connection for recording with Sound Recorder (when no Line-Out exists).

Chapter 6

Capturing and Processing Images

One of the most fascinating uses for computers is creating computer graphics and images. These graphics and images are a major component of multimedia.

In this chapter we'll show you how to store graphics and pictures of all kinds in the computer so that you can use them later as part of a multimedia presentation or database.

6.1 Image Sources

Images must be saved in a graphics file so they can be processed in the computer. Depending on the file format, the image is saved as a pixel table. Information, such as location and color, is assigned to the pixels.

Once you have an image in the form of a graphics file on your computer, you can manipulate the images in various ways.

However, it takes some time to reach this point if you want to use images that require additional hardware before the computer can even access them.

In this section we'll show you the potential sources for saving images or originals in the computer. Depending on cost and use, there are different starting points.

1.   Paint and draw programs

2.   Bitmap graphics

If you use a paint or a draw program to create an image or a graphic, you can save it in a common graphics format. The two general graphics formats are vector graphics and bitmap graphics.

A bitmap graphic displays the elements of the image in pixels, which correspond to the resolution of the graphics card.

Losing information

However, you'll encounter problems if you use a Paintbrush image on a computer where Windows is running in a different graphics mode. If the current graphics mode has a lower resolution (e.g., 640 x 480) than the resolution of the original image (e.g., 800 x 600), you'll lose information.

Conversely, if the resolution is higher, the image will appear smaller on the drawing area. When you enlarge elements of a bitmap graphic, this results in many new pixels. This increases the memory requirements and makes the image look more jagged.

There will also be problems with the number of displayable colors when you use different display modes (see Section 6.2).

Vector Graphics

If you use vector oriented programs like CorelDRAW! to create drawings, the program saves the information separately from the current graphics resolution. The picture consists of lines, circles, rectangles and other geometrical shapes.

Basic shapes

The basic graphics shapes are described as follows:

*   Type of element (circle, line...)

*   Starting pixel and ending pixel

*   Color

When you magnify or reduce a vector graphic, the proportions of the image are recalculated so that you don't lose the quality of the image. This prevents the "jaggies" effect when you change the size of the picture elements.

However, the file formats are designed for one particular program. Good programs have extra modules for converting bitmap graphics to vector graphics.

Hardcopies

A popular way to save the current screen display as a graphics file is to use the hardcopy function. With only this function, you can use an entire series of images and graphics for a multimedia presentation.

Printing the contents of the screen

To create a hardcopy, you need a special hardcopy program. DOS has a special hardcopy key, which is usually the (Prt Sc) key. However, this key only sends screen contents to the printer and works only in text mode. Under Windows, however, this key serves another purpose (see below).

Hardcopy under DOS

To save the screen contents as a graphics file under DOS, you need a special hardcopy program. If you work with graphic oriented DOS applications, however, you can also create a hardcopy directly from Windows (see below).

Using HiJaak

One hardcopy program is HiJaak from Inset Systems. This program consists of two modules, a capture program and a graphics conversion program. This means that you can convert the pictures you capture into one of many popular graphics formats.

Once you've installed HiJaak, use the following to setup the capture portion of the program:

```
HJ
```

After configuring HiJaak to your system, use the following command to call the Resident Process Manager program:

```
LOADRPM
```

This places HiJaak in resident memory, where it requires only 5K of RAM. Use a key combination defined in Setup to "freeze" the current screen and start the resident portion of HiJaak.

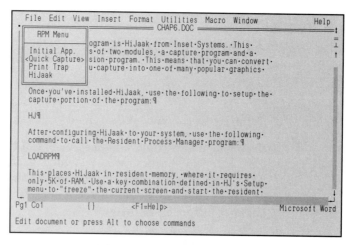

```
File  Edit  View  Insert  Format  Utilities  Macro  Window          Help
                          CHAP6.DOC
  ┌──────────────┐
  │  RPM Menu    │  ogram·is·HiJaak·from·Inset·Systems..This·
  ├──────────────┤  s·of·two·modules,·a·capture·program·and·a·
  │ Initial App. │  sion·program.·This·means·that·you·can·convert·
  │<Quick Capture>│  u·capture·into·one·of·many·popular·graphics·
  │ Print Trap   │
  │ HiJaak       │
  └──────────────┘
     Once·you've·installed·HiJaak,·use·the·following·to·setup·the·
     capture·portion·of·the·program:¶

     HJ¶

     After·configuring·HiJaak·to·your·system,·use·the·following·
     command·to·call·the·Resident·Process·Manager·program:¶

     LOADRPM¶

     This·places·HiJaak·in·resident·memory,·where·it·requires·
     only·5K·of·RAM.·Use·a·key·combination·defined·in·HJ's·Setup·
     menu·to·"freeze"·the·current·screen·and·start·the·resident·

Pg1 Co1          {}            <F1=Help>               Microsoft Word
Edit document or press Alt to choose commands
```

Selection after the snapshot

Use the <Quick Capture> option to save the screen to internal IGF format for later conversion. You can also select the HiJaak option to start the full version of the program and convert the image to the desired format. Choose <Initial App.> to activate the original application, from which you snapped the screen photo.

Converting the image

To convert the image captured in IGF format, start the full version of HiJaak. You can do this from the resident menu or by calling:

HJ

Use the **Capture/Load Screen From...** option to load an IGF file. Choose **Capture/Save Screen As...** to display a dialog box in which you can select the desired destination format.

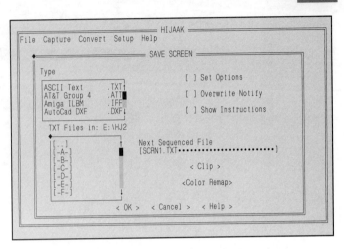

One of the many supported graphics formats

After confirming your selection, you can set a number of options, depending on the destination format you choose. For example, you can set the height and width of the image, resolution and rotation, as well as make settings for colors or gray scales.

Hardcopy under Windows

It's very easy to create a hardcopy under Windows. Everything you need is already integrated in the Windows package. You'll use the same (Prt Sc) key that you use for printing screen output to the printer under DOS.

Full screen or window   When you use this key under Windows, it copies the current screen contents to the Clipboard. Press (Alt) + (Prt Sc) to copy only the current window to the Clipboard.

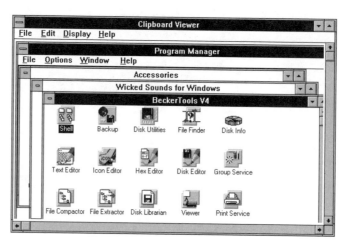

The contents of the screen in the Clipboard

The information in the Clipboard is saved as a bitmap, and can be imported from there into any Windows program. Since Paintbrush is included with Windows, we'll use it in our example:

> 1. Paintbrush composes the image as it should be saved to a file.

You can also start DOS applications that run in graphics mode from Windows, such as GEM or Word 5.5. First, run the DOS application from within Windows. Press [Alt] + [Spacebar] to create a window, then press [Alt] + [Prt Sc] to copy the window to the Clipboard.

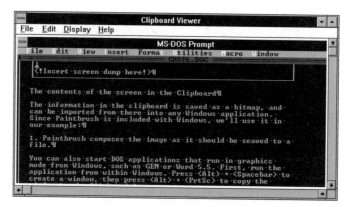

Word 5.5 in the Clipboard

If you use a video overlay card and run the video image in a window, you can also use the [Prt Sc] key to create a hardcopy. Unfortunately, only the Windows screen will be copied to the Clipboard, and not the video image.

This occurs because the [Prt Sc] key can only read from the video RAM of the graphics card. However, the VGA signal overlays the video signal and doesn't access the video RAM of the graphics card.

> To save a video image as a graphics file, you must use your video overlay card's framegrabber or freeze capability (more on this later). However, to create a hardcopy in which the Windows screen, including the video display, appears in the window, you'll have to perform some extra steps. We did the following with Video Blaster, but with some effort, the same steps should work for other systems:

1. Open the video display application. Load or capture the video image, and create a hardcopy of the Windows screen by pressing [Prt Sc], or [Alt] + [Prt Sc].

2. Save the video image you captured (i.e., the picture displayed in the video display application) as a color graphics file using the appropriate software (256 colors, if possible).

3. Exit the video display application. Load the Windows hardcopy into a graphics program. You may have a color background where the video image should be. If so, select that background and cut it.

4. Now paste the video image into the hardcopy. Depending on your system, you may have to load the image file, then copy and paste it, or you may have to use **Edit/Paste From...** or a similar command.

5. Move the image file to the correct position and edit the frame if necessary.

6. Save the montage as a new graphics file.

Here we pasted a video image into a captured window from the Video Blaster's Video Kit software:

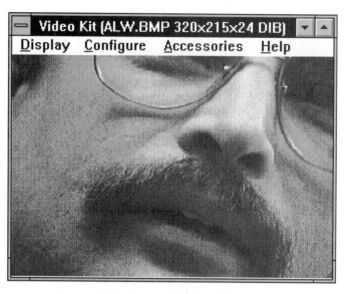

A mounted image with video display

To get an exact copy from pure DOS applications, such as Edit, start them in 386 Enhanced mode of Windows. Press [Alt] + [Spacebar] to change the DOS application into a form Windows can understand. Press [Alt] + [Prt Sc] to copy the image to the Clipboard. This includes the frame of the window in the copy. However, you can edit out the frame with an application such as Paintbrush.

> 2.   Now open Paintbrush and choose Image Attributes... from the Options menu.

Select the option button called "pels" and set the number of pixels for the width and height of the current resolution of your graphics card (e.g., 640 x 480 or 800 x 600).

Since Paintbrush adds only what appears in the display window, you must either increase the drawing area.

> 3.   Select Zoom Out in the View menu.

This makes the entire drawing area visible, so you cannot lose any information.

> 4.   Enable the Paste command from the Edit menu twice to paste the image from the clipboard.

Selecting **Edit/Paste** twice is very important! If you call the command only once, the command pastes the raster without the actual screen contents.

The DOS image in Paintbrush

5. Select Zoom In in the View menu

This returns the image to its original size. You can save it either in PCX or BMP format.

Capturing Video Signals

You can also use images from television or videocassettes in tutorials or multimedia presentations.

With a video overlay card, you can display any video sources you want on the computer screen. If the card has a framegrabber option with the appropriate software, you can freeze a frame and save it as a still image. The image is saved in a common graphics format. The selection of graphics formats can vary. However, you always have the option of saving the image with varying color depths. The lower the color depth, the less disk space the file occupies.

Since only a few graphics cards or programs are currently able to display images in TrueColor, you should use 256 colors. This is sufficient to display the images in photograph quality.

In Sections 6.3 and 6.4 we'll discuss creating image files from video signals.

Scanning

Scanning is similar to using a video overlay card to create graphics files. The difference is when you scan, a solid model (photo, picture, text, etc.) is sufficient for making a graphics file. We covered the basics in Section 2.4.

If you don't want to buy a video overlay card, you could also photograph images from the television or video monitor and then scan the photographs.

We'll discuss the technique for scanning in Section 6.6.

Editing Graphics Files

Obviously creating graphics and image files is useful only if you can edit them. Color separation, false colors and pixel processing are some ways pictures can be modified.

Improving the quality of images

Today's image processing programs have many capabilities. For example, one very important feature allows you to change the focus and contrast. This lets you make significant improvements in the quality of originals digitized by scanners or overlay cards.

Additional effects, fonts and icons prepare a graphics file for use in multimedia presentations. We'll talk about which options are available and how you can best use electronic image processing in Section 6.7.

6.2　Using File Formats

The file format is an important factor in electronic image processing. It determines the type and amount of information that's saved.

Number of colors
is important

The number of colors with which the image is saved is especially important. The maximum number of colors is in the 24-bit file format, which lets you save an image in 16.7 million colors. The minimum number is in 1-bit file format, where each pixel is either black (1) or white (0).

Another important factor is the type of data compression. The greater the color depth of a picture, the greater the amount of disk space it requires. That's why the manner in which you create a graphics file plays a deciding role in the memory requirements of a storage medium. When you compress files, you want as little information to be lost as possible (see Section 2.4).

Most programs for creating image files or graphics files provide an option for saving the information in various file formats. Which format you select depends on the application into which you want to load and use the file.

There is another group of programs designed exclusively for converting existing graphics formats to other formats and then compressing them. One example is the shareware program Paint Shop Pro. It's located in the \SHAREWR\WIN\GFXTOOLS\PSP directory. This directory is in the PSPRO101.EXE self-extracting archive on the companion CD-ROM.

Conversion
option

If you saved a graphics file in a format that isn't supported by the multimedia application, you can use a conversion program to change the graphics file to a supported file format. However, you may lose some information.

For example, if you used a Screen Machine to save a video image as a graphics file in a 24-bit TIFF format (TrueColor) and want to process it in Paintbrush, you'll encounter problems at first.

Depending on which graphics card you installed, Windows works with a specific number of colors (e.g., 640 x 480 with 256 colors or 800 x 600 with 256 colors). There are two ways to use the file in Paintbrush:

1. Load the image file in the SM TV application and save it again in PCX format (requires Screen Machine and the proper software).

2. Use a conversion program (e.g., HiJaak or DoDOT) to change the TIFF file to a PCX file.

Many programs for processing images can save image files in various file formats. To convert an image file, you can import it into one of these programs and save it to the desired file format. However, the algorithm for converting the format may also lose information.

We'll use an example to help explain how information can be lost when you convert a file. If the images are saved in TrueColor in the special TIFF format, the color information must be "trimmed down" to 256 colors in PCX format. A special algorithm checks the image for related colors that can be assigned to a color group.

Instead of being based on per square unit, this is based on a percentage of how often the individual colors occur. If colors were combined per square unit, for example, a face that stood out in contrast to a colorful background would lose nearly all its contours.

Program for conversion

The companion CD-ROM has a professional, extremely powerful, conversion program in the \SM directory called The Ultimate SM Image Converter. This program, manufactured by Fast Electronics GmbH, supports all common graphics formats. A special conversion algorithm ensures that only a minimal amount of information is lost. This application requires the SMPAR.DLL file available only from Fast Electronics GmbH. If you don't have Screen Machine, you cannot use this application.

Install the application using the WININST.EXE application, as you did the other Screen Machine software. The program icon is placed in its own program group. The image converter is divided into the following groups:

Group	Function
Source	Selects the file to be converted
Destination	Specifies the destination file name and graphics format
Dithering	Selects the dithering process
Palette	Manages the color palette
Display	Preview of the image

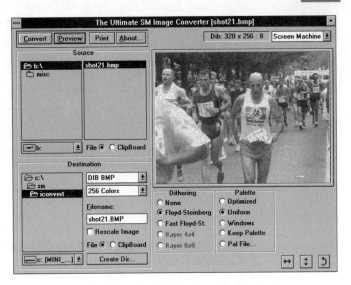

A file being specified

Choose a graphics file in the "Source" group to enable the
remaining options. Click the [Preview] button to display the graphic
in reduced form in the display window. Choose the color mode used
to display the image in the list box in the upper-right of the
display window. The list box in the upper-left lets you adapt the
image to the display window.

Specify the destination directory and the desired file format in
the "Destination" group. The following formats can be selected
from the list:

Format	Colors	TrueColor	Gray Scales
FLM	n/a	24 Bit	256
DIB BMP	16, 256	24 Bit	4, 16, 256, B/W
DIB RLE	16, 256	n/a	4,16, 256
RDIB	16, 256	24 Bit	4, 16, 256, B/W
RDIB RLE	16, 256	n/a	4,16, 256
PM 1.2 DIB	16, 256	24 Bit	4, 16, 256, B/W
EPS	n/a	24 Bit	256
GIF	16, 256	n/a	4,16, 256
PCX	16, 256	n/a	4,16, 256
TGA	256	16 Bit, 24 Bit	256

Format	Colors	TrueColor	Gray Scales
TIF	16, 256	24 Bit	4, 16, 256, B/W
LZW TIF	16, 256	24 Bit	4, 16, 256, B/W

Click the (Convert) button to convert the selected file and save it under a new name. Click on (Print) to print out the file in the display window.

6.3 Video Overlay

Processing external video signals (television, video etc.) was only possible in real time with very expensive hardware. Television on the PC (e.g., made possible by the TV tuner of a VCR connected to the port of a video overlay card) is only one way of processing video signals.

Saving video images in a common graphics format provides various possibilities, ranging from importing digitized images from a home video into WinWord to editing and touching up video images with image processing software.

In this section we'll discuss two video overlay cards that have the framegrabber option: Screen Machine from Fast Electronic GmbH and Video Blaster from Creative Labs.

Screen Machine

The Screen Machine, which was one of the first video overlay cards, quickly became very popular. This product supports the NTSC television standard of the USA and the PAL television standard of most of Europe. You can also buy an option to have the card support the SECAM television standard used in France and the Eastern Bloc countries.

Color Keying option

Screen Machine has three video ports for connecting all common video sources. Screen Machine also supports S-VHS hookups or Hi8 sources, which are higher quality. The built-in Color Keying option lets you select any VGA color for live video.

A special time base corrector ensures optimum synchronization with "mechanical" video sources. For example, the corrector corrects speed fluctuations in VCRs. Digital row correction corrects the striping effect produced by rapid movement in the video image.

Image quality

Screen Machine scans the entire video tape width at a frequency of 13.5 MHz. During this time, Screen Machine completely processes the video tape width of 5.5 MHz. Then the Screen Machine digitizes the video source with a color depth of 21 bits (approximately 21 million colors). The color depth increases when you use a still video source at 24 bits (16.6 million colors).

Audio option

The newer Screen Machines include an audio option that places a separate expansion slot in the back of the case. You could connect the Audio-Out cables from the VCR here, for example. Actually, you should use this option only if you don't have a sound card. Otherwise, connect the audio source directly to the sound card and save room in your computer.

Use the SM-Camera application to display the video image under Windows. This program has three modules:

1. The TV module displays the video signal on the screen. This module is intended for live or still video, although you could also use it to snap pictures and save them.

2. The Camera module contains options for recording and saving images. The camera creates a film (actually a separate subdirectory). You can save as many pictures as you want in this directory in internal FLM format.

3. The Darkroom module is for developing the pictures. You can save the pictures in common graphics formats; a compression procedure (JPEG) provides a compression rate of as much as 50:1. The procedure performs compressions of up to 15:1 without any visible loss in quality.

Easy to program

Because of Microsoft's MCI (Media Control Interface) support, it's easy to instruct the Screen Machine to interact with your own applications. In Chapter 13 we'll show you how to do this by using Visual Basic programming as an example.

Video Blaster

The Video Blaster is a compact 16-bit card to which you can connect up to three external video sources. For example, you can buy a video out cable to connect a home VCR and plug it into the jack of the Video Blaster cable.

When connecting the VCR, you can use an integrated antenna tuner to show television programs as well. To synchronize the video signal of the external source to the VGA signal (also called SVGA), the Video Blaster includes a cable to connect it to the computer's VGA card using the Feature Connector.

Scale to any size   Use the appropriate Windows applications to set up the Video Blaster card. The Video Kit application displays the video signal in a Windows window that you can scale to any size. Use the **Display/Freeze** item to grab single images and save them as graphics. When you freeze the video signal, a separate item, called **Display/Smoothen**, helps prevent blurred images.

IBM MMotion, Windows Bitmap and Targa formats are available for output formats in various color depths. This means that you can continue processing the images in other applications. You can produce other formats by saving the images in the desired format from the supplied image processing program.

You can also process video signals in European PAL or American NTSC format. You could use each of the three video ports for a different format.

From the Video Kit you can use **Configure/Color Control...** to modify the video signal's color, brightness and contrast settings. Use the scroll bars to change the color percentages of red, green and blue separately.

Mask brightness   The **Display/Masks...** item displays a dialog box from which you can mask specific bits of brightness and color value information (luma/chroma) by at the click of a check box. This enables you to exclude disturbing colors or create special effects.

Some versions of Video Blaster include a DOS based program called Tempra GIF. From within Tempra GIF, you can modify stored video images by using special effects to flip, rotate and enlarge cutouts of the images. You can also change colors or delete them.

You can convert the image to different color depths, or save the image in monochrome. Because Tempra GIF supports scanners, you can easily combine digitized video images with scanned models. We captured the following image using the Video Blaster Video Kit.

An example of a processed image with Tempra GIF

You can also display video images and freeze single images from Tempra GIF.

6.4 Recording A Video Signal

Before making the recordings, plug in the video source to one of the three video ports of the card.

Connecting The VCR

To record video or television images, you must connect a VCR to the card. Depending on the port, you may have to purchase a special cable at an electronics store. Most VCRs intended for the home have RCA phono plugs, like the Video Blaster. Upper-end VCRs and VCRs in some parts of the world may require a BNC, DIN A/V or SCART plug.

The other end of the cable should have RCA phono plugs for Video Out and Audio Out. Connect the Video Out plug to one of the three Video In ports of the video overlay card. To listen to sound at the same time, connect the two Audio Out plugs (for right and left channels) to the Audio In of the video overlay card, or to your sound card's Line-in jack using a Y adapter (see Chapter 5).

Now switch on the VCR. Until you press the Play button, the VCR's antenna tuner usually runs. In this case, the television picture appears on the screen, if you plugged in the VCR to the antenna or cable connection. Insert the tape containing the scene you want to capture, and press Play.

Video Camera

The video camera, or camcorder, is used to produce electronic images. Many amateur film makers have been using camcorders for several years. Now it's possible to connect video cameras and computers by using video overlay cards.

Capture individual images

The biggest advantage of a video camera is its ability to capture individual images at any time. Scanners can only capture images from two-dimensional models. With a video camera, you can capture images anywhere and then process them in your computer.

The following are some advantages of owning a video camera:

• Can be used anywhere

• Many different models available

• Record three-dimensional objects

• Zoom allows change of field

• Different perspectives

• Relatively popular

The big disadvantage of a video camera is its low resolution. The camera's video resolution may not be sharp enough for professional level multimedia or desktop publishing.

Video Camera Types

There are two kinds of video cameras and still video cameras.

Camcorders

Camcorders use videocassettes for recording. The VHS-C format, which is very popular, has a playing length of 30 to 45 minutes.

Some camcorders have a Long Play, or Extended Play, function that lets you extend the recording capacity of a cassette. Since these cassettes are smaller than conventional videocassettes, they are suitable for portable use. Some camcorders use 8mm cassettes or even VHS videocassettes.

There are two ways to watch a recording. You can use a connecting cable to plug the camcorder into a VCR to play back the recordings, or buy an adapter to play back the small cassettes onto standard VHS cassettes.

Camcorder controls

Since camcorders have controls, you can track the recordings from the monitor in the viewfinder.

By doing this, you can preselect the part of the recording you play back, since you probably don't want to view the entire tape. This also makes it easier to edit your recordings later on the VCR you plan on using for editing.

Still video cameras

Unlike camcorders, still video cameras provide video images without an option for recording. Still video cameras are connected to a monitor. You can hook up a still video camera to a VCR in order to play recordings.

Still video cameras work like camcorders with the [Pause] button pressed during playback. The light passing through the lens meets an electronic image sensor, called a CCD (Charge Coupled Device) sensor, and is displayed in the viewfinder. The connecting cable to the overlay card displays the captured image in the computer, where you can save it.

Which is better?

Since still video cameras are usually cheaper than camcorders, they are perfect for gathering single electronic images indoors. The camcorder, however, is widely used and has many options, including the same options offered by still video cameras. If you want to shoot motion pictures outdoors and edit them in the computer, you need a camcorder.

It's important to have the right connection when you work with a camera and a computer. Buy a connection cable that sends the video data from the camera to the Video In RCA phono jack of the video overlay card.

You can purchase this type of cable for all camera models. It's usually included with the camera. If the other end of the cable has a BNC or DIN A/V plug instead of the RCA plug, then you must purchase an adapter at an electronics store.

Three video sources

Most overlay cards let you connect up to three video sources. This means that you can connect your VCR and the video camera at the same time. Use the software to switch between the different video sources.

If you connect a camcorder directly to the overlay card, it functions like a still video camera. The subject appears in the video window of the monitor. You can edit the incoming video signal as if you were using a VCR.

For some video sources, you'll need two ports on the video overlay card, since the information for luminance and chroma are transferred separately. If you have a Screen Machine, use the respectively marked cables for luminance and chroma. If you're using a Video Blaster, use any two ports.

Screen Machine

If you're working with Screen Machine, use SM-Camera to convert digitized images into usable graphics files. SM-Camera consists of three modules. Use the Camera module to get snapshots of the video image.

Although you cannot scale the window of this module like a window in the TV module, you can save several snapshots together in a film.

Snapshots with the camera

Follow this procedure for quick results:

1.   Double-click the SM-Camera icon and run the Camera module.

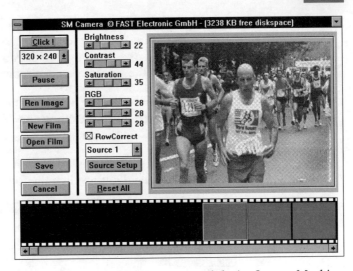

Recordings with the Camera module in Screen Machine

2. Click the [Source Settings] button to select the video source and set the option needed (NTSC, PAL or SECAM). US users would select NTSC, for example. The available video sources are:

Source 1	Black cable
Source 2	Red cable
Source 3	Yellow cable
S-Video	Black + Red cable

    Ensure that the "Composite Colour", "Time Base Correction (VCR)" and "Prefilter" check boxes are checked. Click [Save] to save changes and exit.

3. Select the video signal resolution from the drop-down list box below the [Click!] button:

NTSC	PAL	Mode
640 x 480	640 x 512	Full Screen
320 x 240	320 x 256	Half Screen
160 x 120	160 x 128	Quarter Screen

4. Set the "Brightness", "Contrast" and "Saturation" scroll bars, then enable the "RowCorrect" check box.

5.   Run the tape up to just before the point you want captured. Click on the (Pause) button to freeze the image. Click on the (Click!) button to save the image as a frame in the film display at the bottom of the screen. You can repeat the process often.

6.   Click on the (Save) button to save the film containing the images and your settings. When the "Save Film As" dialog box appears, click on the (Save) button.

7.   Click (Cancel) to exit the Camera module, and run the Darkroom module. Double-click the file name to load it.

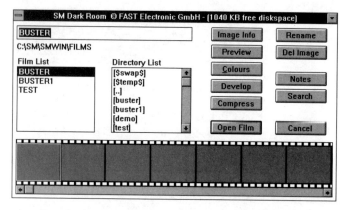

Developing is performed in the SM Dark Room

8.   Enable the image you want to develop by clicking on it and then clicking on the (Develop) button. Use the "Image Format:" and "Image Colour:" drop-down list boxes to set image file format and color layout. Click (OK) to develop the image.

Advanced Settings

Several options in the Camera module can be used to modify video signals. For example, after you call Camera or the TV module, the video signal may move within the window in Windows.

This means that you would have to make corrections to the alignment and scaling of your video image. To do this, open the TV module and select **Misc/Display Setup**.

The settings you make here affect the display of the video image in the Camera module.

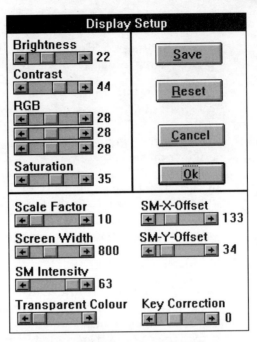

When the video signal moves, you must make corrections

A perfectly synchronized image is produced when you have the correct ratio between the "Scale Factor", the "Screen Width", the "SM-X-Offset" and the "SM-Y-Offset". To display the image correctly, first adjust the size to the window in Windows. Use the Scaling factor and the screen width to do this. Then use the scroll bars for "SM-X-Offset" and "SM-Y-Offset" to position the image in the frame.

If other things besides the video image have shifted in the window (e.g., the check boxes and the slider), then use a graphics card with a resolution higher than 640 x 480 pixels. In this case, you must also make changes to the Windows SETUP.INF file. The necessary changes are described in the Screen Machine documentation.

However, if you have a graphics card that contains an ET4000 chip set, you can choose a high resolution with small fonts using the latest Windows drivers. In this case, Windows displays the check boxes correctly; you don't have to modify a file.

Changing the color percentages

The "Brightness", "Contrast", and "Saturation" scroll bars are located to the left of the image display in the Camera module.

Directly beneath these are three scroll bars for regulating the color percentages of red, green and blue. You can choose from 64 (0 -63) levels. Set all three sliders to the same value for a "normal" color image. As this value increases, the image's contrast becomes brighter or richer.

If you completely remove a color (0), Windows redraws the image in the other two colors. Remove two colors to produce a monochrome image. You can create special effects or remove color imbalances by varying the color percentages.

Interlacing

Since video images are drawn in the interlace procedure, when you record a moving object, the second half frame will probably already contain information about the next movement phase. This causes lines which distort the image.

Although this problem can be used as a special effect, usually you should avoid it. To do this, enable the "RowCorrect" check box in the Camera module. In this case, the program shoots only a half frame and determines the missing lines by interpolation (calculating intermediate values based on known values).

Filtering the input signal

Use filters to correct interferences in video signals. Electronic filters change specific properties of the incoming video signal, depending on the type of electric filter. For example, it's possible to suppress certain frequencies or color and brightness information by having the filter block them.

Both the Camera and TV modules provide different filters. The "Prefilter" check box, which is the default setting, suppresses the noise that causes "snow" on the screen.

You can also optimize your video source with custom settings for the "Sharpness", (emphasizes edges rich in contrast), "Noise Filter", and "Bandpass" filter scroll bars.

Color Keying

You've probably seen interesting visual effects on television. An image or graphic appears with a running video image overlaid in certain areas. For example, a font on a black background may shine through the video image.

To create this effect, define a color that's transparent for the video signal. You can produce the same effect by moving the Transparent slider in the "Display Setup" dialog box in the TV module to define a VGA color as transparent. The selected color is displayed to the right of the slider. Move the "Transparent Colour" scroll bar all the way to the right to choose white as the Color Key.

So if a white area overlays the video image (e.g., a dialog box with a white background), the white area will be replaced by the video signal.

Video Blaster

The Video Kit, VB Setup and Tempra are programs included with Video Blaster. While VB Setup can display live video, Video Kit is intended for capturing video "snapshots."

Snapshots with Video Kit

Win-Video

Follow these steps to get the fastest results:

1. Run Windows, double-click the VB Setup icon and set the "VBW Setup View" window to Maximized status. Check to see whether the **Configure/Sources...** item is either checked, or dimmed, or both. If it is, there should be a set of group boxes for video control.

2. In the "Video Standard" group, click on the "NTSC" or "PAL" option button, depending on your video configuration (US systems run on NTSC, most of the world systems run on PAL). Insert the tape containing the image you want to view in the video device (the VCR or camcorder) and press the [Play] button.

3. In the "Video Source" group box select the video input (the "Video 0" option button is the default). Here are the video input numbers and the color cables used on some Video Blaster systems:

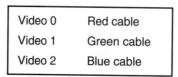

Video 0	Red cable
Video 1	Green cable
Video 2	Blue cable

4. When the video image appears in the display, select **File/Save Configuration**, then **File/Exit Setup**.

5. Double-click the "Video Kit" icon. Using the video device's [<<] and [>>] buttons, find the image you want to capture. Play up to that image, then press [Ctrl] + [S]. This serves the same purpose as selecting **Display/Freeze**, but accesses the capture much faster than selecting the menu and item. Pressing [Ctrl] + [S] a second time serves the same purpose as selecting **Display/Unfreeze**.

6. Select **Display/Save...** to save the still image.

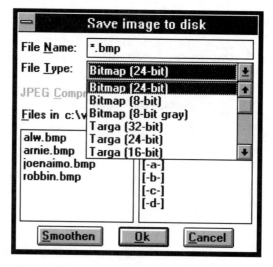

Video Kit's Save image to disk dialog box

7. Choose the file format and type a name for the image. Click [OK] to save the image.

The BMP, TARGA and MMOTION file formats can be used with Tempra. If you prefer to use the PCX or TIFF or EPS formats, capture your video images using Tempra.

Setting the video signal

Video Kit has different options for displaying video images on the screen. The focus, contrast and brightness of the video image determine its quality. Optimum color distribution of red, green and blue color percentages is also important for a good image.

> Experiment with brightness in Video Kit to get the best results. You can improve the display quality of a video film that is out of focus or too dark by setting the parameters properly.

Setting parameters

The **Configure** menu contains the **Color Control...** menu item. Use the scroll bars to set the values for "Bright", "Satura" and "Contra". Choose values between 0 and 255 for these parameters.

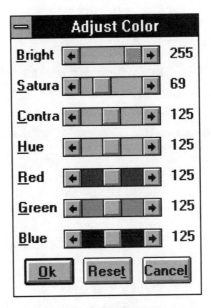

The Adjust Color dialog box

Hue parameter for NTSC signals

If you use an NTSC video source to obtain video signals (USA standard), use the "Hue" scroll bar to set the hue.

Color correction

Use the "Red", "Green" and "Blue" scroll bars to change the color percentages of the RGB components. Set all three scroll bars to the middle (128) for a normal color display. When you eliminate a color (0), the program mixes the video image from the remaining two colors. Eliminate two colors to have the video image drawn in one color. Removing all three colors removes the image from the display. Set all three colors to the highest value (255) to produce an image that's extremely bright and rich in contrast.

Change the color percentages and parameters for the video signal to produce special effects. We'll discuss these effects in more detail in the next section.

Special effects through modification

Follow these steps to create special effects or improve the quality of the incoming signal from the video source:

- When the window is Maximized, the video image appears in the correct aspect ratio. To create special effects by changing the aspect ratio, select **Display/Fit**. This completely fills the window with the video image.

Window isn't Maximized   If the "Video Kit" window isn't Maximized and **Display/Fit** isn't selected, only a section of the actual full video frame appears in the window.

- Select **Display/Zoom** to increase the video image to four times its size. By default, only the upper-left section is displayed in the window. If the window isn't in Maximized mode, use the scroll bars on the right and at the bottom to choose different sections of the image. However, selecting **Zoom** affects the quality of the display.

Window is Maximized   If the window is Maximized, the scroll bars for positioning the section disappear. Exit Video Kit, and run VB Setup. From this application, select **Configure/Align Video...** to change the values of "Display Position X" and "Display Position Y". Exit VB Setup and run Video Kit again.

- If you experiment with the colors to create an alienation effect, use the default settings of **Configure/Color Control...**. You can also use the **Display/Masks...** item, which lets you delete specific bits of brightness (luminance) information and color value (chroma) information from the video image.

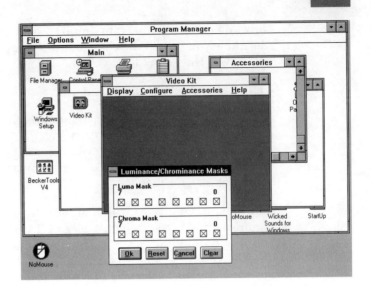

Adjusting luminance and chrominance

You can experiment with different combinations to achieve interesting effects.

Photo Plus (non-US versions)

In Section 6.7 we'll discuss editing image and graphics files. Some non-US versions of Video Blaster include an image processing program called Photo Plus. The advantage of this program is that you can use an extra module to load video images directly into the program for processing.

6.5 Photo CD

If you have not yet purchased a CD drive, make certain that it can take advantage of Eastman Kodak Co.'s Photo CD.

Photo CD allows you to have a roll of film on a CD as a high-resolution scan. Then by using the correct CD drive, you can load your pictures or even import them into documents as professional-quality color images.

The Kodak Photo CD

In September 1992, Kodak introduced their Photo CD. With the Photo CD, you can read still photographs and video images into your computer. Obviously this technology will open a large market in the future.

Now you can have your film digitized on a photo CD-ROM at the same time you have it developed. Instead of prints, you get a small golden CD, the Kodak Photo CD.

CD-ROM Drive With XA Standard

You need a CD-ROM drive that supports the XA standard (XA = eXtended Architecture) to place the Photo CD images in the computer. Not all CD-ROM devices on the market support the XA standard. You also need the proper software so you can display your photos on the monitor.

Powerful PC required

You must have a powerful computer to do this. The minimum requirement is a 386/SX with 4 Meg of RAM, a 100 Meg hard drive and Microsoft Windows 3.1. The faster the processor, the more quickly you'll be able to load or print the photos. The same principle applies to the size of RAM. You need at least 10 Meg of RAM to display a photo CD image in full resolution on your monitor.

Unprecedented photo resolution quality

With 18 million pixels per single frame, the photo CD provides unprecedented photo resolution quality. Using a high performance scanner, it's possible to read and digitize the image information of a 35mm negative or slide. Then the image information is saved to the photo CD through laser technology.

The scanner occupies about as much space as a normal office desk. It's possible to digitize 35mm slides, negatives in black & white or color and paper photos onto the photo CD.

In the future, it will be possible to digitize medium or large format photos. Currently there is only one scanner for these professional formats. Negatives appear as positives on the Photo CD.

Quality Duplicates

It's also possible to produce quality duplicates. The color and sharpness of the photos can be adjusted while the individual frames are digitized. With this process, you can restore old faded photographs to their original quality.

It takes about 30 minutes to make a CD with 100 photos. After the CD is finished, prints of single frames are printed in color as contact prints. You can also create larger prints (e.g., DIN A4 size).

Every CD receives a number that also appears on the contact print. This number is important for finding specific images in a large archive.

100 Photos On One CD

The Kodak CD has the memory capacity of a normal CD (i.e., 600 Meg). The color photo file is 18 Meg, which can be compressed to 6 Meg through a special compression procedure. This means that the maximum capacity of a Photo CD is 100 color images in photo quality.

By the summer of 1993, Kodak will offer CDs with a maximum capacity of 800 color images in TV quality (512 x 768 pixels). You'll also be able to save up to 72 minutes of sound on these CDs.

Although it's possible to make photo quality prints directly from the Photo CD, this process is much more expensive than making prints from slides or negatives.

Now you can have your exposed films developed and get your negatives or slides back in a couple of days along with a Photo CD. The contact print of your single photo is the title of the Photo CD. It costs about $20 to $30 per 35mm film for a CD.

For about 75 cents per image, you not only get the option of viewing and editing your photos in your computer, you also get a new, space saving, reliable method of archiving your photos. The price of the CD decreases as the number of images you want to store increases.

Images do not fade

Unlike conventional film, which ages over time (i.e., the color changes), the images on the Photo CD remain consistent in color and don't age. Because of the low space requirements of a CD, photo albums become a thing of the past.

Also in 1993, Kodak will offer other Photo CD formats. The Pro Photo CD will save images in formats larger than 35mm and in higher resolutions.

The Portfolio Disc will save up to 800 images in television quality, and you can even add sound. The Catalog Disc can store several thousand images in low resolution. All these new formats correspond to the XA Standard and use the same technology as the "regular" Photo CD.

In the future, when you want to read pictures into your computer, you won't need an expensive color scanner. Instead, all you'll need

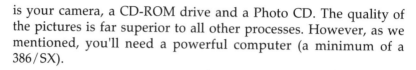

is your camera, a CD-ROM drive and a Photo CD. The quality of the pictures is far superior to all other processes. However, as we mentioned, you'll need a powerful computer (a minimum of a 386/SX).

Hardware

XA Standard drive

Not all CD-ROM drives support the XA Standard. Only XA capable drives can read Kodak CDs.

Multi-Session drive

Eventually Single-Session drives will be replaced by Multi-Session drives. Single-Session technology lets users record on the photo CD several times, but only the first set of images can be read. Multi-Session devices can also read photo CDs that have been recorded on several times.

Organize your photos

Owners of Single-Session mode drives should organize their photos on single CDs.

Before purchasing any hardware, ask questions about the latest developments on the market. One recent kit contains a Multi-Session CD-ROM drive, software, expansion card and a test CD. An internal kit costs around $950 while an external kit costs about $1,200.

Single-Session CD-ROM drives are common. These drives recognize Kodak CDs and read the first-time recordings.

Multimedia Upgrade Kit is an alternative

You can also use Multimedia Upgrade Kits that contain a CD-ROM drive as well as a sound card. To address the CD drive, you need a SCSI adapter and SCSI driver. This is an excellent combination, because you can enjoy both images and sound. Drives with AT buses don't have the right drivers to recognize Photo CDs.

You can also purchase all of these accessories separately. However, ensure that you have the proper SCSI driver. Without an updated version, your Photo CD software won't work on old equipment.

Software

According to Kodak, soon all the important image processing programs will be able to read the Kodak format. Registered users will then receive offers for updates.

Access Software

Kodak offers Access Software for amateurs. This software program is available for under $100. With this program, users can view special image files on the monitor and copy them to an image processor.

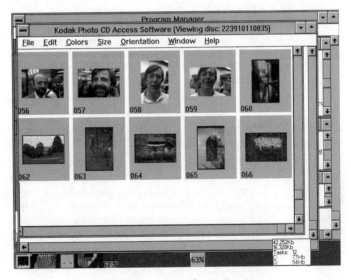

Contact prints from Access

First, a contact print appears with all the slides on the CD. Double-click your mouse to load the desired image in various sizes. The larger the format, the longer it takes to load the image.

The same principle applies to copying the images. The higher the resolution, the more disk space is needed on the hard drive. However, the quality of the picture is also better.

Access also gives users the option of rotating and flipping images, loading them in 24-bit color or with only 256 colors. Users can also load them in black and white.

PhotoEdge

Kodak also has a program called PhotoEdge, which is much more user-friendly than Access. This program is very similar to PhotoVision from Toshiba, which we'll discuss shortly, but doesn't have as many functions.

One of PhotoEdge's special features is a Copyright window, which lets the author of the pictures claim credit for their work. Eventually Kodak will offer a special coding process for securing copyrights.

PhotoVision

As we mentioned, Toshiba also offers a Photo CD program called PhotoVision. You can choose from six different languages when you install this program. PhotoVision has many more options than Kodak's Access software.

You can load single photos using the contact print on the CD or from the hard drive in all the common formats. You can print the photos, in amazing quality, after loading them. Even color ink jet printers produce satisfactory results.

Compared to what was possible up to now, the printouts are outstanding. PhotoVision offers many different printing options.

A computerized darkroom   You can also enlarge, reduce, correct and improve the focus of images, as well as influence the contrast and color saturation. PhotoVision has all the tools you would expect from an image processing program.

However, there are no functions for directly manipulating the image (brush, eraser, etc.). You can also export each PCD file to current image processing software. PhotoVision also includes a comprehensive help function.

Image processing with PhotoVision

Toshiba PhotoVision is available as a separate software product, so owners of a CD-ROM drive can take advantage of this new technology without purchasing a new drive. This software costs about $180.

If you already have a powerful image processing program, Kodak Access is enough. We recommend PhotoVision and PhotoEdge because of their user-friendliness and many options.

Incredible picture quality   The new Photo CD technology is quite fascinating. The picture quality is incredible; we've never seen such excellent image reproduction on a computer monitor. There are still problems with displaying the images. This technology will improve over time, but the best photographs are still created in photo labs.

However, if you're willing to pay about $65 for an almost perfect print, then this is the right technology for you. Ask a graphic artist where you can have your files exposed professionally.

Thermotransfer printers   For about $2,000 you can purchase a small thermal transfer printer that produces acceptable results. However, this printer can produce only wallet size photos. As the photo size increases, so does the price of the printer. In the future, these printers should become more affordable.

You're probably wondering how you can use this new technology. One use is to view photos in your PC. Also, you can modify your photos, make montages and change the colors of the photos.

Then you can import your artwork to texts or print it out. The image CD is also ideal for presentations.

Kodak is trying to attract private consumers by selling photo CD players. With these devices, users can view CDs on their televisions. These devices can also play back music CDs in stereo quality. Photo CD players are reasonably priced, so the average PC owner can afford them. You can purchase one of these players for about $500.

Many of the products we discussed are intended for professional users. However, if you can afford the technology, you may want to experiment with these products.

Currently Available Products

Toshiba

Toshiba is marketing a Photo CD Kit, which contains a CD drive and an image processing software program called PhotoVision.

Toshiba's CD-ROM drives support the XA standard and Multi-Session mode.

Developers are working on motherboards with an integrated SCSI interface. With this interface, users will be able to conduct sound information via the SCSI cable. Multimedia PCs will no longer need add-on cards and there won't be any addressing conflicts.

NEC

NEC has three different CD-ROM drives. They all support the XA Standard, but can support only Single-Session mode.

However, NEC sells a Multi-Session update for $70. Exchanging the EPROM enables the drive to support the new standard. Only experienced users should make the exchange themselves. If you're unsure about doing this yourself, ask your computer dealer to do it for you.

Sony

In early 1993 Sony is planning to introduce two XA CD-ROM drives. Both of these drives support Multi-Session mode.

Phillips

Phillips also has a CD-ROM drive. This is an internal device with an interface card that also supports the XA standard.

Pioneer

Pioneer plans to introduce a sextuple CD-ROM CD changer in early 1993 that will cost about $1,600. The CD changer also supports the XA standard.

None of the other CD-ROM drive manufacturers have products that are guaranteed to be able to read photo CDs.

OEM devices

There are also many OEM devices. These are CD-ROM drives with company names that aren't related to the manufacturer. Often, a quality drive from Sony or Toshiba has been renamed.

All hardware manufacturers offer this option to bulk buyers. This makes it difficult for the customer to determine whether the product actually supports the latest technological options.

You can usually assume that devices with SCSI buses are able to read photo CDs by means of adapted device drivers. Drives with AT Buses cannot be addressed.

Before investing a lot of money in a new drive, experiment with your old CD-ROM drive. With patience and endurance, you may be able to obtain the necessary drivers.

The drives sold in the Sound Blaster Multimedia Upgrade Kit don't support the XA Standard. However, according to Creative Labs, some of these CD players can recognize Photo CDs.

It will probably take some time before all the problems related to the XA Standard have been solved. However, most likely by the end of 1993, all brand name CD-ROM drives will be able to read Kodak Photo CDs.

A Review of CD-ROM Drives				
Mftr	**Model**	**Compatibility w/ Kodak Photo CD***	**Access time (ms)**	**Special features**
NEC	CDR 84	Single-Session	280	Internal
	CDR 74	Single-Session	280	External
Phillips	CM205XRS	Single-Session	375	Internal
Sony Corp	CDU 541	Single-Session	380	Internal
	CDU 3024	Single-Session	380	Internal
Toshiba	3301	Multi-Session	325	External
	3401	Multi-Session	200	External

*   Single-Session refers to Photo CDs which have been written to once. Most users will require Single-Session Photo CDs. However, if you work extensively with Photo CD, you should consider purchasing a Multi-Session Photo CD brand drive.

6.6 Scanners

An earlier method of placing images in computers involved digitizing the original with a scanner. Various kinds of scanners are available.

With scanner software and different settings on scanners, you can change the brightness and contrast with which originals are digitized. Also, image processing programs (see Section 6.7) provide options for touching up originals. However, using a good original (i.e., one rich in contrast) will generate the best results.

Scanner Software

Scanners usually included a scanner program. By using this program, you can read in the original, digitize it and save it as a graphics file. You should use an image processing program to edit these files.

If you're considering buying a new image processing program, pay attention to the integrated scan module supported by your scanner. This eliminates the step with the scanner software and the digitized image is available for editing in a format supported by the image processing program.

In this section we'll explain the basics of using a hand scanner with scanner software and the basics of using a flatbed scanner through the scan module of an image processing program.

Scanner Types

Hand scanner

Because of its limited scan width (approximately five inches or 13 cm), the hand scanner can be used to digitize smaller originals. However, you can also use this scanner to do partial scans and use the scanner software to combine these partial scans into a complete image.

Brightness and contrast

Depending on the original, first you must choose the brightness and contrast settings. Start with medium settings and remember that you won't get the best results the first time you scan. If the original is too dark, you can increase the brightness; if the original is too bright, decrease the brightness.

This also applies to the contrast. For example, if the original is a monochrome line drawing or text, use a higher contrast. With this setting, the scanner won't react very much to subtle transitions (e.g., several gray scales or colors). Use a lower contrast for color pictures or black and white pictures with many gray scales, to scan as many transitions as possible.

For fast results, use the following procedure for scanning:

1. Firmly place the original on the table and use a guide (e.g., a ruler) so you can guide the scanner in a straight line.

2. Set the correct contrast and brightness for the original. Some scanners require that these settings be made through software.

3. Run the scanner program and select the scanning command.

4. Set the desired resolution at which you want to digitize the original.

5.   Put the hand scanner on the guide and hold down the start button.

6.   Pass the hand scanner over the original until the light goes out or you hear a warning beep, signaling the end of the scan.

7.   If the scan was successful, save the original in the desired file format. Otherwise, repeat steps 2-6 after changing the settings for brightness and contrast.

8.   Edit the image with an image processing program.

Flatbed scanners

A flatbed scanner is used the same way. However, with a flatbed scanner, you can scan entire pages at one time. So you don't have to paste together different strips of a page.

Scanner Tips

Before scanning, you should consider the quality of the original and how the image will be used. When you use a high quality scanner, the way you scan the original can affect the quality of the scanned image.

Color format

First, consider the format. Usually you can choose from black & white, gray scales and colors. You can choose from 16, 256 or 64 million (RGB) for color resolution in colors.

The anticipated file size is important, because you must save between 1 and 24 bits of information per pixel.

The format you choose depends on how you want to output the graphic. If you plan to print the image on a normal laser printer, you shouldn't scan the image in RGB format.

However, you should use a different procedure if you want to edit the image before outputting it so certain colors stand out.

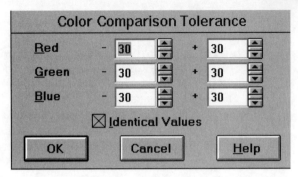

An example of controlling color (in PhotoStyler)

Line drawings   It's also important to think about line drawings before scanning them. If you don't want to output the graphic in the same size and resolution in which it's scanned, don't scan the original in black/white mode. Jaggies (uneven edges) will appear on round or slanted lines on the screen or on a printout after editing a line drawing. This is especially true with lower resolutions.

In this case, choose gray scales instead. The lines will appear much smoother later. Use your image processing program to convert the image to a black and white drawing only after the image is the size and resolution you want printed.

The following table shows the different values between resolution and gray scale for different output devices. The top row represents the halftone resolution and the left column shows the printer resolution.

	50	75	90	100	120	150
300	36	16	11	9	6	4
600	144	64	44	36	25	16
1000	256	178	123	100	69	44
1270	256	256	199	161	112	72
1693	256	256	256	256	199	127
2540	256	256	256	256	256	256

Resolution

Next you should consider resolution. You can choose a value between 60 and 600 DPI (dots per inch). The values depend on the type of scanner you're using.

Think about the quality of the image and the capabilities of your printer. Remember that usually "less is more". If you scan in images from printed masters, also remember that the master is already rastered and isn't in infinite resolution.

The same physical laws apply here that apply for digitizing music. Either the digitizing rate must be much higher than the dot frequency (raster width) of the original or it must be much lower, so that the same number of larger screen dots can be scanned simultaneously. For more information, refer to Section 6.7.

Scanning With A Flatbed Scanner

After determining the correct color and dot resolution, you can begin scanning. Call the scan module of your image processing program. Usually, you can call a prescan. This is scanning at a lower resolution and smaller size. The results appear in a window.

STEP #1

Determine the scanning area

In this window, select the area that you want to scan. Usually you don't want to scan an entire page. Remember that the scanning process takes up time and disk space.

STEP #2

Set the resolutions

Before you begin scanning, set the color and dot resolutions. Once this is done, the program usually displays the estimated file size.

STEP #3

Set the brightness

You can also set the brightness at which the original will be scanned. You must experiment with this setting to obtain the proper results. First scan with the basic setting, then change the setting if necessary.

STEP #4

Scan

Now begin scanning. The results are displayed in your image processing program. Then you can edit the results of the scan. We'll discuss editing options in the next section.

6.7 Image Processing

Selecting The Correct Program

Many programs, which have similar functions, are available for processing digitized or scanned images. The following are the basic requirements for an image processing program:

- Numerous filter and retouch functions

- Support for numerous graphics formats (TIFF, PCX, BMP, GIF, TGA and EPS)

- Support for RGB, CMYK color originals

Aldus PhotoStyler

PhotoStyler from Aldus is considered the standard of image processing programs. Therefore, we used it as the sample program in all of our explanations about functions (filters).

Although PhotoStyler is expensive for most users, you'll find its power and control over your images to be exceptional.

This program provides many useful tools for image processing professionals and runs under Windows, like most image processing software. However, PhotoStyler has the best text and effects tools.

Also, PhotoStyler can handle virtually any type of graphic format needed by professionals. Also, its color correction features are among the most powerful available.

The drawing tools are the only area in which PhotoStyler may be lacking. Other image processing programs have much better drawing tools.

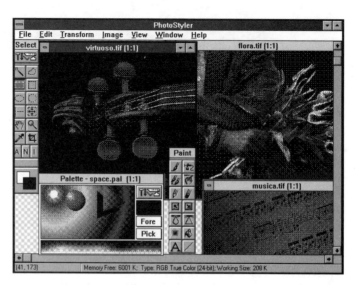

Processing several images simultaneously in PhotoStyler

PhotoStyler also provides excellent support for the different color originals (in addition to RGB, CMYK, HSB and HSL).

Image-In-Color 3.0

Image-In-Color 3.0 from Image-In Inc. in Minneapolis MN, was one of the first image processing programs. This program's documentation is much better than PhotoStyler's documentation. Image-In-Color provides a calibrating function for the monitor, and the many scanners supported by the program to optimize color correction.

For example, you can output a gray scaled sample from the printer and then scan it back in. Image-In-Color will then calculate the calibration curve from the scanned result compared to the printed original.

Simulated gray scales
The only problem with this system is that normal dot matrix printers, ink jet printers and laser printers cannot print gray scales. Instead, they simulate the gray scales with black dots that vary in density (for more information, please refer to the section "Colors and Gray Scales").

Like PhotoStyler, Image-In-Color can also handle important image formats such as TIFF, TGA, GIF, PCX and some others.

Unfortunately, Image-In-Color's options for color separation are quite weak. So, in this area, PhotoStyler is superior. However,

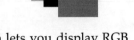

Image-In does have a unique function which lets you display RGB values and CMYK color values for each pixel on the screen.

Better drawing tools

Image-In-Color offers much better drawing tools than PhotoStyler. Its effect options are still lacking, although Image-In-Color also offers many effects, filters and perspective functions.

However, Image-In-Color's ability to create custom filters proves that it's a professional program. Image-In-Color is a good program because of its ease of operation.

Image-In-Color costs less than PhotoStyler. However, since there isn't a major difference between these programs, which one you choose depends on your personal preferences.

Micrografx Picture Publisher

Picture Publisher from Micrografx runs under Windows and, like PhotoStyler, is easy to use. However, it has fewer filters and effects than PhotoStyler.

PhotoFinish

PhotoFinish is an excellent, inexpensive image processing program from ZSoft. Originally, ZSoft sold this program as a paint program called "Publisher's Paintbrush". PhotoFinish costs about $200 and is comparable to the more expensive image processing programs.

Many advantages

This program contains all the basic functions. It lets you change focus, contrast and brightness, like PhotoStyler and Image-In-Color. PhotoFinish also has some effect filters, including filters for contour smoothing and soft drawing. It also supports numerous scanners and has a text tool that even supports TrueType fonts.

Another advantage of using this program is its Clone tool. This is an easy-to-use function for manipulating images. The Clone tool lets you copy a section of one image to another image by using a mouse. For example, you could place a picture of a movie star in a family photo.

No Color Separation

Unfortunately, PhotoFinish also has its disadvantages. For example, the tools for rotating images or cutouts fall short of normal needs. So the program cuts off the corners of an image during complex rotations.

No color
separation tool
Also, there isn't a color separation tool and you can't export images from RGB to the CMYK color original. Although PhotoFinish can output EPS files to PostScript, the program supports only one color original, RGB.

However, PhotoFinish is able to perform almost all the tasks of a professional image processing program. If you want or need a better program, you'll probably have to spend the extra money for Photo-Styler.

6.8 Image Processing Techniques

With manual photo processing, you can change the brightness of photos and touch up the photos. Today's image processing programs provide so many filters (options for processing images) and calibrating functions that it's hard to keep track of them.

Filters

For example, there are filters for brightness and contrast in addition to effect and perspective filters. In the following paragraphs we'll use examples to explain how the different filters work. We used PhotoStyler for all of the effects in the examples. However, there are only minor differences between PhotoStyler and the other image processing programs.

Filters for changing the contrast, brightness and focus are basic functions that should be included in every image processing program. When changing an image's contrast, remember that a higher contrast is only possible for line drawings with as few pixels as possible. Otherwise, fine color spreads in complex images would be lost.

Resizing

The program should also have a tool for shrinking or enlarging the size of the image. Remember that higher resolution doesn't always mean better picture quality. For example, when you increase the resolution, dark areas turn almost completely black.

However, if the resolution is too low, the individual color pixels are too visible. Experiment as much as possible with your photos. Eventually you'll become more familiar with working with images.

This photo is our base original

This image in PCX format is our base original. We created every effect with this original.

The base original processed with the Mosaic effect

One simple effect is called the Mosaic effect. This effect is often used on television to hide a person's identity. In the Mosaic effect, the image is broken down into brightness segments. Since the segments have the same color tone, it's impossible to see the entire image clearly.

Few color spreads because of the Poster effect

Another special effect is the Posterization (Poster) effect. This effect reduces a high resolution image to a few gray scales and brightness scales. For example, all areas with up to 30% black are displayed as white, all areas up to 60% black appear as gray, and all areas over 60% appear as dark gray to black. You can choose your own settings for the intervals in which the color tones change.

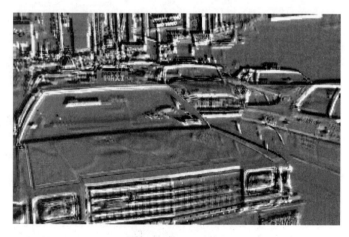

The Emboss effect

The Emboss effect creates a "proof" of the original image. Often the proof has a three-dimensional effect. When you use this effect, all the color information of the image is lost.

You can create the proof inside of a surface or on top of a surface. Specify the intensity of the proof in numbers. Positive numbers project the proof on the surface, while negative numbers "cut" the proof into the surface.

The base original in motion from the Motion-Blur effect

The Motion-Blur effect is perfect for our sample image. This effect uses blurs to create the illusion of motion. The modified image looks like a photo in which something that was moving quickly was snapped with a long exposure time, so the motions are blurry.

3-dimensional taxis with the Cylinder effect

The Cylinder effect is a popular filter. This 3-D filter copies the image onto a cylinder. The horizontal curvature of the cylinder and the resulting long, drawn-out figures create a realistic 3-D effect.

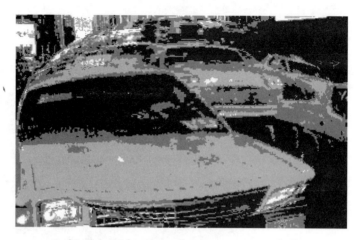

You can also copy the image onto a ball

While the Cylinder effect uses the horizontal curvature to create a three-dimensional effect, the Fish-Eye effect projects the image onto a ball, so that the image is distorted both horizontally and vertically. As a result, the image looks as if it were photographed with a Fish-eye lens. With this type of lens, the focal length (distance) is less than 10 mm and the visual angle of the photograph is greater than 90°. To achieve this effect, the image is copied to a flat surface (paper) as if it were a ball.

We can't discuss all the filters and effects used in image processing programs. So experiment with the ones offered in your program.

You've probably noticed that many of the functions found in image processing software can be used to correct errors that were made when the photograph was taken. For example, photographers can improve the depth of focus, change the contrast and brightness or even add a 3D effect to their photos. It's also possible to change colors or remove objects (Clone function).

Unfortunately, these options for manipulating photos can be dangerous. Since a photograph can be changed so dramatically, it's difficult to distinguish the original photo from an edited photo. So, people and things can be placed in artificial situations. These types of photos often appear on the covers of gossip magazines and tabloid newspapers.

Colors and Gray Scales

The colors you see on your monitor or television screen are usually mixed from the three primary colors (red, green and blue). Since all color tones are mixed from these three colors, this color original is called the RGB original.

RGB original

The RGB original is suitable for the display on the monitor. Scanners also supply the colors in the RGB original. The weaknesses of this color original are noticeable in printouts. That's why almost all image processing programs have an option for color separation.

The programs convert the RGB images to the CMYK original used by printing companies. In this original, color tones are made out of cyan, magenta and yellow. The K stands for an additional contrast component. This component is usually black, since a proper black isn't produced when you mix cyan, magenta and yellow. (This also explains why the HP Deskjet 500c color printer can't print a proper black. It only has cyan, magenta and yellow. Black isn't in its color ink cartridge.)

HLS and HSB originals

While the colors are described in the RGB and CMYK originals, the HLS and HSB originals display the color quality. For example, color quality includes color saturation, color shading, color brightness and color value. There is another original called the YUV original. This original consists of the brightness (luminance) Y and the color difference (chroma) U and V. PAL images (digitized television images, for example, with the Screen Machine) use the YUV original.

Seven color print original

The only color original with better print quality than the CMYK original is the seven color print original. Three colors are added to cyan, magenta and yellow. However, instead of only four printing stages, this original requires seven stages. Because of this, seven color print is a very long, expensive process that's rarely used.

Color Distortions

Color distortions are a major problem in image processing because they aren't noticeable until the images are printed. These distortions are caused in several ways. Usually the first distortion of the color occurs when you digitize the image.

If you create your originals with a still video camera, the problem isn't too bad because the photos are always very similar. Therefore, the color correction for almost every photograph is identical. Distorted colors in scanned photos are a more serious problem. This is especially true with scanners that use red light to scan the original. These images have incorrect RGB values.

Computer monitor reproduction

A second kind of color distortion results from reproduction on the computer monitor. Even expensive monitors usually don't have a display that's color fast. Also, the screen is a self-luminous display device, so it displays colors that don't match the print colors.

You can eliminate such color distortions by correcting the gamma values. You can also avoid such distortions by calibrating (adapting) each device. With the monitor, you must even calibrate the individual color channels. Although programs like PhotoStyler and Image-In now include a calibration function, neither program has perfected it.

The Moiré Effect

Distorts monitor image

This effect distorts the image on the monitor. The Moiré effect, which is created by overlaying asymmetrical patterns, usually occurs when the wrong colors are used in fine color transitions. This effect also occurs when you scan a rastered image (all printed images are rastered) at a resolution that is not an even numbered part of the printer resolution.

The Moiré effect can also occur when the dot pitch on the monitor isn't identical to the phosphorous dots on the glass surface, or when the video line synchronization doesn't match.

Black & White or Gray Scales?

Although the programs we discussed in this chapter can be used for color image processing, most average PC users can't afford to use this process. Normally only magazines use color prints. For most PC users, the usual output medium is an ink jet printer, PostScript or HP Laserjet compatible laser printer.

Unfortunately, normal printers can print in only one color, which is usually black. To display different shades of gray, the printer uses a rastered original of black dots. For example, printing six dots in black results in the color black. Printing four of the six dots in black produces a dark 60% gray, and printing only two of the six dots in black results in a dark white.

Color or Gray

You're probably wondering whether it's actually useful to convert color pictures into gray scale pictures. There are a few reasons why this shouldn't be done. One reason is that problems can occur when these pictures are printed. Also, gray scale pictures take up large amounts of disk space, while black and white pictures are 1-bit images, so they save a lot of space. In addition, printers (especially PostScript printers) can print 1-bit images much faster than 8-bit images.

You should use gray scale images only if you're planning on coloring them later. When you color gray scale images, each gray tone is assigned three RGB values. For example, you could assign gray tone 5 the values Red=20, Green=5 and Blue=0. All the parts of an image having gray tone 5 would then be colored brown. Generally, Lock-up tables convert gray scales into colors. They are also used to convert True-Color images into 256-color or 16-color format. Such converted colors are also referred to as false colors.

Determining The Correct Image Format

Unlike other technical areas, such as video systems and diskettes, there still isn't a definite standard for image formats. Each manufacturer has its own image format, so import-export problems still exist. Although this can be frustrating, being limited to a single image format isn't desirable either because there are so many different applications for processing images.

Most popular image formats   The most popular image formats are PCX, TIFF, EPS, GIF, TGA and BMP. These formats have different storage and space requirements and different color depths.

Vector graphics and pixel graphics

There are two types of formats for saving images: Vector format and pixel-oriented format. In pixel graphics, each pixel is stored with its color information. In vector format, objects instead of pixels are stored. While a circle in a pixel graphic is composed of many dots, in a vector graphic only the information about the shape (circle), position, size and color are stored.

No clear advantage   There isn't a clear advantage to either of the graphic formats. Vector graphics are scalable and don't lose any of their quality, even when you enlarge them. When you enlarge a pixel graphic, the result is a stair-step effect (i.e., jaggies).

However, in practical image processing with pixel graphics, you can simply omit a pixel from the image to create different effects. Since you cannot do the same with vector graphics, they are almost useless for image processing.

Therefore, in the following paragraphs, except for the EPS format, we'll discuss only the most important pixel-oriented graphic formats.

PCX Format

Developed by ZSoft

PCX format was developed by ZSoft for their paint program Paintbrush. This is probably the most widely used format for pixel graphics. While almost all programs (including Windows) can read PCX format, many professional image processors encounter problems with it because True Color display at resolutions of more than 1024x768 pixels are impossible. An 8-bit display is the maximum. However, PCX format is the standard format on PCs.

Remember that you cannot process images in PCX format on other computers, such as a Macintosh. You must convert the images to TIFF format.

TIFF

Versatile graphic format

TIFF (Tagged Image File Format) is an extremely versatile graphic format. The disadvantage to TIFF's versatility is that there are so many different TIFF formats. As a result, one program may not be able to read a TIFF image saved on another program.

Since a DIN A4 image scanned at 300 DPI with 24-bit color depth (True Color) in TIFF format takes up 42 Meg, different compression procedures have been developed for TIFF format. Probably the most well known compression procedure is the LZW procedure from Aldus (makers of PhotoStyler and PageMaker).

Many programs are able to scan LZH compressed files, both on PCs and Macintoshes.

GIF

More versatile format than TIFF

GIF is an even more versatile format than TIFF. You can use this format on various types of systems. Unfortunately, GIF can display only up to 256 colors (8-bit). CompuServe developed GIF.

TGA format is used to save and convert True Color image data on PCs and Macintoshes.

EPS (Encapsulated PostScript)

Most word processors can read EPS format, but usually they cannot display the format on the screen. You can save images in EPS format, and then output them on a PostScript laser printer from any text program without losing much quality.

Although EPS format is frequently used as an intermediate format for converting between different vector formats (PostScript printers work like vectors), this format is also often used in image processing or desktop publishing. Usually a TIFF image in lower resolution is bundled along with the EPS image so you can display it on the screen.

BMP

Used mainly by Windows

BMP is a bitmap format that saves images according to the bit pattern. Windows uses BMP format more than any other program. There are many different bitmap formats, but most of them are very similar. Along with the standard BMP format, there is also DIB format (almost identical to BMP format) and RDIB format, which is used by Windows Multimedia Extensions.

There has been a compression procedure for bitmap files since Windows Version 3.1 was released. RLE format is actually just a compressed version of DIB format.

Memory Requirements of Images

The memory requirements of images mainly depends on the resolution and color depth. Using these data, it's easy to create a formula for calculating the memory requirements.

It's important to remember that the calculated memory requirements are only approximate, since each graphic format also has a header that varies in size, depending on the format. Also, some formats don't save all the image information, which saves memory space, while other formats use internal compression algorithms.

The memory requirements of an image with an 8-bit color depth (1 byte/gray scale graphic) and a VGA resolution of 640x480 = 307,200 bytes.

Here's the formula:

```
Color_depth_in_bytes x resolution (ver x hor) =
memory_requirements
```

For a 24-bit color image with a resolution of 800 x 600 pixels, use the following formula:

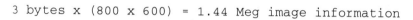

```
3 bytes x (800 x 600) = 1.44 Meg image information
```

If 1.44 Meg of memory for an image is still acceptable, this process becomes more difficult with scanned DIN A4 images with 40-50 Meg memory requirements. If you want to do image processing, you must have at least a 120 Meg hard drive and a fast 386 (33 MHz) processor. For professional image processing, you should have a CD-ROM drive and an effective compression procedure. You can also save memory by frequently deleting files that you no longer need.

Chapter 7

Moving Pictures and Animation

Animation plays a major role in multidimensional presentation graphics and information retrieval. Where a picture may be worth a thousand words, a series of pictures producing a moving image can be worth ten times more. Sometimes, the animated image can fill in those gaps often left by our imagination when we look at a still picture.

Live video is an alternative to animation. However, this method is very expensive to use. So, animated video pictures are a good compromise. We'll discuss this in more detail later in this chapter.

Animation brings life to a presentation or a multimedia database. Also, computer games wouldn't be possible without animation. The most elaborate examples of animation are close to cartoon quality. However, these obviously require an enormous amount of time to create.

7.1 How Does Animation Work?

You've probably seen a flip-book. This is a small book, in which a figure, scene or some other design is drawn on each page. The position of the drawing is slightly different on each page. If you flip the pages one after another with your thumb, the object seems to move.

This effect is also used in television and film. Film segments consist of a number of individual frames (pictures). The finer the gradations between two succeeding frames, and the shorter the time period between the viewings, the clearer and the more fluid the movement appears on film.

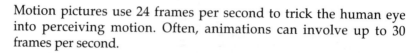

Motion pictures use 24 frames per second to trick the human eye into perceiving motion. Often, animations can involve up to 30 frames per second.

If, for example, only 10 individual frames are shown per second, the motion appears jerky, or even choppy. However, the same effect can also occur with 30 frames per second if the image varies significantly from picture to picture (e.g., if frames 2-4 of a film were removed, and you saw the jump from frame 1 to frame 5).

However, even animations that consist of only a few frames can be effective. For example, to demonstrate how a four-cycle engine works, a sequence of about 10 pictures would be all you would need to demonstrate the piston stroke and the valve movement.

Since the process continually repeats itself, the animation sequence itself is continually repeated and gives the impression of a running motor.

Pictures in video memory

How quickly the pictures can be played back one after another mainly depends on how the program interacts with the graphics card. When a picture is loaded, this process takes several tenths of a second.

Therefore, to guarantee a fluid motion, the program must directly load several pictures into the video RAM of the graphics card and must fade them in one after another.

While the pictures are fading into the foreground, others are being loaded from the hard drive into the background of video memory.

Which applications do I need?

How you create an animated sequence mainly depends on any special requirements you have, and the amount of time you're willing to spend on the project.

Smaller animated segments can be easily generated from several individual pictures, which are displayed one after another. The pictures are created with a drawing program, and then saved with a slightly different file name.

Programs like Autodesk Animator can be used to generate pictures one after another so the result is the impression of movement (see Section 7.4).

Section 7.2 contains a very simple animation based on an existing Sound Blaster accessory program, using four pictures. We drew the pictures using a drawing program that supported PCX (PC Paintbrush) format. The motion is somewhat jerky, but the four pictures do the job that we intended.

Special animated software is needed for more complex sequences. Autodesk Animator and Autodesk Animator Pro are two well-known animation packages.

The Autodesk 3D Studio program provides professional results. This program lets you generate objects and give them near-photographic quality by adding surfaces and light sources. We'll discuss both of these programs in more detail later in this chapter.

Follow a written script

Before you start designing your animated sequence, determine what you want the sequence to convey. You may want to write out the sequence in text form, then build upon the graphics from this script. Creating a script to act as a rough draft also helps you set realistic goals.

By accessing the program's capabilities, you can avoid future problems that may occur because of unrealistic expectations.

Playing Back Animation Data

The animated sequences that you've generated with Autodesk Animator or Autodesk 3D Studio (flics), can be played back within Windows using the MCI Animator driver with the Microsoft Windows Media Player.

This driver is located in the WINDOWS\ANIMATE directory on the companion CD-ROM and it can be installed using the Windows Control Panel (Drivers option).

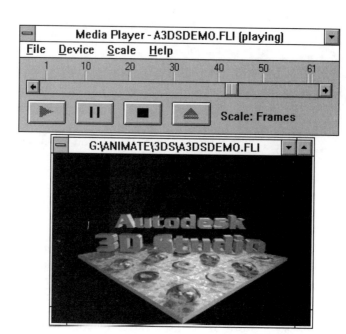

Animation in a window

Start the Media Player and select the **Animation1...** item from the **Device** menu. The file select dialog box appears, and you can activate the desired flic file (*.FLI). The animation is started by clicking the [Play] button of the Media Player.

Animation under DOS

If you want to play back the animation files at the DOS level, you can use the animation player AAPLAY.EXE. This is located in the \ANIMATE\PLAYER directory on the CD. Besides displaying animation, you can also view individual pictures in GIF format. Also, by using a script file, several animation files and GIF pictures can be played back as a complete presentation.

To load the animated sequence into the player, open the **FILE** menu and select the **FLI LOAD...** item. Select the file you want loaded from the file selector and click [OK]. Click the double-arrow (>>) to run the flic file. You can change the playback speed using the right slider bar. A value of 1 provides the fastest playback speed; a value of 120 is the slowest option.

The lower-left slider bar displays the frame on display. Pressing the ◄ and ► keys displays the previous and next frames. If you want to directly play back an animated sequence, the Player can be loaded by indicating the appropriate file:

```
AAPLAY [path]<filename>
```

Presentation
using a script file

A script provides an interesting way of playing back combined flics and GIF files. A script is a normal ASCII file; the commands contained in it are executed consecutively by the Player. The following parameters and commands are available:

Action	Parameter	Options	Default
Transition	-T	Fadein/Fadeout/Cut	Cut
Speed	-S	0..120	
Pause	-P	0..14400	GIF=5, FLI=0
Loop	-L	0..999	0
Action	Command	Options	
Complete loop	LOOP	0..999	
Return to Player	EXITTOPLAYER		
Return to DOS	EXITTODOS		
Link external script file LINK <script file>			

The L and S parameters cannot be used with GIF files. However, several parameters can be used, one after another.

In its simplest form, a script file contains several filenames that must be played back in order. If the files aren't in the same directory as the script file, the complete path must be indicated:

```
E:\ANIMATE\3DS\MORPH.FLI
E:\ANIMATE\3DS\SCALE.FLI
C:\TEST\MERLIN1.GIF
D:\ANIMATE.FLI
```

You can call the script file by using the **FILE/SCRIPT LOAD...** item in Autodesk Animator Player, or by entering it as a parameter at startup. The following runs the script file SCRIPT.TXT:

```
AAPLAY SCRIPT.TXT
```

If the parameters and commands are included in the script, the process can be controlled correspondingly:

```
ANI1.FLI -L4 -S10
TEST1.GIF -P10
```

```
TEST2.GIF -T FADEIN, FADEOUT
LOOP 2
ANI2.FLI -S30
LINK C:\DOS\SCRIPT2.TXT
ANI3.FLI
EXITTODOS
```

In the example file listed above, the ANI1.FLI file is played back a total of four times with a speed of 10. The TEST1.GIF file is then displayed on the screen for 10 seconds. The TEST2.GIF file is faded in from a white background and is faded back out in a white background.

The command LOOP 2 indicates that the previous action must be repeated two more times before the subsequent commands can be executed. The file ANI2.FLI is executed at a speed of 30, before the commands in the script file SCRIPT2.TXT are executed.

When execution of the SCRIPT2.TXT script file is completed, the file ANI3.FLI is played back. The presentation ends by the EXITTODOS command and you're returned to the DOS prompt.

7.2   The Talking Wizard

The Sound Blaster card provides a short animated program called The Talking Parrot. This is an impressive demonstration on how to use a sound card.

You can view the parrot's four images or listen to the parrot speak. Sometimes the parrot will mimic what the user says into the microphone plugged into the sound card.

The Talking Parrot

The parrot gets boring after a while. Fortunately, it's possible to change the sentences spoken by the parrot, as well as the graphic images used. Since we have a certain fondness for wizardry, we decided to change our Talking Parrot to suit our own needs.

Changing The Graphics

We'll demonstrate one alternative by using our wizard, who will replace the parrot images. Any four pictures will do - the Parrot consists of four images, so you're not limited to only open beak, close beak.

You can use any PCX graphics instead of the parrot, drawn with any graphics program that supports PCX files (e.g., Microsoft Windows Paintbrush).

As we mentioned, the Talking Parrot consists of a total of four separate pictures, which are located in the \ANIMATE\PARROT directory.

Parrot Pictures		
Filename:	**Eyes**	**Beak**
PARROT.E0	OPEN	CLOSED
PARROT.E1	OPEN	HALF-OPEN
PARROT.E2	OPEN	OPEN
PARROT.E3	CLOSED	CLOSED

Remember to rename the original parrot files. The files must be named PARROT.E0, PARROT.E1, PARROT.E2 and PARROT.E3 for the PARROT.EXE program to read the files.

If you want to create your own graphic, it must be stored as an EGA graphic image (i.e., it should have a resolution of 320 x 200 with a maximum of 16 colors).

But who still has an EGA card according to the MPC definition? Well, since VGA cards are downwardly compatible, you can generate the graphic images in the desired format using Windows.

To do this, go to Windows Setup and install a graphics driver with 16 colors if you haven't already done so.

You must do this because Paintbrush always saves pictures using the current graphics resolution. Another way to do this is to reduce the number of colors by using a conversion program like Paint Shop Pro (included on the companion CD-ROM).

Scanned pattern   We took our wizard from a drawn image, scanned him using a hand scanner, cleaned up the image using Microsoft Windows Paintbrush, then saved him as a PCX file.

However, the problem is to match the size of the original parrot drawing with the new drawing, since the original and the new pictures probably have different dimensions.

For the final result, you need a picture file of 320x200 pixels with 16 colors. So the final version of the desired picture fills the entire screen, you should adjust it to the desired size at the normal VGA resolution, or better yet, at a resolution of 800x600. The current cursor position should be indicated so you know when you've reached the correct size.

To do this from PC Paintbrush, select **View/Cursor Position**. Mark your picture with the rectangular cutout tool. Open the **Pick** menu and select the **Shrink + Grow** option. Now move the crosshair into the upper-left corner of the picture and, while pressing the mouse button, open up a frame that is within the position 320, 200. If you also press the (Shift) key, even the same aspect ratio will be used with the changed copy.

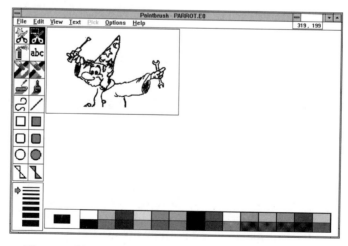

The graphic must be reduced to the appropriate size

After you've adjusted the graphic to the correct size, transfer it into the Clipboard. Click on the rectangular cutout tool again and define a border around the graphic. Then select **Copy** from the **Edit** menu.

Then make the picture the required size. Select **Options/Image Attributes...**. A dialog box, in which you can adjust the picture size, appears on the screen. Select the "pels" option button, and enter 320 for the width and 200 for the height.

If you select (OK), you'll immediately see why you saved the graphic in the Clipboard. Paintbrush informs you that the current picture contents will be lost. Since you're prepared for this, confirm the loss.

Then an empty picture with the desired dimensions appears. Now you must fill in the picture. Select **Edit/Paste**, and the stored graphic appears on the screen again. Now you can use the mouse to move it wherever you like, and then anchor it by selecting a tool. Save the picture using a new name.

If you want to change the picture, you should do this now so you can use it as the first picture in the animated sequence. Save this picture under the name PARROT.E0.

Now change the graphic's mouth or eyes to change the expression on the face during the animation. We've changed the position of the mouth, the eyes and the right arm in each picture to make the animation work.

To rotate the arm, you can either redraw the arm in Microsoft Windows Paintbrush, or use a more powerful graphics editing program capable of rotating selections in small increments. Save each of the resulting pictures with the appropriate name (PARROT.E1, PARROT.E2, PARROT.E3).

Once all four drawings have been saved, copy them into your Sound Blaster PARROT directory. You can also copy these files from the \ANIMATE\PARROT directory on the companion CD-ROM into the corresponding directory on your hard drive.

When you run the PARROT program, the animation begins. Unfortunately, the wizard still says things that the parrot says. Let's change that.

Creating New Speech Files

The MAKEPV program, which is located in the PARROT directory, can be used to generate sound files that can be used with the Talking Parrot. MAKEPV creates a master file, PARROT.VCB, out of a series of VOC files that contains the Parrot's comments.

The master file consists of a total of 21 subfiles, which must have a specific name. The following is a list of these files:

Introductions:

PVOC-A.VOC	"Hello there!"
PVOC-E.VOC	"I'm a talking parrot"
PVOC-F.VOC	"Please talk to me"

If nothing has been spoken into the microphone for a while:

PVOC-B.VOC	"Hi! How are you?"
PVOC-D.VOC	"Welcome to the show"
PVOC-I.VOC	"Have a nice day"
PVOC-G.VOC	"Nice to see you"
PVOC-C.VOC	"Good day"

Closing:

PVOC-J.VOC	"Goodbye"
PVOC-H.VOC	"Please say something"

The Parrot occasionally says the following:

PVOC-K.VOC	"Oh! You sound terrible!"
PVOC-L.VOC	"Yak! You have bad breath!"
PVOC-M.VOC	"What are you saying"
PVOC-N.VOC	"What are you saying (annoyed)"
PVOC-O.VOC	"Don't talk nonsense"

When a key is pressed:

PVOC-P.VOC	"Ouch!"
PVOC-Q.VOC	"Ooo..h!"
PVOC-R.VOC	"Don't touch me"
PVOC-S.VOC	"Go away!"
PVOC-T.VOC	"Hee..Hee..Hee"
PVOC-U.VOC	"Herr..Herr..Herr"

Remember, you need a total of 21 separate files to generate a master file. These data files can be recorded using the Voice Editor. Start the Voice Editor and adjust the sampling rate to 10,000 Hz (the User Defined option) by using the **Record/Setting** command.

Start recording by selecting **Record/To Memory**. Speak clearly and distinctly into the switched-on microphone. To stop recording, press the Stop button.

Blank spots occur before and after talking when you're recording, so you should edit the recording. This is especially true when you forget to switch on the microphone until after you've started recording.

When you switch on the microphone, a disturbing noise is produced later. It's best to record several sentences simultaneously and then separate the desired segments into individual blocks, which you can edit separately and then save.

The blank spots before and after the actual speech recordings interfere with the synchronization of the mouth movements in the motif.

To fix this, select **Edit/Modify**. The recorded speech will appear in the window.

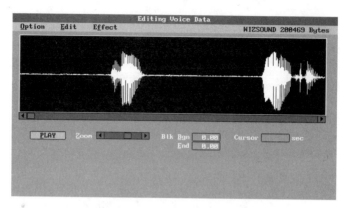

Blank spots must be cut out

Use the mouse to mark the blank spot before the first block of speech and select **Edit/Cut**. Then click after the first block of the recording and select **Option/Split Block**.

Suddenly everything to the right of the cursor position disappears. However, it was only moved into another block, instead of being deleted. Now if you exit the Edit screen using **Option/Exit**, you'll see another block in the listing box. Now you can select this block and edit it using **Edit/Modify**.

Cutting out the blank spots also reduces the file size considerably.

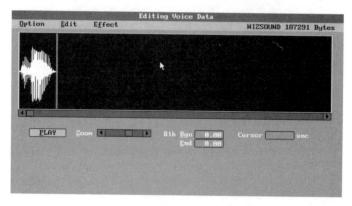

An edited file is also smaller

You can save this block by selecting it and using the **File/Save as** command. Remember to use names matching the original VOC file names previously stated (PVOC-A.VOC, PVOC-B.VOC, etc.).

When you've generated all 21 files in this way, copy them into the directory containing your Talking Parrot program (usually

SB\PARROT or SBPRO\PARROT). To create the master file, run the following program:

```
MAKEPV
```

First you're asked if you want to overwrite the existing PARROT.VCB file. Press Ⓨ. MAKEPV reads the 21 files and creates the new PARROT.VCB file.

You'll find all the files needed for the Talking Wizard in the ANIMATE\PARROT directory of the companion CD-ROM.

Now if you run the PARROT.EXE program, the Wizard appears, speaking in the voice you recorded.

7.3 Animations With ToolBook

 As a development system for multimedia applications, Multimedia ToolBook from Asymetrix Corporation has ideal features for creating animated sequences. Various methods can be used to animate your pictures.

Video Animation

In our example, we animate a sequence from a video of a marathon. The individual pictures, with a size of 320 x 200 points, were created with Screen Machine. Each picture was stored in DIB/BMP format using the Dark Room, and it was reduced to 256 colors (8-bit CLUT = Color Look Up Table). The size of the picture on the hard drive is around 82K per picture with average compression.

A total of 32 pictures were generated for the sample sequence. Every third picture from the video sequence was "snapped". You can do this by using the still frame and frame advance functions of the video recorder. Record a picture using the still frame function. Use the frame advance function to let the sequence run for three more pictures, then freeze the picture again using the still frame function. This method can be used to break up video sequences and to save them as individual pictures.

The more individual pictures recorded for a given period of time, the smoother the animation will be. Since video uses about 25 frames per second, several pictures are used. Depending on your needs, you can use every other picture or, as in our case, every third picture. By doing this, you can save a tremendous amount of memory. Later we'll see how the course of the animation changes when additional intermediate pictures are removed.

> When recording individual pictures, you may not have to record every third picture. For example, if there is little or no movement in a longer sequence (e.g., a landscape scene), then you need only one recording. Later on in the animation, this one recording can be displayed long enough to create the same effect as on the video. This also saves a lot of storage space.

Storage space   In addition to the number of pictures, the quality and size of the pictures are also important. Using 256 is perfectly sufficient for photorealistic animation, but these pictures also take up a large amount of memory.

The pictures must be stored in memory so they can be displayed smoothly, because reloading from disk requires enough time that you will notice a jerking effect.

Again, the size of the picture determines the amount of the memory needed and also, ultimately, the speed of the animation. If you have problems with memory at this point, you should experiment with another graphics format or a different picture size.

Arranging The Page

The applications created in ToolBook are page-oriented. This means that each page can contain several objects (i.e., buttons, fields, hotwords, draw objects, paint objects and groups). The objects are arranged on different layers and can partially or completely overlap each other.

Similar to Visual Basic, objects can be linked to events to which the object reacts, according to a predefined script. If you click on a hot button, an associated script is executed.

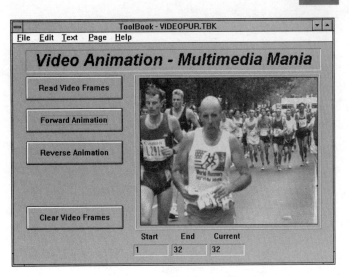

A sample ToolBook application

This technology is used in animation by loading all of the pictures as objects on a page.

How our books work

The ToolBook books we've included on the companion CD-ROM load in a series of graphics as pages, or as object layers (a group of objects stacked together). For example, the VIDEOPUR.TBK book loads a series of graphics, starting from last to first. Then when you click the ⌈Forward Animation⌉ button in the VIDEOPUR.TBK book, the graphics are displayed in proper order (first to last).

You'll find a series of RACE*.BMP files in the \ANIMATE\TOOLBOOK\V16 (16-color animation) and the \ANIMATE\TOOLBOOK\V256 (256-color animation) directory. If you look at the script which applies to the ⌈Read Video Frames⌉ button using **Object/Button Properties...**, you would find the following (we added our own remarks to the code below):

```
to handle buttonUp
system PNull,SName,SNumber,eNumber
--PNull is defined in the page script and indicates the
--first number than can be given to a paint object.

--Ask for the root name, starting and ending BMP file numbers
  ask "Enter the root name, first number and last number of the BMP file
  set" with "race 1 32"
--Save the input as system variables
  put the first word of it into SName
  Put word 2 of it into text of field "SNumber"
  put Word 3 of it into text of field "ENumber"
```

```
--Write the starting and ending numbers in variables
  put Text of field "SNumber" into SNumber
  put Text of field "eNumber" into eNumber
--Loop with import routine
  step I from ENumber to SNumber by -1
--modified import routine, filename consists of
--root name and incremented variable i
    importGraphic Sname & i & ".BMP"
    move the selection to 3405, 915
--Display which graphic is being imported
    Put i into text of field CurNum
--Disable drawDirect for better performance
    set drawDirect of selection to false
--Assign name to graphic
    set Name of selection to PNull+i
--Hide the graphic
    hide selection
  end

end buttonUp
```

The lines beginning with "--" are comment lines. After all the pictures have been loaded, save the book under any name. Now you've created an object stack where the first picture of the sequence is on the lowest layer and the last picture is on the uppermost layer. Since the complete pictures are stored in the ToolBook file, you no longer need the individual pictures.

To display this sequence, simply display the individual pictures one after another in the same order in which you loaded them. To display the first, or bottom-most picture, all of the pictures on top of it must be faded out.

You can do this in a loop, either before each display of the animation or else immediately after you've displayed a new picture. The following script instructs the [Forward Animation] button what to do:

```
to handle buttonUp
system PNull,SName, SNumber, ENumber, Curnum, sortup
--The current picture number is stored in Curnum
--SortUp is true if the animation is displayed in ascending order.
--To display the animation backwards, the pictures must be restacked.

--Fill in the display fields
  put Text of field "SNumber" into SNumber
  put Text of field "eNumber" into eNumber
  put Text of field "CurNum" into Curnum
--Hide the picture just shown
  hide paintObject (PNull+Curnum)
--if sortup is not true
```

```
--Set the pictures in ascending order on continuous
--layers
  step Curnum from sNumber to eNumber by 1
    set layer of paintObject (PNull+Curnum) to 400
  end

  set sortup to true
--end
  set curnum to sNumber

--Show first picture
  show paintObject (PNull+Curnum)
--Loop through all pictures
  step Curnum from sNumber+1 to eNumber
    Show paintObject (PNull+Curnum)
    hide paintObject (PNull+Curnum-1)
  end
  set Text of field "Curnum" to Curnum-1

end buttonUp
```

As you can see, with only a few lines, you can bring video images to life using ToolBook. You can use other programs on the companion CD-ROM in the \ANIMATE\TOOLBOOK\ directory to link video pictures from the Screen Machine directly into ToolBook.

VIDEO.TBK is an empty book that you can fill with pictures using Screen Machine; VIDEOANT.TBK runs a brief sequence of an ant carrying an object along a log; and VIDEOALE.TBK displays a brief sequence of daughter Alexandra showing us an insect. VIDEOPUR.TBK is a sequence of one of the authors running the Berlin Marathon.

A few items you should know about these companion CD-ROM files:

1. The VIDEO.TBK, VIDEOANT.TBK and VIDEOALE.TBK books require the DLLs provided by Fast Electronics GmbH's Screen Machine software.

   These DLLs are SMPAR.DLL, SM.DLL, SMWB.DLL, SMTT.DLL, SMJPEG.DLL, SMIP.DLL, SMCLIP.DLL, and SMHOOK.DLL.

   In addition, you'll need the WINMEM32.DLL file to run VIDEO.TBK and VIDEOALE.TBK. VIDEO.TBK and VIDEOALE.TBK require the Screen Machine for loading in video images.

If you don't own a Screen Machine and have no intention of buying one, VIDEOPUR.TBK is a ToolBook book you can use to view video images without the Screen Machine's DLLs.

2.   These books load data very slowly, because of the way multiple BMP images are handled. Be patient.

Alexandra shows a bug from VIDEOALE.TBK

This book consists of two pages. The first page displays the animation and the second page is used for recording video information using Screen Machine.

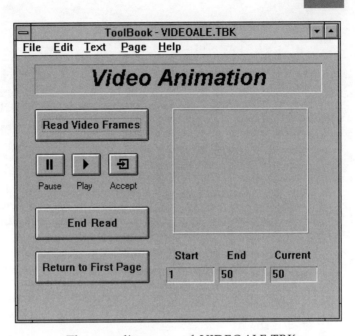

The recording page of VIDEOALE.TBK

Clicking the Read Video Frames button starts your Screen Machine Video Workbench. The Workbench will ask whether you have Colorkey (click No if you aren't sure). The video picture appears in the window next to the three control buttons. Using these buttons, you can play, pause or accept (save) the video image.

To record a video sequence, use your video recorder to get to the first picture and then click the Pause button when the videotape reaches the image you like (we suggest you press the video recorder's Pause button as well, just after you click the Pause button on the VIDEOALE.TBK book.

Click on the Accept button to copy the frame into ToolBook. This simply copies the video image from the Screen Machine into the Clipboard.

The script for the "Accept" button changes to page 1, stores the video image in the Clipboard, and returns you to page 2.

Using the VIDEOALE.TBK Play button and the video recorder's Play button, advance to the next image, and repeat the process described in the preceding paragraph. After you've read in all of the pictures, disable the Screen Machine using the End Read button.

Click on [Return to First Page]. Now you can view your work forwards and backwards.

The programming is almost the same as it was in the last example, except that this example has an additional slider control for regulating the speed. This controls a delay loop within the playback loop.

7.4 Autodesk Animation Programs

With the Autodesk Animator and Animator Pro programs, you can create two-dimensional animated sequences. These animated sequences, which are called flics, can be built into many other multimedia applications.

Unlike Animator, Animator Pro provides a higher screen resolution and an expanded list of features. Animator Pro has all the features found in Autodesk Animator (it's downwardly compatible, meaning that it will accept Autodesk Animator FLI files).

We'll discuss and illustrate both products in this section.

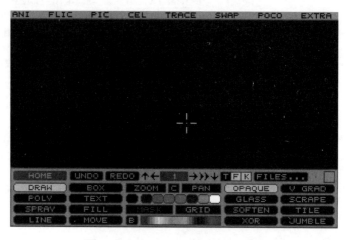

The Animator Pro environment

Cartoon animation

The **TRACE** menu offers the traditional concept of animation, as seen in animated cartoons produced by Walt Disney Corporation and Warner Brothers. In this method, you would start in the Autodesk programs by inserting frames (right-clicking on the bottom center of the Home panel, where frame control occurs).

Then you would load an initial graphic in the first frame. By copying this graphic to succeeding frames and changing the image a bit in each frame, the illusion of movement is created.

> If you want to animate existing cartoon figures, read them in using a scanner. Then convert them to the GIF format. Appropriate picture editing software (see Chapter 6) is used to edit the scanned pattern. This pattern is then used as a basis for the trace function.

If you're using Animator, make certain that you're using a picture resolution of 320 x 200 pixels. Higher resolutions can be selected with Animator Pro, depending on the installed graphics driver.

If a series of pictures is already available, they can be converted into GIF format using the Animator module CONVERT.EXE. Then these pictures can be loaded as a frame into Animator. The sequence of the frame can be stored as a flic. For our first example, we'll use the four Merlin drawings from earlier in this chapter.

You'll find GIF versions of the four Merlin files in the \ANIMATE\MERLIN directory on the companion CD-ROM. You can also use any other graphic editing program or conversion program to convert files to the GIF format.

Creating A Cartoon

To produce a simple animation, an appropriate number of frames (pages) must be made available in Animator (in the case of Merlin, we'll need four frames). The corresponding picture is loaded into each frame and is animated using the Frames panel. The animation results from the changes in the state of motion in the individual pictures.

In the section on the talking wizard, we used four files, which display different stages of movement. We'll create an animated sequence now using these four files. The files were already converted into the GIF format for this purpose.

These files, named MERLIN1-4.GIF, are located in the \ANIMATE\MERLIN directory.

After Animator is started, a menu bar and the Home panel appear on the screen. Select **FLIC/RESET** to clear memory.

You should determine the number of frames that will make up the animation. To do this, activate the Frames panel using **ANIMATOR/FRAMES**.

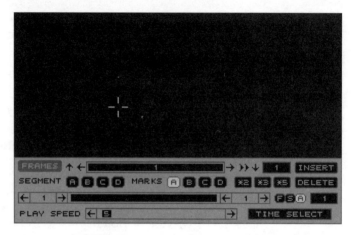

The Frames panel in Animator

In the Frames panel, you can move among the separate frames and make adjustments to the animation's course. Look at the box containing a number, located just to the left of the [INSERT] button. By clicking in this number box, you activate a dialog box in which the desired number can be adjusted using a slider bar. Since we want to use four GIF files, set the number to 4 and click [OK].

The button in the Frames panel now shows the total number of frames as 4. The number can also be read in the frame bar, which indicates the current frame number.

You can move between the individual frames by moving the slider bar. If you move the mouse pointer into the drawing screen and click the right mouse button, the Home menu panel reappears. The frame indicator and the control icons are visible above the color palette. You can use them to move among the individual frames.

If you aren't already in frame 1, click on the up arrow until frame 1 appears. Open the **PIC** menu and select **FILES...**. This opens the Files panel, which is used to load the first picture file. Make sure the [PICTURE] option is highlighted. Click the [LOAD] button to load the MERLIN1.GIF file into frame number 1.

Click on the single right arrow in the Files panel to advance to frame 2. Click on the [LOAD] button and load the file MERLIN2.GIF as described in the preceding paragraph. Load the two remaining files in the remaining frames.

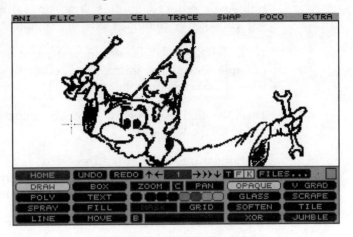

The first file is loaded

Playback

After all four frames contain picture files, you can start the animation by clicking the double arrow >> icon. The sequence executes continuously (i.e., the animation starts all over again after the last frame is displayed). If the sequence is played back too quickly, you can slow down the playback speed with the speed slider in the Frames panel. The number of pictures per second is adjusted here.

> You can insert as many frames as you want into an existing sequence by using the [INSERT] button in the Frames panel. An animated sequence can easily be expanded in this way.

You can save the animation now as a flic. Select **FLIC/FILES....** The Files panel appears again, but this time the [FLIC] button is highlighted. Click on [SAVE], give the animated sequence a name (e.g., MERLIN.FLI) and click [OK].

·The final animation file is in the \ANIMATE\MERLIN directory on the companion CD-ROM.

Producing A Cel Animation

Cel (celluloid) animation is another animation function that's easy to use. With it, you can animate various objects and combine them to make a movie.

For example, characters can be arranged on the screen in an animated fashion to form a logo, and the entire logo can then be rotated or reduced. In this way, several smaller cel animated sequences can be combined to form a complete presentation.

We'll use the creation and animation of a company logo as an example. During the animation, a rectangle slides from the bottom edge of the screen into the middle of the screen.

Then the characters of the company name appear, one by one, inside the rectangle.

Additional information (address, etc.) is faded in using another effect. After the logo is complete, it rotates around its own axis and disappears to the edge of the screen by becoming smaller.

You can use the following script for this animation so you know how the individual frames can be used.

Frame	Presentation
1-20	Rectangle slides from the bottom edge of the screen into the middle of the screen
21-28	Presentation of the company name, in animated fashion within the rectangle
29	The telephone number is faded in above the rectangle
29-38	The address develops letter-by-letter below the rectangle on both sides of the middle axis
39-58	No further movement (rest interval)
59	Screen is cleared
60-100	Object disappears over to the edge of the screen as it is rotated and reduced in size
Repeat of the animation	

To be on the safe side, after Animator has started you should use FLIC/RESET to restore all the default values.

An animation can consist of several segments. Each segment includes a group of frames, which in turn can contain a cel animation.

Now we'll create the first segment, which contains the movement of the rectangle to the middle of the screen.

The Rectangle First

We'll start by drawing a filled rectangle at the center of the screen. Right-click (click the right mouse button while the pointer is on) the ⌧BOX⌧ button. Click on the ⌧FILLED⌧ button if it isn't already selected. Right-click the drawing screen to return to the Home panel.

Click on the color white in the mini-palette at the top of the Home panel. Draw the rectangle. Now select **CEL/CLIP** to copy the rectangle into the cel buffer for later animation. Now select **PIC/CLEAR**.

Select **ANIMATOR/OPTICS**. This panel is where you animate objects stored in the cel buffer. The buttons provide various options. First you should erase any movements that might still exist by selecting **PRESETS/CLEAR ALL**.

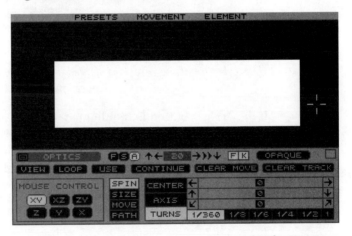

The rectangle in the Optics panel

Select **ELEMENT/CEL** to activate the rectangle in the cel buffer so you can refer to it.

We want the rectangle to move from below the bottom border of the screen to the center of the screen. Select the ⌧MOVE⌧ button, then click on the ⌧Y⌧ button in the MOUSE CONTROL box. Click on the drawing screen; the rectangle appears as a dotted frame with an L shape drawn in this frame.

Click on the top of this frame, and move the frame down, out of screen view. When the frame is pushed completely out of the way, set the new position by clicking the mouse.

To demonstrate the movement, right-click on the frame icons in the Optics panel. Set the total number of frames to 20 in the Frames panel. Right-click the drawing screen to return to the Optics panel and click the [USE] button. The Time Select panel appears.

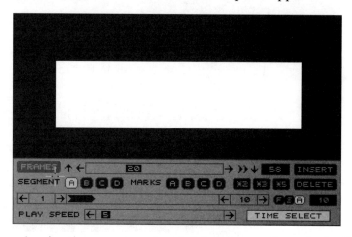

The cel animations are transferred to a segment through the Time Select panel

If the [TO ALL] button is highlighted, the movement that's produced will be distributed among all the set frames. Click the [PREVIEW] button. This shows our movement from center to bottom. Since we want the opposite action, click the [REVERSE] button. This gives us the desired movement.

Click the [RENDER] button to convert the movement into a complete animation.

In the next segment, we'll place the company name in the white rectangle, letter by letter. Since the company name consists of eight letters, you should add another eight frames using the Frames panel.

Click on the down arrow to reach frame 20. Select Click on the [INSERT] button eight times to add frames 21 through 28. Select the first frame of the new segment (frame 21). This will help you orient yourself. The rectangle will appear on the screen.

Make certain to select a new color. Otherwise, the writing will be displayed in the same color as the rectangle. Since the writing will overlap the rectangle, you must select another color. We used dark green.

Titling

Select **ANIMATOR/TITLING** to enter the Titling panel. Click on the LOAD FONT item. Click on a font name (we used SUPBOL22.FNT) and click [OK]. Click on the NEW TEXT item. Place the cross hairs near the upper-left corner of the white rectangle and click the left mouse button. Now move the cross hairs to the lower-right corner of the white rectangle and click the left mouse button.

Type the letters "MM MANIA" in the text box that appears. You can use the cursor keys, [Del] and [Backspace] keys to edit the text. If the text doesn't quite fall where you want it to fall, click on the text box and move it to where you want it. If the text box is too big, right-click outside the text box, click NEW TEXT again, and draw a different size text box. Repeat the text entry process as needed. This takes practice, so be patient.

Right-click on the text box to freeze the text. Clicking on the mouse (the right button) outside of the text box freezes the text. The text will disappear (don't panic).

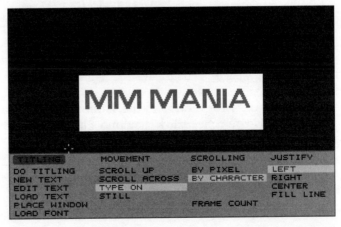

Titling texts overlap the rectangle

In the Titling panel, click on TYPE ON for the type of movement and BY CHARACTER for the type of display. Click on DO TITLING to return to the Time Select panel. Now there's a total of 28 frames. Since the first 20 frames contain the movement of the rectangle, the appearance of the letters should be transferred to the last eight frames. To do this, click on the [TO SEGMENT] button.

Two smaller scroll bars, in which the number of a frame appears, are located to the left and the right of the scroll bar. These scroll bars define the start and the end of a segment. Using the left scroll bar, set the start of the segment to the frame with the number 21. Use the right scroll bar to set the end of the segment to 28. The segment is indicated in the center scroll bar with a filled-in area.

Segments are clearly defined

If the [REVERSE] button is still highlighted, click that button to disable it. Now click [PREVIEW] to observe the execution of the character movement. If the process is correct, right-click to return to the Time Select panel and click the [RENDER] button to render the sequence.

Animator returns to the Titling panel. Right-click to return to the Home panel. Click the double arrow to see the animation at work.

Click on the down arrow to move to frame 28. Select **ANIMATOR/FRAMES**. Click on the [INSERT] button ten times to add 10 frames.

Click on the right arrow to move to frame 29. Right-click to display the menu bar and the Home panel. Select a new color (we used orange). Select **ANIMATOR/TITLING** to enter the Titling panel. Click on the LOAD FONT item.

Click on a font name (we used ARCHP14.FNT) and click [OK]. Click on the NEW TEXT item. Place the cross hairs near the upper-left corner of the drawing screen and click the left mouse button. Now move the cross hairs slightly down, and to the right border of the drawing screen. Click the left mouse button.

Type the letters "52nd ST SE" in the text box that appears. Right-click on the text box to freeze the text. Clicking on the mouse (the right button) outside of the text box freezes the text. The text will disappear.

In the Titling panel, click on TYPE ON for the type of movement and BY CHARACTER for the type of display Click on CENTER for the alignment of the display. Click on DO TITLING to return to the Time Select panel. Now there's a total of 38 frames. Click on the TO SEGMENT button.

Two smaller scroll bars, in which the number of a frame appears, are located to the left and the right of the scroll bar. These scroll bars define the start and the end of a segment. Using the left scroll bar, set the start of the segment to the frame with the number 29. Use the right scroll bar to set the end of the segment to 38. The segment is indicated in the center scroll bar with a filled-in area.

Click PREVIEW to observe the execution of the character movement. If the process is correct, right-click to return to the Time Select panel and click the RENDER button to render the sequence. Animator returns to the Titling panel. Right-click to return to the Home panel. Click the double arrow to see the animation at work.

Stop the animation. Move to frame 29. Select a new color (we selected powder blue). Select **ANIMATOR/TITLING**. Click on the NEW TEXT item. Place the cross hairs just below and to the left of the white rectangle and click the left mouse button. Now move the cross hairs slightly down, and to the right of the white rectangle. Click the left mouse button.

Type the letters "Grand Rapids MI" in the text box that appears. Right-click on the text box to freeze the text. The text will disappear.

In the Titling panel, click on TYPE ON for the type of movement and BY CHARACTER for the type of display. Click on CENTER for the alignment of the display. Click on DO TITLING to return to the Time Select panel. Make sure the TO SEGMENT button is active, and that the sliders indicate frames 28 through 38.

Click [PREVIEW] to observe the execution of the character movement. If the process is correct, right-click to return to the Time Select panel and click the [RENDER] button to render the sequence. Animator returns to the Titling panel. Right-click to return to the Home panel.

Select **ANIMATOR/FRAMES**. Change to frame 38. Click on the [INSERT] button 20 times. This displays the ending text for two seconds or so. Click the double arrow to see the animation at work.

The results so far

Change back to the Home panel and run the complete animation.

The object's movement

You'll find this animation in the companion CD-ROM's \ANIMATE\ANI directory under the name LOGO1.FLI.

The actual animation of the object is created with the help of the Optics screen. Currently the last frame has the number 58, which is the last of the 20 rest frames. Switch to the Home panel and select **CEL/CLIP** to copy the complete object to the cel buffer. Select **ANIMATOR/FRAMES**. Click on [INSERT] to add an additional frame (number 59). Move to that frame using the down arrow, and right click on the drawing screen to return to the Home panel.

The contents of frame number 59 are deleted with **PIC/CLEAR**. This is necessary because if you remove the object in the Optics panel from the image area by rotating, moving and scaling down, the object would still be visible on every frame.

Basically a copy of the object would be animated. Although this might be useful in some situations, in our case we want to avoid this effect.

After you've cleared the screen in frame number 59, select **ANIMATOR/FRAMES**. Right-click the number box to the left of the INSERT button. Enter the number 100 and click OK.

So the last animation segment can be generated, you should activate frame number 59. Select **ANIMATOR/OPTICS**. Select **PRESETS/CLEAR ALL** to clear any movements that might have been preset. Use **ELEMENT/CEL** to refer to the object that was previously copied into the cel buffer. The animation consists of a combination of rotation, reduction and moving across a segment range of 41 frames (100-59).

Click on the SPIN button. Set the MOUSE CONTROL box to Y. Double-click on the drawing screen to activate the object. Drag the cross hairs to the right, rotating the dotted form twice around its Y-axis.

Click the SIZE button. Double-click the drawing screen to activate the object. Again the object is activated by clicking twice. By dragging the mouse, the object can be reduced to a few square millimeters. Click. Now select the MOVE button and click on X in the MOUSE CONTROL box. Double-click, and drag the object to the right and off the screen.

Transfer to the segment

Click USE. This activates the Time Control panel. Click on the TO SEGMENT button, and adjust the segment from frame 59 to frame 100. Click PREVIEW to double-check this is what you want, then click RENDER.

The complete animation is located under the name LOGO2.FLI in the \ANIMATE\ANI directory on the companion CD-ROM.

7.5   3D Animation

The 3D Studio program is a professional solution for creating three-dimensional, photograph-quality animations. Three-dimensional objects can be assigned a variety of materials. The surfaces of these materials realistically reflect light when light sources are appropriately placed. For example, the reflection of a sphere with a glossy surface will differ from the reflection of a sphere with an unfinished wooden surface.

3D Studio includes modules such as:

- The modeler for creating models

- The renderer for rendering three-dimensional objects

- The materials editor for editing or generating new surface textures

- The keyframer for animating the created objects

Let's generate a small animation with the 3D Editor. The Flic that we produce can be played back with the Animation Player AAPLAY.EXE or Media Player under Windows. If you don't have a 3D Studio available, you can see how things look by using the specified example flics.

For example, let's create simple, three-dimensional objects which have a material surface. Also, light sources and a camera are positioned and are used to view the entire animation.

The 3D Studio Environment

After startup the 3D Studio environment appears, with a total of four viewing windows. Each window provides a different viewing angle for the three-dimensional object. The corresponding views are displayed in the upper-left corner of each window. The object is seen from the user's perspective (i.e., three-dimensionally), in the lower-right window.

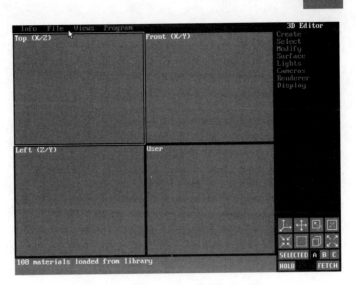

The components of 3D Studio

The menu bar along the top appears only when the mouse is moved into this area. Otherwise the current coordinates of the mouse pointer are indicated when you move in one of the viewing windows.

The command column is on the right, next to the viewing windows. If a command group is selected, other commands, which belong to this group, will also be displayed. If you move the mouse over a command, its color changes.

After it has been selected, the command is displayed in another color, so it's easy to follow the active command sequence at any time. The last executable command in a group is displayed in yellow.

You can execute an action directly with a "yellow" command. You can activate some commands directly by using the icon strip.

Creating An Object

You should reset 3D Studio before creating the first object. To do this, use **File/Reset**. This returns any settings, which might have been changed, to the default settings. This isn't absolutely necessary immediately after starting the program, but it is necessary if you're creating a second or third animation. This also means that the contents of memory will be erased. Therefore, be sure you save any needed data before doing this.

Object selection The objects must be created first. This is done in one of the four viewing windows. By default, the upper-left window is active. This is indicated by a brighter border. Simply click in the appropriate area to activate a different window.

Since we want to generate several different objects, we'll need a lot of space. However, the animation will be crossing the entire screen later. Because of this, the size of the window used for generating objects can become very narrow.

The Full Screen icon (top icon, second from the right) in the icon bar will expand the active window to the size of the full screen so you'll have enough space in which to draw the object.

Making a sphere **Create** generates a list of all available objects. Two commands can display a sphere:

- LSphere... (simple mesh)

- GSphere... (complex mesh)

If you select **GSphere...**, the lighting effects will be more obvious and the color gradations will be finer. After you've made a selection, you must choose a type of display:

- Faceted (faceted grid surfaces)

- Smoothed (smoothed grid surfaces)

- Values (indicates the number of parallels and meridians)

Select the **Smoothed** option. Later, if you want to display the system of coordinates of the earth, for example, you can indicate the exact figure for degrees of longitude and latitude by using the **Values** option.

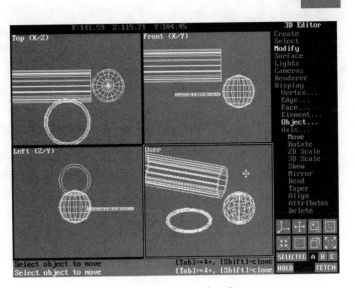

Different kinds of spheres

Now the object can be created in the window. The next action to be executed always appears in the command bar at the bottom of the screen. The sphere is defined using a central point and a radius. Establish a central point by clicking the mouse in the window.

The circumference of the circle is displayed when you move the mouse. By using the coordinates indicator, you can establish an exact radius of, for example, 100, by clicking the mouse a second time.

Then a dialog box appears in which you must enter a name for the object. The objects are automatically numbered sequentially. However, if you want to refer to an object by name, you must use logical names, like we have done with sphere, tube, cylinder, etc.

Deleting objects   If you've drawn an object incorrectly, you can delete it at any time. Select **Modify** from the command column. Highlight the **Object...** option so you're referring to the entire object. With **Delete**, you can remove the object from the window by clicking and confirming the prompt that appears.

Now generate several objects. Always refer to the status line, since the next step is indicated there. The objects can be in a line, since the orientation will be performed in a later step.

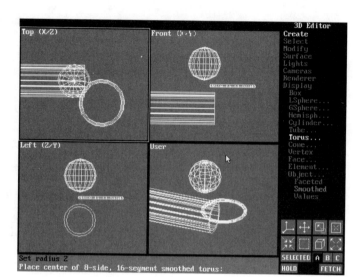

Several objects are created

*Object
Placement*

You can place the objects anywhere on the surface. An object's distance from another object and its position can change depending on the other objects. Depending on the change in the distance or the height, relative to each other, you should make these placements in the appropriate window.

The distance between objects is clearly displayed in the **Top (X/Z)** window and relative heights are displayed in the **Left (Z/Y)** window.

To move an object, select the command sequence **Modify/Object/Move**. The cursor changes into a cross made of four arrows. This shape indicates that an object can be moved in any desired direction. Pressing the ⬚Tab⬚ key changes the cursor shape to two horizontal arrows.

If you press ⬚Tab⬚ again, the cursor changes into two vertical arrows. The selected objects can be moved depending on the appearance of the cursor.

If you then click on an object, a frame, which can be moved in the appropriate direction with the mouse, appears.

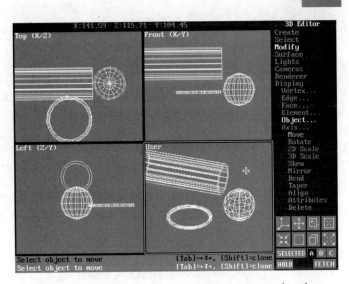

Position of the objects with respect to each other

To change the height of the objects in relation to each other, you shouldn't use the currently active view. We're looking at the objects from above in that window. So, activate the **Front (X/Y)** window and change the height.

If you're still in the full screen mode, you can use the View icon (second icon from the upper-right) to activate the display of the four windows.

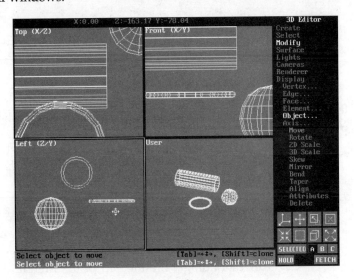

Various distances

Don't forget to
save your work

Now you must save the results. Use **File/Save** to display a dialog box, in which you can enter a file name. Select the name OBJECTS. The extension 3DS will be added to the file name to indicate that the file is an object file from 3D Studio. These files contain the basic elements that can be animated by using Keyframer.

Assign Material

By default, the objects you create have a neutral white surface. This looks a little boring after a while. In our example, we want to distinguish the individual objects by their color as well. Therefore, we'll assign different materials to the surfaces of the individual objects. There is an extensive selection of materials available in 3D Studio. Also, existing materials can be edited or new ones can be created.

Select **Surface/Material/Choose**. A dialog box appears with a list of all the available materials. You should do some experimenting here and try different materials.

The selected material can be assigned to as many objects as you want later. After you've decided on one, activate the Assign option in the Select/Surface/Material menu. Now click on the sphere to which you would like to assign the selected material. After confirming the verification question, a message like the one below will appear in the status line:

```
Object "Sphere" assigned Material "CYAN METALLIC"
```

Now select other materials for the remaining objects so they are different from one another.

Objects can be represented as boxes instead of the actual objects. For complex objects, this lets you move or select things more quickly. In this case, only the position of the box must be recalculated, instead of the complete object. To switch over to this kind of display, select **Display/Geometry/Box**. You can also accomplish the same thing by pressing ⎇Alt + Ⓑ, which you can also use to switch back to the normal display.

Locate A Light Source

Now we need a realistic lighting reflection for our picture. To do this, place several light sources in a view window. The objects are correspondingly illuminated from different directions.

Select **Lights/Omni/Create** and click in one of the four corners of the active viewing window. A dialog box, in which you can select the type of lighting, is displayed. The default setting is suitable for our example. To accept the default setting, click the (Create) button. By changing the color slide, you can make the light source radiate in color.

Even light sources are objects, so they must also be given a unique name. The default name "Light01" can be used since it's unique for our example. Now there is a yellow dot in the views, which symbolizes the position of the light source. Define a second light source, and position it in another corner.

> If you set up only one light source, the object will look dark later, depending on the material you use. You should use many light sources here; light objects from several sides and heights.

The light source can be adjusted at any time using the command sequence **Lights/Omni/Move**.

Establishing A Visual Angle

You must assign a camera so you can view the animation from a particular angle. The camera looks from a location in a defined line of sight. The position of the camera can be changed later. This changes the visual angle.

Activate the **Top (X/Z)** window and select the **Cameras/Create** command. Establish the location of the camera by clicking the mouse outside of the outermost object. Now move the mouse toward the center of the objects and define the direction of view by clicking on the mouse. A dialog box appears; accept the default values by clicking on the (Create) button. The camera is represented by a blue line in the windows.

Select a window as the camera lens

The ability to use one of the windows as a camera lens is very helpful. In this window, the presentation appears similar to the location site and the directional view of the camera. Select **Views/Viewports** from the menu bar at the top of the screen. Select **Cameras** and click within the iconized view window on the lower-right field, which is labeled U (User).

The label changes to C (Camera) and you can confirm the selection. The window is now identified as Camera01 and it contains the directional view of the camera. The position and the angle can be changed at any time with **Cameras/Move**.

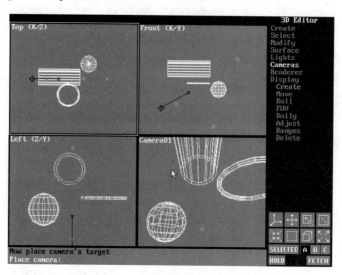

Light sources and a camera

7.6 Creating A Three-Dimensional Model

Since the assigned surface materials must reflect the positioned light sources to create a realistic effect, they must be calculated using the Rendering process. To do this, select **Renderer/Render** and activate the camera window (Camera01). A dialog window, in which you can adjust the Render options, appears. Experiment with the options and confirm the adjustments with the [Render] button. This starts the process and calculates the model.

The finished model is displayed and you can determine if any additional changes are needed. For example, you can move individual objects. While the calculations are being made, you can observe the results with the [Spacebar]. In this case, the rendering process is limited to the current picture. Later, you must also render the animation sequence so the changes in the reflection of light during the movement stage can be calculated.

> By clicking on the mouse, you can return to normal display mode and you can interrupt the calculation process with [Esc].

Your first three-dimensional scene is finished. The rendering process can be repeated at any time (e.g., when you want to observe the effect of different surfaces).

Animating Objects

The last step is the actual animation. You must activate the Keyframer module to execute this process. This is done by using the option of the same name in the **Program** menu. Keyframer is similar to the 3D Editor. The previously generated 3D scene appears in the four viewing windows.

> Before experimenting with different kinds of animation, you can use the key combination [Alt] + [L] to hide the icons for the light sources. You can do the same thing with the camera icon by using the key combination [Alt] + [C]. Activate the user view window and change it to the camera window by typing [C].

A certain number of frames (pages) per time interval must be specified so an object can be animated. By doing this, each frame contains changes to the object based on the previous page. If all the pages are played back sequentially, an animation is created. By default, 30 pages per second are used in the Keyframer. If you want to change the value, use **Time/Total Frames** and enter an appropriate value.

Selecting the pages

If you move the mouse to the lowest line on the screen, the page counter appears as a horizontal scroll bar. If you click on a particular location, the corresponding page number opens. The representation of the object hasn't changed because changes haven't been entered yet.

Five transformations are available:

- Move

- Rotate

- Scale

- Squash

- Morph

It's very easy to use the transformations. For example, if a sphere must be moved, a starting position and an ending position must be indicated. The starting position is automatically the original position of the sphere. The ending position can be the opposite side of the viewing window, for example. If you set the ending position to page 30, the position on the intervening pages will be average. Otherwise, nothing would happen until page 29 and then suddenly on page 30 the sphere would jump into the new position.

Obviously, you don't want this to happen. Since the entire animation starts over again after page 30 has been reached, the object makes a big jump from page 30 back to the first page. In some cases, this effect may be intentional. However, it's much better to arrange a smooth transition with a continuous animation.

This is done by having the object reach the furthest position somewhere in the middle pages and by having it move back in the direction of the original position towards the end of the sequence.

Checking the animation

The icon bar contains a symbol with a double arrow pointing to the right. This is the playback symbol. You can activate this symbol at any time to observe the animation. Depending on which viewing window is active, you can observe the animation from a different angle. The playback is stopped with the right mouse button.

Assign movements

To move an object from one position to another during an animation sequence, use the following procedure: Select page 15 and activate **Object/Move**. Click on an object and establish the new position with a mouse click. Allow the animation to play back. Select page 30 and return the object to the original position. This ensures that the object will move smoothly during the animation.

The file MOVE.FLI in the \ANIMATE\3DS directory of the companion CD-ROM shows the movement of the sphere.

Generate rotations

To rotate an object, select **Object/Rotate**. Activate page 30 and click on a long-shaped object so the rotation will be more noticeable. Use the Tab key to select the axis of rotation. It will appear in the menu bar on the upper border of the screen. Select the Y-axis in the same way and move the mouse until an angle of rotation of 360° is indicated. Confirm the setting by clicking on the mouse. Use the playback key to display the animation.

Refer to the ROTATE.FLI file in the \ANIMATE\3DS directory on the companion CD-ROM.

Changing An Object Size

To change the size, select page 15. Activate the **Object/Scale** command and click on a particular object. Use the (Tab) key to select the axis to which the change in size will refer. Move the mouse to establish the size factor. For example, input a factor of 200%. Make the adjustment by clicking on the mouse. In this case, select Objects/Tracks/Loop to automatically return to the original size near the end of the animation.

Squashing objects

The SCALE.FLI file in the \ANIMATE\3DS directory on the companion CD-ROM contains this animation.

With this feature, you can change the shape of an object so it's either proportionally drawn out or compressed. Select the desired page and activate **Object/Squash**. Again, use the (Tab) key to select the reference axis. Use the mouse to display the effect on the screen. Set the final position by clicking on the mouse.

Transforming objects

Refer to the SQUASH.FLI file in the \ANIMATE\3DS directory of the companion CD-ROM.

Another way to animate an object is to transform it to the size of another object. To do this, both objects must be the same kind of object. So you cannot change a sphere to a rectangle. To start the process, select a page and activate **Object/Morph/Assign**. Indicate the object that must be changed. A dialog box, containing all the objects to which the highlighted object can be transformed, appears. Select an object and watch the results.

Additional effects

This transformation is located in the MORPH.FLI file in the \ANIMATE\3DS directory of the companion CD-ROM.

To really liven up the animation, you can assign as many manipulations to an object as you want. You aren't limited to only one.

Other interesting effects are created when the camera position or the light position is changed during the sequence. To test this, change the position of the camera within the 30 page sequence on pages 5, 10, 15, 20, and 25. On page 25, after repositioning the camera, select **Object/Tracks/Loop** to restore the original position of the camera. You can also do this with the light sources.

The A3DSDEMO.FLI file in the \ANIMATE\3DS directory on the CD shows the additional effects.

Generating The Flic

The last step involves generating the animation file, or the flic. Use **Preview/Make** to convert the animation scene. Use **Play** to play back the complete animation in full-screen mode. If this file is saved as a flic (Save option), you obtain an animation sequence from the "mesh" models.

For the complete animation, including the representation of surface materials and the coloration of the background, the scene must be recalculated for the individual pages by using the **Renderer/Render** command. Activate the appropriate window and highlight the **Disk** option in the accompanying dialog box to save the complete model as a flic (*.FLI).

The sample flics on the companion CD-ROM demonstrate how you can use 3D Studio.

Chapter 8

Composing Electronically - MIDI

The synthesizer is an electronic device that generates synthetic notes or sounds. Today the synthesizer is used extensively throughout the music world, especially in popular and rock music. Some well-known synthesizer musicians include Howard Jones, Danny Elfman, Wendy Carlos, and Michael Oldfield.

You're probably wondering what the synthesizer has to do with your Multimedia PC. The sound card of the Multimedia PC also has a synthesizer that's capable of generating electronic notes.

Certain musical instruments can be imitated by sounds generated on the basis of frequency modulation, or FM (see Chapter 2). Several instruments (voices) can be played on a synthesizer simultaneously. So, when the synthesizer is played, it may sound like an entire orchestra or band is playing.

A musical piece that is generated with a synthesizer can be an excellent background for a multimedia presentation.

The Sound Blaster Pro 2.0's OPL3 chips support a number of modes, and four-operator FM instruments. These modes are:

• Nine melodic and five percussion instruments.

• 15 melodic (two-operator) and five percussion instruments.

• Six melodic (four-operator) instruments.

• Three melodic (two-operator) and five percussion instruments.

When we refer to instruments, we mean the synthetically generated sound that imitates the actual instrument, such as a piano. However, purely synthetically generated instruments seldom sound as realistic as the originals.

We previously mentioned the word operator. In FM synthesis, operators interact to produce instrument sounds. The more the operators, the better the sound quality. For example, the four-operator instruments generated using Sound Blaster Pro will sound better than the two-operator instruments.

The tone color, sound quality, or timbre (pronounced "TAM-brr" or "timber", depending on who you ask) of a synthetic sound depends on the kind of sound generation. Some methods synthesizers use to generate sound are:

• PCM (pulse code modulation). The Casio CZ series and Kawai K series synths use this method of sound generation.

• FM (frequency modulation) through operators. The Sound Blaster Pro card and the Yamaha DX series synths use this method.

• Digital sampling (sounds digitized from real life). The Ensoniq Mirage sampler and some church-model electronic organs use this method.

The sound card's synthesizer capabilities are controlled by sequencer programs, such as Voyetra Sequencer Plus and Midisoft Studio. These programs can be used to record note data and to play them back through the sound card, or through external MIDI devices.

To provide contact with the outer world, a MIDI interface was integrated into the MPC sound card. Because of this connection, it's possible to interface with external devices that support the MIDI interface, such as keyboard synthesizers or other MIDI controlled instruments or keyboards.

All MIDI-compatible devices can be attached to the MIDI interface of the sound card. These can be keyboards (Roland), MIDI guitars (Casio) or drum machines.

Advantages of using MIDI

The advantage of the MIDI interface is that the computer can control the external devices, or it can process and output data generated by these devices.

Therefore, musical selections that are generated on the computer can be played on an attached MIDI synthesizer. However, pieces played on a MIDI synthesizer can be played through the sound card's synthesizer in the computer.

Also, MIDI files are much smaller than comparable WAVE files. So you can use longer musical pieces without affecting the capacity of the hard drive. It's even easier to compose your own music because of the variety of instruments that are available.

8.1 What Is MIDI?

The term MIDI (Musical Instrument Digital Interface) refers to a standardized hardware interface for connecting MIDI-compatible devices with each other. In addition, MIDI is a more-or-less standardized data format by which MIDI-compatible devices communicate with one another.

The MIDI concept wasn't developed for the MPC. The music industry has used MIDI for communication between musical instruments since 1983. For example, MIDI made it possible to generate sounds from two connected keyboards that were significantly better than the sounds produced from just one keyboard.

MIDI data doesn't contain the actual sounds. Instead, MIDI data provides the basic values needed to play the sound, such as pitch, volume, timbre, the start and end of the sound, and information about the instrument that plays the notes.

Note on/off

Therefore, the most important messages relate to the start and end of the note as played on an instrument. This can be an external device attached via the MIDI interface or a keyboard simulated on the computer screen. When the musician presses a key, the note on message is generated. When the key is released, the note off message is sent.

Unlike WAVE files, which contain the information in the form of digitized sounds, this process requires much less storage space.

A MIDI file that is about two minutes long requires approximately 40K. If this file was sampled with the Windows Sound Recorder and saved as a WAVE file, considerably more disk space would be required. See the PASSPORT.MID and WAVE files in the MIDI\MAPPER directory of the companion CD-ROM.

The MIDI
Channels

The MIDI standard includes a total of 16 channels, which are numbered consecutively from 1 to 16. You can send and receive via any of the channels. A specific synthesizer instrument can be assigned to each channel. So, MIDI files contain the number of the instrument, as well as the channel. The channels transfer MIDI data from the sequencer or keyboard to the synthesizer.

We'll use an example to help explain this process. Let's use an external keyboard that's connected to the sound card of the computer by a MIDI adapter. The keystrokes on the keyboard are sent (e.g., through channel 7) to the MIDI port of the sound card. The keystrokes are then recorded in the computer by a sequencer program, which reads the MIDI port for incoming MIDI data.

If you want to play back the recorded MIDI data via a synthesizer (e.g., the internal one on the sound card), it must be able to receive data on channel 7 and to play back data through channel 7 as well.

You can change the playback or record channel assignment to another channel (e.g., channel 1), but you must also remember to change the synthesizer to channel 1. If you leave the synthesizer set at channel 7, the information sent to channel 1 may not play back through the synthesizer (with some exceptions).

Imperfect
Standard

Unfortunately the MIDI standard, which Microsoft established for Windows, doesn't always provide full compatibility with other MIDI devices.

All manufacturers support the control of 16 channels in MIDI format. However, the assignment of instrument numbers isn't included in this standard.

This causes a problem when MIDI files are played on systems with different instrument assignments; the files sound completely different.

For example, a number that specified a piano sound on a Kawai K1 may call a percussion sound on a Casio CZ-1000.

Microsoft Windows 3.1's MIDI Mapper application "re-routes" MIDI sounds, based on the General MIDI Specification of instrument sounds.

The MIDI Mapper Patch Map has the following assignments:

Piano

0	Acoustic Grand Piano	1	Bright Acoustic Piano
2	Electric Grand Piano	3	Honky-tonk Piano
4	Rhodes Piano	5	Chorused Piano
6	Harpsichord	7	Clavinet

Chromatic Percussion

8	Celesta	9	Glockenspiel
10	Music Box	11	Vibraphone
12	Marimba	13	Xylophone
14	Tubular Bells	15	Dulcimer

Organ

16	Hammond Organ	17	Percussive Organ
18	Rock Organ	19	Church Organ
20	Reed Organ	21	Accordion
22	Harmonica	23	Tango Accordion

Guitar

24	Acoustic Guitar (nylon)	25	Acoustic Guitar (steel)
26	Electric Guitar (jazz)	27	Electric Guitar (clean)
28	Electric Guitar (muted)	29	Overdriven Guitar
30	Distortion Guitar	31	Guitar Harmonics

Bass

32	Acoustic Bass	33	Electric Bass (fingered)
34	Electric Bass (picked)	35	Fretless Bass
36	Slap Bass 1	37	Slap Bass 2
38	Synth Bass 1	39	Synth Bass 2

Strings

40	Violin	41	Viola
42	Cello	43	Contrabass
44	Tremolo Strings	45	Pizzicato Strings
46	Orchestral Harp	47	Timpani

Ensemble

48	String Ensemble 1	49	String Ensemble 2
50	Synth Strings 1	51	Synth Strings 2
52	Choir Aahs	53	Voice Oohs
54	Synth Voice	55	Orchestra Hit

Brass

56	Trumpet	57	Trombone
58	Tuba	59	Muted Trumpet
60	French Horn	61	Brass Section
62	Synth Brass 1	63	Synth Brass 2

Reed

64	Soprano Sax	65	Alto Sax
66	Tenor Sax	67	Baritone Sax
68	Oboe	69	English Horn
70	Bassoon	71	Clarinet

Pipe

72	Piccolo	73	Flute
74	Recorder	75	Pan Flute
76	Blown Bottle	77	Shakuhachi
78	Whistle	79	Ocarina

Synth Lead

80	Lead 1 (square)	81	Lead 2 (sawtooth)
82	Lead 3 (calliope)	83	Lead 4 (chiff)
84	Lead 5 (charang)	85	Lead 6 (voice)
86	Lead 7 (fifths)	87	Lead 8 (bass + lead)

Synth Pad

88	Pad 1 (new age)	89	Pad 2 (warm)
90	Pad 3 (polysynth)	91	Pad 4 (choir)
92	Pad 5 (bowed)	93	Pad 6 (metallic)
94	Pad 7 (halo)	95	Pad 8 (sweep)

Synth Effects

96	FX 1 (rain)	97	FX 2 (soundtrack)
98	FX 3 (crystal)	99	FX 4 (atmosphere)
100	FX 5 (brightness)	101	FX 6 (goblins)
102	FX 7 (echoes)	103	FX 8 (sci-fi)

Ethnic

104	Sitar	105	Banjo
106	Shamisen	107	Koto
108	Kalimba	109	Bagpipe
110	Fiddle	111	Shanai

Percussive

112	Tinkle Bell	113	Agogo
114	Steel Drums	115	Woodblock
116	Taiko Drum	117	Melodic Tom
118	Synth Drum	119	Reverse Cymbal

Sound Effects			
120	Guitar Fret Noise	121	Breath Noise
122	Seashore	123	Bird Tweet
124	Telephone Ring	125	Helicopter
126	Applause	127	Gunshot

MIDI-
Synthesizers

Each of the instruments previously listed can be assigned to a channel. If the synthesizer works in a multitimbral mode, several instruments can be played simultaneously. However, one instrument, such as a flute, can always generate only one sound; this instrument is monophonic. So, multitimbral capability for polyphony (i.e., the ability to play more than one sound) is one indication of a synthesizer's abilities.

There are two kinds of synthesizers: base-level and extended synthesizers. Every MPC contains a base-level synthesizer as a component of the sound card. The MPC can be converted into an extended synthesizer with hardware expansions, such as a connection to a MIDI keyboard. The main difference between these synthesizers is the number of notes that can be played:

Base-Level Synthesizers			
Melodic		**Percussive**	
Instruments	Polyphony	Instruments	Polyphony
3	6 Notes	3	3 Notes

Extended Synthesizers			
Melodic		**Percussive**	
Instruments	Polyphony	Instruments	Polyphony
3	16 Notes	8	16 Notes

The sound cards that correspond to the multimedia specifications contain a base-level synthesizer.

The melodic instruments in these synthesizers are located on different channels, but the percussive voices are on a single rhythm channel. To obtain an ordered series when generating MIDI files, the individual channels should be used as follows:

Channel	Synthesizer	Description	Polyphony
1	Extended	Melodic	16 Notes
2	Extended	Melodic	16 Notes
3	Extended	Melodic	16 Notes
4	Extended	Melodic	16 Notes
5	Extended	Melodic	16 Notes
6	Extended	Melodic	16 Notes
7	Extended	Melodic	16 Notes
8	Extended	Melodic	16 Notes
9	Extended	Melodic	16 Notes
10	Extended	Percussive	16 Notes
11	unused		
12	unused		
13	Base-Level	Melodic	6 Notes
14	Base-Level	Melodic	6 Notes
15	Base-Level	Melodic	6 Notes
16	Base-Level	Percussive	3 Notes

For the MIDI standard for Multimedia Windows, the individual percussive instruments are assigned to the keys of a MIDI keyboard. The starting point of the assignments is the B below middle C on the keyboard.

Key	Number	Instrument
B	35	Acoustic Bass Drum
C	36	Bass Drum 1
C#/Db	37	Side Stick
D	38	Acoustic Snare
D#/Eb	39	Hand Clap

Key	Number	Instrument
E	40	Electric Snare
F	41	Low Floor Tom
F#/Gb	42	Closed High Hat
G	43	High Floor Tom
G#/Ab	44	Pedal High Hat
A	45	Low Tom
A#/Bb	46	Open High Hat
B	47	Low-Mid Tom
C	48	High-Mid Tom
C#/Db	49	Crash Cymbal 1
D	50	High Tom
D#/Eb	51	Ride Cymbal 1
F	52	Chinese Cymbal
F	53	Ride Bell
F#/Gb	54	Tambourine
G	55	Splash Cymbal
G#/Ab	56	Cowbell
A	57	Crash Cymbal 2
A#/Bb	58	Vibraslap
B	59	Ride Cymbal 2
C	60	High Bongo
C#/Db	61	Low Bongo
D	62	Mute High Conga
D#/Eb	63	Open High Conga
E	64	Low Conga
F	65	High Timbale
F#/Gb	66	Low Timbale
G	67	High Agogo
G#/Ab	68	Low Agogo
A	69	Cabasa
A#/Bb	70	Maracas
B	71	Short Whistle
C	72	Long Whistle

Key	Number	Instrument
C#/Db	73	Short Guiro
D	74	Long Guiro
D#/Eb	75	Claves
E	76	High Wood Block
F	77	Low Wood Block
F#/Gb	78	Mute Cuica
G	79	Open Cuica
G#/Ab	80	Mute Triangle
A	81	Open Triangle

8.2 Using MIDI Files

As we mentioned, the MIDI file format is a standardized format. The MIDI files contain musical pieces or sounds in the form of MIDI language commands. When the MIDI files are played, these commands are directed to the synthesizer, which interprets the commands and generates the sounds. MIDI files are generated and played by a sequencer. These files have the file extension .MID.

The Media Player in Windows is an example of a simple sequencer. It can be used to play MIDI files, but not change them. However, to play MIDI files with Media Player, the **MIDI Sequencer...** item must be specified in the **Device** menu.

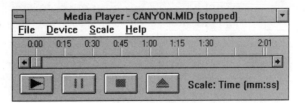

MIDI files in Windows

Real-time Sequencer

With this kind of sequencer, the data are input via an external MIDI keyboard, and they are recorded via the sequencer in real time. These recorded data can be saved as MIDI files. The ability to change the playback speed or to change the values or lengths of notes are characteristics of this type of sequencer.

Single-Step
Sequencer

A basic characteristic of a single-step sequencer is a notation program. With this program, music is created by entering the MIDI information by typing the instrument number, note values, tone values, etc. using the computer keyboard.

In simpler programs, the notes are entered through the computer keyboard (e.g., Sequencer Plus Pro), either as "blocks" or as text. More advanced programs have a graphical user interface, in which the notes are graphically displayed like in true music notation (e.g., Midisoft Studio and Cakewalk Professional). However, to use this kind of composition, you must be very familiar with music and notes.

Modern applications combine both methods of creating MIDI files. This way, the music can be input by a MIDI keyboard, a computer keyboard, or both. This means that larger pieces can be input very quickly and the detail work is performed in single-step mode.

> In single-step mode, the finest definition of the tone values can be used to create musical pieces that can be played back only by the synthesizer itself. Even if the corresponding notes are displayed in their final format, a musician wouldn't be able to play the piece on the actual musical instruments. This gives you the key to an entirely new world of music.

8.3 Using External MIDI Devices

If you want to change your MPC to an extended synthesizer, there's an entire series of MIDI-compatible accessories that can turn your computer into a powerful music machine. In this section we'll show you how to attach external MIDI devices to your computer.

Interface Construction

Data are transmitted serially with MIDI connections. However, to save space, the MIDI connectors of "genuine" MIDI devices are different from those of the sound card. These connectors consist of a 15-pin plug. The plug combines the functions of a MIDI port and a joystick port.

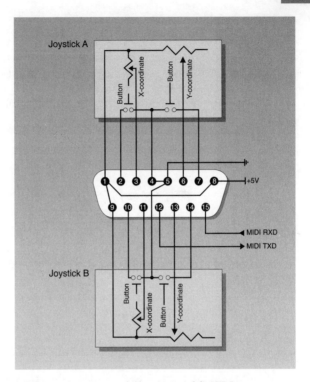

Pin assignment of the joystick/MIDI connector

Pins 14 and 15 are used for transmitting MIDI data. You need a separate MIDI box to connect with an external MIDI device. These are sold as add-ons by the sound card manufacturers.

5-pin is the standard

The standard connector for an external MIDI device is a 5-pin DIN plug. MIDI devices always contain only connector jacks, so cables with the appropriate plugs are used for connecting several devices.

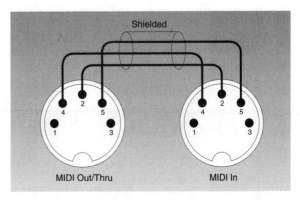

Connection of two MIDI plugs

Only three of the total five pins are needed. Pins 4 and 5 are used as conductors for MIDI data. Pin 2 is used to connect the cable shield with the plug. MIDI cables consist of a shielded, twisted pair of wires so electronic waves cannot be radiated outward.

However, the shielding of audio cables also protects against electric radiation from the outside.

XLR Connection   Some MIDI devices, which were created for portable application, have a 3-pin XLR connector instead of the 5-pin DIN plug.

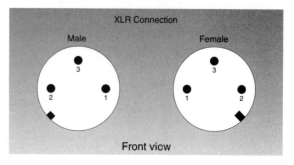

Pin assignment of the XLR connection

This is a much more stable connection (designed for concert use) that contains only the three pins that are needed. With these adapters, you'll always have the right connection, even if different devices with DIN and XLR jacks are used.

Connecting External MIDI Devices

When connecting a MIDI device, like a MIDI keyboard, you must use a special MIDI connector with the sound card. The Sound Blaster MIDI Kit includes a MIDI connector. One side of this connector connects to the 15-pin port of Sound Blaster. The opposite end of this connector has two 5-pin DIN MIDI jacks.

MIDI Input and   There are three kinds of MIDI connections:
Output

MIDI Connections	
Name	**Function**
MIDI IN	Input
MIDI OUT	Output
MIDI THRU	Throughput

The MIDI OUT must always be connected to the MIDI IN of the device that must be controlled. For example, if an external keyboard, including a synthesizer, is connected to the sound card, you can transmit the data in only one direction (from the keyboard to the sound card).

However, since even external synthesizers can be driven with sequencer programs, a connection, which allows data transfer in both directions, is needed.

When connecting the computer (or the MIDI Adaptor) to the MIDI device, make certain the MIDI IN port of the MIDI Adaptor is connected with the MIDI OUT port of the MIDI device.

The MIDI OUT port of the MIDI Adaptor is then connected with the MIDI IN port of the MIDI device.

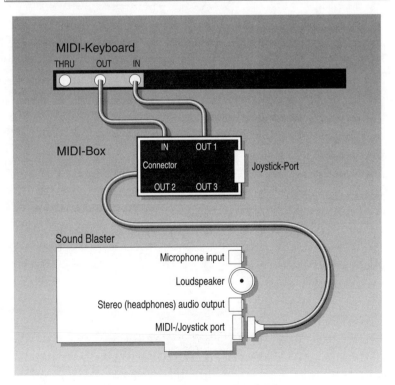

Port design of the MIDI Adaptor

The Sound Blaster MIDI Adaptor connects to the joystick port. However, you can still use your joystick because there is another joystick port in the MIDI Adaptor.

Chaining
multiple devices

With the MIDI THRU port, you can daisy chain several MIDI devices. The THRU actually sends the same signal traveling to the MIDI IN port.

By plugging a MIDI cable into the first device's MIDI THRU port and a second device's MIDI IN port, a user can control both devices from the first device.

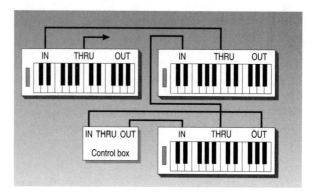

Daisy chaining MIDI devices

Daisy chaining can cause data deterioration from device to device. Devices can be more usefully connected in a star network by using a special MIDI THRU box with one or more MIDI IN ports and several MIDI THRU ports.

This interface can be purchased as an accessory from several sound card manufacturers, most of them for $100 or less.

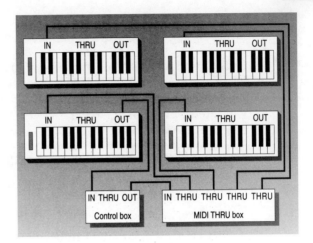

Star network with MIDI devices

However, simply connecting the devices isn't enough. You can play all the connected devices from the "master" device, but you still require sequencing software to optimally control the synthesizers (see Sections 8.4 and 8.5).

Overview of MIDI devices

There are many ways to connect external MIDI devices with the computer via the MIDI interface.

> When purchasing a MIDI instrument, you should consider its MIDI capabilities. Simply knowing that a MIDI interface is present doesn't provide any information about which data can be transmitted across the interface.
>
> For example, a few companies can physically retrofit (i.e., revamp) a non-MIDI instrument for MIDI capability.

These firms have retrofitted grand pianos, Moog analog synthesizers, organ pedalboards, etc., for connection to MIDI IN or MIDI OUT. Even with the retrofit, it's possible that the device's full capabilities cannot be controlled through the interface.

MIDI Keyboards

Keyboard synthesizers are the most popular MIDI devices. The reason for this popularity is that most MIDI systems have a keyboard for control.

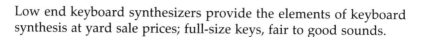

Low end keyboard synthesizers provide the elements of keyboard synthesis at yard sale prices; full-size keys, fair to good sounds.

Higher end instruments provide higher quality sounds, larger keyboard range (up to 88 keys), velocity-sensitive keyboards (i.e., the harder you press a key, the louder the sound), and keys with a weighted, piano-like "feel." All these instruments are self-contained, so you can use them with or without the MPC computer.

The most likely addition to the MPC MIDI standard will probably be the MIDI keyboard controller. Unlike the keyboard synthesizer, a keyboard controller has no onboard sound synthesis modules.

In fact, the keyboard controller can only transmit MIDI data played by the user. The keyboard should have a wide key range (a minimum of five octaves [61 keys]) and should be velocity-sensitive. A few major electronic musical instrument manufacturers (e.g., Roland Corporation) make keyboard controllers.

It's helpful to split (divide) the keyboard into different ranges. This allows the keyboard to be divided into zones, each of which can be assigned to a different MIDI channel. So the musician can play one instrument with the left hand and another instrument with the right hand.

The zones should be divided so they each include an entire octave; usually a split into three parts is enough.

The following illustration is an example of three zones and possible instruments:

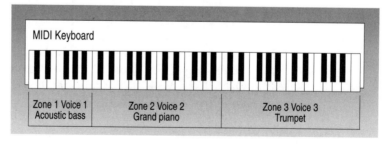

Division of the keyboard into zones

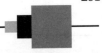

MIDI Expander

This device is basically a synthesizer without an attached controller—a black box, with MIDI IN, MIDI THRU and MIDI OUT ports.

You can connect the expander to an existing MIDI instrument, and play it from the existing instrument. The "expansion" is a sonic one as well as a physical one, as the sounds from the existing instrument are enriched by the expander's sounds.

Pitch-To-MIDI Converters

The pitch-to-MIDI converter is a very interesting device. This device can turn almost any kind of note and sound into MIDI data. The input note is converted into the corresponding command, similar to digitizing. This makes it possible to store guitar sound, wind instrument sound and even the human voice as MIDI data for processing through a sequencer.

This converter has its disadvantages. With many waveforms, it's difficult to identify the exact pitch. Also, noticeable time delays can occur, since the input signal for the pitch determination must be sampled over several periods.

Besides strictly monophonic devices, there are numerous polyphonic units. Since these have several voices, each guitar string can be assigned to a different channel, for example.

MIDI Guitars

Casio Corporation sells an actual MIDI guitar. Sensors sample the strings, and convert the notes into MIDI data. This produces a more exact result than a pitch-to-MIDI converter used with an electric guitar. With a MIDI guitar, notes can be generated simply by touching the strings.

MIDI Wind Instruments

As its name implies, the MIDI wind instrument is a keyed instrument with a key layout similar to those found on wind instruments such as saxophones. The player blows through a mouthpiece and fingers notes; the MIDI wind instrument makes its own sound, or controls an external MIDI expander through the wind instrument's MIDI OUT port. The harder the player blows into the instrument, the louder the note.

Drums

MIDI drums can be connected to other MIDI instruments. Each drum can control a separate channel. When used with a synthesizer, each one can generate a different timbre. However, all of the drums can also be directed to a single MIDI channel. In this case, each drum plays a different note.

8.4 Sequencer Programs

In this section, we'll discuss different sequencer programs.

When you generate your own MIDI data, you should follow these guidelines:

*   Generate MIDI files directly for base-level and extended synthesizers according to the division of the channels (Section 8.1).

*   Important instruments should be assigned to the channels with lower numbers (creating priorities).

*   Limit the polyphony of the percussive channels to three notes (channel 16) with base-level synthesizers and to 16 notes (channel 10) with extended synthesizers.

*   Limit the polyphony on the melodic channels to 6 notes (channels 13-15) with base-level synthesizers and to 16 notes (channels 1-9) with extended synthesizers.

*   Use a value of 80 as an initial volume. You can always change it later.

*   Use the standard channel assignment and the standard instrument assignment (Section 8.1).

Tracks   Most sequencer programs use tracks, similar to studio tape recorders. Although this concept isn't part of the MIDI standard, it simplifies editing an individual MIDI file. Each instrument is recorded on its own track. The individual tracks are distributed among the channels and they are played together.

You're probably wondering why there are so many tracks if there are only 16 channels. The explanation is simple—flexibility. For example, if you wanted an improvised saxophone solo in a piece, you could record 10 different versions of the solo on 10 different tracks.

One after another, you can assign the individual track to a channel and retrace the effect on the entire piece. Also, every solo or every instrument can be changed. However, if several instruments are recorded on a single track, then the changes apply to all the instruments on the track. So you can no longer differentiate between them.

Sequencer Plus

Sequencer Plus is a user-friendly sequencer program that can be used to generate MIDI files using an external keyboard (real-time sequencer) or by direct processing (single-step sequencer). In the first mode, a piano keyboard appears on the screen. This keyboard can be controlled from an external MIDI keyboard instrument, or from the computer's QWERTY keyboard.

Installation

Sequencer Plus is easy to install. Insert the program disk in the disk drive and type the letter of the hard drive on which the software should be installed:

```
INSTALL C:
```

The program automatically identifies which Sound Blaster version you're using. Then the appropriate driver for initializing the card is copied to the hard drive. The batch file SP.BAT, which starts the sequencer, loads the Sound Blaster driver before loading the actual program.

Problems During Installation
If you're using a version of Sound Blaster Pro, the installation program copies the initialization file TAPISB3.COM to the hard drive. If only a whistle is emitted from the speaker when you start the driver (using SP.BAT), the driver isn't working with the card. One way to avoid this is to emulate an older Sound Blaster version.

The installation program obtains the current version of the Sound Blaster card from the following line in the AUTOEXEC.BAT file:

```
SET BLASTER A220 I7 D0 T4
```

Change the value to "T3" and execute AUTOEXEC.BAT again. Now if you install Sequencer Plus again, the TAPISB.COM driver will be installed and will work properly.

Sequencer environment

After start-up, Sequencer Plus displays a very dense, line-oriented environment (50 lines). The main screen consists of 9 columns:

Column	Description
Trk	Number of the track
Name	Name of the track
Port	MIDI port used
Chan	MIDI channel used
Prg	Instrument number
Transpose	Transposition of the pitches
Quantize	Adaptation to the beat
Loop	Repeat function
Mute	Replay priority

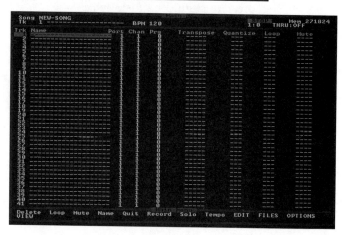

The main screen of the sequencer

The commands are located along the bottom of the screen. To activate a command, type the first letter of its name.

Playing a MIDI File

If you want to load a finished MIDI file into the sequencer, you must activate the file selection screen using (F)ile.

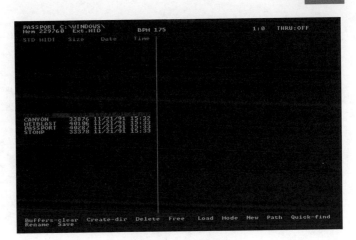

Selecting a MIDI file

The sequencer supports three file formats:

Format	File extension
Standard MIDI	.MID
Adlib songs	.ROL
Voyetra songs	.SNG

When you enter the (M)ode command, the desired file extension appears in the second line on the screen. So, if you want to load a standard MIDI file, the "MID" extension must be displayed.

After this has occurred, all files ending with .MID appear in the file selection window (if there are any in the current directory). Use (L)oad to load the file and press Enter; the MIDI data will be displayed on the screen.

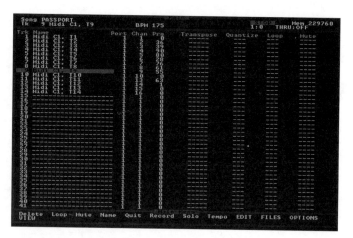

A MIDI file

A metronome is extremely helpful for recording a MIDI file. This timing device generates a rhythmic beat through the speaker to help you orient yourself. However, you should turn off the metronome if you want to play back a piece.

Select (O)ptions to display the options screen and (M)etronome to toggle metronome operation on or off. You can also activate this dialog box by pressing ⌊F3⌋. Use the ⌊+⌋ key to turn off the metronome and ⌊Esc⌋ to exit the dialog box.

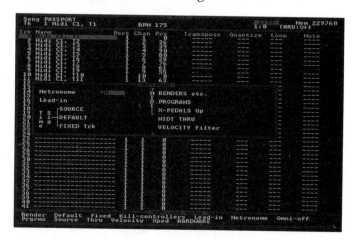

Turning off the metronome

Starting and   The playback of a MIDI file is controlled with ⎡Spacebar⎤. To start
Stopping   playing the file, press this key once and to stop the playback, press
                 this key again.

Generating MIDI files

An easy way to generate your own MIDI files without an external
keyboard is to control the sound card's synthesizer from the
computer keyboard. With this method, a piano keyboard is
displayed on the screen. Its key designations match those of your
keyboard. The notes that are generated when a key is pressed are
displayed next to the keyboard.

To record a song, first use **(D)elete/(A)ll** to clear any existing tracks.
However, if you want to add a new track to an existing file, load the
file and highlight the next empty track.

You must set the Port option of the current track to 2 so the
keystrokes played on the keyboard can be heard. Otherwise, you
won't hear anything. Also, you must activate the MIDI THRU
option. To do this, select **(O)ptions** and set the MIDI THRU option
to "ON" by using the ⎡+⎤ key.

Switch the sequencer into recording mode with (R)ecord. The labels
REC and STOP are displayed at the top of the screen. This indicates
that, although you're in recording mode, the recording hasn't
started yet.

Keyboard Display   Use ⎡Shift⎤ + ⎡F1⎤ to display the graphical keyboard on the screen.

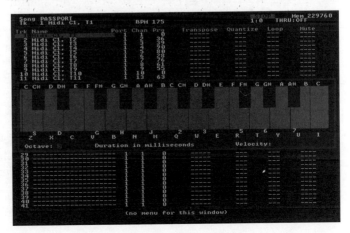

The piano on the screen

Start recording by pressing (Spacebar). You can type the song out on the keyboard. Let's enter "Twinkle, Twinkle, Little Star." Each key corresponds to one syllable:

```
Q    Q    T    T    Y    Y    T
Twin-kle, twin-kle, lit-tle star!
R    R    E    E    W    W    Q
How I won-der what you are.
T    T    R    R    E    E    W
Up above the world so high
T    T    R    R    E    E    W
Like a dia-mond in the sky,
Q    Q    T    T    Y    Y    T
Twin-kle, twin-kle, lit-tle star!
R    R    E    E    W    W    Q
How I wonder what you are.
```

> If some of the tracks have already been used, their data will be played back during the recording. This makes it easier to add a new accompaniment to an existing piece, since you can estimate the insertion point by ear.

Stop the recording by pressing (Spacebar). The top line on the screen will display STOP again. REC no longer appears on the screen. Change back to the main screen by pressing (Esc). Now you can play back the piece as usual and save it as a file.

Selecting an Instrument

Now you can experiment by perhaps marking the next empty track for the example previously given and by selecting another instrument in the Prg column. The instrument names for General MIDI were listed in Section 8.1.

To select a separate instrument for each track, first you must assign another MIDI channel to it with the Chan column. If the instrument number of a track is changed, all the other tracks that refer to the same channel number will automatically be adjusted.

The Loop column on the main screen is also very interesting. If you switch the option to ON, the data of the track will be permanently repeated. So you don't have to input the entire piece in an accompanying melody if a rhythm must be continually repeated.

Midisoft Studio

Midisoft Studio for Windows is a powerful sequencer program that can help you record keystrokes from an external keyboard (real time sequencer) and edit complete MIDI files, note-for-note, on the screen (single-step sequencer).

Installing Midisoft

Midisoft is installed on the hard drive using an installation routine. Start this routine with the command:

```
INSTALL
```

A dialog box, asking for a source drive, appears. If you're installing Midisoft from a CD, specify the complete path where the files are located. Start the program by using its icon from the Program Manager.

Midisoft Studio versions earlier than Version 3.02 use their own MIDI drivers to control the MIDI port with Multimedia Windows. The MIDI Mapper of Windows isn't used. If you want to drive an external keyboard using the cards mentioned, you must copy the SEQUEN.DLL file from the Midisoft installation diskette to the Midisoft directory on the hard drive.

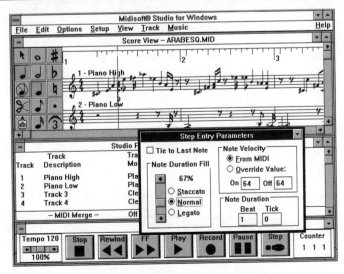

The different views in Midisoft

Midisoft environment

The Midisoft environment consists of different components:

Score View

In the Score View window, the music is displayed in the form of notes. If you use a keyboard to record the keystrokes, the corresponding notes appear on the screen. When you play back the piece, the notes that are being played are displayed in a different color, so you can always follow the current situation.

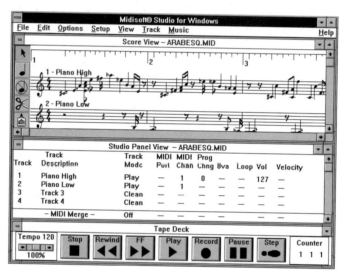

A song in Score View

Toolbox

The Score View contains a Toolbox that contains icons for the functions used in editing the notes. In addition to a highlighting function, you can add new notes, erase existing notes and erase and add highlighting.

If you select the Add Note function, the Toolbox is enlarged and a dialog box, in which you can indicate the note or icon to be added, appears.

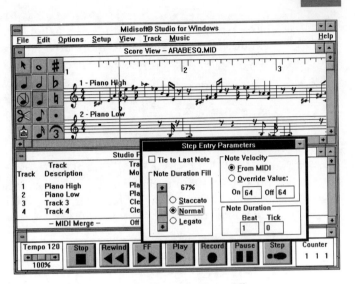

The Toolbox in the Score View

Studio Panel View   The use of the individual tracks is displayed in the Studio Panel View window. This is where you name and match the recorded tracks. You can also modify the playback characteristics of each separate track.

Track	Track Description	Track Mode	MIDI Port	MIDI Chan	Prog Chng	8va	Loop	Vol	Velocity
1	Piano High	Play	—	1	0	—	—	127	—
2	Piano Low	Play	—	1	—	—	—	—	—
3	Track 3	Clean	—	—	—	—	—	—	—
4	Track 4	Clean	—	—	—	—	—	—	—
5	Track 5	Clean	—	—	—	—	—	—	—
6	Track 6	Clean	—	—	—	—	—	—	—
7	Track 7	Clean	—	—	—	—	—	—	—
8	Track 8	Clean	—	—	—	—	—	—	—
9	Track 9	Clean	—	—	—	—	—	—	—
10	Track 10	Clean	—	—	—	—	—	—	—
11	Track 11	Clean	—	—	—	—	—	—	—
12	Track 12	Clean	—	—	—	—	—	—	—
13	Track 13	Clean	—	—	—	—	—	—	—
14	Track 14	Clean	—	—	—	—	—	—	—
15	Track 15	Clean	—	—	—	—	—	—	—
16	Track 16	Clean	—	—	—	—	—	—	—
17	Track 17	Clean	—	—	—	—	—	—	—
18	Track 18	Clean	—	—	—	—	—	—	—
19	Track 19	Clean	—	—	—	—	—	—	—
20	Track 20	Clean	—	—	—	—	—	—	—
21	Track 21	Clean	—	—	—	—	—	—	—
	— MIDI Merge —	Off	—	—	—	—	—	—	—

The Studio Panel View

Tape Deck View   The playback and recording of a MIDI file is controlled by using buttons that are similar to those on a tape recorder. There is also a slide to regulate the playback speed (Tempo Box).

Buttons provide the controls

MIDI List View   In the MIDI List View window, the music is played as a MIDI event. If you feel more comfortable with conventional MIDI sequencers than with composing using notes, you can change and expand MIDI files like you can in programming.

Type	Chan	Start Time	Duration/Data	Pitch	Vel On	Vel Off
Controller	[1]	1 | 1 | 1	64	127		
Controller	[1]	1 | 1 | 1	10	64		
Controller	[1]	1 | 1 | 1	91	64		
Controller	[1]	1 | 1 | 1	93	0		
Note	[1]	1 | 1 | 1	0 | 1 | 72	C#4	67	64
Note	[1]	1 | 1 | 40	0 | 1 | 8	E4	86	64
Note	[1]	1 | 1 | 70	0 | 0 | 73	A4	90	64
Note	[1]	1 | 2 | 1	0 | 0 | 48	E4	64	64
Note	[1]	1 | 2 | 1	0 | 0 | 48	A4	64	64
Note	[1]	1 | 2 | 1	0 | 0 | 37	C#5	91	64
Note	[1]	1 | 2 | 34	0 | 0 | 37	E5	92	64
Note	[1]	1 | 2 | 67	0 | 0 | 11	F#5	65	64
Note	[1]	1 | 3 | 1	0 | 0 | 74	G#5	70	64
Controller	[1]	1 | 3 | 27	64	0		
Note	[1]	1 | 3 | 32	0 | 0 | 62	D#5	80	64
Note	[1]	1 | 3 | 62	0 | 0 | 71	B4	68	64
Controller	[1]	1 | 3 | 80	64	127		
Note	[1]	1 | 4 | 1	0 | 0 | 30	G#4	70	64
Note	[1]	1 | 4 | 30	0 | 0 | 26	D#4	77	64
Controller	[1]	2 | 1 | 20	64	0		
Note	[1]	2 | 1 | 32	0 | 0 | 90	C#4	81	64
Note	[1]	2 | 1 | 59	0 | 0 | 58	F#4	74	64

Midisoft© Studio for Windows — File Edit Options Setup View Track Music Help

MIDI List View – ARABESQ.MID

1 - Piano High   Insert Delete

An overview of MIDI commands

Playing a MIDI file

To play a file, it must be present in memory. You can either load a complete file or you can record a piece using an external keyboard. With **File/Open...** you can select among several formats. Midisoft supports the following file formats:

Studio File

> This is the internal Midisoft format. These files have the .SNG extension.

Midi File

> Three types of MIDI files are supported. These types can be generated when the file is saved. The extension .MID is used:

Type 0	All information is on one track. This format is used by older sequencers.
Type 1 (Default)	MIDI data and channel information are stored in different tracks.
RIFF	This Microsoft format was developed in conjunction with multimedia. It makes it possible to store various kinds of information. The .RMI extension is used for this format.

To play back a piece, either use the mouse to click on the Play button or press (Spacebar). You can use the space bar to toggle between the Play and the Stop function. When the piece is playing, in Score View the segment being played is indicated with a specific color. The position within the piece can also be determined from the counter box, which is located to the right in Tape Deck View.

During playback, you can change the playback speed by clicking on the tempo slide. You can use the fast forward and rewind buttons to move around in the piece, even during playback. These keys are useful when you want to play only the modified section of a song you've changed.

Recording a piece

If you've attached an external keyboard, you can record the keystrokes and save them as a MIDI file. This function can be used only if an external keyboard is connected to the computer through the MIDI interface of the sound card.

Clear the Memory First   Before you start recording, you should clear the contents of the memory and restore the default values using **File/New**. You can use the **View** menu to activate the Score View, the Tape Deck View and the MIDI List View if you aren't already located in this screen.

When you press the button for recording, a rhythmic beat is played over the loudspeaker. This is the metronome, which should help you stay on beat. The metronome's default setting is a 4/4 beat, but you can change this at any time using **Setup/Metronome**.

To determine whether Midisoft Studio is in Record mode, look at the (Record) button. It will have a different color. Press a few keys on the keyboard.

By default, the input is recorded on track 1. At the same time, the note symbols appear in Score View. Each line of notes in Score View represents a separate track. Therefore, the first line represents Track No. 1, the second line represents Track No. 2, etc.

Activate the Studio Panel View and click in the line below Track Description to label the track. You can edit the entry as needed. If the recording isn't what you had expected, you can clear the track with **Track/Delete**.

	Track	Track	MIDI	MIDI	Prog				
Track	Description	Mode	Port	Chan	Chng	8va	Loop	Vol	Velocity
1	Rhythm	Clean	–	–	–	–	–	–	–
2	Kbd	Clean	–	–	–	–	–	–	–
3	Bongos	Clean	–	–	–	–	–	–	–
4	Trombone Solo	Clean	–	–	–	–	–	–	–
	– MIDI Merge –	Off		–	–	–		–	–

Track descriptions provide a quick overview

Overdubbing

You should use an empty track to record a new instrument. Obviously the new instrument should harmonize with the one already recorded so the entire rendition sounds pleasant. The process of synchronizing a new instrument with one that's already recorded is called "overdubbing".

With this technique, you can re-edit MIDI files at almost any time. You can use the overdubbing process to change existing files by filtering out certain instruments, erasing the track and then adding new ones.

The easiest way to do this is to record an instrument on a separate track while the existing piece is being played back. In this way, the beginning can be reconstructed. A second method is to place an already existing track into the Overdub mode and mix the newly generated data with the existing ones.

Recording While Playing Back

Open the MIDI file you want to edit and click on the Record button. If the metronome is active, you'll hear the beat over the speaker. Then recorded tracks are played back. At the same time, the next free track becomes active. Move to the appropriate position of the piece and play the desired section with the keyboard. Stop the recording and save the piece.

Recording in Overdub Mode

To use the second method, activate the Studio Panel View and click on the label for the Track-Mode of the appropriate track until the Overdub label appears. Now you can activate the Record button and record the new input via the keyboard. The information that already exists on the tracks will also be played back while recording.

The first method is much easier than the second. If you make a mistake during recording, it's much easier to undo this mistake by using a separate track. Detailed editing is also considerably easier. To mix the track later with another track, you can still use the Track/Combine function. However, you should be sure that both tracks contain error-free data.

Composing Your Own Songs

If you have a sound card installed in your computer but you don't have an external keyboard, Midisoft provides a powerful tool for composing your own musical pieces. The individual scores can be developed in standard note form on the screen just like in a notebook and then played with the synthesizer of the sound card. Also, the pieces can be printed in note form. This is a big advantage over Sequencer Plus, which lets you edit only pure MIDI data.

Another advantage of Midisoft Studio is that you can take existing musical pieces, which are available in note format, and easily store them with Midisoft Studio by inserting the notes in a MIDI file. You can do this without any musical knowledge and you can then use these pieces for your multimedia presentation. You can also add your personal touch to these pieces by changing them this way.

When composing or when editing individual tracks, you can refer to a specific instrument. For example, if you've created a song by using the keyboard or by inserting notes, you can use the ProgChan option of the appropriate track in Setup Panel View to change the desired instrument number.

At least until Version 3.02 of Midisoft Studio, instrument numbers are assigned by its own DLL library instead of by the MIDI Mapper of Multimedia. Therefore, in this case, adjusting the MIDI Mapper doesn't have any effect on the playback under Midisoft Studio.

Also, the values for Vol (volume) and Velocity (tempo) of the track can be changed. To change an entry in the Setup Panel View, move the mouse pointer to the original value (the sign "-" is the default setting).

Use the left mouse button to decrease the value and the right mouse button to increase it. When you arrive at either end of the scale, the display returns to the starting point.

Editing functions

Midisoft Studio contains an entire series of editing functions for changing completed musical pieces. To edit individual notes or note groups, first highlight them in Score View:

Highlighted Range	Action
Individual note	Single mouse click.
Several notes	Hold down [Shift] while clicking.
Range	Hold down the left mouse button and highlight the desired range. The starting point of the highlighting cannot be within the line of notes.

Cutting and pasting a highlighted range

Highlighted notes or ranges can be cut or copied in the usual way by using the Windows Clipboard. Then they can be inserted anywhere you want in the same track or in any other track using the Paste tool. However, if you want to delete only individual notes, you should use the erase function from the Toolbox to remove individual notes.

If you select the Splice Cut function instead of the Edit/Cut command, all the notes following the cut out area are moved to the left. Otherwise the cut out section would remain empty and would be very noticeable as a break during playback.

Cakewalk Professional for Windows

Cakewalk Professional for Windows, from Twelve Tone Systems, is a 256-track MIDI sequencer for Windows 3.1. This program helps you use powerful MIDI sequencing to create various types of music, such as film scores and radio spots.

By using its graphical user interface, you can easily control all aspects of music production on your PC. With Cakewalk Professional you can view and edit MIDI notes using three methods: Piano-roll format, staff notation format, and event-list format.

Installation

To install Cakewalk Professional on your hard drive, simply use the installation program located on disk 1 of the Cakewalk package. Insert this disk in the drive and then select **File/Run...** from the Windows Program Manager.

In the dialog box that appears, type the letter of the drive containing the Cakewalk Professional diskette, the name SETUP, and press (Enter). For example, if you placed the diskette in drive A:, type

A:SETUP

and then press (Enter).

The following window and dialog box appears:

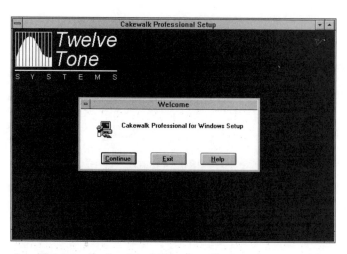

Complete the installation by following the instructions that appear on the screen.

Special Note On Roland MPU-401 or Compatible Interfaces

If your system is using a Roland MPU-401 or compatible interface, and you already have the "Roland MPU-401" driver installed, you'll need to run Drivers from the Windows Control Panel. Remove the Microsoft "Roland MPU-401" driver from the driver list. Click on the [Add...] button. Select "Unlisted or Updated Driver" and click [OK].

Enter the drive in which the Cakewalk Professional installation diskette is located, and click [OK]. Click on the "Twelve Tone Systems MPU-401" listing and click [OK].

You may be prompted for the base address and interrupt; if you don't know these numbers, select the defaults and click [OK]. When prompted, click [Restart Now].

At the time of publication, Twelve Tone Systems recommends this, as Cakewalk Professional uses its own driver. If both drivers are present, problems may occur.

Starting Cakewalk Professional

Once Cakewalk Professional is installed, an icon representing the program will appear in the Windows Program Manager, within its own program group. To start the program, double-click this icon.

When Cakewalk Professional starts, you may be prompted to modify MIDI input and output. Respond as needed, and click OK. The Track/Measure view appears within the Cakewalk Professional window.

"View" is the generic term used by the Cakewalk Professional documentation to describe the windows within the Cakewalk Professional window. You can select views by clicking on a track using the right mouse button. This displays a menu, from which you can select a view.

The Track/Measure view is divided into several rows and columns, similar to those you might find on a worksheet application such as Microsoft Excel.

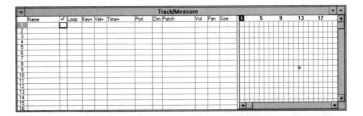

Cakewalk Professional's main window

The menu bar is located at the top of the screen. You can select the Cakewalk commands by selecting the appropriate menu titles in the menu bar. The Control bar is located below the menu bar. This bar contains buttons and information that are frequently used, such as timing, measure of music, and other data. At the bottom of the screen is the Message line. This line displays various temporary messages.

We defined views earlier in this section. When you start Cakewalk, the Track/Measure view is automatically displayed.

Track/Measure view

This window is divided into two sections, called "panes:" the Track pane and the Measure pane. You can specify different parameters for all 256 tracks in the Track pane. For example, you can assign channels, patch names or numbers, ports, and other parameters to tracks. This is also where you can adjust individual track offsets (e.g., MIDI key number transposition and velocity number transposition).

Files can be loaded into Cakewalk Professional by selecting **File/Open....** The following illustration shows the Track/Measure view with the ROWROW.WRK file in memory.

Track/Measure view

In the Measure pane you can see which measures of each track contain events (i.e., MIDI instructions). This pane makes it easier to edit tracks and measures. You can easily copy or move selected measures and also see how a command, such as **Edit/Cut**, will affect many tracks.

Piano-roll view

Similar to a player piano roll

Another view is the Piano-roll view. Moving the mouse pointer to the track named Theme and clicking the right mouse button displays a menu. Select **Piano-roll**. In the Piano-roll view, notes from a single track are displayed in a grid format that's similar to a player piano roll. Notes are displayed as horizontal bars. The pitch is represented in the left margin as piano keys.

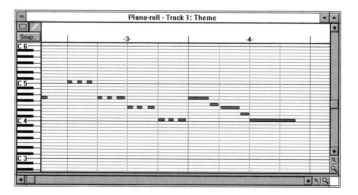

Piano-roll view

Note and Velocity

This view is divided into two panes: Note and Velocity. When the Piano-roll window is opened, the entire Note pane is displayed and the Velocity pane is hidden at the bottom of the window. To display the Velocity pane, double-click on the gray bottom border just above the horizontal scroll bar, or simply drag the border up until this pane is displayed.

Note pane modes   The Note pane has two modes. In the Select mode, you can set the From and Thru markers. In the Draw mode, you can insert new notes and change existing notes.

Event-list view

The Event-list view is another window in Cakewalk Professional. This window displays different events in a list format. In this window you can insert, delete or modify any event, such as those that control notes, velocity, and WAV file playback.

Trk	Hr:Mn:Sc:Fr	Meas:Beat:Tick	Chn	Kind	Values		
1	00:00:00:00	1:1:000	1	Note	C 4	91	92
1	00:00:00:20	1:2:000	1	Note	C 4	88	106
1	00:00:01:10	1:3:000	1	Note	C 4	98	79
1	00:00:01:23	1:3:080	1	Note	D 4	88	35
1	00:00:02:00	1:4:002	1	Note	E 4	90	91
1	00:00:02:20	2:1:000	1	Note	E 4	88	89
1	00:00:03:04	2:1:082	1	Note	D 4	80	29
1	00:00:03:10	2:2:001	1	Note	E 4	88	71
1	00:00:03:24	2:2:082	1	Note	F 4	73	27
1	00:00:04:01	2:3:003	1	Note	G 4	84	1:037
1	00:00:05:10	3:1:000	1	Note	C 5	80	21
1	00:00:05:17	3:1:041	1	Note	C 5	70	20
1	00:00:05:23	3:1:078	1	Note	C 5	61	23
1	00:00:06:00	3:2:000	1	Note	G 4	80	21
1	00:00:06:07	3:2:040	1	Note	G 4	72	20
1	00:00:06:13	3:2:078	1	Note	G 4	76	34
1	00:00:06:20	3:3:001	1	Note	E 4	80	24

Event-list view

Controllers view

In the Controllers view, the MIDI controller events for a track are graphically displayed. These events adjust volume, pitch modulation, sustain pedal and panning. You can edit these events in this window.

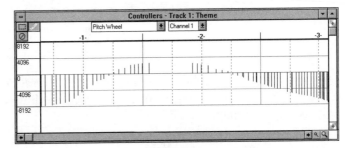

Controllers view

Staff view

The Staff view displays sequencer data as musical notation. This window also provides editing capabilities.

Staff view

The Minimized Window Views

The remaining views appear as Minimized windows at the bottom of the Cakewalk Professional window. You can access each view either by double-clicking the Minimized window or by selecting the window title from the **Window** menu.

Comments view

In the Comments view you can enter comments about your work. These comments are saved along with the file.

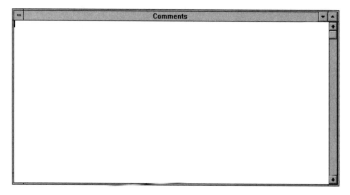

Comments view

Tempo view

The Tempo view graphically displays any tempo changes in your work file. Using your mouse, you can draw or plot tempo changes on a map.

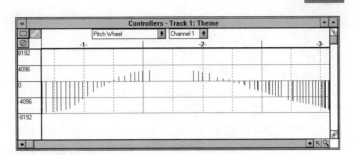

Tempo view

Meter/Key view

In the Meter/Key view, you can enter meter and key changes on measure boundaries.

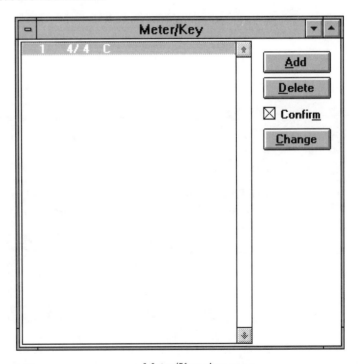

Meter/Key view

Sysx view

The Sysx view (or System Exclusive view) lets you enter System Exclusive messages for various pieces of equipment. This window provides 256 banks, in which you can insert messages. These messages contain a manufacturer ID and information about the product that is supplied by the manufacturer.

Markers view

The Markers view displays a list of markers, which are used to associate text with a time. One way markers can be used is to name sections of your work.

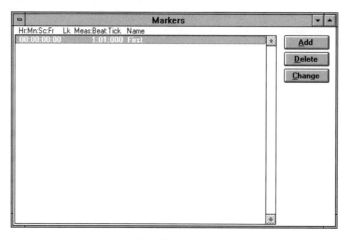

Markers view

Faders view

The Faders view displays 16 graphical faders (sliders). These faders generate MIDI Controller events when you move them.

Faders view

Playing a file

To play a file, first it must be loaded. To do this, select the **Open...** command from the **File** menu. A dialog box with a list of file names appears. A number of demo files exist. Select the appropriate file and then click OK. When the file is loaded, some names and numbers will appear in the lines of the Track/Measure view.

Before playing the file, you must ensure that the synthesizer is switched on and that it is set to receive on MIDI channel 1. Refer to your synthesizer documentation for instructions.

Now, to play a file, press the Spacebar or click the Play (>)button, which is located in the Control bar. The file will begin to play. At the bottom of your screen you should see some numbers changing. The Now marker shows the current count of measures, beats and ticks.

To stop the playback, press the Spacebar or click the Play (>) button again. Now if you want to continue the playback from the place where the file stopped, simply press the Spacebar or click the Play (>) button.

However, if you want to play the file from the beginning, you must press W or click the Rewind (<<) button in the Control bar. Then you can start the file again.

Recording tracks

Before recording a track, ensure that Cakewalk Professional is sending the notes you play on your keyboard to the proper MIDI channel. Your synthesizer must be set to respond on this channel. Again, refer to your synthesizer documentation for instructions.

Pick an empty track. If a zero appears in the Size column, the track is empty. Then move the highlight to this row. Next, move the highlight to the column labeled Chn (Channel).

Now press a key on your synthesizer. If you don't hear any sound, change the MIDI channel number. To do this, use the computer's addition and subtraction keys while pressing keys on the synthesizer. Continue to do this until you hear a sound.

If, after doing this, you still don't hear any sound, you should check your MIDI cables. They may not be connected properly.

To start recording, press R or click the Record button in the Control bar. When you do this, the metronome starts to beep. At this point, there is a one measure count-in before the actual recording starts. If you play any notes at this time, they won't be placed in the track until the recording actually begins.

The recording begins after the fourth metronome beep. Now play some notes on your MIDI instrument. The original tracks (if any exist) will play along with you.

To stop recording, press ⓇR or click the ⟮Record⟯ button again. Cakewalk Professional will then ask you whether you want to keep the "take" you recorded. If you want to save it, click ⟮Yes⟯; if you don't, click ⟮No⟯.

If you decided to keep the take, you'll notice that the screen changes. The right half of the Track/Measure view indicates that something has occurred in the measures of the track. This is what you just recorded.

Now rewind and play back the file. Your track will be played along with the originals.

8.5   Changing Instrument Assignments

The MIDI standard established in Microsoft Windows contains a series of assignments so problems with external MIDI devices don't occur. For example, the MIDI standard specifies which instrument is assigned to which number.

There is also an established key assignment that specifies which rhythm instrument can be played with which key of a MIDI keyboard. In the last step, the channel assignment for Base-level- and Extended Synthesizers is established.

> In Windows, these assignments are maintained in the form of tables (MIDI maps). In Multimedia Windows, if a MIDI file is played by a Windows sequencer (e.g., the Media Player) over the MIDI port or the synthesizer of the sound card, the assignment tables are activated. DOS-only sequencers cannot access these tables; they normally use their own module for the assignments.

Problems with Assignments

If you use only programs, files and MIDI devices that are compatible with the Multimedia Windows requirements, you don't need to modify the tables. However, if you use devices that have different instrument numbers, it's possible that the MIDI files might sound completely different than if standard MIDI devices were used.

For example, if you hear a cello instead of an oboe, the synthesizer is using the instrument number 68 to generate the sound of a cello. However, standard MIDI uses this number to generate the sound of an oboe. In standard MIDI, the cello is under instrument number 42.

So, to ensure that the MIDI file is played back correctly, you must assign the instrument number 68 of standard MIDI to number 42 of the synthesizer in the appropriate table. Then assign number 42 of standard MIDI to the number 68 of the synthesizer.

> If the devices work without any problems, you don't need to make any changes. However, by modifying the tables, you can create some interesting effects. For example, by deactivating individual channels or by changing instrument numbers, you obtain a completely different sound.
>
> So if you're using only the MIDI sequencer option of Media Player, which only allows the playback of MIDI files, this is one way to expand your possible options.

Editing The MIDI Mapper

In Multimedia Windows, the assignments we just discussed are made with the MIDI Mapper option in the Control Panel. These tables are stored under the name MIDIMAP.CFG in the Windows system directory. Existing tables in MIDI Mapper can be changed as desired.

However, to be safe you should create a new table when needed so you still have access to the original data. Tables can be named and activated using a selection list.

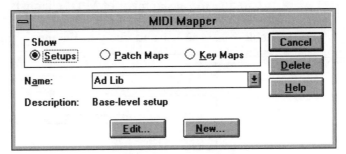

The MIDI Mapper environment

MIDI Mapper has three options, which refer to the corresponding assignment tables:

Option	Assignment
Setups	Maps and activates the MIDI channels
Patch Maps	Maps the instrument numbers
Key Maps	Maps the rhythm instruments to keys on the keyboard

Only one mapping function can be selected at a time. In each option, you can access several tables from a list. The currently active table appears in the display in the selection list.

Sound Blaster Tables

If you install Sound Blaster or Pro Audio Spectrum, the appropriate tables are automatically provided. When you install the corresponding driver, a modified MIDIMAP.CFG is copied into the Windows system directory. Therefore, the individual displays might be slightly different, depending on which sound card you install.

> Before making changes in the tables, perhaps because the MIDI files aren't being correctly played back by a synthesizer, you should ask the manufacturer if a suitable MIDIMAP.CFG file has already been created for the device.

Changing the Setup Table

Changing the assignment of MIDI channels is done in the Setups option. If you want to edit an existing file, select the appropriate table from the list and click on the [Edit...] button. Use the [New...] button to generate a completely new table.

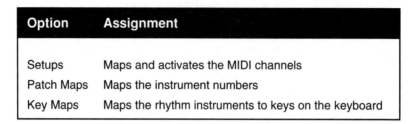

New MIDI Setup ...

Name: SoundBlaster

Description: Test

[OK] [Cancel] [Help]

Name and description for the new table

Then a dialog box, in which you can enter the name and description of the table that must be created, appears. The entry in the Name: text box will appear in the selection list of the appropriate option. The entry in the Description: text box appears below the Name: list

box. Always use meaningful keywords here so you can immediately determine the table's purpose.

Making Changes   The Setup tables consist of four columns and a function switch:

Src Chan (Source Channel)
> This column contains the individual MIDI channels as they are used by standard MIDI. The entries in this column cannot be changed.

Dest Chan (Destination Channel)
> This is where you specify the channel that will be used by the sequencer for data output from the source channel to the synthesizer. You can select all channels here.

Port Name
> The output port, through which the channel data will be output, is selected here. With Sound Blaster, you can direct the output to the internal synthesizer (SB Pro 2 Synth) or to the MIDI port of the sound card (SB MIDI Out). You must always use the second option when the data of one or more channels must be output to the channels of an external MIDI synthesizer. It's possible to have a combined output within the table so data can be directed to the Sound Blaster FM synthesizer and to an external synthesizer simultaneously.

Patch Map Name
> A different patch map table, which contains the assignments for the instrument numbers, can be activated for each channel. The selection of the patch maps relates to the corresponding tables of the Patch Maps option.

Active
> If this check box is enabled, the data of this channel are transmitted. Individual channels are deactivated by disabling the check box.

A number of setups are offered for the Sound Blaster card, communicating through the onboard FM synthesizer and through the sound board's MIDI ports.

To test the effects of changing setup, we changed the assignment and the activation of individual channels. The MIDI Mapper window must be closed after each change so the changes will be activated. The same file was played back each time with Media Player. We recorded the results using the Sound Recorder.

The files are in the \MIDI\MAPPER directory on the companion CD-ROM. Since we used Sound Blaster Pro to play the MIDI file, the setup table went through some modifications. You can listen to the results with the Sound Recorder.

File	Setup Table changes
PASSPORT.MID	MIDI file from Windows
MIDI1.WAV	Default setup
MIDI2.WAV	All channels assigned to channel 1
MIDI3.WAV	Channels 1-10 were deactivated
MIDI4.WAV	Only channel 16 was activated
MIDI5.WAV	Only channel 15 was activated
MIDI6.WAV	Only channel 14 was activated
MIDI7.WAV	Only channel 13 was activated
MIDI8.WAV	Only channel 10 was activated
MIDI9.WAV	Only channel 5 was activated
MIDI10.WAV	Only channel 3 was activated
MIDI11.WAV	Only channel 2 was activated
MIDI12.WAV	Only channel 1 was activated

This example makes it very easy to reconstruct the creation of a MIDI file. When individual instruments must be changed, the advantage of using MIDI files becomes obvious. In this case, the MIDI file is edited with a sequencer program so a new instrument is output through the appropriate channel. These kinds of changes are impossible with WAVE files.

It's also possible to vary the tonality of a MIDI file significantly by changing the table.

Changing the Patch Map Table

If you play a MIDI file on a synthesizer that has a different instrument assignment than the Microsoft MIDI standard, you'll probably get a completely different set of timbres from what you intended. If this happens, refer to the user's manual for the device to determine the appropriate assignments. The instrument numbers that are used must be re-mapped to the numbers for standard MIDI.

		MIDI Patch Map: 'AdLib'		
		1 based patches		
Src Patch	Src Patch Name	Dest Patch	Volume %	Key Map Name
0	Acoustic Grand Piano		100	[None]
1	Bright Acoustic Piano	1	100	[None]
2	Electric Grand Piano	2	100	[None]
3	Honky-tonk Piano	3	100	[None]
4	Rhodes Piano	4	100	[None]
5	Chorused Piano	5	100	[None]
6	Harpsichord	6	100	[None]
7	Clavinet	7	100	[None]
8	Celesta	8	100	[None]
9	Glockenspiel	9	100	[None]
10	Music Box	10	100	[None]
11	Vibraphone	11	100	[None]
12	Marimba	12	100	[None]
13	Xylophone	13	100	[None]
14	Tubular Bells	14	100	[None]
15	Dulcimer	15	100	[None]

OK	Cancel	Help

The Patch Map table

The Patch Map table consists of the following:

Src Patch (Source Patch Number)
> This column lists the 127 original numbers (patches). The entries in this column cannot be changed.

Src Patch Name
> This column lists the names of the instruments associated with the original numbers in the first column as they are assigned in the MIDI standards. You cannot change these names either.

Dest Patch
> This column lists the patch numbers sent to the synthesizer to generate the appropriate instrument. For example, suppose that you use a church organ under number 19 of the MIDI standard in a MIDI file. However, when you play this file through a synthesizer, you hear a trumpet instead of an organ.

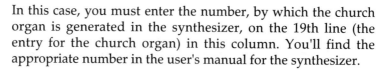

In this case, you must enter the number, by which the church organ is generated in the synthesizer, on the 19th line (the entry for the church organ) in this column. You'll find the appropriate number in the user's manual for the synthesizer.

Volume %

A separate volume can be specified for each instrument. A value of 100 is the default setting. A value between 1 and 200 can be used. Therefore, the melodic instruments could be brought into the foreground using volume control in the patch map table by increasing the volume. However, it's better to change the volumes of the instruments in the file yourself using a sequencer.

Key Map Name

You can use a different key map for rhythm instruments for each item or entry. However, by default no table is used. The list contains all of the tables that are contained in the Key Maps display.

We also tested the effects of changing instrument assignments in this case. A new Patch Map table was created to do this. For the appropriate patch maps to be used, you must select the appropriate patch map table in the fourth column of the active Setup table.

Several WAVE files are located in the \MIDI\MAPPER directory of the CD. These files demonstrate the effects of making changes.

Name	Description
PASSPORT.MID	Original MIDI file
MIDI20.WAV	Standard assignments
MIDI21.WAV	DestPatch values were set in the opposite direction (0 becomes 127, 1 becomes 126, etc.)
MIDI22.WAV	DestPatch values were each increased by 10 (10 becomes 20, 11 becomes 21, etc.)

Again, the changes are obvious. You can create interesting effects in this way. However, the changes aren't retained in the MIDI file itself and it's always time-consuming to change the MIDI maps. In this case, it's easier to use a sequencer program that lets you store the use of other instruments as a separate MIDI file.

Changing the Key Map Table

With the Key Maps option, you see the table for assigning rhythm instruments to the keys of a keyboard. The default assignments were listed in Section 8.1. If you don't use an external keyboard, you don't need to make any changes in the table.

Src Key	Src Key Name	Dest Key
35	Acoustic Bass Drum	47
36	Bass Drum 1	48
37	Side Stick	49
38	Acoustic Snare	50
39	Hand Clap	51
40	Electric Snare	52
41	Low Floor Tom	53
42	Closed Hi Hat	54
43	High Floor Tom	55
44	Pedal Hi Hat	56
45	Low Tom	57
46	Open Hi Hat	58
47	Low-Mid Tom	59
48	High-Mid Tom	60
49	Crash Cymbal 1	61
50	High Tom	62

MIDI Key Map: '+1 octave'

OK   Cancel   Help

The Key Map table

Src Key (Source Key)
> This column contains the numbers of the rhythm instruments as defined by the Microsoft MIDI standard. Values between 35 and 81 are used. The values cannot be changed.

Src Key Name (Name of the rhythm instrument)
> This column lists the names of the 41 instruments that correspond to the numbers in the first column. You cannot change these names either.

Dest Key (destination key)
> The key numbers, by which the MIDI keyboard generates the appropriate rhythm instrument, are entered here.

Chapter 9

Multimedia Presentations

A multimedia presentation, such as a Point of Sale (POS) or Point of Information (POI) presentation, is an excellent example of integrating various multimedia components. With multimedia presentations, information can be displayed impressively. From a run-time demonstration to an interactively controlled information system, multimedia presentations always have an impact.

Presentation Components

You can easily create your own multimedia presentations. However, the appropriate components must be available. The amount of animation, sound, graphics, text, and images in a presentation depends on the information that you want to present.

It's also important to know how the individual components will be received before using them in a presentation. The following is an overview of the individual components.

Generally you can create components or use existing libraries. In any case, you should know which file formats are supported by your presentation program.

In some cases, you can convert existing files into other formats.

Speech and Sound Effects

You can easily use recorded speech or sound effects in your presentation. However, even relatively short sound pieces require large amounts of disk space.

See Chapter 4 and 5 for more information on:

*   Sound recorder and WAV files

See Chapter 5 for more information on:

*   Voice editor and VOC files

Music

If you want to add background music, use a MIDI file to do this. A MIDI file plays longer than a Wave file and uses much less storage space.

See Chapter 8 for more information on:

*   Midisoft Studio and MIDI files

*   Sequencer Plus and MIDI files

Text

Many presentation programs contain their own text functions. You can also create text slides with graphics programs and include them in a presentation.

See Section 9.4 for more information on:

*   Paintbrush   Clipboard/PCX/BMP files

Graphics

Graphics and diagrams can increase the effectiveness of your presentations. A diagram is often much more powerful than several pages of text. Graphics can also be used as background images during the presentation.

See Section 9.4 for more information on:

*   Paintbrush Clipboard/PCX/BMP files

*   Excel Clipboard

See Section 6.5 for more information on:

*   Handling PCX/TIFF/BMP/GIF files

Hardcopy

Screen displays (or portions of them) can be used in the presentation by saving and manipulating them with print key programs.

See Section 6.1 for more information on:

- Windows
- Paintbrush
- Screen capture
- SCR/PCX files
- Clipboard/PCX/BMP files

Photographs and Images

If photos or images are included, either as background or as primary presentation data, a scanner can be used to store them as graphic files.

See Chapter 6 for information on scanner programs and TIF files.

Video and TV

Images that have been saved on videotape can be digitized and saved as graphics using a video overlay card. Three-dimensional objects and images from television can also be captured with a video camera and saved in a file with an overlay card.

See Chapter 6 for more information on:

- Video Blaster   TIF/BMP/PCX files
- Screen Machine   TIF/BMP/TARGA/BMP/PCX files

Animation

Animation sequences make multimedia presentations truly "multimedia." Templates captured by animation programs represent movement on a series of frames. These programs can also create completely new animation sequences.

See Chapter 7 for more information on:

- Animator   FLI files

- 3D Studio   FLI files

Before you use a presentation program, become familiar with its commands. This will give you an idea of the program's capabilities.

The next step is to create a script. The sequence of the presentation must be assembled step-by-step and tailored to the capabilities of the program. When a script has been created, converting files to run in the program is much faster when you've already planned the next effect.

While you're creating the script, consider such factors as colors, fonts and type faces.

In this chapter, we'll demonstrate how to use some multimedia presentation programs. It's a quick overview of procedures you can use to create your own multimedia presentation.

9.1 Creating Presentations With MMPLAY

The Sound Blaster card provides a simple but fairly powerful presentation program that can be used to create your own multimedia presentations.

Combines animation and sound files

MMPLAY.EXE combines animation and sound files with a series of commands and functions. You can also include audio CDs. By using just a few tricks explained in this chapter, you can get quite a lot out of this program.

To create a presentation with MMPLAY, use the following components:

- Sound   .VOC Creative Labs format (See Chapter 5)

- Music   .CMF

- Music   Audio CD function call

- Animation   .FLI Animator/3D Studio (See Chapter 7)

Example files used in this chapter are located on the companion CD-ROM in the \PRESENT\MMPLAY directory.

Setting up and Starting the Presentation

Each presentation follows a script. This script, which is an ASCII file, contains commands and functions that are executed in the specified order. The script file can be created using any text editor, such as EDIT.COM or EDLIN. Some commands require certain parameters that must follow the command.

Spacing between the command and its parameters isn't specified, so commands and parameters can begin at certain screen positions to provide a better overview. You can use empty lines to subdivide groups of commands that belong together.

```
Command1        Parameter1
Command2        Parameter1        Parameter2
Command3

Command4
Command5        Parameter1

Command6
```

When you save the text file, .ACT is the default file extension. You can use any extension, but other extensions must be explicitly entered.

Preparing to start

Script file name   When you run the presentation, you'll be prompted for the script file name. Therefore, when you create a presentation, ensure that all components are located in the same directory. This makes handling the file names in the script file easier, since otherwise full path names must be entered in the script file. However, if necessary this option is available.

```
MMPLAY EXAMPLE.TXT
```

If you used an alternate extension, the script file extension must be entered here. Usually, the MMPLAY.EXE file is located in \SBPRO\MMPLAY directory after installing Sound Blaster Pro software. To create a new presentation, create a new directory. Copy all the necessary files, along with the script file, into the new directory. The presentation is called from this directory by entering the path when running the MMPLAY.EXE file.

```
C:\SBPRO\MMPLAY\MMPLAY EXAMPLE.TXT
```

> This method maintains a better overview of individual presentations. The previous presentation can run much faster if you use an appropriate batch file, especially when you include CMF files in the presentation.
>
> To use CMF music files in the script, the FM driver SBFMDRV.EXE, normally located in the directory \SBPRO, must be loaded before calling MMPLAY.

The batch file appears as follows:

```
C:\SBPRO\SBFMDRV
C:\SBPRO\MMPLAY\MMPLAY EXAMPLE.TXT
C:\SBPRO\SBFMDRV /u
```

The final call to the FM driver removes it from memory.

Interrupting a presentation while it is running

To interrupt the presentation before it ends, press Ctrl + End. The presentation interrupts after completing the current sequence and returns to DOS. You cannot continue from the point where the presentation was interrupted.

A presentation runs in a special screen mode. This mode uses a resolution of 320 x 200 pixels and 256 colors. By using .SCREEN 0, you can delete the screen during the presentation and the existing mode is maintained. If you use .SCREEN 1, the screen is also deleted but the original VGA mode is activated.

Creating A Presentation

Tips on how to write a script file

Commands and parameters can be written in upper or lowercase characters. If the files are in the same directory as the script file, you don't have to enter a path. File extensions aren't entered either, since file formats are assigned to specific commands. Commands automatically use standard suffixes, as listed earlier in this section (CMF, VOC, etc.).

Commands are identified by an initial period. If the period isn't encountered, the presentation will stop at the line with the unknown command and an error message will appear.

Since the construction of the script file is now clear, we can begin working on a presentation. Open any editor and enter the following lines:

```
.volume    master     100 100
.vout      classic
.aplay     rotate
```

Copy the CLASSIC.VOC and ROTATE.FLI files from the companion CD-ROM into the MMPLAY program directory (or into a separate directory).

Save the file using the name DEMO.ACT, in the appropriate directory, change to that directory and start the presentation by entering:

```
MMPLAY DEMO.ACT
```

A classic melody should now be audible and a continuous animation sequence should be running. When the animation sequence ends, the music continues. This occurs because .APLAY indicates continuous execution of the animation sequence, while .VOUT plays the VOC file once. The animation can be interrupted by pressing Ctrl + End, since it is the last command to be executed.

To use artificial music (i.e., music created with an FM chip and the Sound Blaster Pro card), you must save this music in CMF file format, then run them using .PLAY.

CMF files

CMF files are a type of MIDI file. Unlike regular MIDI files, CMF files contain instructions for playing, as well as instrument definitions for FM chips in the Sound Blaster card. They cannot be played by all MIDI machines; they can be used only with the Sound Blaster cards. The advantage of using these files is that, with an instrument editor, the sound of the instruments can be optimized for the sound card.

Shareware products exist for converting CMF to MID files, WAVE files to VOC files, and other format conversions.

Regulating the volume

The volume of the music is controlled with .VOLUME. Each output channel is entered separately, as are the volume of the right and left stereo channels. The following options are available:

.VOLUME	VOICE	0-255 0-255
.VOLUME	LINE	0-255 0-255
.VOLUME	CD	0-255 0-255
.VOLUME	MUSIC	0-255 0-255
.VOLUME	MASTER	0-255 0-255

Matching sound files and animation sequences

To time musical output to match an animation sequence, limit the animation sequence with a loop. Experiment (or calculate) how often the sequence plays before the music ends. Try the following solution for this script file:

```
.volume       master 100 100
.vout         classic
.repeat       5
.aplay1       rotate
.end
```

Running through the loop

Instead of .APLAY, .APLAY1 was used. So the animation sequence played only once. The loop was executed five times with .REPEAT 5. Finally, .END limited the functions included in the loop. With loop commands, several functions can be repeated.

The animation now ends with the music. There was some luck involved in getting exactly five repetitions to take the same time as the VOC file.

If you use another sequence or another sound file, the animation and the music may no longer be coordinated. Because of this, there is a more exact procedure for matching a sound file to an animation sequence.

Adding markers to a sound file

Several sampling programs, such as the Voice Editor 2, enable a user to add markers to a sound file. The Sound Blaster driver CT-VOICE.DRV, which is called by MMPLAY every time, can recognize and read these markers.

An animation sequence then stops exactly when the driver encounters the mark while playing the sound file. To add a marker to a sound file, load it into the Voice Editor 2.

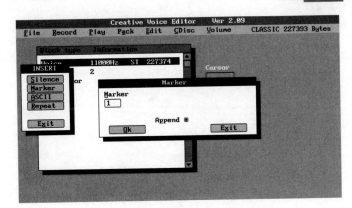

Marking in the Voice Editor

Select **Edit/Insert** to open a dialog box. Select (Marker). In the next
dialog box, type ①(Enter). Click on the "Append" button and click
(OK). A mark of value 1 is added to the file.

To make the ending smooth, edit the file further. Marks can be
placed at any position in the file with the Voice Editor. To place a
mark, you must split the file at the desired location. Select the
block, in which you want to insert the mark, and select
Edit/Modify. This opens an editing window. Click on the desired
position in the waveform. A vertical line appears. Select
Option/Split Block.

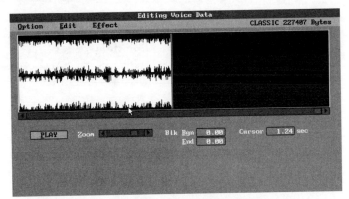

The block is now split in the editing window

Everything to the right of the line is now moved to a new block.
Now exit this screen. Click on the marker and drag it up one row,
then drag the pointer back to the marker. A double-border should
be surrounding the marker. Select **Edit/Move**. This moves the block
to the proper location.

Select **File/Save** and exit the Voice Editor 2.

You can refer to the marker by name in the script file. Change the script file as follows:

```
.volume         master 100 100
.vout           classic
.sync           v1
.aplay          rotate
```

The .SYNC command reads markers for .APLAY. The parameter "v" represents the VOC file. To use marks in a CMF file instead, use the "f" parameter instead of "v". Immediately after the parameter, specify the desired mark (in this case, enter "1").

The animation is now synchronized on the mark in the sound file. When the mark is reached, the animation repetition ends and returns you to DOS.

Matching music to animation

To stop the music immediately after completing the animation sequence, use .STOP. This command can be executed as soon as the animation ends:

```
.vout           classic
.aplay1         rotate
.stop           v
```

The V parameter interrupts output of a VOC file. The F parameter ends output of a CMF file (with .PLAY). In the previous example, the animation sequence is executed only once. Using loops, the process can be repeated several times:

```
.vout           classic
.repeat         3
.aplay1         rotate
.end
.stop           v
```

Interrupting a presentation

Another effect can be created by starting an animation when the driver encounters a mark in a sound file. In this case, the screen remains dark as threatening sounds emerge. By waiting until a specific mark is reached in the music, the animation appears as a climax of the presentation.

```
.vout     classic
.wait     v1
.aplay    rotate
```

The .WAIT command is used here. It operates in the same way as
.SYNC. Animation isn't executed until the sound driver encounters
the mark. This command not only starts animations, but works on
all subsequent output commands.

Controlling the presentation

A presentation is usually intended not only to influence, but also to
inform. Information must remain on the screen for a certain period
of time, or until a specific event has occurred.

Since MMPLAY plays only animation sequences, and is unable
to display graphic files, informative text pages must be
displayed indirectly.

You have several ways to do this:

Text Animation

FLI files can be created using Autodesk Animator or 3D Studio (see
Chapter 7). Display a text page during a presentation by creating
it with one of these programs and saving it as an FLI file, without
adding any movement. Using MMPLAY, the text starts as an
animation sequence, but since no movement was assigned, the text
remains motionless on the screen. The command list could appear
as follows:

```
.aplay1    text
.pause
```

Waiting for a keystroke

An animation sequence that displays a text page using .PAUSE
remains on the screen until a key is pressed. If you want subtle
fading in and out, create two text animations. In the first file, the
text is faded in. In the second, it is faded out. Control is
maintained with the keystroke:

```
.aplay     text1
.pause
.aplay     text2
```

Executing DOS commands

Using .EXECUTE   Another method is to use .EXECUTE. Any DOS command can be executed during a presentation. For example, you can call a graphic display program to display a text. By using the animation player AAPLAY.EXE, which is discussed in Chapter 7, you can display picture files in GIF (Graphic Interchange Format). These images could appear during a presentation.

```
.vout       rooster
.execute    aaplay merlin1.gif
```

Now the AAPLAY program determines how long the display appears on the screen. Control it in a separate script file (Chapter 7). The presentation continues after the DOS command is executed.

If you play large music files before executing a DOS command, you may encounter memory problems. In this case, the DOS command isn't executed properly.

Using Audio CDs

During a presentation, you can access any audio CD in the CD-ROM drive to add background music to the animation. MMPLAY uses two control commands to do this. Since, in this case, there are no marks, a piece from an audio CD can be limited only by length of time.

To match the music output to an animation sequence, measure the length of the sequence and adjust the loop. For example, if the animation lasts five seconds and you want to run through it six times, cancel the music after ending the animation loop with the following commands:

```
.volume     CD 100 100
.playcd     4 0 30
.repeat     6
.aplay1     demo
.end
```

The animation sequence plays six times with the loop. Each sequence takes five seconds. So running it six times will take 30 seconds. Using .PLAYCD, the fourth track (parameter 4) of the CD is played between 0 and 30 seconds, which covers the necessary total duration of 30 seconds.

To end the presentation with a piece of music from an audio CD, use a delay loop. If .PLAYCD is the last command in the script file, the presentation's execution is immediately interrupted after executing the command. For example, to end a presentation with a minute of Mozart from track 6 of a CD, use the following commands:

```
.playcd     6
.delay      6000
```

In this case, the program sequence runs without a time limit after the seventh repetition. The time limit is set by .DELAY, which is controlled by a parameter showing time in hundredths of a second. One second would have a value of 100; one minute a value of 6000, etc. The .DELAY command can also be used with other functions.

To stop the program sequence at a certain point during the presentation, use the .STOPCD command.

Slow fades

If you're using a sound file or a piece of music from an audio CD and want to interrupt it at a specific point, the ending would be very abrupt. If, as in the previous example, you want to end the presentation with a few bars of Mozart, a softer ending would be important. This can be done with a combination of .VOLUME and .DELAY commands:

```
.volume     cd 100 100
.playcd     6
.delay      6000
.volume     cd 90 90
.delay      20
.volume     cd 80 80
.delay      20
.volume     cd 70 70
.delay      20
.volume     cd 60 60
.delay      20
.volume     cd 50 50
.delay      20
.volume     cd 40 40
.delay      20
.volume     cd 30 30
.delay      20
.volume     cd 20 20
.delay      20
.volume     cd 10 10
.delay      20
.volume     cd 0 0
.stopcd
```

You can create a fade effect by lowering the volume. Appropriate delays are created with .DELAY 20; otherwise the music ends abruptly.

The .STOPCD command should be used only if additional commands must be executed after the music ends.

The following table lists all the commands:

Fade Effect Commands				
Command	**Par 1**	**Par 2**	**Par 3**	**Effect**
.SCREEN	0, 1			Screen control 0 cancels the screen without changing the mode, 1 erases the screen and switches to VGA mode.
.VOLUME	MASTER	0-255	0-255	Volumes of left and right channels. If only one is indicated, both channels are set to this value.
.VOLUME	VOICE	0-255	0-255	Volume of VOUT for left and right channels. If only one is indicated, both channels are set to this value.
.VOLUME	LINE	0-255	0-255	Volume of line input signal in the left and right channels. If only one is indicated, both channels are set to this value.
.VOLUME	CD	0-255	0-255	CD volume for left and right channels. If only one is indicated, both channels are set to this value.
.VOLUME	MUSIC	0-255	0-255	Music volume (for CMF files) in the left and right channels. If only one is indicated, both channels are set to this value.
.VOUT	VOC file			Plays the given VOC file.
.APLAY	FLI file			Repeatedly plays animation from Autodesk Animator or 3D-Studio format.
.APLAY1	FLI file			Plays animation in Autodesk Animator or 3D-Studio once.
.PLAY	CMF file			Plays a music file.
.PLAYCD	t	s	e	Plays track t of the inserted CD from second s to second e.
.EXECUTE	Program	Program parameter		Executes a given DOS program.

Fade Effect Commands (continued)			
Command	**Par 1**	**Par 2 Par 3**	**Effect**
.REPEAT	Repetitions		Repeats all commands until the following .END, the given number of repetitions.
.SYNC	Vn		Synchronizes the following animation in the script and stops repeating when the n mark is found in the VOC file.
.SYNC	Fn		Similar to the above command, but the synchronization is set on marks in a CMF file.
.WAIT	Vn /Fn		Waits to execute the next command until the n mark is reached.
.STOP	V / F		Stops output of a VOC file (V) or CMF file (F).
.STOPCD			Stops output of a CD.
.DELAY	1/100s		Delays execution by the given value in 1/100 seconds.

9.2 Q/Media for Windows

Q/Media for Windows by Quorum Computer Corporation is a complete authoring system that lets you create multimedia shows with video, animation, graphics, and audio. The uses for Q/Media are limited only by your imagination.

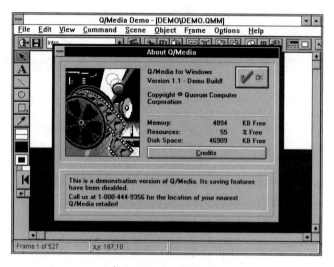

Q/Media for Windows

Q/Media imports presentations from popular Windows presentation packages such as Microsoft PowerPoint, Aldus Persuasion, Harvard Graphics for Windows, and Lotus Freelance for Windows. You can add power to your presentations with animation, sound, and video.

A special demo version of Q/Media 1.1 for Windows is included on the CD-ROM with this book. You can experiment with the tools we describe and watch a self-running demo created with Q/Media.

Before you can experiment with the endless possibilities offered by Q/Media 1.1, you must install it onto your hard drive from the companion CD-ROM. This version will require about 6 megabytes of storage space.

To install Q/Media, place the companion CD-ROM in your CD-ROM drive, then select **Run** from the **File** menu. Enter the path for your CD-ROM drive and the name of the Multimedia Mania interface program, CDSTART in the text box as shown below.

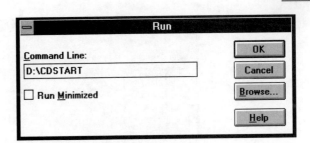

Starting the Multimedia Mania user interface

When the Multimedia Mania interface is displayed, open the **Sampler** menu and select the **Q/Media** menu item. You can do this by pointing and clicking with your mouse or by pressing Alt + S to open the **Sampler** menu and Q to select the **Q/Media** menu item.

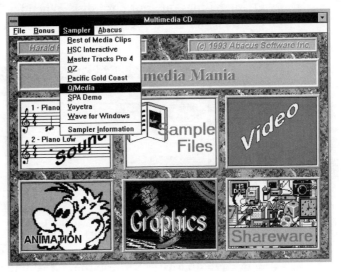

Selecting Q/Media from the Sampler Menu.

An information dialog box will inform you that you are about to install Q/Media. Select OK and then choose Open from the File Selector as shown below:

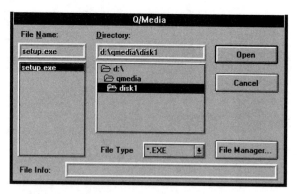

Selecting the Q/Media SETUP program

Follow the prompts from the setup program to install the
Q/Media files on your hard disk. When the installation process is
complete, a new group will appear in the Program Manager. This
is the Q/Media group.

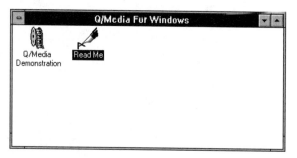

The Q/Media Group

Select the Q/Media Demonstration icon to start the self-running
demo and Q/Media. To stop the self-running demo, just press the
Esc key. After watching the demo and reading this section,
experiment with the many features of Q/Media. Remember, this is
a demo version and you won't be able to save anything you create;
contact Q/Media to purchase a full-featured version (use the
special coupon at the back of this book).

If you have any questions about Q/Media, call Q/Media customer
support at (604) 879-1190.

The Q/Media self-running demo highlights   many features

Q/Media doesn't require a laborious scripting process or time consuming file conversions. Files from popular Windows, DOS, and Macintosh applications can be used in your multimedia presentations.

The full-featured version of Q/Media includes over 10 Meg of multimedia files and an assortment of templates designed for business, training, and entertainment.

It's easy to create to create special effects with the graphical timeline. You can easily determine when each object will appear on the screen. Objects can be repositioned and synchronized simply by clicking on them with your mouse, then dragging them along the timeline.

Q/Media includes a complete set of drawing tools for creating diagrams, arrows, and text. Online help on any feature is available by selecting **Help** from the Menu bar.

Other useful features include:

• Align and Size Tools
   An align tools palette has been added to the **View** menu for easy access to aligning objects on the screen. Align and size menu items have also been included in the **Object** menu. The new tools let you automatically space objects evenly in a given area, align objects, and increase and decrease them to conform with other selected objects.

- Nudge Features
  Objects can be moved in small increments by holding down the
  [Shift] key and using the cursor keys.

- Automatic Text Sizing
  The text titling tool now will automatically resize text when
  you drag the size box.

- Selecting and moving multiple objects around the stage
  In previous versions only multiple draw objects could be moved
  around the stage.

- Support for High Color Cards
  Q/Media supports 4,8,16, and 24-bit color cards. When you are
  dragging and dropping images, animations, or video files onto
  the stage in 16 and 24 bit modes, Q/Media will no longer
  prompt you to merge or replace the palette. The color dialog
  has also been updated to allow for the selection of more than
  256 colors.

Q/Media is one of the easiest to use authoring systems, but it does
not sacrifice power for convenience.

9.3 Presentations With Authorware Star

Authorware Star is a component of the Sound Blaster Multimedia
Upgrade Kit, and can be found in other multimedia kits. This
Windows application was designed as a system for creating both
sequentially run and interactively controlled presentations. You
don't need any programming experience to work with Authorware
Star. Building a presentation is an object-oriented, mouse-
controlled process.

The files used in this section are located in the \PRESENT\ASW
directory on the companion CD-ROM. The presentation was
created with a resolution of 640 x 480 in 256 colors. The complete
animation is located in the file MERLIN.ASW. If you don't have a
complete version of Authorware Star, there is a stand-alone
version named MERLIN.EXE that will start from Windows.

Creating A Presentation

The first step in creating a presentation is to consider the direction you want the presentation to take. We prefer writing down the steps needed, then basing the Authorware Star application on these steps.

The MERLIN.ASW file performs the following tasks:

Task	Effect
Step 1:	Sound effect welcoming the user
Step 2:	Play first drum vamp (repeated solo)
Step 3:	Display Merlin graphic
Step 4:	Display WELCOME TO... title
Step 5:	Display MERLINMEDIA title
Step 6:	Wait for three seconds
Step 7:	Clear Merlin graphic from scene
Step 8:	Clear WELCOME TO... title
Step 9:	Play second drum vamp (repeated solo)
Step 10:	Move MERLINMEDIA title
Step 11:	Display animated bird
Step 12:	Move animated bird across screen
Step 13:	Clear bird when it reaches final coordinates
Step 14:	Display final screen

Once you add the basics as previously stated, you can add different features to the ASW file, such as wipe effects.

Program Preparation

After starting Authorware Star

An "Open File" dialog box appears. You can choose an existing file and edit it. To create a new file, click on the [New...] button and type a name in the "Filename:" text box (for this example, we entered TEST.ASW). Click [OK].

A new design window is created. The vertical line in the left border of this design window is called a flowline—this is where you place your presentation sequence.

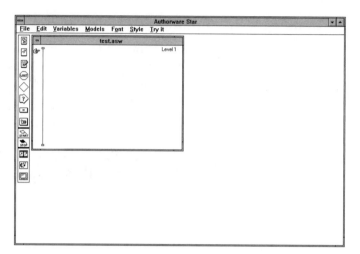

The Authorware Star design window

An icon palette, containing icons for individual commands, is located on the left side of the screen. These icons have the following meanings:

Icon	Name	Description
🗒	Display Icon	Placing texts and objects
↗	Animation Icon	Assign movements
🗒	Erase Icon	Delete objects
(WAIT)	Wait Icon	Insert pauses
◇	Decision Icon	Make decisions
[?]	Interaction Icon	Request input
[=]	Calculation Icon	Perform calculation
🗺	Map Icon	Define branches
START	Start flag	Starting point of an area
STOP	Stop flag	End point of an area
🎬	Movie Icon	Insert animation
🔊	Sound Icon	Insert sound file
💻	Video Icon	Control CD player

The icon palette

You can use these icons to create a presentation. These icons, which represent interactions (components), are arranged sequentially on the flowline by dragging the desired icon from the icon palette to the flowline. When you double-click on an icon lying on the flowline, either a dialog box or a presentation window appears. This allows you to add more specific options for the objects.

Screen Arrangement

The screen display should be specified first. There are several ways to display the presentation window. The size of the window can be either full screen size or it can be adjusted manually.

Using the full screen size helps focus people's attention on the presentation, but assigning a specific resolution may solve other problems.

Select **File/Setup...** to open the "Setup" dialog box.

Setup
Title:
test
Wait button title:
Continue
Presentation window size:
VGA (640x480) ⬇

Presentation window style:
☒ user menu bar   [Color:]
☒ title bar

When user returns to the file:
○ resume   ◉ restart at beginning

[Video device...] [OK] [Cancel]

Arranging the presentation window

When selecting a display type, remember that VGA (640 x 480) and EGA (640 x 350) create problems if you're using a computer running Windows with a resolution of 800 x 600 pixels.

The window can be expanded to full screen size, but the presentation is moved into the upper-left area of the screen.

However, a presentation with a resolution of 800 x 600 pixels and 256 colors running on a computer that can display only 16 colors in normal VGA mode displaces individual objects. Also, full-saturation colors appear with a superimposed grid pattern.

The least problems occur if you arrange the settings for the graphics card under which the presentation will run. These options are controlled from the "Presentation window size:" drop-down list box and the "Presentation window style:" group. We selected VGA 640x480 for the size. Click on (Color:) to select a background color (we selected a light to medium gray). Once you've selected these factors, click (OK).

Transferring The Script

The steps outlined in the script are performed as follows:

Using the mouse, drag a Sound Icon from the icon palette to the flowline. When you release the mouse button, the icon appears at the top of the flowline with the title "Untitled". Double-click this icon to open the "Load Sound" dialog box.

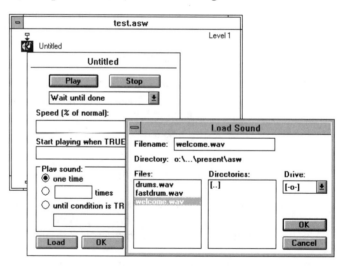

Loading a sound file

Load the WELCOME.WAV file, located in the \PRESENT\ASW directory of the companion CD-ROM. This file contains a short greeting. Make sure that "Wait until done" is selected in the drop-down list box. This indicates that no other actions are performed until this file is executed. Click (OK).

You can edit the text to the right of each icon. Click on the word "Untitled" to the right of the sound icon you just inserted. The entire text is selected. Now type "Welcome statement as sound effect" and press (Enter).

STEP #2
Play first drum vamp (repeated solo)

Once this resonant voice says, "Welcome to MERLINMEDIA," we can add some music to accompany some visual information. Drag a sound icon from the icon palette to a point below the first icon on the flowline. Double-click the placed icon to open the "Load Sound" dialog box.

Load the DRUMS.WAV file, located in the \PRESENT\ASW directory of the companion CD-ROM, and click (OK). To repeat the rhythm, click on the "Until Condition is TRUE" option button.

We still don't need to add a condition, since we'll replace the rhythm with new background music that lasts until the end of the presentation.

To play this sound while Authorware Star displays information on the screen, select "Concurrent" from the drop-down list box and click (OK).

Click on the "Untitled" icon title. Type "First drum vamp" and press (Enter).

STEP #3
Display Merlin graphic

To display the first image of the presentation, drag the display icon to a point on the flowline below the two sound icons. Double-click this icon to open the presentation window and the graphics toolbox. Select **File/Import Graphics...**. The following formats are supported:

Format	Extension
Bitmap	BMP
Bitmap	DIB
Metafile	WMF
Paintbrush	PCX
Macintosh	PIC

Select the MERLIN1.PCX file from the \PRESENT\ASW directory and click (Paste). Increase the size of the magician by moving the selection handles at the corners of the graphic.

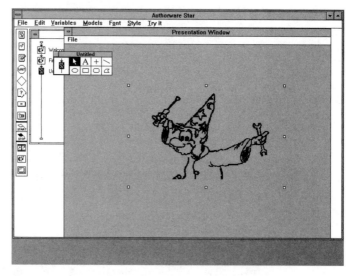

Adding the first graphic image

The graphics toolbox contains the usual tools for creating lines, circles, angles, etc.

Assigning Fading Effects

Once you've placed Merlin's picture in the presentation window, select **Edit/Effects...** You can display an image in different ways. Select "Venetian Blind" from the "Effect:" drop-down list box and click (OK).

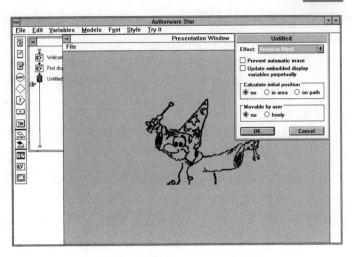

Many effects are available

To close the presentation window, click on the close box in the upper left corner of the graphics toolbox.

Click on the text to the right of the display icon and type "Display Merlin". Press ⟨Enter⟩.

STEP #4

Display WELCOME TO... title

Now we want a text to appear in the same screen as Merlin. Drag a display icon to a point on the flowline below the "Display Merlin" icon. Double-click this icon to open a presentation window.

Select **Edit/Color...** and the color purple. Select **Font/Modified Helv**, then **Style/Plain**, **Style/Left justify**, **Style/18**. Click the text icon in the graphics toolbox and click on the presentation window. Type "Welcome to the World of...". The graphics toolbox text function can also be used to edit texts.

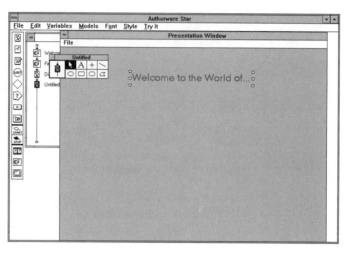

The first text

To make the background of the text box the same as the background color of the window, select **Edit/Modes...** and click on the "Transparent" option button. Click OK.

Now, we want the text to fade in, instead of simply popping onto the screen. Select **Edit/Effects...** again. This time select "Build to Right"; the text is now displayed from left to right. Click on the graphic toolbox's close box to return to the flowline.

STEP #5

Display MERLINMEDIA title

Add another display icon. Select **Font/Arial**, **Style/Center**, and **Style/48**. Select the text icon and type "MERLINMEDIA" in the text window. Select each character and assign each character a different color using **Edit/Color....** Click the pointer icon and select the MERLINMEDIA text. Select **Edit/Effects...** and use "Barn Door Close".

Click on the text to the right of the display icon and type "MERLINMEDIA title". Press Enter.

STEP #6

Wait for three seconds

Drag the wait icon to a point beneath the display icon created in step #5. Double-click the wait icon you just placed on the flowline. The "Wait Options" dialog box appears.

Wait Options

Wait until:
- ☐ mouse click
- ☐ keypress
  - ☐ Show prompt

Time limit: 3 seconds

☐ Show time remaining

[OK] [Cancel]

Setting delays

Disable all three check boxes in the "Wait until:" group. In the "Time limit:" text box, type "3". Click OK.

Click to the right of the wait icon and type "Three-second delay". Press Enter.

STEP #7

Clear Merlin graphic from scene

Drag two erase icons onto the flowline. Double-click the first erase icon. Click on the Merlin graphic. Select "Venetian Blind" from the "Effect:" drop-down list box and click OK.

Click on the "Untitled" text to the right of the first erase icon and type "Clear Merlin". Press Enter.

STEP #8

Clear WELCOME TO... title

Double-click the second erase icon. Click on the "Welcome to..." text. Select "Remove to Left" from the "Effect:" drop-down list box

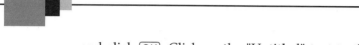

and click OK. Click on the "Untitled" text to the right of the first erase icon and type "Clear WELCOME TO... title". Press Enter.

STEP #9

Play second drum vamp (repeated solo)

Drag a sound icon to a point on the flowline beneath the remaining icons. Double-click the sound icon and load the FASTDRUM.WAV file. Click OK. Select "Concurrent" and "until condition is TRUE". Click OK.

Click on the "Untitled" text to the right of the sound icon and type "Second drum vamp". Press Enter.

STEP #10

Move MERLINMEDIA title

To move the "MERLINMEDIA" text from the bottom of the screen to the top, drag an animation icon onto the flowline. The animation icon doesn't actually create true animation—it just moves the selected object.

There are several ways to indicate movement of an object across the screen. You can indicate a starting point and an end point, or draw a route along which the object must be moved. To move the text, use the starting point/ending point method.

Moving To New Positions

Double-click the animation icon. In the dialog box that appears, enter "2" in the "Seconds:" text box, click on the "time" option button, and select "Wait until done" in the drop-down list box. The upper-right border of the window should say, "Fixed Destination".

If it doesn't, click the Change setup... button and select that mode. Drag the "MERLINMEDIA" title from the bottom of the window to the top of the window. Click the Replay button to see the movement. Click OK.

Click on the text to the right of the animation icon and type "Move MERLINMEDIA title". Press Enter.

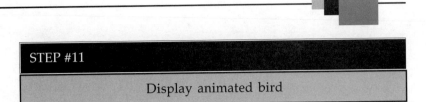

This step calls a "real" animation into the application. Drag a movie icon to the point on the flowline below the animation icon. Double-click the movie icon to open the "Import Movies" dialog box. Select the BIRDRT.MOV file. Click (Preview) to check out the movement and click (Load).

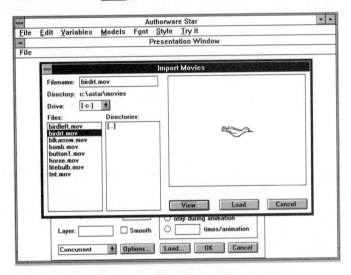

Previewing animations

Place the bird at the left edge of the screen. Make sure that the "Concurrent" list item is selected, and that the "repeatedly" option button in the "Play movie:" group is active. Click (OK).

Click on the "Untitled" text to the right of the movie icon and type "Display animated bird". Press (Enter).

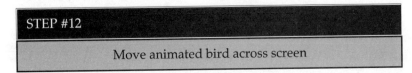

Assigning A Flightpath

Now we want to move the bird from the left to the right, in a fixed path rather than a straight line. Drag an animation icon to the bottom of the flowline icons and double-click it.

Click the (Change setup...) button. Select the "Fixed Path" option button and click (OK). Type "5" in the "Seconds:" text box. There you can choose a direction of motion. Use the Fixed Path option to enter a fixed route. The dialog box for the Animation icon opens. Click on the bird and, in the center of the image, a small triangle, called a "point," appears.

Drag the point to the right edge of the screen. The path you followed is now indicated by a line. Now, double-click on the point you first created. The point changes from a triangle to a circle point. Move the mouse pointer to different locations on the line and click. This produces a series of circle points. Clicking on any location in the line and dragging the point up or down, you can create an interesting flightpath. The following is a sample flightpath we drew for TEST.ASW.

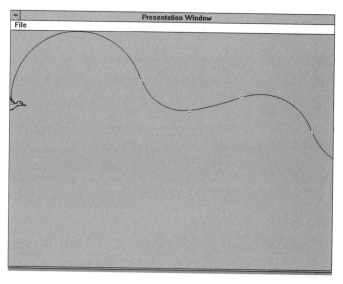

The completed flightpath

Click (Replay) to view the flightpath. Click (OK) to accept the movement.

Click on the "Untitled" text to the right of the animation icon. Type "Move animated bird across screen" and press (Enter).

STEP #13

Clear bird when it reaches final coordinates

To delete the bird after its flight has ended, drag an erase icon to the set of flowline icons. You may have to Maximize the presentation window first, as you dragged the bird off-screen. Double-click the erase icon, click on the bird, make sure "Effect:" states "None", and click OK.

Click on the "Untitled" text to the right of the erase icon. Type "Clear bird when it reaches end coordinates" and press Enter.

STEP #14

Display final screen

The final step is to display a page of information. We created the final screen as a PCX file. Drag a display icon to the bottom of the flowline. Double-click the display icon. Select **File/Import Graphics....** Select the BOOK.PCX file and click OK.

The last page

Move and size the graphic using the selection and editing handles.
Now select **Edit/Effects....** Select "Mosaic" in the "Effect:" drop-
down list box and click OK.

Click on the "Untitled" text to the right of the display icon. Type
"Final screen" and press Enter.

You've just completed an Authorware Star application. You can
save this file, and compare it to MERLIN.ASW found on the
companion CD-ROM.

Running Presentations

The **Try it** menu contains commands that control an application.
Start a run-though at any time during the development phase to
check completed steps. Most effects assigned to an object are
immediately executed after the object is selected.

To start the presentation, select **Try it/Run**. The display appears
in the display mode you selected at the beginning. Use **Try
it/Pause** to interrupt a sequence and use **Try it/Proceed** to resume
execution.

Mark an area in the presentation by setting a start flag and a stop
flag. These symbols are also taken from the icon palette and
placed at appropriate positions on the flowline.

This is useful for testing longer presentations by running through a
small sequence. In this case, start the presentation from the start
flag by selecting **Try it/Run**.

Executable Files

An Authorware Star application can be saved as a stand-alone
runtime module. This is an EXE file that can be executed on any
Windows device.

Therefore, you can pass on your presentation to Windows users who
don't own the presentation program.

Make sure TEST.ASW is in memory. Select **File/Package....** Click
[Save File & Package]. A dialog box appears, defaulting to the name
with an .EXE extension. Click OK to create an executable file from
TEST.ASW.

9.4   An Excel Slide Show

The Microsoft Excel 4.0 worksheet application can create slide show presentations. The "slides" are normal screen graphics displayed, on command or in a timed sequence, one after the other.

Special fading effects make the transitions between the individual slides more interesting. Sound files in Wave format (e.g., created using Sound Recorder) can be included in the presentation and tend to create a casual presentation atmosphere.

> Any information that can be imported through the Clipboard can be displayed in an Excel presentation. This means that you're not restricted to Excel data; any data from Windows and DOS environments can be added. However, existing graphics cannot be imported directly; you must always use the Clipboard.

Excel Presentation Components

To create a slide show, open the SLIDES.XLT template file. This file has several special buttons. You can use these buttons to paste slides, specify display options, and run the slide show.

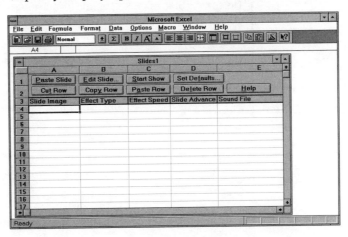

Creating a template for the presentation

The first two rows of the template contain buttons for creating and changing the presentation. The third row contains a column header describing the individual slides and their parameters. Graphics are pasted into the slide show worksheet starting at row 4.

Slide Image

This cell contains a smaller version of the graphic. Therefore, you can look at the graphics in the first column, in the sequence in which they are displayed, to check them.

Effect Type

This cell shows which effect is used for the transition to the next graphic. The following options are available:

Option	Function
None	Shows the next graphic without a transition.
Cut through Black	Erases the screen between the two graphics.
Fade	Fades in the next graphic.
Vertical blinds	Makes transition to next graphic using vertical venetian blind effect.
Horizontal blinds	Makes transition to next graphic using horizontal venetian blind effect.
Box in/Box out	Makes transition to next graphic using a box effect similar to a photographic iris.
Dissolve...blocks	Graphic dissolves in blocks.
Wipe...	Original graphic is wiped from screen from border, revealing new graphic.
Corner...	Original graphic is wiped from screen from corner, revealing new graphic.
Uncover...	Original graphic slides off the screen, uncovering new graphic.
Cover...	New graphic slides onto the screen, covering over original graphic.
Scroll...	Original graphic scrolls off the screen, while new graphic scrolls onto the screen.
Diagonal...	Original graphic is wiped from screen diagonally, revealing new graphic.

After making your selection you can preview the effect. Some effects contain a direction indicating the side of the screen where the movement should begin.

Effect speed

Enter the length of time the effect should take to be completed in this cell. Use a value from 1 to 10, but remember that these aren't seconds. Experiment until you find an optimal value.

Changing slides

This cell contains the graphic control option. Choose between "Manual" (change when the mouse is clicked) or "Timed" (displaying each slide for a specific number of seconds).

> Use manual control if the slide show contains text tables and graphics. Timed presentation is used for self-running demos.

Sound File

If you have a sound card in your computer (Sound Blaster, Pro Audio Spectrum and compatible products), you can assign sound to the graphics. Any sound file in Wave format (*.WAV) can be used. Enter the file name, including the complete path, in the cell.

Inserting slides using the Clipboard

All graphics included in the presentation are displayed on the entire screen. Appropriate graphics are needed for the presentation. Under Excel and Windows, there are several ways to create graphics. Most likely you'll want to display Excel worksheets or charts, which is possible by converting them into graphics.

As we mentioned, all graphics are added to the template using the Clipboard. To use Excel documents, you must copy the information to be displayed into the Clipboard.

> Before you copy graphics to the clipboard, save them as separate Excel files (*.XLC). If you want to use the same graphic later, you cannot access information deleted from the source file unless it has already been saved.

Information from Excel

After creating a chart in a worksheet, double-click the chart to place the chart in its own window. Select **Chart/Select Chart** to select the entire chart, then select **Edit/Copy** to copy the chart to the Clipboard. Now it's in the clipboard as a bitmap graphic format.

To place worksheet information in the Clipboard, select part of the worksheet and select **Edit/Copy**. Open the Clipboard Viewer application. If **Format/Auto** is selected in the Clipboard Viewer, only the Excel cell references appear (e.g., Copy 1R x 3C). Make sure **Format/Bitmap** or **Format/Picture** is selected. This will display the selected range as a graphic.

In bitmap format the table displays the same font and format as in Excel. Worksheet column and row labels are also copied to the clipboard. However, the grid pattern can be distracting. Avoid these effects by disabling the "Gridlines" check box, or the "Row & Column Headings" check box, found in the **Options/Display...** menu item. Then the table converts to a bitmap in its most optimal form.

	A	B
1	Multimedia Mania Co	
2	Category	Company
3	Animation/Video	
4		Autodesk Inc
5		Animating Apothecary
6		Creative Labs
7		FAST Electronics US
8	MIDI	
9		Passport Designs Inc
10		Sparks Media
11		Twelve Tone System

Using information from the screen as a graphic image

Creating slides

A presentation conveys many types of information. Speakers can use slides (text overlays that contain written information) to summarize or emphasize important points. You can integrate graphics with text in these slides.

The easiest way to create slides is by using Windows Paintbrush. This application provides a complete palette of font and graphics options.

A slide created with Paintbrush

As we showed earlier in this section, an Excel worksheet can be copied as a bitmap image, for placement in a presentation.

To copy slides from Paintbrush, select **View/Zoom Out**. Select the Pick tool and select the entire graphic. Pressing Ctrl + Ins copies the selection to the Clipboard.

DOS Applications

To use information from DOS applications in a presentation, use the Clipboard. Start the DOS application from Windows and prepare the information you want to display. Press Alt + Spacebar to display the DOS application as a window in Windows. Press Alt + Prt Sc to move the entire DOS screen to the Clipboard as a graphic.

Creating a presentation

To create a slide show, select **File/New...** and select "Slides" from the "New:" list box. Click OK to open the "Slides1" template. You can paste graphics beginning at cell A4.

There are several example Paintbrush files, called SLIDE1.PCX, SLIDE2.PCX, etc., as well as Clipboard files of the same names, on the companion CD-ROM in the \EXCEL\SLIDES subdirectory.

Switch to the Program Manager and load the first Clipboard file into the Clipboard. You can paste any graphic on the Clipboard.

If a graphic is in the Clipboard, click on cell A4 and click on the Paste Slide button. A dialog box, in which you can make entries regarding the display effects, appears.

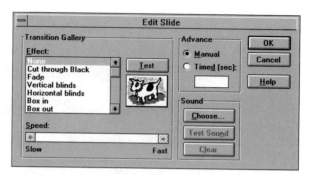

Many options create interesting presentations

We discussed individual components in the previous section. After you choose an effect, preview it on a small graphic by clicking the [Test] button. The speed at which the effect is displayed can be set with the "Speed:" scroll bar.

Control Between Graphics

In the "Slide Advance" column you control the transition between two graphics. Choose between "Timed" and "Manual". If you use "Manual", the slide changes to the next graphic on a key stroke or mouse click. If you choose "Timed", you enter a value in seconds, indicating the length of time that should pass before the next graphic.

Finally, in the "Sound File" column, you can paste a Wave file for playback when the slide is displayed. Double-click the respective "Sound File" cell to play back the sound file.

After you've made all the settings and confirmed them, this information is added to the template on a new line. Now click on cell A5 and paste in another graphic. Save the template regularly to prevent data loss. The entire template is saved with the .XLS file extension.

Running the presentation

To display the presentation, load the desired presentation template. Click on the [Start Show] button. The following dialog box appears:

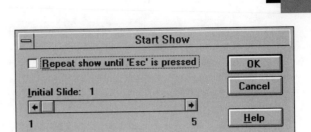

Determining the course of the presentation

Use the "Initial Slide:" scroll bar to determine which graphic should start the presentation. Usually this is the first graphic. Occasionally, when you're testing a presentation, you may not want to watch the entire presentation. In these instances, you can start at the fifth graphic, for example.

If you enable the "Repeat show until 'Esc' is pressed" check box, the presentation will be repeated continuously. Interrupt it by pressing Esc. When the presentation is interrupted, another dialog box appears.

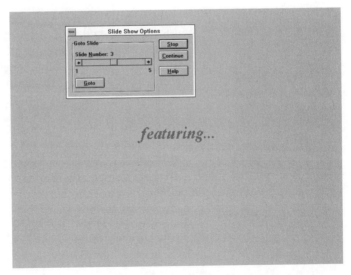

Controlling the presentation after an interruption

You can either continue the presentation or stop it completely. To continue, start it at any graphic by moving the scroll bar. If you use timed display, the template automatically appears on your screen when the presentation is complete.

Editing presentations

A presentation template can be edited at any time. You can edit the order of display or the display parameters. You can also add or delete graphics from a presentation.

Changing display parameters
There are two ways to change a graphic to another effect or a different time setting. First, you can go to the cell you want to change and edit it by clicking Edit Slide...

> Enter the new value in the appropriate cell to change only the speed of the effect or the display time. Exception for the first cell of each row, you can add or change the contents of the cells.

Changes to the rows
Changes that affect the order of the presentation, such as deleting or adding graphics, always apply to the entire row. A series of buttons enable you to work directly on an entire row, even if only one cell is marked.

Use Cut Row, Copy Row and Paste Row along with the Clipboard. These commands work like cutting, copying or inserting areas in a worksheet. They let you change the order of display by cutting a line and inserting it at a new position. When inserting, other lines are moved down. Use Delete Row to completely delete the active row from the template.

If you frequently use the same effects, such as synchronous display, set default display parameters. Default values are always used when you insert or edit graphics. Click on Set Defaults... to access the "Set Defaults" dialog box. Set the desired options and click OK to confirm your settings.

You'll find the complete presentation in the PRESENT\EXCEL subdirectory under the file name SLIDES.XLS.

9.5 PictureBook Professional

PictureBook Professional by Digithurst provides a multimedia development system that, like Fuzzy Logic, builds connections among images, texts, video sequences, animations, sound, and speech, using rules derived from artificial intelligence.

This program is an object-oriented authoring system. As its name implies, the application structure resembles a book. A PictureBook application consists of a "book," containing several display pages. Each page can be assigned objects.

Several objects, such as texts, still photos, video sequences, animations or digital sound files can be arranged on the display page. Each object can call actions, make connections to other pages and activate them.

With PictureBook, you can create multimedia information systems on an object-oriented basis. Even without programming knowledge, it can manage and control live and static images, texts and sound, as well as arrange the user interface.

A demo application is located in the \PRESENT\PICTURE directory on the companion CD. Install it by running INSTALL.BAT from a DOS prompt.

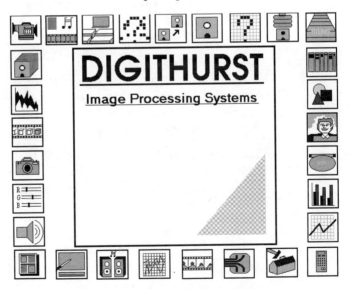

Main screen for the PictureBook Professional demo

How PictureBook Professional Works

Since an application created with PictureBook Professional is clearly structured, planning this type of application is easy. PictureBook Professional structures its multimedia applications as follows:

The author creates a Book (PictureBook) in which users can browse or search for specific information.

Each page in the Book can be different from any other page. Different multimedia components appear as objects on the page. The author determines the appearance, position and function of these interactive elements.

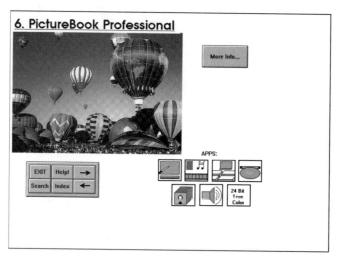

A typical PictureBook Professional page

Author mode and User mode

The system works in two modes: Author Mode, with editing functions, and User Mode, in which the editing features are disabled. In Author mode, a page with different objects is created.

Each object can be a live or still image, a text, a graphic or a WAVE file, or an animation. In User mode, users can interactively call desired information pages, but no changes can be made (as system designers intended).

Picture disk and video recorder control

With PictureBook Professional Software, an author can control all media, such as images, sound, text, animation, speech or film sequences, as objects, without any programming knowledge. Visual input from media, such as picture disks or video recorders, can be controlled via PictureBook in various ways.

The functions that are usually found on a remote control are available. This includes fast-forward, reverse and slow-motion replay. However, the appropriate hardware is needed.

In versions after 1.4, the MCI (Media Control Interface) is supported by Microsoft. This means that all sound cards (e.g., Sound Blaster) that support the Microsoft interface are directly accessible.

Similarly, animations in FLI file format (from Animators or Animator Pro) can be included in PictureBook applications because they also support MCI.

Chapter 10

Authoring Systems and Hypertext

An authoring system is usually a development environment that creates applications. These applications are either interactive learning programs or multimedia databases.

The advantage of a good authoring system is that you don't have to have any programming knowledge to use it. You design the display and all actions are mouse-controlled and object-oriented. The result is an application that's easy to use.

User access to interactive tutorial applications and multimedia databases is no longer entirely sequential (as in a book). Instead, cross-references are used to access all levels. This programming technique, called Hypertext, can be created with authoring systems. These systems are used to create interactive learning programs and multimedia databases.

Depending on structure, these two application types can overlap and become indistinguishable. An interactive tutorial learning program is usually attached to a database. So, by adding a few control commands, a database can become a learning program.

In this chapter, we'll discuss the features of these applications and explain how to create these applications.

10.1 Learning Program Structures

The main difference between applications and presentations is interaction (see Chapter 9). When a user can control the program path, depending on the program's features, he/she can interact with the program.

Interaction   Interaction is especially important in interactive tutorial learning programs. Transmitting knowledge is much easier if the user can interact with the program through dialog boxes. A self-running presentation manages information, assuming that all the users have the same level of knowledge and the same ability to comprehend information.

Interactive tutorial programs are constructed so that the starting point can be chosen by the user. Information can be played as often as necessary, until the user is ready to move to another topic. Test questions or practice exercises also help the user understand the information. A user can also cancel the program at any time and resume working at the same place later.

Teaching techniques and lesson plans also need to be considered when planning a multimedia presentation. If you yield to the temptation of using flashy graphics and following technological advances, these may lead to developing complicated networks of non-related topics, or to using test questions that don't relate to the main ideas in the lesson.

Keep in mind that multimedia can make learning much more interesting when animations and sound files are used to explain the topics. Also, a quiz is more fun when set up as a game.

If the information is presented in a poorly structured interactive tutorial program, an experienced user or a system developer can adjust the information. The amount a user can work with the program independently depends on the quality of the program. If the user can't interact efficiently and easily with the tutorial program, then the tutorial program won't be effective.

Interactive tutorial programs are useful for training employees in various fields. Purchasing good interactive tutorial software can save companies money on training and continuing education classes, which often are very expensive. Interactive training programs can provide employees with the latest information quickly, without requiring time away from the job.

Unfortunately there are some disadvantages to using learning programs at work. In the workplace, there are too many interruptions, such as telephone calls and requests from colleagues. Any learning program requires concentration to be effective. This means no interruptions. Because of interruptions, many workers will rush through the program. The end result is that more time and money is required. Employees have to ask others for help and sometimes use the program several times before they understand it completely.

Interactive tutorial programs are often components of standard programs. For example, the tutorial programs for Excel, Word for Windows and PageMaker are excellent. Look at these programs to get an idea of the components and the teaching concepts behind their arrangement.

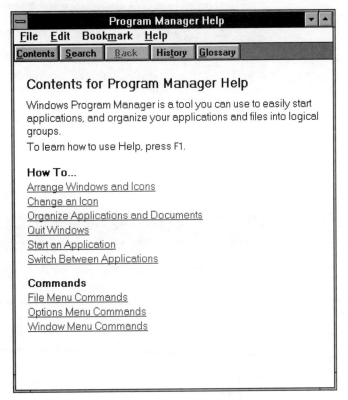

Even Windows includes a tutorial program

A learning program's development can be divided into seven steps:

STEP #1

Conceptualization

First, decide which concept will be used and how it will be constructed. The concept must be suitable for the information that will be taught.

STEP #2

Task Folder

The task folder contains a detailed list of the client's needs. You should determine what previous knowledge can be assumed, which topics should be included, and the projected budget for the project. Also determine possible designs for the learning program.

STEP #3

Collecting materials

Since learning programs always contain practical materials, you must begin collecting the materials you'll need. Company-specific topics could use photos and videos from the company. Information from manuals or other documentation can also be used. Sound files, such as alarms which indicate errors in an actual process, must be recorded or imitated (if creating the error is too costly).

STEP #4

Script

As we mentioned in our discussion of animation and presentations, writing a script is extremely important. This step is essential when creating a learning program because the teaching concept must be determined in the script. For example, you must decide which topics to present first, how to connect different themes, which test questions to use and in how much detail the material will be covered.

STEP #5

Production

Next, you must decide which hardware will be used. For example, can you use CD-ROM disk drives, picture disks or compression boards? Perhaps you're restricted to a hard drive and a VGA screen. Depending on the components, the display outlined in the script may not be possible technically. Consider these concerns when you're creating the script.

STEP #6

Software development

The next step is to convert the script with an authoring system. The files selected from the collected materials are connected and possible interaction points are added at appropriate places.

It's also important to make the program easy to use and crash-proof, especially by new users who panic if they encounter errors by pressing the wrong button. The result could be that the user never wants to see the program again.

STEP #7

Distribution

When the program is completed, it must be distributed to the users, or installed by the system administrator or a data processing professional.

Although the program should be easy to use, information on how to use the program should still be provided.

It's also important to receive feedback about the program. You should ask the users for their comments about the program. This will help you determine whether the program fulfills its purpose and how it can be improved.

10.2 Multimedia Database

Less demands are placed on a multimedia database than on an interactive tutorial program. With multimedia databases, the desired information must be accessed quickly. Also, supporting information must be available through cross-references.

Animations, video sequences and sound files enhance multimedia database capabilities beyond conventional printed sources, such as encyclopedias. Although these sources also contain cross-references, you must look them up manually.

A path through a multimedia database may lead to many levels. Each level has additional cross-references. For example, if a person is mentioned in an explanation of a topic, additional information about this person can be accessed with a mouse click. Then, when a button is pressed, the person's voice can be played from the speaker.

After retrieving the information, you can return to the original topic and continue from there. With the Hypertext technique, the pages of information appear to be on a stack on top of each other. When a page is selected, it moves to the top. Usually there is a complex network of other, equivalent, levels.

Using point and click for selecting topics is another unique feature. For example, if a map is displayed, information about mountains, cities, etc. can be accessed by clicking on the appropriate positions in the map.

In the following illustration, from the Space demo program included with ToolBook from Asymetrix, you would click on the space suit to learn more about its components.

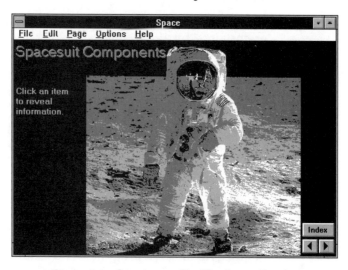

Space travel using a ToolBook application

When you're creating a multimedia database, first you must determine what terms or information will be on the main level. Then you must determine what secondary information will be included for each term.

An excellent example of this is the structure used by HyperGuide, the multimedia help system component of the Multimedia Extension for Windows 3.0. Windows 3.1 users will not have this example, but may follow the description in the following section.

If you're using Windows 3.1 and have the Microsoft Multimedia Development Kit, you may examine HyperGuide by opening Help. Then Select **File/Open...** and change to the CD-ROM directory which contains the CD-ROM for the Microsoft Multimedia Development Kit.

Then change to the HYPER directory and select HGCD.HLP. The next section describes the results and subsequent options available after opening this file.

Using HyperGuide

The information in a multimedia database is usually available on a CD. Program software is installed on the hard drive for speed and configuration reasons.

HyperGuide includes four main groups. If you click an icon for a group, a list of additional topics appears.

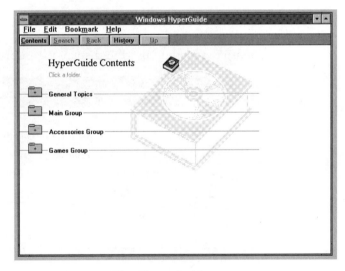

The HyperGuide screen

To display a topic, click on its label or icon. The changed appearance of the mouse pointer indicates the action that can be performed.

When the mouse pointer has changed, for example, into a hand, you can click on an area underneath the mouse pointer and activate it. If you click on **Accessories Group**, a selection menu, in which additional themes are displayed as icons, appears.

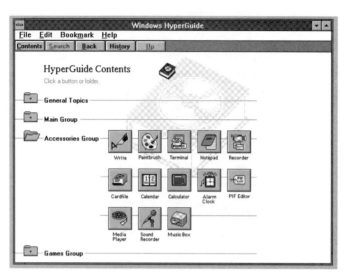

Sub-topics are displayed as icons

To move to another level of the selected topic, click on an icon. Another window lists additional possibilities related to the topic. Choose the method used to display the information:

Type	Function
Quick Look	Short, keyword-oriented examination
Concept	Basic work methods
Procedures	Step-by-step explanation of use
Commands	List of all commands and functions
Keys	List of keyboard functions
Tools	Explanations of individual components

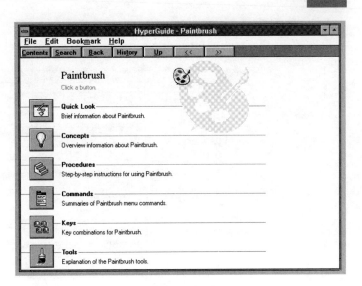

Various topics

Up to this point, selections were based on a search for specific information. By continuing in this way (step-by-step in HyperGuide), you'll eventually, awkwardly, reach the appropriate topic. This occurs when looking for the solution to a specific problem.

We'll use a Paintbrush example to explain this. To learn the procedures for Color eraser (in HyperGuide it's called Color Eraser), the following steps are necessary:

• Choose Accessories Group

• Choose Paintbrush

• Choose Tools

• Choose Erase

By using the icons for Paintbrush and Eraser, even a beginner can quickly reach the desired page. An index search is faster, because the path to the desired information is usually more direct. Use **Search** to activate a dialog box in which you can enter the search word.

There are several ways to access the search word from there. One helpful function is a corresponding list display after each input letter. For example, when you enter an "E", the entries beginning with "E" are placed at the beginning of the display. If you type the next letter of the search word, a more detailed search begins.

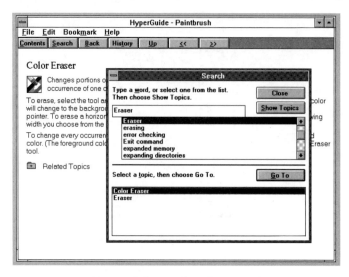

Successful searches for a topic

Searching For Information

Term is known

If you know the exact label for the function, enter it in the input field. The term will be marked in the list field.

Partial term is known

In the Color Eraser example, you could also search for the term "Eraser". This entry is sufficient since the index search provides both the normal Eraser and the Color Eraser for selection.

Using cross-references

Related information can be connected with cross-references. You can use cross-references to access different levels:

Related topics
These topics are displayed in green and underlined. When you click this kind of cross-reference, the related topic is displayed.

Definitions
After being activated, definitions or explanations for certain key words are displayed in a small window. This type of information is displayed in green letters and underlined with a dotted line.

Graphic cross-references

In this case, the cross-reference appears as a graphic icon. True Hypertext applications can include cross-references to additional information in the graphic.

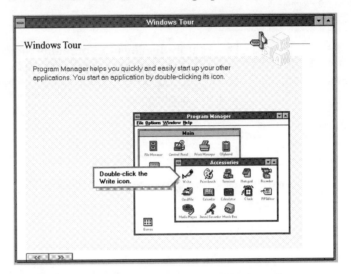

Areas in graphics can be activated

Control Buttons

A HyperGuide window contains several buttons. By pressing them, you can move between individual pages.

Contents

This button leads to the HyperGuide main menu, regardless of your current location.

Search

This button opens a dialog box for an index search. When an entry in the topic list is selected, the appropriate topic entry is displayed.

Back

This button displays the previous page. The order of pages depends on the entries in History.

History

This button lists all the topics that have been called since HyperGuide was started. By using this feature, you can repeat a topic quickly, without going through the cross-references again.

If you want to mark a specific page for later reference, use **Bookmark/Define....** An entry is made in the **Bookmark** menu. You can select it at any time to access the appropriate page.

This button displays the previous topic within the term. For example, if the help text for **File/Copy** is currently displayed and you activate <<, the help text for **File/Cut** will be displayed.

This button moves you to the next command in the topic.

Inserting Your Own Comments In Help Texts

The HyperGuide window contains brief and precise explanations of many topics pertaining to Windows. The entire system is based on an extensive collection of help texts, which are located on the Multimedia Extension CD.

Select **File/Open...** to load the normal help files available for Windows applications. Help files have the file extension .HLP.

These help files aren't text files. So, they cannot be read by normal text editors. However, it's possible that an explanation is incomplete or didn't include all the information you need.

Perhaps you want to add a few tricks or shortcuts you've discovered that may help other users. This can be helpful if many users have network access to HyperGuide.

Each topic can include an Annotation (comment) that's inserted into the help text. These annotations aren't inserted randomly on the page. Instead, they are stored on their own level.

A paper clip symbol appears in front of a topic header that has an annotation. The paper clip is treated like an underlined term and can be opened by clicking on it with the mouse.

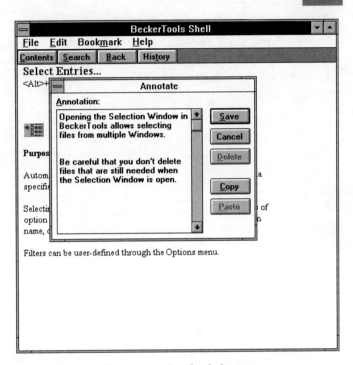

Comments in the help text

A comment can be assigned only to a topic heading. To create an annotation, choose the page that will contain the comment. Select **Edit/Annotate...** to activate a dialog box, in which you can enter any text. Press [Save] to save it to the hard drive (since you cannot save to a CD).

Removing Annotations

Each page can contain only one annotation. To erase a comment, choose **Edit/Annotate...** again and press [Delete]. The paper clip and the annotation disappear.

10.3 Using Authorware Star

In Chapter 9 we explained how to create a presentation with Authorware Star. In this section, we'll show you how to add interactive control. With these procedures, you can create learning programs and multimedia databases.

We'll explain the basic procedures. You can use equivalent command sets with other authoring systems.

The program is controlled by buttons that are always displayed on the screen. Special information is arranged according to topic. This information can be called only from a specific page. To do this, click on an icon or a keyword.

As an example, we'll create a short Windows tutorial that contains three topics. Each topic consists of three pages. You can always access the controls by choosing from the button bar. For example, to repeat a topic or exit the program at any time, press a button.

The files used in this example are available in the \LEARNER\ASW directory on the companion CD-ROM. If you don't have Authorware Star, you can display this presentation by activating the appropriate EXE file.

Program Conception

Regardless of the methods used by the authoring software, you must determine the structure of the learning program. If you're not sure of the structure, you'll quickly become confused and frustrated while you're creating the program.

Basically, you should create an event tree that shows the steps involved in the program, at various levels. The following exercises and examples refer to our example program LEARNING.ASW (LEARNING.EXE). This program is stored ready-to-run on the companion CD-ROM.

To create a preliminary event tree, concentrate on the basic structure. For the moment, don't worry about the opening music, effects, etc. The following structure was used for this example program:

Level 1	Level 2	Level 3
Main menu	Topic 1	Main menu
		Page 1
		Page 2
		Page 3
		End
	Topic 2	Main menu
		Page 1

Level 1	Level 2	Level 3
		Page 2
		Page 3
		End
	Topic 3	Main menu
		Page 1
		Page 2
		Page 3
		End
	End	

Level 1
> The first level is displayed after starting the learning program. In this level, choose one of the three topics or end the program.

Level 2
> The three topics are located on a second level, independent of one another. From here, select an individual page, end the program or return to the main menu to select another topic.

Level 3
> The third level contains individual pages of information. If you want to activate areas on the page with a mouse click or keyboard entry (for example, to play a sound file or show a graphic object), additional levels can be created.

Using levels ensures that the program has an effective structure and helps the author maintain an overview of the program.

However, use levels carefully. It's possible to lose sight of the overall program if the information is nested too deeply.

Converting In Authorware Star

When you want to create a new file, the upper-right corner of the window displays the flowline and a description of the present level (Level 1).

Use a map icon, placed on the flowline, to create a new level. If you add a map icon to the second level, you create access to the third level, etc.

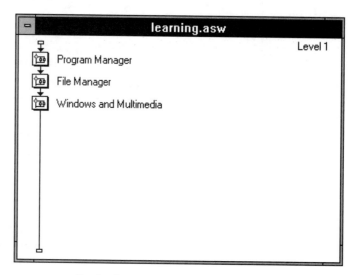

Beginning to create the application

Before a selection can be made, an interactive query must appear so that the user can make a decision. Two icons are used:

Decision Icon
    A selection is made on the basis of a specific decision.

Interaction Icon
    A branch to the appropriate level is made on the basis of a user selection.

Our example uses the interaction icon, which is placed on the flowline. The next step assigns selection options. Since we provide three topics, three map icons are placed directly under the interaction icon.

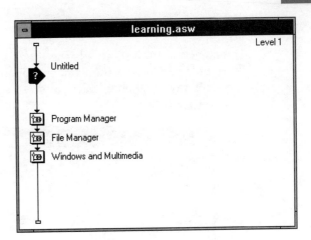

Selecting the interaction type

After the first map icon is placed, a dialog box, containing possible interaction types, appears. Since we want to use button selection, click on the "Pushbutton" option button. A small symbol above the map icon indicates the selected interaction type.

After placing the icons, the connections between the icons and the flowline are automatically generated. Change the text for the map icon. Select a description that refers to the appropriate selection. By using clear connections, you'll maintain an overview of the function of each symbol.

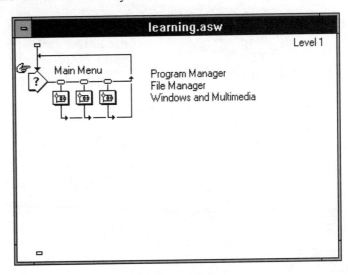

Complete selection

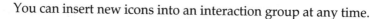

You can insert new icons into an interaction group at any time.

To enable a button that ends the program, add a calculation icon. By double-clicking on the icon, you open a window in which you can enter any function or calculation. To send an end command, use the Quit() function.

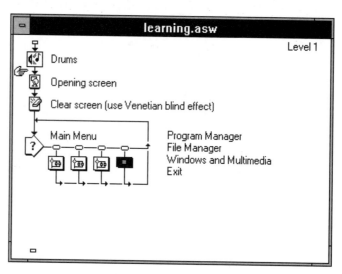

The end function is set

The selection menu is almost complete. To finish the first level, add a sound file to the beginning of the flowline and create a starting page using a Display Icon. Mark all elements on the starting page with **Edit/Select all** and connect them with **Edit/Group** to a single group. This makes it easier to delete all the elements on the starting page with one stroke.

Continue On Key Stroke

In this case, the starting page should be displayed until either a key is pressed or a mouse click occurs. (Don't forget to indicate this somewhere on the page.) Place a wait icon under the starting page and activate it by double-clicking.

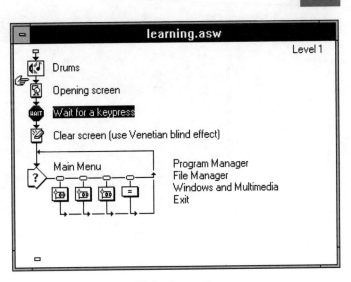

Wait for action

Enable the "keypress" and "mouse click" check boxes. Disable the "Show prompt" check box; otherwise a button will appear in the starting window.

The last icon in the start procedure is an erase icon. Add it under the wait icon. To define the object to be erased, click on the grouped elements on the starting page.

This will remove all elements from the starting page and leave room for the main menu display. The erase procedure can be changed to make the next image fade in more gently.

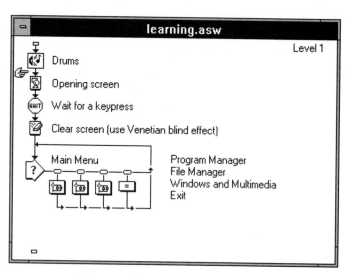

The complete starting procedure

Creating The Main Menu

In the next step, you create the main menu. When you double-click on the interaction icon, a window, which contains several selection options, is displayed.

We're interested in only the "Erase interaction:" drop-down list box. Select the text "after each entry". This indicates that, after selecting an interaction function (in our example, a button), the main menu will be deleted. This occurs so that it doesn't cover the subsequent display. Click on [OK - Edit display] to design the main menu.

This demonstrates the strength of Authorware Star. The button you previously created is already in the selection window, including its label. Move this button to the desired position and enhance the menu with texts or added graphics.

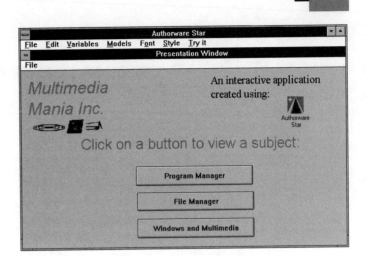

The main menu is created

Now the first level is created. If you let the program run to this point, you still cannot make a selection, but you can end the program by pressing (End).

Creating Individual Topics

Next, an individual page of information for one of the topics must be created. Our example contains three pages for each topic. Within a topic, you should be able to call any individual page, return to the main menu or end the program.

The same elements are used here as in the main menu. To create the first topic, open a new level by double-clicking on the map icon.

Use a display icon first. It should contain the first page of the topic. Then place an interaction icon. To return to the main menu, add a calculation icon to the interaction icon.

As with the interaction icon, click on the "Pushbutton" option button again. The three individual pages are indicated as map icons because the topic contents are deleted before showing the actual page of text.

The end of the sequence is a calculation icon with the Quit() function. The Restart() function for the calculation icon returns you to the starting page of the program.

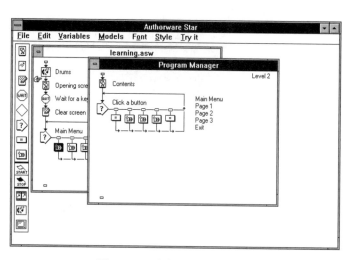

The second level is defined

By double-clicking on the interaction icon, you can create a title page for the available topics. Arrange the buttons at the bottom of the screen. The topic header should be displayed in the upper area.

The elements of this screen should be displayed whenever you're in a topic. Therefore, select "upon exit" from the "Erase interaction:" drop-down list box. Then the menu won't be deleted until you exit the topic.

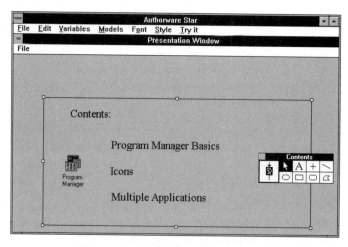

The control page for the first topic

Information that should appear only on the title page should be in a display icon. This information can indicate the information that's located on a certain page. All elements of this page should then be grouped so that they can be deleted together later.

The final step is creating the individual page. By double-clicking on the map icon for the first page, the third level is opened. This level contains an erase icon that can erase the contents and a Display Icon that contains the information on the page.

Copy Groups

Creating branches

After the first topic is completed, you must create branches for the next two topics. Since they have the same structure as the first topic, you can copy the complete group and simply insert the other topics. With this method, you must change only the labels and perhaps add some graphics. This method is much faster than creating groups from scratch. You should create the new topic pages after the group structure has been copied.

Activate the second level for the topic "The Program Manager". Choose **Edit/Select all** to mark all icons on this level. Copy the icons to the clipboard with **Edit/Copy**. Activate the map icon in the file manager and add the complete group using **Edit/Paste**. Repeat this step for the final topic. Now you simply must make the necessary changes to specific topics. Once you do this, the program is complete.

Special Effects

CHIMES.WAV file

You can add special effects to the program to make it more interesting. One way to do this is to accompany each click on a button with a sound. For example, we could use the CHIMES.WAV file.

This sound file must be added wherever actions are executed as a result of activating a button. This doesn't occur in the first level of the example program. If you select the [File Manager] button, you simply branch to the appropriate level.

The click must be heard before the topic contents are audible, to create a reference to the button. Add a sound icon in front of the first display icon and choose the file CHIMES.WAV. Set "Play sound:" to "one time".

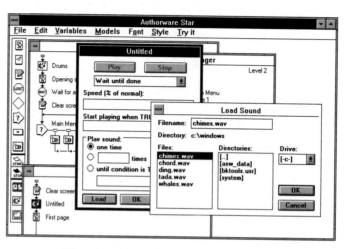

The click for the File Manager button

This means that the opening music stops after the button is pressed. If you want the music to continue playing, a new sound icon command must be added after the click. To add a click to the buttons within individual topics, you must insert the sound file into each level that contains a text page. The quickest way to do this is to copy the sound file onto the Clipboard and insert it into the appropriate levels.

Map icons

It's more difficult to use a button to execute a command contained in a function, such as the buttons used to end the program or return to the starting page. The calculation icons must be replaced with map icons. By using the map icon, you can reach a new level, in which you can place both the sound icon and the appropriate calculation icon.

If you change the icons in an interaction group, check the arrangement of buttons. Activate the outline by double-clicking on the Interaction icon and then edit the presentation window.

10.4 Using Hypertext with Microsoft Viewer

Microsoft ViewerViewer is one component of the Microsoft Multimedia Development Kit (MDK). It can create multimedia Hypertext applications. Viewer's screen and operation are identical to the Windows help system and HyperGuide, which was created with Viewer. This means that you can access Bookmark, Annotation and Keyword search.

Applications created with Viewer range from Help systems to extensive multimedia databases that include sound, animation and graphics files.

Building A Viewer Title

A Viewer title is a collection of pages (topics) that contain text, graphics or sound. A summary of all text appears in the title. Cross-references to other pages connect information via *Context Strings*. You've probably seen underlined single terms in the Windows help system. Cross-references are also displayed in green letters.

Information windows (popup windows) display information that's not displayed on a separate page (e.g., background information or the definition of a term).

Information windows are also used in the Windows help system. You can identify these windows by the dotted underlining and green writing.

A Viewer title is structured as follows:

Title	Page	Cross-reference
Info Window		
	Page	Cross-reference
Info Window		
	Page	Cross-reference

Using a mini-glossary, we'll show you how to create a title. For this purpose, we've created several pages of information, with cross-references, an information window, sound files and graphics.

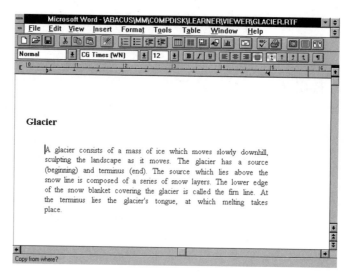

A geographical glossary

All examples used here are located on the companion CD-ROM in the \LEARNER\VIEWER directory. All components of the viewer runtime module are located in this directory (all DLLs).

Run SETUP.EXE, then open and examine the example file GLACIER.MVB during the following discussion. This will provide you with a point of reference even if you do not own Microsoft's MDK.

Creating Viewer Titles

The first step in creating a document is to create the title page. The document will hold many items with text information later: pointers on images, cross-references, display windows and sound files.

The file format is RTF (Rich Text Format). You should create the title page in Winword or some other word processor capable of saving text as an RTF file.

When files are formatted in this way, RTF formatting retains character formats and type styles.

Dividing The Page

Our example uses the first line of a page as a glossary; the actual text appears starting at the third line. To start a new page, add a hard page break by typing [Alt] + [I] [B] [P] [Enter]. Indent the main text with paragraph format and use various type styles as desired.

When you create pages, notice which texts will contain jumps or activate information windows. The following character formats must be added to these keywords:

Keyword	Formats
Jumps	Word must be double underlined
Info window	Word must be single underlined

The appropriate marks will be added later. The last lines of a page can also contain related topics. These entries should be marked as cross-references also, so the information can be called when needed. The text in the following illustration is located in the GLACIER.DOC file.

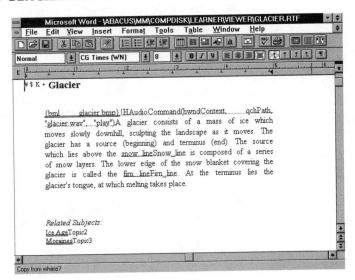

Basic page structures

Next, an information text window is created. The information can be attached to the rest of the text on its own page. Pages with information window texts aren't displayed in the Viewer again as separate pages. The data used here are located in the GLACIER.DOC file.

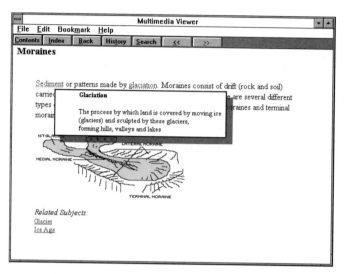

Displaying text in an information window

The text is now created. Unfortunately, you cannot indent the text; all titles are displayed as left justified. Titles displayed in the Viewer are always left justified. However, all other character fonts and styles are transferred.

Defining References

Pointers for jumps and cross-references and information windows must be added to the normal text information in the file and are generated when the application is compiled. Pointers are created as footnotes.

The following footnote symbols are used:

Symbol	Meaning
#	Defines a reference to a page as a context string.
K	Assigns a given number of keywords to the page. The index function can access this page through these keywords.
$	Topic Title defines a page header, which appears in the History window of Viewer.
+	Browse sequence defines the sequence for >> (Forward) and << (Back) buttons.

First a page must be assigned a context string (#) so that it can be accessed later using cross-referencing. The procedure is simple.

Place the cursor in front of the first keyword on the page (in our example, the word "Glacier") and select **Insert/Footnote...**. Click on the "Custom Footnote Mark:" option button and use the number sign (#) as the mark.

The footnote window opens. Enter a unique description that refers to the page following the first footnote entry, for example, "Topic1" (note that there is no space) or "Glacier".

Continue this procedure for the following pages.

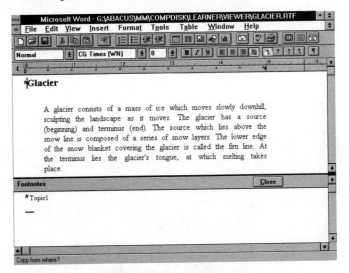

Footnotes as references

Footnotes for the index and page headers are generated in the same way. For keywords (K), enter all terms that access this page as footnote references.

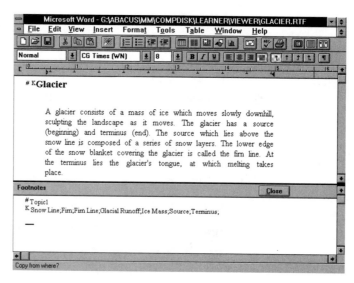

Indexes make searches easier

Setting The Page Browse Sequence

To set the Browse order of pages, use the "+" (plus) symbol as the footnote marker, then enter a term followed by a colon and a three digit number. For the number, enter numeric values in increments of 10. Then you can insert more pages later if necessary.

The following descriptions were used for the footnotes in the example application:

Footnote	Description
#	Topic1
$	Geography: Glacier
K	Snow Line; Firn; Firn Line; Glacial Runoff; Ice Mass; Source; Terminus;
+	Ice:005
#	Topic2
$	Geography: Ice Age
K	Mountains; Ice Age; Climatic Change; Shift in vegetation; Drop in Temperature;
+	Ice:010
#	Topic3
$	Geography: Moraine

Footnote	Description
K	Ground Moraine; Terminal Moraine; Lateral Moraine; Medial Moraine; Sediment;
+	Ice:015
#	Snow_Line
#	Firn_Line
#	Sediment
#	Glaciation

Marking Context Strings and The Information Window

To generate an information window, mark it as a keyword in a footnote. Activate the pages with an appropriate context string and text and place the cursor in front of the first keyword. Again, use the number symbol as the footnote mark and enter a unique description to access the information window.

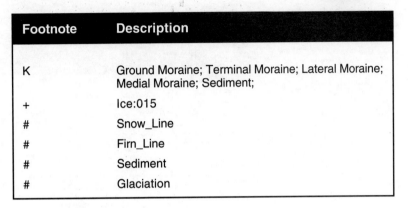
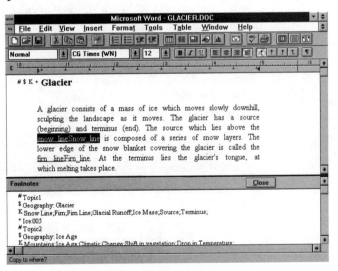

A reference to the information window

Terms that activate an information window must be underlined in the text. You still must create context references to the term on the page that contains the text of the information window.

Place the cursor immediately behind the underlined term and enter a label for the footnote in the information page. This term must be formatted as hidden text.

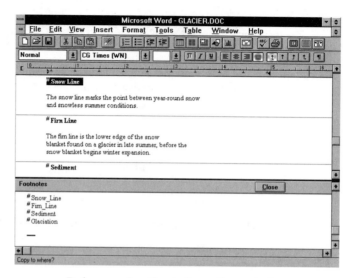

Reference for the information window

Depending on the screen setting in Winword, hidden formatted terms are displayed with dotted underlining. This establishes a connection to the pages.

Designating Cross-Topic Jumps

Terms for Cross-Topic jumps are double-underlined. Immediately after the term, enter the context string in hidden text which identifies the page references.

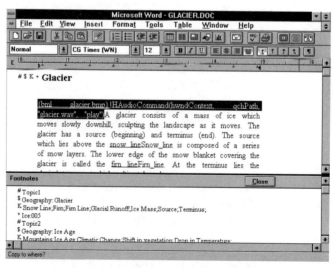

Now the Cross-topic Jumps are complete

Now the text page is complete, but the multimedia components are still missing. These components can be added as sound files, screen files or animations.

Using Sound and Screen Files

Image files use bitmap graphic BMP format. Sound files are bundled as two WAV files that were created using the sound recorder. These files aren't part of the text file. They can be called with a reference.

To add an image file, enter the following:

{bml	*file*.bmp}	Left justified
{bmc	*file*.bmp}	Centered
{bmr	*file*.bmp	Right justified

You can make any entries in the text. When using large screens, use slider bars to see information that doesn't completely fit on the screen.

If you make an entry immediately in front of text, the entry (in our example, GLACIER.BMP) will move to the right screen edge. You can use this effect only for screen files that are smaller than 64K.

Reference To Sound Files

Sound files are called with a similar command:

```
!HAudioCommand(hwndContext,qchPath,"glacier.wav","play")
```

This entry must immediately follow a double-underlined term and must be hidden. To activate the audio sequence with an image, double-underline the image.

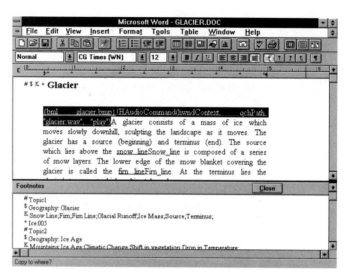

Assigning a sound file to an image

This completes our example. When formatting with hidden text, be careful of paragraph markers or line breaks. If end of paragraph marks or line breaks are included in the hidden text, an error occurs during compilation. Individual references between terms and pages must be equal. To compile the application, save it in RTF format and give it the file extension .RTF.

The complete file can be found under the file name GLACIER.DOC or GLACIER.RTF in the \LEARNER\VIEWER directory of the companion CD-ROM.

Compiling The Text File

To use a text file in the Viewer, it must be compiled. This requires a Control file, which contains information to guide the compilation process.

An example of a control file is called GLACIER.MVP (also on the companion CD-ROM). When creating your own applications, modify this file and save it with the file name of the RTF file you have created for your application. Note that the MVP file extension is necessary. The file structure is as follows:

[FILES]
glacier.rtf

```
[CONFIG]
RegisterRoutine("mvaudio", "HAudioCommand", "USSS")
RegisterRoutine("ftui","InitRoutines","SU")
InitRoutines(qchPath,1)
RegisterRoutine("ftui","ExecFullTextSearch","USSS")
CreateButton("ftSearch","&Search","ExecFullTextSearch(hwndApp,qchPath,`',`
')")
BrowseButtons()

[BAGGAGE]
bag.ini
```

If you use the MVP file on the companion CD-ROM, you must change only the entry for the [FILES] option. All other entries can be transferred intact.

If you continue to explore Viewer, you'll discover many possible entries for this file. Even the limited number of entries previously described provide many possibilities.

The last file that must be changed is BAG.INI, which is also on the companion CD-ROM.

Ensure that all files (text, image and sound files) are in the same directory.

Start The Compiler

To compile the sample file, you'll need the MVC.EXE program from the Viewer directory of the Microsoft Multimedia Development Kit. This call can be made from the DOS level. It's not necessary to enter the filename extension of the RTF file:

```
MVC GLACIER
```

If errors occurred during text creation, you'll receive warnings or error messages. If the compilation process runs properly, a file with the extension ".MVB" will be created. This is a complete ready-to-run Viewer file. To see our example, use the GLACIER.MVB file.

Start the Viewer and the MVB file. If all references and pointers are correct, you can move all around the text in any direction.

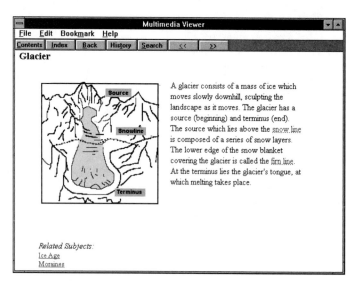

The complete glossary

You can also use bookmarks and annotations as provided by the Viewer.

10.5 MacroMedia Action!

MacroMedia Action! is an authoring system that lets you create multimedia presentations that combine sound, motion, text, and graphics. You can also include interactive elements in your presentations. These elements let the user determine the course of the presentation by clicking certain buttons on the screen.

Action! is different from many other multimedia programs because it uses shapes, graphics, and text that move around the screen instead of staying in one place. You can also add sound to these moving images.

Using MacroMedia Action!

Installing Action!

To install Action! on your hard drive, use the Install program that's located on Disk 1. Insert this diskette in your disk drive and then start Windows. From Windows, choose **File/Run....** Then type the following

```
A:Install
```

and press Enter.

Complete the installation process by following the instructions that appear on the screen.

Starting Action!

Once Action! is installed, an icon representing the program appears in the Windows Program Manager. To start Action!, double-click this icon. When you do this, an empty presentation window appears:

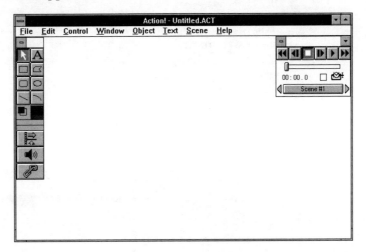

Presentation window

The top line of the window is the title bar, which displays the name of the current presentation. The line below this is the menu bar. The Tool Palette is used to create objects and apply motion, sound, and linking. To determine where you are in the presentation, use the Control Panel. The stage is the part of the window where presentations are played.

Elements of Action!

Action! presentations consist of scenes. Each scene contains objects. These tools are either drawn with the tools from the Tool Palette, imported from other applications, or imported from ClipMedia, which is included with Action!.

Besides the tools that are normally included with drawing programs, Action! also provides tools for adding motion (action tool), sound (sound tool), and interactivity (link tool) to your presentations.

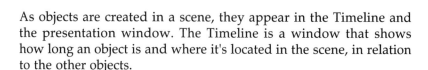

As objects are created in a scene, they appear in the Timeline and the presentation window. The Timeline is a window that shows how long an object is and where it's located in the scene, in relation to the other objects.

The Content List displays a list of all the scenes in the presentation and all the objects in each scene. This provides an overview of your presentation; it also helps you edit text objects in a scene.

The Scene Sorter displays an image of each scene in the presentation, the scene's name, and its associated template. It also shows what happens at the end of the scene and any sound that plays between scenes.

Action!'s Views

Action! has several views, or windows, in which you can work. Usually the Scene view is used.

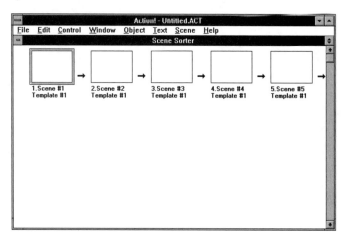

Scene view

In this view, the objects are displayed as they occur at a specific scene time. At a certain scene time, some objects are in transition and some have the stage or haven't appeared yet.

Use the Template view when you're creating and editing a template. A set of templates is included with Action!; these are ready-to-use scenes that contain objects, motion, transitions, and text. These templates can be edited by changing the text and graphics so they can be used in your own presentations.

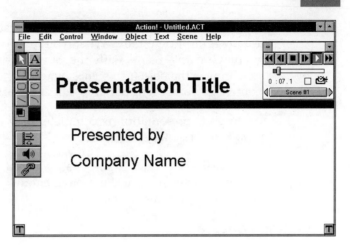

Template view

Compressed view is used when you open an existing Action! presentation. In this view, all scene and template objects are displayed in their Hold positions. This helps you align objects, change positions, and re-size objects.

Creating Multimedia Presentations

The following is a brief overview of the steps involved in creating an Action! presentation. We don't have enough space in this book to discuss these steps in detail. However, simply remember there are three basic steps:

• Creating objects

• Creating scenes

• Creating presentations

Before starting There are several things you must do before you actually work with Action!. First you must determine what the presentation will be about and how long it will be. Once this is done, create an outline for the presentation. Based on this outline, divide the presentation into scenes. Next check the Action! Template Guide for a template you could use for your presentation. Also, collect the graphics and sounds you'll need.

Now you're ready to use Action!. First load or create a template if you want to use the same objects in several scenes. Then, in the presentation window, draw objects or import objects using the Tool Palette.

If you want to add motion, sound, or interactivity to your objects, use the appropriate tools. When you're finished, check the results by playing the scene with the buttons on the Control Panel. Synchronize the objects in scenes by using the Timeline and use the Content List and Scene Sorter to edit and rearrange scenes.

When your presentation is complete, play it on your monitor or print it to videotape.

Now we'll use a brief example so you can become familiar with Action!. Obviously, we don't have enough space in this book to discuss this program in detail.

Creating Objects

As we mentioned, once you determine the type of presentation you want to create and then develop a plan, you can begin by creating objects.

With the Tool Palette, you can create text objects or graphics objects, such as rectangles and arcs. Let's create a text object. In the presentation window, click the Text tool in the Tool Palette. The mouse pointer changes to a text cursor. In the stage area of the presentation window, click where you want the text to begin. Since we want to create a box, drag the mouse to create a box in which the text will appear. Now type the following:

```
Announcing our new products!
```

Creating a box

Then click outside of the box. You'll see that the cursor changes back to a pointer and the text box is selected.

Now that we've created an object, we can apply actions to it. This adds excitement because the object isn't displayed in just one static scene.

In this step, we'll determine how our box appears in the scene and how it's moved while in the scene. First click the Action! tool in the Tool Palette. Then move to the presentation window. You'll see that the pointer changes into the Action! cursor. Click the box you just created.

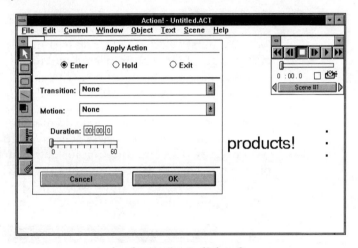

Apply Action! dialog box

Now click on the "Enter" option button and select "Reveal Left" from the "Transition:" drop-down list box. This specifies how the box enters the scene. Then select a motion for the box's entrance. Select "From Left" from the "Motion:" drop-down list box.

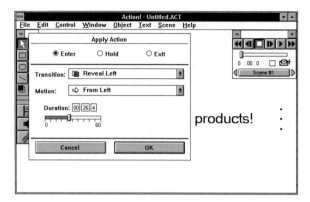

Selecting a motion

Next we must select a transition and motion for Exit. To do this, click on the "Exit" option button and select "Push Left" from the "Transition:" drop-down list box. Then select "To Lower Left" from the "Motion:" drop-down list box.

Once you've selected a transition and motion for Enter and Exit, you must determine how long these actions will occur. In our example, we'll use a two second duration for both Enter and Exit. Enter this time in the "Duration:" text box either by using the boxes, using the slider, or clicking the arrows. You'll need to click on each option button ("Enter" and "Exit"), then set the duration for each.

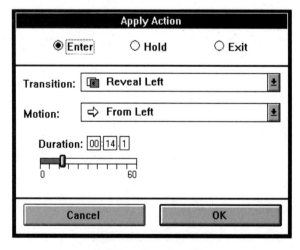

Setting the duration

Each object has a default duration of 10 seconds. The object stays in its Hold position for this amount of time. The time you set for Enter and Exit is added to this value. So, in our example, the duration is 14 seconds.

Action! provides ways for including sounds, animation, and images in your multimedia presentations. It's quite powerful and has an extensive array of commands and functions. You might prefer to show the Action! Help system while you are working, as the following illustration shows.

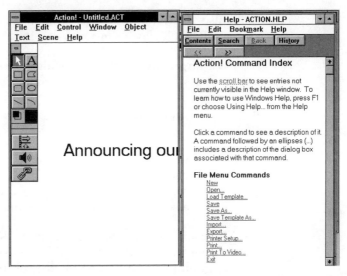

Each Action! scene consists of objects, such as text, graphics, sounds and animation clips.

10.6 Microsoft Multimedia Development Kit (MDK)

The Microsoft Multimedia Development Kit is an add-on to the Microsoft Windows Software Development Kit (SDK) or the Borland C++ Compiler. With this kit, you can develop multimedia titles and applications for Microsoft Windows graphical environment with Multimedia Extensions 1.0 or the Windows 3.1 operating system.

All the kit's contents are located on a CD-ROM disc. This development kit contains APIs (Application Programming Interfaces) that can be used to access the power of Windows' graphical environment with Multimedia Extensions. MDK also contains header files. These files are needed to use the Multimedia Extensions in Windows programs written in C.

The Microsoft Multimedia Development Kit also contains various development tools that can be used to prepare data. These tools include the Microsoft BitEdit, which is used to edit bitmap images; Microsoft PalEdit, which is used to adjust color palettes; Microsoft WaveEdit, which is a sound editor; Microsoft FileWalker, which is used to view and edit resource interchange file format (RIFF) and other data files; and Microsoft Convert, which is a file format conversion utility.

You'll also find an on-line Help system. Sample applications and sample MIDI and waveform audio files are also included.

Multimedia Viewer   The most impressive tool is the Multimedia Viewer, which is an authoring system. By using this program, you can create "content-rich" multimedia titles. An example of a title is an encyclopedia multimedia application. To create a Viewer document, you must use Microsoft Word for Windows.

Topics   To create a title, organize the text and bitmaps into topics. These topics are then linked into "books". To do this, you must specify "hotspots", which can be text strings or areas of bitmaps. These hotspots can also activate audio files or animations.

The Microsoft Multimedia Development Kit can be used by C programmers and regular users who are using authoring tools to develop multimedia titles. The MDK is useful for C programmers because it provides the additional elements that are needed to write Multimedia Windows programs.

These tools also make it possible to add multimedia capability to existing Windows applications. For regular users, the MDK provides useful documentation on the Media Control Interface (MCI) and tools like Multimedia Viewer.

MDK Components

The Microsoft Multimedia Development Kit is divided into four parts.

Multimedia Extensions

One part is the Multimedia Extensions, which are a set of libraries, drivers and applications. These items make it possible for Windows 3.0 to support the multimedia features that are included with Windows 3.1. These features include support for waveform audio playback and recording, MIDI and joystick input.

Data Preparation Tools

Another part of the MDK are the Data Preparation Tools. These are programs that are used to prepare and edit sound and image files for multimedia applications.

BitEdit tool

Use the BitEdit tool to edit bitmapped graphics. With this tool, you can crop a bitmap, change the size or color depth or rotate selected areas in a bitmap. Use the PalEdit tool to create or edit color palettes for bitmaps or stand-alone palette files. For example, you can apply a new color palette to an existing bitmap.

WaveEdit tool

The WaveEdit tool can be used to edit and play waveform audio files. For example, you can cut and paste between waveforms and adjust sound characteristics. Use the FileWalker tool to view and edit various types of files. The Convert tool lets you convert data files from one format to another.

Multimedia Viewer Author Toolkit

The Multimedia Viewer Author Toolkit is another part of the MDK. This is a multimedia authoring and presentation program. It lets users create and distribute on-line documents, called titles, that contain text, pictures, audio and animation and run in Windows. Multimedia Viewer titles can contain multimedia elements, such as text with various fonts, sizes and colors. Titles can be stored on magnetic (hard drive) or optical media (CD-ROM).

Contains various elements

This toolkit contains various elements. The Build Utilities build the Multimedia Viewer data files that contain text, hypertext links and references to multimedia data. Hotspot Editor lets you add hypertext hotspots to bitmaps. The Runtime Viewer displays Multimedia Viewer files. The USA Tour is a sample title. It demonstrates the Multimedia Viewer features. These source files should help you build your title.

Multimedia Development Environment

The final part of the Microsoft Multimedia Development Kit is the Multimedia Development Environment. This is a collection of programming libraries, source files and debugging tools.

Installing

These are needed to develop applications for the Windows operating system. If your development platform uses Windows 3.0, install these tools from the MDK. If your development platform uses Windows 3.1, use the Windows 3.1 Software Development Kit (SDK).

The Multimedia Development Environment includes C header files and libraries, a debugging version of the multimedia extensions, and sample applications that demonstrate the multimedia extensions API. There are also on-line reference files that provide complete information about Multimedia Extensions functions, messages, commands and data structures.

Installing Microsoft Multimedia Development Kit

To install the data preparation tools, Multimedia extensions 1.0 (for Windows 3.0 only) and Multimedia Development Environment (on Windows 3.0 systems only), use the Setup program that's located in the root directory of the MDK CD-ROM.

First insert the MDK CD-ROM in the CD-ROM drive. Change directories to the root directory of the MDK CD-ROM. At the DOS prompt, start the Setup program by typing:

SETUP

Then press (Enter). The installation process begins. During this process, you'll be asked for the directory path for MDK files and whether you want to install the multimedia data preparation tools and sample multimedia data files.

You'll also be asked whether you want to install the Multimedia Development Environment (Windows 3.0 only) and the directory paths for the library and include files and the debugging and non-debugging versions of Multimedia extensions. Also, you must specify whether you want to install sample C programs.

Installing the Runtime Viewer, Build Utilities and USA Tour

To install the Runtime Viewer, Build Utilities and USA Tour, use the Setup program in the \VIEWER directory of the MDK CD-ROM. First insert the CD-ROM in the CD-ROM drive. Since you must start the Setup program from Windows, make the Program Manager the active application.

Choose **Run** from the **File** menu. Then type the letter of CD-ROM drive, followed by:

\VIEWER\SETUP

Then select (OK). During this installation process you'll be asked for the directory path from Multimedia Viewer files and whether you want to install the sample files used to build the USA Tour title.

Multimedia Titles

Basically, you can use the MDK to create multimedia applications. These applications consists of titles. As we mentioned earlier, a title is an on-line document. This means that a title is an electronic document that exists on a computer screen.

There are various kinds of titles. The type of titles you use depends on the purpose of the multimedia application you want to create.

Titles can be divided into five categories:

Productivity titles

Productivity titles enhance productivity applications, such as spreadsheets and databases.

Information titles

Information titles are usually reference materials, such as dictionaries and encyclopedias.

Entertainment titles

Entertainment titles are used to create games and other leisure multimedia applications.

Creativity titles

Creativity titles help users increase their creativity by providing the appropriate tools, such as sound and images. With these tools, you can create interesting presentations for business or personal use.

Education titles

Finally, there are education titles. These titles enhance educational applications by making them interactive and including references to related topics.

Multimedia Viewer's Basic Components

In this section we'll briefly discuss the elements found in the Multimedia Viewer user interface.

The various units of information found in a title are called "topics". All related information is placed together in one topic. The first topic that appears when a title is opened is the Contents topic. All the topics contained in a title can be accessed from this topic.

Another element of Viewer is "jumps". These are cross-references to related topics. Certain text and pictures can be specified as "hotspots". When these hotspots are activated (i.e., clicked on), Viewer displays the related topic.

Popup windows

Popup windows are used to provide additional information about a term or explanation. You can associate definitions and other information with specific terms in a topic. When these terms, which are also hotspots, are clicked, the appropriate popup window appears on the screen.

Viewer menus

The Viewer has four menus, which appear in every Viewer window. Use the commands in the **File** menu to display titles, print topics, specify printer information and exit the Viewer. With the commands in the **Edit** menu, you can copy text and add text to a topic. The **Bookmark** menu allows you to define bookmarks that are placed in titles. Use the commands in the **Help** menu to access on-line Help.

The final element in the Viewer interface is the Viewer buttons. These buttons are located below the menu bar in the Viewer window. Use these buttons to access topics in a title.

Creating a Viewer Title

The companion CD-ROM contains two ready-to-compile Viewer titles. The title we're discussing here is in the \LEARNER\VIEWER\MUS_DICT directory. In this directory you'll find a series of files needed to create the MUS_DIC Viewer title.

Our sample is called MUS_DICT (short for Music Dictionary). These topics present a little information about the pipe organ. We'll look at each element and how they fit into the Viewer title.

MUS_DICT.DOC:
> This file was created using Microsoft Word for Windows. Like the GLACIER.DOC file, we included context strings using footnotes, keywords, and topic titles. MVC doesn't access this file—it's the form in which you can create your title easily.

MUS_DICT.RTF:
> Selecting **File/Save As...** while MUS_DICT.DOC is in memory lets you save this file as a Rich Text Format (RTF) file. MUS_DICT.RTF is needed by MVC.

Files accessed by the MUS_DICT.DOC and MUS_DICT.RTF files are:

ORGAN.BMP:
> A scanned image of an organ console. We scanned this from a clip art book using a hand scanner, then converted it to a BMP file.

PIPES.BMP:
> A drawing of the two basic types of organ pipes (flue and labial). We drew this using Microsoft Windows Paintbrush, then cropped it using BitEdit.

TOCCATA2.WAV:
> This is a recording of the opening bars of the Bach Toccata in d minor. When you click on the ORGAN.BMP bitmap file, this Wave file plays. We recorded this file using the Windows Sound Recorder, then edited it using WaveEdit.

MANUALS.WAV:
> A spoken-word brief description of manuals (organ keyboards). This plays when you click on the (Info) context string in the "Manuals and Pedals" page.

BAG.INI:
> This is a "Baggage" file, used for storing temporary information. Make sure this file exists before compiling using MVC.

SETUP.INF:
> This controls setup for installing the file.

MUS_DICT.ICO:
> The icon for the music dictionary, used by SETUP.INF.

To view this file, you can run Viewer, then select **File/Open....** From the "Open File" dialog box, change to the companion CD-ROM and select the MUS_DICT.MVB file. From there you can read this file and test it.

Chapter 11

A Home Film Studio

Personal computer video technology is one of the most interesting areas of multimedia. While processing any video source with an overlay card results in a single image, live video provides completely different possibilities:

- Storing video sequences on hard drives or CD-ROMs

- Mixing video sources with computer graphics

- Computer graphics, output to video

- Cutting and mixing video sources, combined with computer graphics, output to video

Live Video

Live video refers to recording and transmitting a moving object with a frame rate of at least 25 pictures per second in real time.

Overcoming two problems

For computers and video to work together, two problems must be solved. Computers, video cameras, video recorders and televisions usually don't send the same video signals. However, converting to a different signal is time-consuming and often results in decreased quality.

> The basic difference between VGA and video signals and the compression techniques now being used are described in Chapter 2.

Another problem occurs when live video is stored on data carriers, such as hard drives. Digitized images require a tremendous amount of memory. This memory usage is increased by the length of the video sequence. Therefore, you must use effective compression techniques, which results in a minimum loss of quality.

11.1 Computer to Video

To record a VGA signal on a conventional video recorder, you can insert a special add-on card in the PC. This type of add-on card is known as a video output board.

There are also small external computer interfaces that allow you to display your multimedia creations on a standard TV or even record them to a VCR.

Due to the differences between the computer graphics signal and the television signal, the picture quality is not very good. These devices overcome these shortcomings with special flicker reduction circuitry, special fonts for television use and advanced software to improve the television picture quality.

The Presenter Plus

Consumer Technology Northwest, Inc. makes The Presenter Plus. It allows you to operate a standard TV or VCR from any DOS- or Windows-based computer that can display VGA graphics. It's portable and can be used with a notebook or laptop computer to make presentations.

Includes software and fonts

The Presenter Plus includes software to enhance the quality of the television image. The quality of the video image must be taken into consideration when creating presentations. Special fonts are included for television output.

A notebook computer with a portable CD-ROM drive and this device allows you to make multimedia presentations anywhere.

The Presenter Plus is an external interface which sends a VGA signal to a VGA monitor and to video. An inexpensive alternative to a video output board, this black box lets you display computer output on a television set, or send the output to a video recorder for recording and playback.

Installing The Presenter Plus hardware and software is literally a ten-minute job. Here are the steps involved.

1.   Turn off your computer and monitor. Unplug your monitor from the VGA card.

2.   Remove The Presenter Plus and its components from the carton. Plug the power cube (power supply) into an outlet, and connect the power cube to the DC IN jack on The Presenter Plus. A red light marked POWER should glow on The Presenter Plus.

3.   Connect the longer of the two VGA cables to the VGA IN jack on The Presenter Plus, and to your computer's VGA card. Connect the shorter of the two VGA cables to the VGA OUT jack, and to the VGA monitor plug.

4.   To interface to a VHS video recorder, connect the RCA cable to the VIDEO OUT jack on The Presenter Plus, and to the VIDEO IN jack on your video recorder. For an S-VHS video recorder, use the other connecting cable and plug this cable into The Presenter Plus' S VIDEO OUT jack and your S-VHS video recorder's input jack.

Once you run the software (provided both as DOS and Windows implementations), you're set; output travels direct to your VGA monitor, and out the VIDEO OUT and S-VIDEO OUT jacks.

Video Output Boards

With a video output board, a genlock device mixes the two signals (computer and video). In the genlock process, a VGA graphic signal is transformed to a television standard, NTSC or PAL, and sent, via a video output connection, to a video recorder or a standard television.

All types of animation, presentations or information on video can be recorded or prepared for various add-on video devices (such as video mixers).

Genlocking

The process of adapting the VGA signal to the video signal is called genlocking. In this process, various parameters are synchronized, such as line frequency, resolution, color palettes, etc. The VGA signal is connected to the video output board using the feature connector of the graphics card. A NTSC or PAL signal is converted and output via the video output interface.

External video signals An additional option enables you to take external video signals, such as images from a video camera, mix them with VGA graphics and output them together to videotape. This offers many interesting multimedia possibilities, such as adding titles to your vacation video with a PC title generator and recording them together.

To use this method, a second video recorder is connected. Use the video input interface of the video output board to receive the incoming video signal. The video output board will synchronize and mix it with the VGA signal from the feature connector of the VGA graphics card.

Defining colors When mixing computer and video images, you can define a color the computer displays as transparent. Areas displaying this color on the computer image can then be changed in the video signal or displayed on a video camera. With additional coloring techniques and by using a conventional add-on video device, you can create professional demos and learning programs.

Since so many people own video recorders, advertisements in the form of multimedia computer animation on VHS videocassettes can be distributed much more effectively than a diskette or a CD.

Installing a Video Output Board

You can quickly install a video output board. In this chapter we'll use the MicroEye Video Output Card as an example. However, this process is similar for all cards. Install the 8-bit card in a free slot close to the graphics card. Then connect the graphics card to the feature connector using the flat wire cable included with the video output board.

The PC monitor isn't connected to the video output board, as is often true with video overlay cards. It continues to receive information directly from the graphics card port.

Three connections A video output board usually has three connections. You can connect professional quality monitors, with RGB input, via a 9-pin RGB port. An RCA jack is available for composite input and output. Using these ports, practically all video input and output devices can be connected.

Other connection types, such as BNC twist connectors or DIN A/V connectors, can be attached using commercially available adapters. A normal configuration of the video output board is displayed in the following illustration:

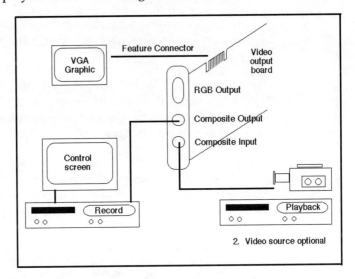

Video output board connections

If you want to record a VGA signal from a computer on videotape, connect the input of the video recorder with the video out port of the video output board. To do this, you need an additional cable for the video recorder to record incoming video signals. Several cables are available, including RCA, Scart, BNC and DIN-AV connectors for the video recorder side.

For the other end, there are several RCA connectors with labels for video in, video out, audio out, etc. The plug labeled "video in" must be connected with the video out port on the card. To record the incoming video signal on the video recorder, activate external video input. For information on how to use the video recorder, refer to its user manual.

Technically, it's possible to connect the video output of the card to the antenna input of the video recorder with a commercial cable antenna. However, this connection isn't acceptable. The cable itself would act as an antenna and add so much interference that the signals created on the card wouldn't be displayed clearly.

A Television as Control Monitor

To monitor the condition of the VGA signal, connect a television set to the video recorder. This allows better control of the final VGA output signal combined with images from a second video recorder or a video camera.

If you use a video recorder, using a television is unavoidable. To display the incoming signal, switch on the video replay channel (TV).

The video output card is completely controlled with the software that accompanies it. The most important task for the software is to determine what function the video output board executes, as well as to set the display parameters.

The following examples are from the MicroEye Video Output Card. The software supplied with other cards may differ slightly. With the MicroEye Video Output Card DOS program VPANEL.EXE, you can easily set display parameters by using menus.

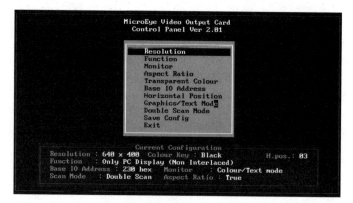

Setting up the screen

Using the cursor keys, select the desired entry and activate it by pressing Enter. An additional menu appears, in which you can select the desired option.

In the Current Configuration field, the options currently being used are displayed. If you make another selection, the new status appears.

Depending on what you're working on, you can change some parameters. Choose an appropriate configuration using VPANEL and save it as a file. Use a distinctive file name and indicate a file extension at the same time.

This file can be activated from other programs without using VPANEL:

```
SETVOB -D<FILE.TXT>
```

The following output functions are available through Function on VPANEL. They are described in more detail later in the chapter.

Function	Input signal	Use
Blank Display	VGA and Video	Transitions between two presentations
Only PC Display (Non-Interlaced Output)	VGA	Output of a VGA signal with line Goto processing
Only PC Display (Interlaced Output)	VGA	Output of a full-screen VGA signal
Only PC Display	VGA	Genlocked to input video
Through Video with overscanning	VGA and Video	Only input Video signals are output
Through Video with black border	VGA and Video	Only input signals are output in a black frame
Overlay with overscan	VGA and Video	Both signals are output together
Overlay with black border	VGA and Video	Both signals are output together in a black frame

Recording a Video Signal

Recording a normal VGA signal from a computer onto videotape is useful because it lets you create a presentation or software demonstration that can be shown without expensive equipment.

For example, many convention centers provide a video recorder but a PC isn't always available. As we mentioned, video recorders are widely used. So, a videocassette is often more effective than a diskette for promoting a product or service.

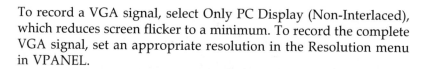

To record a VGA signal, select Only PC Display (Non-Interlaced), which reduces screen flicker to a minimum. To record the complete VGA signal, set an appropriate resolution in the Resolution menu in VPANEL.

If you choose normal resolution of 640 x 480 pixels, start programs like Windows in the same mode. If you use Windows with a resolution of 800 x 600 pixels, some areas of the screen won't appear.

> If the image isn't positioned properly in the center of the screen, adjust it horizontally by selecting from Horizontal positions. Seven settings are available.

When the settings are correct, switch the video recorder to Record. The signal prepared via the MicroEye Video Output Card is recorded by the video recorder. Each action performed on the screen will appear on the video. In this way, you can create learning programs in which you record individual steps first and later add sound to the video.

You should create a script before actually recording the video. Spoken text, which will be added later, should be recited while the image is recorded, to better estimate the required length of time.

Transitions

When creating videos, it's difficult to manage transitions between two topics. For example, to record a word processing procedure first, then the operation of a spreadsheet, you should make an effective transition between the two topics. Theoretically, this is easy. After displaying the word processing screen, pause the recording video recorder. Now continue as follows:

*   Call an animation

*   Display a full screen graphic

You can create the animation with Animator (see Chapter 7). Design the animation so it fits the new topic. A PC graphic is even easier to create.

Use Windows
Paintbrush

Simply use Windows Paintbrush and display the graphic on the full screen using **View/View Picture** menu item of Paintbrush.

Switch on the video recorder again to record the graphic for a few seconds.

Using a Paintbrush graphic as a transition

Graphics can also be used for opening titles in your videos. With this method, you don't need a title generator. Instead, simply draw a full-screen graphic.

Mixing VGA Graphics and Video Sources

If you simultaneously display video and VGA graphics, several effects are possible. First, a video source must be connected to the video input connection of the video output board. The video source can be a video recorder or a video camera.

When you mix a VGA signal with a video source and record them together on videotape, the quality will significantly decrease if the input video signal comes from a video recorder. Each generation of copies taken from a video film further decreases quality. If the signal is from a camera, the quality will be acceptable.

Beautiful effects can be created using transparent color. When you define a transparent color, the video image appears through the transparent areas of the VGA screen. For example, if you run Word with a blue background and define blue in VPANEL as a transparent color, the Word background can display a video image.

A Video Image in a Window

To display a video image in a window, with a product such as the MicroEye 2C Movie Board, use the following trick. Define a color, which normally isn't used for displaying the Windows elements (e.g., brown), as transparent.

If you use Windows with the Standard VGA resolution, access this color in Paintbrush. Simply fill the entire screen in Paintbrush with the transparent color and reduce the window to the desired size.

The video signal is now displayed in the Paintbrush window. A disadvantage of this approach is that the video signal cannot always be scaled correctly. The Paintbrush window will display only a portion of the video image.

Fading Effects

The same effect can be used to create fades between two topics. However, the effect is much better in this case. This method involves recording presentation programs, such as QuickShow or the Excel slide show (see Chapter 9), where the transition between two pictures uses fading effects.

With this technique, a Paintbrush graphic is created as described above. This graphic contains, for example, a reference to the next topic or the title of the video. A second Paintbrush graphic contains only the transparent color defined in VPANEL.

Then a presentation can be created with the Excel slide show using the title graphic as the first image and the graphic file with the transparent color as the second image. The desired fading effect, going from the title graphic to the graphic with the clear color, can now be selected. The slide show should be changed to manual slide change.

Start the presentation with the graphic that contains the title and switch the video recorder to Record. When you switch to the next graphic, during the fade the video image from the connected video source appears.

An example application using an Excel slide show is on the companion CD-ROM under the name SLIDES.XLS in the \PRESENT\EXCEL directory. You can run this slide show and send it to video as it plays back.

Video Titles

Besides adding titles to videos, you can also use this technique in many other applications. For example, this technique can be used to create subtitles for foreign language films.

Theoretically, you can create a title with Paintbrush, use clear color as the background and display the letters in another color. Frequently it's difficult to create the appropriate title and add it to the proper location.

Using TITLE.EXE A special program for creating titles is included with the MicroEye Video Output Card. Use TITLE.EXE to choose from several different character fonts.

Choose settings for foreground, background, and clear color to vary the display. Enter the desired phrase in the text field and display it using Print. Use the Clear button to fade the display and then enter a new phrase.

11.2 Video To Computer - A Software Solution

Video integration is a magical phrase for multimedia users. However, many users are discouraged by the additional costs involved in this process. The hardware needed for importing video films to programs and displaying the films on a PC's monitor is expensive.

Hardware Requirements

Video overlay boards, such as Screen Machine (manufactured by a company named Fast), are currently the most important MPC hardware add-ons for displaying video films in real time. Another important hardware component is a video source, such as a video recorder or CD player.

As you can see, a large investment is needed just to display a few video images on an MPC monitor with good stereo sound. These devices also occupy a large amount of hard drive space. However, video recordings involve sending pure analog signals.

If the image material is available in digital format, for example DVI (Digital Video Interactive), you can treat it like an ordinary file, address it as an object and import it to an existing Windows application.

However, because of the expenses involved, DVI isn't really intended for amateur multimedia users. DVI also requires an add-on board, called the Actionmedia board, for playing back films. Microsoft is developing a new software product for playing back only video images.

Microsoft Video for Windows

Microsoft has developed a pure software solution, called AVI (Audio Video Interleaved), for playing back, recording and compressing video data. It's similar to Quicktime, which is used with Apple computers.

AVI gives MPC users the option of playing back video films with sound from CD-ROM or directly from the hard drive and displaying them with a VGA card on the monitor without any hardware add-ons.

Microsoft released a set of AVI devices and tools in the Microsoft Video for Windows package. In the following pages, we'll provide a brief introduction on how AVI works and the different tools that are available.

With AVI, you can play back sound and animations simultaneously. The recorded compressed data is stored so image and sound data are alternately called, similar to interleaving. Each sound matches the corresponding image.

Without interleaving (i.e, if the audio and image data were saved separately), the images wouldn't be synchronized with the sound. For example, it would take too much time to find and link the individual data on different areas of the hard drive or CD-ROM. The image would flicker on the screen and the sound information would be incomplete. Therefore, the interleave function is vital for a continuous image and sound sequence.

Special Data Compression

Managing the data set of the video images requires an appropriate compression procedure. Since AVI uses only the internal processor of the PC for this purpose, additional chips aren't needed.

In a video film, an average of 25 images per second are displayed. This means that a data set of 20 Meg is needed for one second of film in single frame storage.

Problems   However, a CD-ROM drive cannot transfer this data set. At the same time, no hard drive can accept the resulting data sets for long film sequences. Reducing the amount of data is the Video for Windows' biggest advantage.

The potential data transfer rate of a CD-ROM is still 150K per second. This means that the video data set must also be compressed in this format to guarantee a flowing image sequence from the CD-ROM.

Playback options   AVI provides several options for optimum film playback. Users can reduce the data set for the filming by selecting 8, 16, or 24-bit color resolution. Films in 8-bit format require the smallest amount of disk space.

The program creates a color palette that's responsible for converting the true colors of the video image to a total of 236 colors for the AVI film. The selected window size is also noticeable in film playback. The smaller the video window, the smoother, more flowing the film will play back.

In recording film sequences, AVI doesn't tape all 25 images. Instead, it saves only the 10th or 15th image as a frame. This frame is referred to as a keyframe, which is adjustable. Finally, only the image differences between the individual keyframes are saved, which drastically reduces the amount of data.

Playback Quality

Up to now, the playback of recorded video images with the VGA graphics card has been limited to a maximum size of 160 x 120 pixels and 15 images per second. However, a capture board and driver are also necessary for recording video films.

FAST includes this driver with Screen Machine. A driver for Videoblaster from Creative Labs is also available. Sound recordings can be made for film via different settings, both in full stereo quality and in mono. The quality depends on the sound card.

Linking Through AVI Drivers

After installation, the AVI driver is available to the Media Control Interface (MCI) of Windows. The new OLE capable Media Player included with Video for Windows enables users to call any recorded video film under the object type "Media Clip" and link it to any Windows application as an OLE (Object Linking and Embedding) object.

Double-click the icon of the linked object to start the film. In addition, in **Edit/Options...** you can choose to record the film in a frame, only as a full-screen or, for example, with different operating buttons.

Video for Windows lets users play back and add sound to animations created with Autodesk Animator. Microsoft added a special conversion program for converting film sequences from Apple's Quicktime.

Video for Windows Components

Let's take a closer look at the software:

After you've installed Video for Windows with the Multimedia Data Tools, Windows adds a new program group with these new programs: VidEdit, VidCap, PalEdit, BitEdit and WaveEdit.

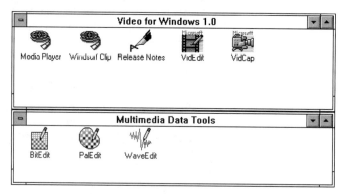

Video for Windows consists of these program tools

VidCap

This program tool is used for recording the video data. However, this tool requires an installed video overlay card and the appropriate driver for Video for Windows.

Define two options first

Click the mouse on one of the icon buttons to record anything in the displayed video window, from a single frame to a long video sequence. However, before you begin recording you must define various options.

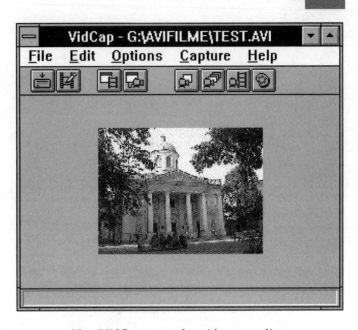

Use VidCap to make video recordings

First, determine the size and color depth of the desired video format. For sound recordings, you can also select the appropriate audio options. Three different options are available for storing the data.

You can save the video film directly on the hard drive, in RAM or from RAM to the hard drive. Depending on the setting you select, you'll notice a difference in the speed at which the program saves the video data.

First, the overlay video is displayed in the window. To determine how the defined settings will affect the recording, preview a video from the **Options** menu. The sequence of single frames will clearly show the difference from the live video.

The images will flicker because of the low number of images per second. After video taping is complete, the film is saved in uncompressed format.

VidEdit

This tool is used to compress and resave previously recorded data. Select the number of keyframes, type of saving, compression method and the exact video cutout.

It's also possible to cut out specific video sequences and paste them elsewhere in the video tape.

You can also paste in other video sequences from existing films. The Copy, Cut and Paste buttons help users quickly edit videos. This makes it easy to combine individual scenes into a whole film.

The scenes can be taken from Autodesk Animator sequences or sequences from a Microsoft Multimedia movie.

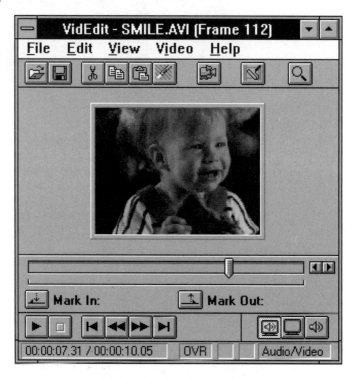

Compression with VidEdit

AVI is able to convert and then process all these different formats. Users can also specify the transfer rate, recording format and memory area AVI uses.

PalEdit

If the video tapes are saved in 8-bit format, a color palette is saved along with them. Different colors of the video recording can be corrected from the color palette, if the film doesn't play back with the proper colors.

PalEdit lets users retouch video sequences with a color palette of 236 colors. Users can edit every color and change the colors in the film.

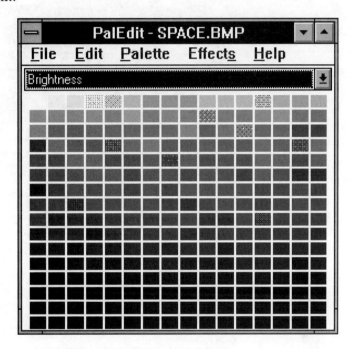

The color palette lets you influence the video film coloration

BitEdit

Use this tool to edit images and image sequences pixel by pixel. The program supports a variety of formats, such as AVI, DIB, BMP, WMF,GIF, PCX, PIC, TGA, EPS, DRW and many other formats.

The Editor helps you change, copy, insert, rotate and flip cutouts. The program is ideal for editing images from different applications.

BitEdit can edit images of any graphics format

WaveEdit

WaveEdit is used for editing recorded sound sequences. This program allows you to change sound data. To mix a new sound into an existing film sequence, use sound formats from the following:

- AVI Waveform

- Microsoft Waveform

- Microsoft PCM Waveform

- Apple AIFF

Different effects, such as fade-ins and fade-outs, are possible during editing.

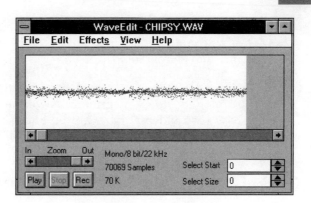

Editing Wave files

Use the mouse to select a sound segment to be edited and pasted into the film. You can also add other sound data or comments from a microphone.

Media Player

The new Media Player is a revised, adapted version of the Windows 3.1 Media Player. Use it to control AVI sequences.

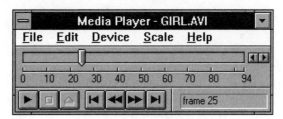

Media Player

What Can I Do With Video for Windows?

When combined with an overlay board, AVI is ideal for creating small video productions. The film can be played back on any computer equipped with a VGA card.

Video for Windows' ability to process a variety of image formats also makes it possible to create small cartoons. In 1993, a company named Multicom will present the first comic on CD-ROM created with Video for Windows.

Video for Windows is especially well suited for integration in different applications for visualization. With the support of the OLE capable Media Player, it's very easy to link existing video

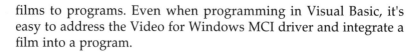

films to programs. Even when programming in Visual Basic, it's easy to address the Video for Windows MCI driver and integrate a film into a program.

Video for Windows represents only the beginning of software supported video integration. Nevertheless, this software shows how easy video editing can be under Windows. All developers have to do now is solve the problems of high data transfer rates and disk space requirements.

11.3 Cutting and Mixing - Video Machine

Video MachineVideo Machine, developed by Fast, is currently the closest thing to a complete video studio for your PC. This program mixes and cuts video and graphics on a computer, changes the image with extensive trick effects and adds titles. Unlike a conventional video board, Video Machine can also add live video, mixed at the computer. So, with Video Machine, you can create a complete video production with your PC.

As the success of camcorders indicates, many people are interested in recording videos themselves. Until recently, only professional video studios could produce high-quality edited video. The equipment was too expensive for video amateurs. Currently, video mixers and simple interface devices are available only as stand-alone solutions.

New Presentation Techniques

Video Machine opens up an entirely new world for presentations. For example, suppose that you're an architect working on a new office complex. You could create a video presentation that shows the planned complex.

At your PC, you can cut and mix recorded video clips of the planned site, a video drive through the model, and a 3D animation rendered from a CAD program. Single images, animated titles, color diagrams and statistics can be added from a presentation program. Finally, you can place yourself in the video by using the blue-box technique.

As you can see, Video Machine can be used in various ways. For example, it's useful for independent studios and television studios that want to produce videos without investing in additional equipment.

Also, companies, educational institutions, and public relations and advertising agencies can create their own video productions. Because of the new developments in desktop video (DTV), the following will occur:

•   Lower production costs

•   Stimulation of supply and demand

•   Lower entry level for video producers

•   More small studios

•   Segmentation of the video market

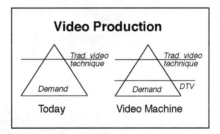

The development of desktop video

Video Machine will definitely have an effect on professional video cutting and editing techniques. Currently, there are some professional, non-linear cutting systems.

In these systems, the image content of a film or videotape is stored on the hard drive after being recorded in digital form. Then video cutting and editing techniques can be performed with the PC.

Not acceptable quality   However, the resulting quality still isn't acceptable for professional applications. After editing, the program cannot be played back from the hard drive to a videotape and then broadcast. When the program is finished, the original tape is re-recorded with time coding and transitions.

At least theoretically, the second generation is already available as broadcast tape. The image data must be highly compressed for a larger file to be stored, or output in real time, or to ensure fast access.

Using Video Machine

Signals are digitized in real time

Unlike the non-linear editing systems previously described, the Video Machine doesn't display the image on the monitor or save it on the hard drive.

Signals from two video sources are digitized in real time, and any fading, mixing or trick effects are selected using the accompanying Windows software.

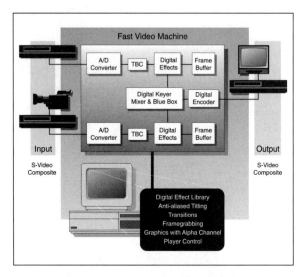

Desktop video and the Video Machine

Cutting time marks can also be saved. The result is converted into an analog signal and output on the attached monitor or played to a connected video recorder.

The Video Machine has the following capabilities:

- Video titles with anti-aliasing

- Digital video effects between two live video sources

- Digital video processing in a 4:2:2 studio format

- Digital RGB video mixer

- Audio supports sound card

- Inputs and Outputs for S-Video (other components optional)

- Digital linear keyer to generate effects

- FBAS and S-Video output signals are coded by a digital encoder chip

- Synchronization to external sources

- Combined operation of NTSC and PAL sources

- Frame grabbing

- Comprehensive effects library

As an extension of Video Machine, a digital recorder/player is currently being developed. This will enable live video to be written in full resolution on the hard drive and to be played from the hard drive in real time.

Calculated single image animations can be decompressed and output to a normal video recorder (without single images) as a moving sequence.

Chapter 12

Virtual Reality and Cyberspace

The multimedia interface between a computer and its user lets the computer react to interactive input by the user. If we take a much larger step toward this interaction of person and machine, we arrive at virtual reality (VR) or cyberspace. Simulation becomes tangibly realistic, bringing a new dimension to computer applications, namely space.

Person - Computer Interaction

These virtual 3D worlds react dynamically to the user's interaction. A conventional CAD (Computer Aided Design) program is used to create the virtual world, including the objects contained within this world. The user can then move within this world by using special VR hardware.

Realistic simulations

Cyberspace tries to create simulations that are as realistic as possible. NASA has done some of the most ambitious development in this field. Until recently, the high cost of VR systems has made this application area available only to large research projects.

However, two companies, MEGABRAIN in Hamburg, Germany, and Sense8 Corporation in Sausalito, California, are now marketing complete VR systems for PCs that have been implemented using Intel's DVI technology.

In this chapter we'll discuss the development of Virtual Reality (VR)/Cyberspace. We'll also discuss how virtual worlds are created by using the WorldToolKit system by Sense8.

12.1 An Example of Virtual Reality

The following describes one person's VR/Cyberspace experience.

The room is dimly lit; computers, monitors, and other devices are carefully arranged on an ornate desk. Finally, on a golden Styrofoam head, I see the data mask. Soft sounds emanate from the system's loudspeaker. I place the helmet onto my head and make one final adjustment. This is my last chance to get my bearings before the cyber trip begins.

The Emerald City created with WorldToolKit by Sense8

As the system is started, I begin to see an infinite space. In the background, I catch glimpses of a city in the distance. Slowly I turn my head in this direction and begin to move toward the city. I can fly above the city, between buildings and can even land on a city street.

I notice an open doorway in a nearby building. I think it's some kind of hotel. I climb the stairs and see a room, perhaps the hotel lobby. Slowly I turn my head in this direction and begin to move toward the entry. My initial approach is too high, and my head hits the door frame. Instinctively I duck. This movement is too quick for the system, the world vanishes, and the program resets.

On my second approach, I'm better prepared. To enter the virtual room, I use my knees—a slight stoop—and turn slightly to the left. Finally I'm standing inside my first virtual room.

The Lobby created with WorldToolKit by Sense8

A plant is in the room. Using slow body movements, I see an overview of the room. Swooping to the base of the plant, I can see the world from a child's perspective. Then I stand up by the plant. From here I can see the chandelier above me.

During my cyber trip my perception of time has completely disappeared. Slowly, I remove the helmet and re-enter the real world.

12.2 Virtual Reality Development

Since 1969 Myron W. Krueger, professor of Information Technology at the University of Connecticut, has been developing interactive environments in collaboration with electronic artists.

Such environments consist of spaces in which the presence of a person is registered in many different media. The data gathered through these devices is then processed by a computer, which in turn creates effects within this environment.

An interactive space might register the presence and movement of a person through in-floor sensors and video cameras. Synthesized images can be projected onto all four walls of the room, which helps create synthetic spaces.

With supercomputers and powerful animation techniques, the visitor's physical form and movements can be integrated into the virtual environment in real-time. The floor sensors can also be linked with a sound synthesizer.

Regardless of the visitor's actions, the cyber-environment will respond in some way. The visitor is confronted with an integrating, sensing, and responding system. Professor Krueger refers to this as a dialogue between two individuals.

Concept of cyberspace transit

In 1968 at the University of Utah, Ivan E. Sutherland had already developed the concept of cyberspace transit as we know it today.

He created a helmet that could simulate a person's sense of sight and sound. The impulses received by the eyes and ears were processed by the brain and registered the first virtual environment, or the first cyberspace.

Unfortunately, Sutherland's helmet was so heavy that it had to be suspended from the ceiling. Also, the computer systems of the day were limited to simulating a virtual ping pong game. More complex simulations weren't possible.

.Electronic sensory input system

However, since 1985 this field has grown rapidly. Michael W. McGreevy recognized the potential of creating a complete electronic sensory input system for human eyes by using the small LCD screens of Citizen's mini TVs.

With his colleagues Scott S. Fisher and James Humphries at NASA's Ames Research Center, McGreevy developed a helmet that integrated these LCD screens.

The person wearing the helmet would be able to see exactly the same images that a robot on a distant planet was registering. If the person's head turned, the robot's camera eyes would move in the same direction.

The sensor that's used to register the helmet's position and orientation has also been used in other virtual reality systems.

Apparently, the U.S. Air Force also has been trying to develop electronic battlefields for a long time. These various developments of virtual reality demonstrate that cyberspace can no longer be explained as simply territory and landscape simulations. An example of this is the cruise missile, which independently finds its target and destroys it.

VPL Research Also in 1985, VPL Research, Inc. was founded in Redwood,
DataGlove California. Within two years, Tom Zimmermann and Young
Harvill developed the DataGlove. This device, originally
designed for US astronauts, translates hand and finger movements
into electronic signals. The DataGlove is made of flexible Lycra®.

Optic fiber wires are sandwiched between two layers of fabric,
following the shape of the fingers. Both ends of each of these
cables are anchored in a connector plate. Into one end of the cables,
LEDs feed light, which is received by a phototransistor at the
other end and transformed into an electrical signal.

The optical fibers are treated so light can escape when the fingers
are bent. This reduces the amount of light received by the
phototransistor. The position and orientation of the hand are
registered by a sensor.

The movements of the user's hand are transferred to the virtual
hand of the computer. This makes it possible to influence and
control the occurrences in a virtual space. With the DataGlove,
you can move objects, open doors, and even play a game of cyber-
squash.

An underlying goal of VR/cyberspace technology is to apply this
technology to robot control. For example, instead of a human being
traveling in a hostile environment to repair machinery (e.g., in an
intensely radioactive area, or in space), a robot controlled by a
human from a virtual environment can perform the same task
without risk to the human.

Organizations such as NASA, are very interested in this
development for its tele-robotic planning and operations.

Taking the DataGlove several steps further leads to the data suit,
which uses the same technology to translate the movements of the
entire body into electrical signals.

Body Electric Jaron Lanier, the head of VPL Research, Inc., and Chuck
Blanchard have written a software program called Body Electric.
This software allows the movements of the DataGlove and the
VPL Eyephone (the only commercial data mask that permits the
view into cyberspace) to be translated into actions within virtual
reality.

VPL isn't the only commercial manufacturer of cyberspace devices.
In the fall of 1988, there were rumors that Autodesk was working

on a project called "Cyberia". Unfortunately, the project was abandoned by the end of 1989. Eric Gullichsen and Pat Gelband subsequently formed their own company, Sense8.

Why Cyberspace?

The sensory interaction with virtual environments can be used in various ways.

Simulation

One of the main uses of cyberspace is the flawless simulation of the real world. Not only can such simulations save enormous amounts of money, they may also help make real life safer. One way cyberspace can be used is for training medical personnel. For example, doctors could practice performing complex operations on cyber-patients.

Communication

Cyberspace will also open new dimensions in communication technology. Networked cyberspace will let audiences and actors interact in a virtual world. Participants will be able to select the form in which they appear.

For example, since 1986 NASA has been developing tele-robotic systems that allow operators to control robots remotely so that they can be programmed and controlled interactively.

Work

Cyberspace will enable people to work together in a virtual room. This type of tele-work will let the participants communicate even if they are miles away from each other.

Virtual reality technology will revolutionize tele-work in the next 20 to 30 years. Virtual offices will be created in which people can work right out of their homes.

Medicine

As we mentioned, cyber technology will also be used in the medical field. Three-dimensional images of the human body can be created. Then these bodies can be traversed and dissected virtually. So, the different parts and relationships of the body can be illustrated and taught much more clearly.

At the University of North Carolina (Chapel Hill), computer science researchers have developed a virtual research system that allows biochemists to test the pharmaceutical properties of specific molecules. This virtual world allows the scientists to easily experiment with creating drug molecules that can bind to the right receptors.

Education

Virtual learning is action-learning. Virtual machines, such as the ones offered by VPL and Sense8, will eventually be able to bring a classroom to life. For example, when a teacher lectures about a distant country, the class will be able to travel to the country.

Recreation

Today cyberspace gloves are already available for under $100 in the U.S. and Japan. Walt Disney and other companies are in the process of transforming their entertainment parks into "experience" parks. Many toy manufacturers, such as Mattel, are also developing VR products. The Japanese company Nintendo has already introduced its first version of a cyberspace game, selling 700,000 games within nine months of its release.

Architecture

Also at the University of North Carolina (Chapel Hill), a virtual reality program allows architects to use a treadmill and head mounted 3-D displays to "walk" through virtual corridors and rooms.

This allows architects, builders, and potential clients to view the building, house, or room before actual construction begins.

Aerospace

The Human Interface Technology Laboratory (HIT Labs), founded by Dr. Thomas Furness in 1989, has developed a VTOL (Vertical TakeOff and Landing) aircraft simulator for Boeing Aircraft.

When a new airport or expansion of an existing airport is being considered, the authorities will hear from both proponents and opponents of the plan. To avoid potential problems, HIT Labs is creating a virtual third runway for the Seattle-Tacoma airport which includes realistic sound simulation. This virtual runway can be used to test different ideas from all sides concerned.

Advertising and marketing

The ability to transmit virtual impressions and sensory perceptions also opens up entirely new dimensions for the advertising industry. While today's advertising is dominated by audio-visual techniques, tomorrow's advertising strategy may enable you to test virtual products at home before actually purchasing the item.

12.3 Creating Virtual Worlds

A joint research project by the Advanced Human Interface Group, which consists of the software company Sense8 and the chip manufacturer Intel, and VPL resulted in the virtual reality system VR1.

Based on a specially upgraded 486 workstation equipped with the necessary peripherals, graphics board and the WorldToolKit software, this system gives you the ability to create your own virtual worlds.

SPEA Fire RISC
i860

The DVI graphics board SPEA Fire RISC i860 produces an extremely high quality image. It features real-time texturing and adaptive resolution.

For stereoscopic visual output, a second PC and delivery board are needed. If you want to incorporate your own illustrations, textures, or other pictures into your virtual world, you'll need the DVI capture board from Intel. This board digitizes and compresses large amounts of picture data.

The VR1 data helmet includes two color LCD screens and a pair of stereo headphones. Each of the two screens has a resolution of 360 x 240 pixels. This helmet provides the user with realistic sensory input.

An ultrasonic movement sensor at the top of the helmet registers the user's movements. This enables the virtual world to respond according to the user's movements.

The system uses a spaceball to allow input through a three-dimensional trackball.

WorldToolKit

With the WorldToolKit by Sense8, virtual worlds can be created by using the VR1 system. This kit is a programming library consisting of C statements and functions, from which the developer can quickly and easily create 3D simulations and virtual worlds in real time.

Since its software is structured modularly, applications can be constructed on PCs as well as on SUN or SiliconGraphics workstations.

WorldToolKit from Sense8

The WorldToolKit allows developers to build complex virtual environments. It simplifies the effort of interfacing to devices such as the Spaceball from Spaceball Technologies and the Flight Helmet from Virtual Research.

The WorldToolKit integrates the following modules in a flexible and object-oriented library:

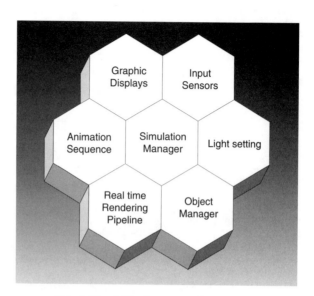

WorldToolKit integrated modules

Realistic object surfaces

With the texturing functions of the WorldToolKit, applications with texture mapping in real time can be developed. Video-realistic textures can be applied to the surface of objects in any desired orientation and size. Using surface textures that correspond to the real-world material makes virtual worlds seem more real.

The system's data import and export functions permit models and data to be imported, rendered and intuitively edited. The package also includes an extensive DXF file reader that permits AutoCAD DXF files to be transformed into 3D objects automatically.

The WorldToolKit library includes various drivers for many devices that allow the user to configure the system's input and output specifically for his or her own applications. By combining various sensors to graphical objects, the following functions are possible:

• Head Tracking (measuring the position of the user's head within the space)

• Gesture Tracking (measuring the manipulation of objects)

The WorldToolKit also features the following functions:

• A fast renderer with the dynamic control of viewpoints, objects, textures, and light setting

- The ability to import 3D objects from DFX, STL and ASCII formats

- Device drivers for Advanced Gravis Mousestick, Polhemus 3Space, Logitech "Red Baron" 2D/6D ultrasonic headtracker/mouse, Ascension Bird, Spatial Systems Spaceball, CiS Geometry Ball Jr., and others

- Linked Hypertext structure for the support of large virtual environments

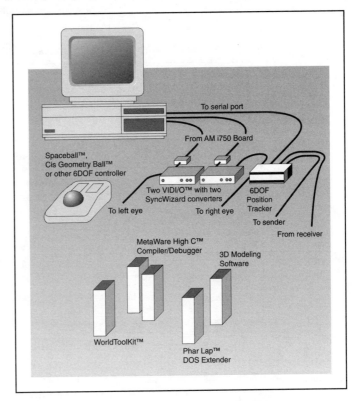

Functions of the WorldToolKit

Command set   The WorldToolKit contains over 200 object-oriented functions that help create prototypes and complex applications. These functions are grouped into the following categories:

Universe   The Universe contains all the objects. Users create their virtual worlds by adding objects to the "universe", subsequently defining their individual actions and interactions.

Command	Function
universe_new	Defines a new universe
universe_delete	Deletes an existing universe and all the objects contained therein
universe_go	Starts the simulation
universe_stop	Ends the simulation
universe_setactions	Defines actions that can be called at any point within the simulation loop
universe_load	Readies the universe for a simulation
universe_pickobject	Selects an object with a 2D viewpoint

Textures

To texture an object, the user selects a picture from the texture data base and places it on the surface of the object. This texture can then be modified to achieve the desired effect.

Command	Function
texture_apply	Applies a texture to an object
texture_remove	Removes a texture
texture_translate	Moves a texture to a new position
texture_rotate	Rotates the texture by a specified angle
texture_scale	Enlarges or shrinks an existing texture
texture_mirror	Mirrors the texture onto the remaining surfaces of the object

Graphical Objects

Graphical objects are the basic building blocks of virtual worlds under the WorldToolKit. The kit provides an extensive set of functions for constructing, using, and organizing objects. Tasks can be assigned to these objects to provide them with a function or a certain action or behavior.

Command	Function
object_new	Creates a new object from a 3D model
object_delete	Deletes an existing object
object_settask	Adds a task to an object that can be called at any point within the simulation loop
object_save	Saves an object to a file
object_translate	Locates an object at a new position
object_rotate	Rotates an object about any desired axis
object_stretch	Enlarges or shrinks an object along any desired axis
object_addsensor	Adds a sensor to an object
object_removesensor	Removes an existing sensor from an object
object_attach	Sets the object to a lower position in the hierarchy
object_detach	Sets the object in a higher position in the hierarchy
object_intersect	Looks for collisions between two objects
object_levelofdetail	Reduces the object to a lower level of complexity
object_copy	Copies an existing object
object_setpivot	Sets the rotational center of an object

Animation   Animation sequences are an easy way to add dynamically changing objects to your virtual world. An animation sequence is a set of objects that's displayed sequentially.

Command	Function
animation_new	Creates a new animation sequence
animation_delete	Deletes an existing animation sequence
animation_go	Starts an animation
animation_stop	Ends an animation
animation_setframe	Sets the current frame number
animation_setframerate	Sets the number of frames per second
animation_getobject	Reduces the animation back to the object

Light Sources   Light setting is both flexible and easy to use. Ambient as well as direct lighting can be placed dynamically anywhere within your virtual world.

Command	Function
light_new	Produces a new light source
light_delete	Deletes an existing light source
light_addsensor	Adds a sensor to the light source
light_setintensity	Sets the brightness of a light source
light_setposition	Sets the position of a light source
light_setdirection	Sets the direction of a light beam
light_setambient	Sets the ambient lighting level

Sensors   Assigning sensors to the objects within your virtual world makes it easier to interact with these objects. A sensor object registers the input of a device for each frame of the simulation.

Command	Function
sensor_new	Produces an object sensor for a specific device
sensor_delete	Deletes an existing sensor
sensor_setsensitivity	Sets the sensitivity of the sensor
sensor_setangularrate	Sets the sensor's rotational point
sensor_setconstraints	Returns the values that were read by the sensor

Viewpoint   Viewpoint functions allow you to add viewpoint objects to your universe. These functions let you select several options, such as monoscopic or stereoscopic display.

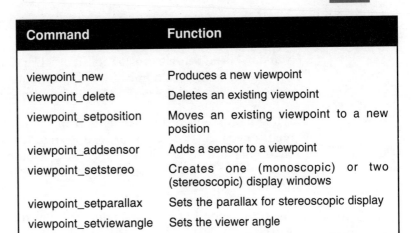

Command	Function
viewpoint_new	Produces a new viewpoint
viewpoint_delete	Deletes an existing viewpoint
viewpoint_setposition	Moves an existing viewpoint to a new position
viewpoint_addsensor	Adds a sensor to a viewpoint
viewpoint_setstereo	Creates one (monoscopic) or two (stereoscopic) display windows
viewpoint_setparallax	Sets the parallax for stereoscopic display
viewpoint_setviewangle	Sets the viewer angle
viewpoint_getposition	Returns the current viewer position
viewpoint_getdirection	Returns the current viewing direction

With only a few lines of C source code, you can create a WorldToolKit application that creates a universe and its view-objects, initializes these objects and assigns an input device to the viewpoint.

The following sample program produces a fully functional "walk-through" application:

```
/* sample walk-through program written with WorldToolKit
#include <stdio.h>
#include "wt.h"
main()
{
    Posn6d p;          /* Model viewpoint */
    sensor *sensor     /* Spaceball sensor */
        /* A new universe is created */
    universe_new();
        /* The "Heavens" universe file is loaded with a size of 1 */
    universe_load("Heavens", &p, 1.0);
        /* Moves the viewpoint to the model viewpoint */
    viewpoint_move_(universe_getviewpoint(), &p);
        /* Initializes the spaceball sensor to COM1: */
    sensor = spaceball_new(COM1);
        /* Readies the universe */
    universe_ready();
        /* Adjusts the sensor speed to the size of the universe */
    sensor_setsensitivity(sensor, 0.01 * universe_getradius());
        /* Starts the simulation */
    universe_go();
        /* Deletes the universe once the simulation is finished */
    universe_delete();
```

12.4 A Virtual World of Your Own

You don't need Sense8, WorldToolKit or a DataGlove to get a sense of virtual reality. A number of public domain and shareware programs exist that create low-level virtual reality environments.

While more awkward to navigate than the commercial products mentioned in this chapter (i.e., you "walk" through the environment using keyboard, joystick or mouse, instead of using data helmets or data suits), these programs still provide elements of virtual reality.

The companion CD-ROM contains a virtual reality demonstration stored in the SHAREWR\DOS\GFXTOOLS\3DHOUSE directory.

This demonstration, a reproduction of author Charles Carr's log house in Valley Center CA, was created using DoMark's Virtual Reality Studio. If you wish to use a mouse, run your mouse driver from DOS, then run the RUNME.BAT file. If you prefer to use the keyboard, just run the RUNME.BAT file from the DOS prompt.

The keys producing movement in this program are as follows:

Key(s)	Movement
Q	Turn left
W	Turn right
P	Turn upward
L	Turn downward
O	Move forward
K	Move backward
H	Move left
J	Move right
R	Raise viewing height
F	Lower viewing height
U	U-turn
I	Center view vertically
Shift + Esc	Return to DOS

If you prefer using a mouse, click on a control at the bottom of the screen to move around the environment, or change your viewpoint.

In either case, pressing Shift + Esc returns you to DOS and reality.

Chapter 13

Multimedia and Visual Basic

By now you've learned a lot about multimedia. You're probably anxious to learn how to program your own multimedia applications.

This chapter will show you how easy it is to use the Multimedia Extensions for Windows 3.1 and Visual Basic. We'll use Visual Basic Professional 2.0 for the example in this chapter, but only minor changes will be required in order to use earlier versions of Visual Basic with the Multimedia Extensions.

In this chapter we've assumed that you have some knowledge of programming with Visual Basic. Therefore, we won't discuss programming principles. Refer to the documentation and tutorials supplied with Visual Basic if you need additional information about programming practices.

The descriptions of the following MCI commands can also be applied to other programming languages, such as Turbo Pascal for Windows or Borland C++.

13.1 MCI Devices

The MMSYSTEM.DLL dynamic link library from Microsoft provides several functions for managing multimedia devices such as waveform, MIDI and timer hardware. The correct driver must be installed for each of these devices. Drivers for the Media Control Interface (MCI) provide high level control of media devices.

The MMSYSTEM.DLL library contains several MCI functions that can be used for the following predefined devices.

animation

A multimedia movie player lets you play back a series of graphic images, simulating motion. Animation can be frame based or cast based. This player doesn't necessarily consist of a hardware device. There are also special software drivers, which enable you to play back, for example, Autodesk Animator files (see Chapter 7). These drivers don't require additional hardware.

cdaudio

A cdaudio is a CD audio player that can be used as a CD-ROM drive as well as a conventional audio CD player. This adds to this device's usefulness in multimedia.

dat

Digital Audio Tape, or DAT, hasn't been as popular as audio CDs. However, its sound quality is equal to a CD.

In the future, DAT may also receive additional competition from the recordable CD. Therefore, DAT devices are rarely found in computer applications.

digitalvideo

This device consists of an expansion card that lets your screen display digital video signals.

overlay

Overlay devices are cards that allow analog signals, such as TV or video signals, to be spliced into the computer picture. These analog signals can even be digitized.

scanner

Image scanners can be accessed with MCI functions.

sequencer

MIDI sequencers are used to record and play back music data in the MIDI format.

vcr

With the correct hardware, it's also possible to control a videotape recorder or player.

videodiscs

These are large laser disks, which operate the same way as CDs. These disks are used to store video information.

waveaudio

This is probably the most commonly used MCI device. This audio device plays digitized waveform files. MCI drivers are available for almost all sound cards under Windows 3.1. With the proper driver, it's even possible to use your on-board PC loudspeaker to play back digital audio signals.

We'll discuss waveaudio devices in more detail later. However, the basic procedure is almost identical for each of these devices.

Simple Device/Compound Device

These devices are usually divided into two types: Simple devices and compound devices.

Simple

A typical simple device is a CD-ROM, a CD audio player or a Videodisc player. Only one storage medium (CD) can be inserted into one player at a time. So only one CD can be played at a time. Simple devices do not require a data file for playback.

Compound

A sound card or a MIDI sequencer are examples of typical compound devices. The data file associated with a compound device is called a device element. Compound devices can be used to access many different sound files (e.g., on a hard drive, a disk, a CD-ROM player or other data carriers). This can be done without physically switching from one medium to another.

Accessing MCI functions

There are two ways to access MCI functions through Visual Basic. One method is difficult while the other is simple.

MCISend Command() function

The difficult method uses the MCISendCommand() function. To use this function, you must be familiar with pointer programming and complex data structures.

An advantage of this method is that even the most minute information about the progress of MCI functions can be determined.

Unfortunately, it's extremely difficult to use this method in Visual Basic. Use the MCISendCommand() function with C compilers and Turbo Pascal for Windows.

Simple method in VB

The way to access MCI functions through Visual Basic is much easier. The MCI provides functions that achieve almost the same results without requiring complex programming maneuvers.

This method requires using only two MCI functions, MCISendString and MCIGetErrorString, to control all MCI devices. We'll explain this procedure in detail in the following section.

13.2 Global Definition

The two MCI functions that you'll need are MCISendString and MCIGetErrorString.

You must define these functions within your global module so they can be used anywhere in your Visual Basic project. The file GLOBAL.BAS demonstrates the best way to do this.

In addition to MCISendString and MCIGetErrorString, the function sndPlaySound is also incorporated.

```
' ***********************************************************************
' *  Microsoft Windows 3.0 + MM Extensions / Windows 3.1 Sound Interface *
' ***********************************************************************
' *              Copyright (C) 1992 DATA BECKER GmbH                    *
' *                         (c) 1993 Abacus Software Inc.               *
' *              Author    : Axel Stolz                                 *
' *          Created with Microsoft Visual Basic Professional 2.00      *
' ***********************************************************************


' ********************************************
' ***          MCI Constants           ***
' ********************************************

Global Const NoMCIError = 0

' ***************************************************************
' ***          Declaration of desired MCI Functions      ***
' ***************************************************************

Declare Function MCISendString Lib "MMSystem" (ByVal CommandStr$, ByVal
ReturnStr$, ByVal ReturnLen%, ByVal hWndCallback%) As Long
Declare Function MCIGetErrorString Lib "MMSystem" (ByVal ErrValue&, ByVal
ErrMessage$, ByVal ErrLen%) As Integer

' ***************************************************************
```

```
' ***    Bindings for the High Level Audio Routine sndPlaySound ***
' ***************************************************************

' *******************************************
' ***    Constants for sndPlaySound()    ***
' *******************************************

Global Const SND_SYNC = 0          ' Play Synchronous Sound (Default)
Global Const SND_ASYNC = 1         ' Play Asynchronous Sound
Global Const SND_NODEFAULT = 2     ' Do not use .INI Sounds if no
                                   ' .WAV files can be found
Global Const SND_MEMORY = 4        ' Pointer to data in memory
Global Const SND_LOOP = 8          ' Repeat sound until next SndPlaySound
Global Const SND_NOSTOP = 10       ' Do not interrupt playing sound

Declare Sub sndPlaySound Lib "MMSystem" (ByVal Filename As String, ByVal
Flags As Integer)
```

13.3 Defining Functions

To define a new function, use Declare Function. This statement is followed by the function name, for example MCISendString. This name must correspond exactly with the function name from the MMSYSTEM.DLL library.

Then you must tell Visual Basic that this function is located in the MMSYSTEM.DLL library. To do this, use the simple statement Lib MMSYSTEM.

Passing parameters

Enter all the necessary parameters for the function within the parentheses that follow this statement. Ensure that each parameter variable is marked with "ByVal". Unlike the function name, individual parameter names can be selected freely.

Function return

Finally you must specify which value the function should return. In the case of MCISendString, this is a 32-bit value because its parameter declaration ends with "AsLong".

Let's take a closer look at the individual functions:

MCISendString

This function is used to address any desired MCI device. It requires four parameters for callback functions and return strings.

Parameter 1: command string

The first parameter is a string. In our example it's named
CommandStr$. This string takes the form of:

command device_name arguments

This parameter is used to pass a command to the MCI device. This
command tells the device what action to perform, such as Open,
Play or Close. Additional commands can be used to further modify
these commands. We'll take a closer look at these individual
commands later.

Parameter 2: return string

The second parameter is a string used for returning information
from the MCI. The contents of this string will vary depending on
the device and command. In our example this pointer is named
MCISendRet.

Parameter 3: length of return string

The third parameter, ReturnLen%, specifies the maximum number
of characters that the buffer can contain. You can suppress the
return information by setting the value of this parameter to NULL
or 0.

Parameter 4: window number

The fourth parameter, which is hWndCallBack% in our example,
tells the MCI the handle of the window that receives the
message. This is important for functions that access video devices.
This parameter isn't as important with audio devices.

Return value : error number

The function value returned by MCISendString is the number of any
error that has occurred. If the value zero is returned, the function
has been executed successfully.

The command used in our example program in the VBEXAM1.BAS
module is:

```
MCISendTest = MCISendString(CommandStr$, MCISendRet, 255, 0)
```

MCIGetErrorString

This function returns the error string associated with an error number. This function uses three different parameters.

Parameter 1: error number

The parameter ErrValue& is used to specify the error number of the error for which you're trying to obtain information. It's possible to assign the return value of MCISendString to this parameter whenever an error occurs. This automatically assigns the current error number to the parameter.

Parameter 2: error text

The parameter ErrMessage$ is used to specify the string in which the error text will be returned.

Parameter 3: length of error text

The parameter ErrLen% is used to specify the number of characters that the error text may contain. This parameter is identical to parameter 3 of MCISendString.

Return value : error during execution

The return value of MCIGetErrorString is declared as an integer. It specifies whether the corresponding error number could be found.

The previous information completely describes the only two functions you need in order to work with the MCI. However, you need more information in order to use these functions.

Now we'll describe the individual MCI commands.

13.4 Using The MCI Commands

The following description of MCI commands specifies the syntax that you must use in order to construct a character string that will be recognized by the MCI.

Optional parameters are listed within square brackets ("...[parameter]..."). These parameters can be omitted if they aren't needed.

MCI Command OPEN

Almost all MCI devices that can be connected to your PC recognize the OPEN command. This command tells the device to prepare itself to receive additional commands.

Open Simple

For simple devices, the following Open command is used:

```
OPEN device [SHAREABLE] [ALIAS name]
```

One way of opening a CD player would be:

```
OPEN cdaudio ALIAS CD
```

SHAREABLE lets you specify whether the device may also be used by other Windows applications. If this parameter is omitted, other programs won't be able to access this device following the OPEN command. Remember that some devices cannot be used simultaneously by more than one program.

The parameter [ALIAS name] is used to abbreviate the name of an opened device in order to save unnecessary work. This isn't especially important with simple devices. However, it's a useful feature when you need to access compound devices, as you'll see later.

Open Compound

The OPEN command for a compound device looks like this:

```
OPEN filename TYPE device [SHAREABLE] [ALIAS name]
```

The following is one way this command could be used:

```
OPEN C:\WIN31\WAVES\RINGRING.WAV TYPE waveaudio ALIAS Ring
```

As you can see, the ALIAS can simplify this process. Using the single word "Ring" produces the same result as using:

```
C\WIN31\WAVES\RINGRING.WAV
```

Generally the parameter TYPE device can be omitted, since the MCI independently recognizes the file type.

Therefore, our example could also look as follows:

```
OPEN C:\WIN31\WAVES\RINGRING.WAV ALIAS Telephon
```

You could open an Autodesk animation file in the same way, once you've installed the corresponding device driver:

```
OPEN C:\ANIM\PLANET.FLI ALIAS PLANET
```

MCI Command PLAY

If you've opened a WaveAudio or CD device with OPEN, you'll probably also want to play back something. This is exactly what the PLAY command does. Its syntax is as follows:

```
PLAY name [FROM start] [TO    end]
```

The parameters FROM and TO specify the range of the file that will be played back. If you omit these parameters, the function will play the data from the current position to the end of the data file.

The values for FROM and TO are interpreted according to the most recently specified time format.

PLAY Wave Audio

The PLAY command for a Wave file might look like this:

```
PLAY Ring FROM 12000 TO 18000 [WAIT]
```

This command will play the time range of 12000 to 18000 in the data file "C:\WIN31\WAVES\RINGRING.WAV", which is represented by the alias "Ring".

If you use the optional parameter WAIT, your program will be paused until the PLAY command has been completely executed. With shorter playbacks this shouldn't be a problem. However, with longer sounds your program will be paused for much longer periods of time.

You can play back WAV files as often as you like. However, remember that these files must be "rewound" after their first playback, just like an audio cassette.

Therefore, if you've entered

```
PLAY Ring
```

the file will be played the first time. However, if you enter the command again, nothing will happen. This occurs because the entire file has already been played back once.

If you want to hear this sound again, use the following command:

```
PLAY Ring FROM 0
```

You can also use this version of the command for your first playback. This ensures that the file is played back from the beginning.

PLAY CD

With a CD device, the following command

```
PLAY CD FROM 5 TO 9
```

would play tracks five through nine consecutively.

MCI Command CLOSE

This command closes an MCI device that has previously been opened. Its syntax is as follows:

```
CLOSE name
```

For our example, the command would be used like this:

```
CLOSE Ring CLOSE CD
```

These are the three most basic commands. However, the MCI provides many other commands. Some of these commands are common to all MCI devices and some are used only with specific devices.

13.5 MCI Sample Program

You've already seen a small portion of our sample program. This was the global definition file GLOBAL.BAS. In this section, we'll take a closer look at the rest of the program.

The sample program is located in the \PROGDEV\VB directory on the companion CD-ROM. If you want to try the VBEXAM1.EXE sample program, you must copy both the program and the WAV and FLI files into the same directory and start the program from there. The file MCI.VBX must also be copied. This is necessary because the MCI commands are called without path specifications. If you do not already have VBRUN200.DLL in your SYSTEM folder, you may copy this file also.

To execute MCI commands for playing back FLI files, the Animation1 driver must be installed in your Control Panel (see Section 7.1 for information on this driver).

The Animation1 driver can also be found on the companion CD-ROM in the \WINDOWS\ANIMATE directory.

This Visual Basic program has three parts.

Part 1 - GLOBAL.BAS

This part contains the definitions that enable the MCI functions to be accessed and was previously shown.

Simple sound playback

However, another function, called sndPlaySound, is defined in this module. This function isn't related to the MCI functions, even though it can be used to control WaveAudio devices. sndPlaySound is a "High Level Audio" function and can play back only Wave files.

At certain points within your programs you may want to play back short sounds. In these instances, it isn't always necessary to send OPEN/PLAY/CLOSE to your sound card through the MCI. sndPlaySound can perform all this in one function. Its syntax is as follows:

```
sndPlaySound (pointer, flag)
```

The parameter pointer can be either a character string, such as "C:\WIN31\WAVES\RINGRING.WAV", or an actual pointer to a Wave file that's in memory. It can even be a name from the [sounds] WIN.INI section, such as SystemStart.

This sound automatically plays when you start Windows. Which file is actually represented by this name can be determined by examining the Sound settings in the Windows Control Panel (found in the Main Group).

As you can see, sndPlaySound has some useful features. However, the command can be used only with WaveAudio devices.

The flags parameter specifies the factors that should be considered during the sound playback. Several constants have been defined for this parameter.

Since the individual constants are additive, additional parameters can be added to the SND_SYNC or SND_ASYNC flags using OR. The resulting parameter is then passed to sndPlaySound.

Parameter flag SND_SYNC

This parameter has a value of 0 and is the default value. If you pass this flag with the function call, the execution of the remaining program will be paused until the WAV file playback has been completed. Since the sound is played synchronously with the program, the flag has been abbreviated as SYNC.

Parameter flag SND_ASYNC

This parameter, which has the value 1, is the exact opposite of SND_SYNC. When this flag is passed with the function call, the output of the WAV file is started. Then the program execution continues immediately. So, program and sound are processed simultaneously, or asynchronously.

Parameter flag SND_NODEFAULT

If sndPlaySound is called with a file name that Windows cannot locate, Windows automatically emits the system tone that has been specified in WIN.INI under [sounds]. If you add the flag SND_NODEFAULT to the parameter SND_SYNC or SND_ASYNC, this tone won't be played when a WAV file cannot be located.

Parameter flag SND_MEMORY

When this flag is used, you don't have to pass a pointer to a string with the file name. Instead, a pointer to a memory area, in which the loaded WAV is resident, must be passed.

This flag must be used with SndPlaySoundMem; the pointer must identify a WAV data file in memory. Otherwise the function call is identical to that with a file name.

Parameter flag SND_LOOP

When this flag is set, the sample is played back repeatedly until either the playback is stopped or until another playback is started.

SND_LOOP should be used only with SND_ASYNC, not with SND_SYNC.

Parameter flag SND_NOSTOP

When a sample playback is started with this flag, playback begins only if another file isn't currently being played. Therefore, it isn't possible to interrupt a sample that's being played back with SND_LOOP by calling a new sample file with the NOSTOP flag.

So you understand how these flags work, we'll present a few examples that demonstrate some ways they can be used.

The following command line will start the asynchronous playback of the WAV file ALARM.WAV by using a playback loop:

```
SndPlaySound('Alarm.WAV',SND_ASYNC OR SND_LOOP);
```

This alarm will sound until a new file is played or until you enter SndPlaySound(0,SND_SYNC). Otherwise, this sound will be played back continually, even if you've already terminated your program.

You can also use command lines such as these:

```
SndPlaySoundFile ('COUGH.WAV', SND_ASYNC OR SND_LOOP
                 OR SND_NODEFAULT OR SND_NOSTOP);
```

This command will start the looped playback of COUGH.WAV, if another sound isn't currently being played. If this file cannot be found, the system sound is suppressed.

As you can see, sndPlaySound is a very useful command for sound output functions.

Part 2 - VBEXAM1.BAS

The VBEXAM1.BAS module contains functions that make using MCI commands even easier.

MCISimpleCommand

The first function is called MCISimpleCommand. With a normal MCI command, you must specify the return string as well as its length and window handle. Since these parameters remain unused with many of these function calls, they cause an unnecessary amount of work.

MCISimpleCommand requires only the actual MCI command. It returns the MCI error number as its function value, for example:

```
Errornumber = MCISimpleCommand("PLAY Ring FROM 0")
```

The return string is obtained and then simply displayed within a text box of FORM1.

MCIErrorCheck

The second function is MCIErrorCheck, which makes it easier to identify an error that's occurred. The value returned by MCISimpleCommand simply must be passed to this function. Technically, this function is a procedure, since it doesn't return a function value. It simply displays the identified error's text in FORM1.

Part 3 - VBEXAM1.FRM

The third portion of our sample program consists of the FORM shown below. It's the main screen of our sample program.

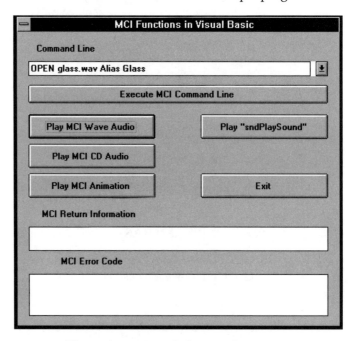

The main screen of the sample program

Experimenting With MCI Commands

At the top of this window is a text box in which you can enter and execute MCI commands. Simply type the desired command and click the [Execute MCI Command Line] button or press [Enter].

So you don't have to retype a command each time you want to execute it, the text box is linked with a list box. To open this box, simply click the arrow to the right of the text box. From this list you can select one of the commands that you've previously entered and executed.

If you don't want to experiment with MCI commands at this time, you can also click one of the example buttons that are located below the command line.

Three of these buttons are for Wave Audio, CD Player and Animation. The fourth button is reserved for sndPlaySound.

MCI Error Messages

Errors displayed in the text box

If an error occurs during the execution of an MCI command, the corresponding error message will be displayed in the text box at the bottom of the window. If the command was executed flawlessly, this text box will contain the text "The specified command was carried out."

The text line above this box is reserved for the MCI command return texts. Only a few of these commands actually return text messages. The OPEN command, for example, returns the number of the opened Wave Audio file; "1" is for the first file, "2" is for the second, etc.

Ending the program

The final element of this form is the Exit button. You can end the program by clicking this button. Remember that any devices that you've opened will remain open, even after the program has been terminated, until a proper CLOSE command is issued.

To see how easy it is to use the MCI commands, you may want to start modifying our sample program. Perhaps your system includes an MCI device that wasn't used in the example. In that case, simply add another example button, perhaps for your video disk.

MCI programming lets you access complex multimedia devices easily. This enables you to create powerful applications quickly. The following is a listing of VBEXAM1.BAS and all the event procedures of the sample program:

VBEXAM1.BAS

```
Sub MCIErrorCheck (ByVal TestValue&)

  Dim TestErr As Integer
```

```
    Dim ErrorText As String * 255


    TestErr = MCIGetErrorString(TestValue&, ErrorText$, 255)

    Form1.MCI_ErrorText.Caption = ErrorText

End Sub


Function MCISimpleCommand (CommandStr$) As Long

    Dim MCISendTest As Long
    Dim MCISendRet  As String * 255

' Test MCI Command

    MCISendTest = MCISendString(CommandStr$, MCISendRet, 255, 0)

    If (Len(MCISendRet) = 0) Then
        MCISendRet = "No text returned"
    End If

' Display the Returned Text in FORM1

    Form1.MCI_ReturnText.Caption = MCISendRet

' Return the Error Number

    MCISimpleCommand = MCISendTest

End Function
```

VBEXAM1.FRM

```
Sub CmdLine_Click ()

End Sub

Sub MCI_Input_KeyDown (KeyCode As Integer, Switch As Integer)

' Execute the command when 'Enter' is pressed

    If KeyCode = &HD Then
        MCIExecCommand_Click
    End If

End Sub

Sub MCIExecCommand_Click ()

    Dim TestSend As Long
    Dim MCIExecStr  As String * 255
```

```
' Copy text from the Combo Box

    MCIExecStr = MCI_Input.Text

' Copy Input line to list and then
' delete in input line

    MCI_Input.AddItem MCI_Input.Text
    MCI_Input.Text = ""

' Erase MCI ErrorText field

    MCI_ErrorText.Caption = ""
    MCI_ErrorText.Refresh

' Send input command

    TestSend = MCISimpleCommand(MCIExecStr)

' If Error, display error message

    Call MCIErrorCheck(TestSend)

End Sub

Sub MCISendStringAnim_Click ()

    Dim TestSend As Long

' Delete an existing error text

    MCI_ErrorText.Caption = ""
    MCI_ErrorText.Refresh

' Close any open file

    TestSend = MCISimpleCommand("CLOSE Animation")

' Call desired file

    TestSend = MCISimpleCommand("OPEN Testshw2.FLI alias Animation")

' In case of error, output corresponding text
' otherwise playback file

    If (TestSend <> NoMCIError) Then

        Call MCIErrorCheck(TestSend)

    Else
        Call MCIErrorCheck(TestSend)
        TestSend = MCISimpleCommand("PLAY Animation from 1 wait")
        TestSend = MCISimpleCommand("PLAY Animation from 1 wait")
        TestSend = MCISimpleCommand("PLAY Animation from 1 wait")
```

```
            TestSend = MCISimpleCommand("PLAY Animation from 1 wait")
            TestSend = MCISimpleCommand("CLOSE Animation")
        End If

End Sub

Sub mciSendStringAudio_Click ()

    Dim TestSend As Long

' Delete any existing error text

    MCI_ErrorText.Caption = ""
    MCI_ErrorText.Refresh

' Close any open file

    TestSend = MCISimpleCommand("CLOSE Glass")

' Call desired file

        TestSend = MCISimpleCommand("OPEN glass.wav TYPE waveaudio ALIAS
Glass")

' In case of error, output corresponding text
' otherwise playback file


    If (TestSend <> NoMCIError) Then

      Call MCIErrorCheck(TestSend)

    Else
        Call MCIErrorCheck(TestSend)
        TestSend = MCISimpleCommand("PLAY Glass wait")
        TestSend = MCISimpleCommand("CLOSE Glass")
    End If
End Sub

Sub mciSendStringCD_Click (Index As Integer)

    Dim TestSend As Long

' Delete any existing error text

    MCI_ErrorText.Caption = ""
    MCI_ErrorText.Refresh

' Close any open file

    TestSend = MCISimpleCommand("CLOSE CD")

' Call desired file
```

```
    TestSend = MCISimpleCommand("OPEN cdaudio ALIAS CD")

' In case of error, output corresponding text
' otherwise playback file


    If (TestSend <> NoMCIError) Then

        Call MCIErrorCheck(TestSend)

    Else
        Call MCIErrorCheck(TestSend)
        TestSend = MCISimpleCommand("SET CD TIME FORMAT tmsf")
            TestSend = MCISimpleCommand("PLAY CD FROM 2:00:00:00 TO
2:00:30:00")
        TestSend = MCISimpleCommand("CLOSE CD")
        End If

End Sub

Sub Program_End_Click ()
    End
End Sub

Sub sndPlay_Click ()
    Call sndPlaySound("cough.wav", SND_ASYNC)
End Sub
```

13.6 MCI Commands

The following lists the most important commands for the two most popular MCI devices: The sound card and the CD player.

Accessing WaveAudio Devices

OPEN name TYPE WAVEAUDIO [SHARABLE] [ALIAS aliasname] [BUFFER size]

name

    NEW   With this command, a new, temporary Wave file is opened for recording. The recording process is started by using RECORD. The file name is then specified with the SAVE command. When New is used, a name must be set with the ALIAS parameter.

    FILENAME   If the name of an existing Wave file is specified, the file is opened. The file is then ready to be played back using PLAY.

Options

[SHARABLE]   Using this parameter makes the sound card accessible to other applications as well.

[BUFFER size]   Determines the buffer size, in seconds, that will be available for the Wave Audio device in conjunction with the Wave file specified by the command. The default value is 4 seconds.

PLAY name [FROM start] [TO end]

name

FileName or AliasName
The playback of the specified Wave file is started using PLAY. The playback begins at the start of the file, unless a previous PLAY or SEEK command has been used to reach a certain position within the file. In this case, the playback starts at the most recent file position.

Options

[FROM start]   With this option, you can determine the exact file position where the playback will begin. The units in which this parameter is evaluated are determined using SET (see below). If the [TO end] option is omitted, the file is played to the end.

[TO end]   This option lets you determine the file position where the playback will stop. Similar to the previous parameter, the units for this parameter are determined using SET. You can also use TO without the FROM option. In this case, the starting position is determined by the conditions previously explained.

STOP name

Name

FileName or AliasName
This command stops any playback or recording that's in progress. The playback or recording can be resumed by using PLAY or RECORD again.

CLOSE name

Name

WaveAudio or FileName or AliasName
> If you use the WaveAudio parameter, this command closes the entire connection to the MCI device. By specifying a WaveFile or an AliasName, you can close that particular file.

DELETE name [FROM start] [TO end;]

Name

FileName or AliasName
> This command deletes the entire segment, unless PLAY or SEEK were previously used to reach a certain position within the file.

Options

[FROM start]
> With this option, you can determine the exact position from which the file contents will be deleted. The units in which this parameter is evaluated are determined using SET (see below). If the option [TO end] is omitted, the file contents are deleted to the end of the file.

[TO end]
> This option specifies the file position from which the file contents will be deleted. The units in which this parameter is evaluated are determined using SET. The option TO can also be used without FROM. In this case, the starting position is determined by the conditions previously explained.

PAUSE name

Name

FileName or AliasName
> This command interrupts the playback or recording. By using RESUME, you can continue the playback or recording at the point where it was paused.

RESUME name

Name

FileName or AliasName
> This command resumes a playback or recording that has been interrupted with PAUSE.

RECORD name [FROM start [TO end] [INSERT]

Name

FileName or AliasName
> This command starts the recording process of sound data to a file. The position at which the recording is started is determined by a STOP or SEEK command that may have been executed before the recording began. If this position is located within the current contents of the file, the following contents will be overwritten. To prevent this, use the INSERT option.

Options

[INSERT]
> With this option, you can insert the recording into the file at the current file position. The existing file contents after the current position will simply be shifted by the length of the recording.

[FROM start]
> This option allows you to select the exact location where the recording will start. The units in which this parameter is evaluated are determined using SET (see below).

[TO end]
> This option determines the file position up to which the sound data will be recorded. The units in which this parameter is evaluated are determined, as with the previous parameters, using SET. The option TO can also be used without FROM. In this case, the starting position is determined by the conditions previously described.

SAVE name

name

FileName or AliasName
> This command saves the file, under the specified name, in the Wave format using the .WAV file name extension.

SEEK name TO position

Name

FileName or AliasName
> This command locates a specified position within the file. PLAY, RECORD, and DELETE are executed beginning at this position, if FROM isn't specified for each of these commands.

TO

START or END or position
> The beginning of the file can be reached by using TO START. Use TO END to specify the end of the file as the current position. The parameter position is used to locate a certain point within the file by specifying a value. The units of this value are determined with SET.

SET name TIME FORMAT units

Name

FileName or AliasName
> This command determines the units that will be used for the FROM and TO options when specifying file positions.

Units

Bytes or milliseconds or samples
> The units specified with this command are used as the time format. Use milliseconds since sound recording devices generally use this format.

CAPABILITY name CAN RECORD

Name

WaveAudio or DateName or AliasName
> This function determines whether a recording can be made. If it can, the function returns the value TRUE; otherwise it returns FALSE.

CAPABILITY name CAN SAVE

name

WaveAudio or DateName or AliasName
> This function determines whether the file can be saved. If it can, the function returns the value TRUE; otherwise FALSE is returned.

INFO name PRODUCT

name

WaveAudio or DateName or AliasName
> This command returns the name of the appropriate MCI driver for the WaveAudio device being used.

INFO name FILE

name

FileName or AliasName
> This command displays the file name of the specified element.

STATUS name object

name

FileName or AliasName
> This command returns certain information or conditions about the specified object.

Objects

Bitspersample   This object provides the file resolution, which is specified by the number of bits (8/16) used per sample.

Bytespersec	This object provides the number of bytes per second stored in the file.
Channels	This object returns the number of channels stored in the file. The value 1 indicates a mono signal and 2 indicates stereo.
Length	This object returns the file length in the specified time format.
Level	This object returns the currently sampled value.
Position	This object returns the current file position in the specified time format.
Ready	This object returns the readiness mode of the WaveAudio device being used. If the device is ready, the value True is returned; otherwise the function value is False.
Samplepersec	This object returns the file's sampling rate in samples per second.
Time format	This returns the current time format that was specified using SET.

Accessing The CD Player

OPEN Name [SHAREBLE] [ALIAS AliasName]

name

cdaudio	This command opens the CD player for further operations. Using the ALIAS option, you can assign an AliasName to the device.

Option

[SHARABLE]	This parameter lets other applications access the CD player as well.

PLAY Name [FROM start] [TO end]

name

cdaudio or AliasName
> The audio CD is played back, starting with the first track, using PLAY.

Options

[FROM start]   This option determines the exact file position where the playback will start. The units in which this parameter is evaluated are specified using SET (see below). If the [TO end] option is omitted, the CD is played until the end.

[TO end]   This option determines the file position where the playback will end. The units for this parameter are, as with the previous parameter, specified using SET. The option TO can also be used without FROM. In this case, the starting position is determined by the conditions previously described.

CLOSE name

name

cdaudio or AliasName

    This command closes the CD player. Additional access isn't possible until another OPEN command is sent.

STOP name

name

cdaudio or AliasName

    This command interrupts the playback of the audio CD. Playback can be resumed only by using PLAY.

PAUSE name

name

cdaudio or AliasName

    In its present version, this command actually stops the audio CD playback. Therefore, it's identical to STOP.

INFO name

name

  cdaudio or AliasName

This command returns the name of the appropriate MCI driver for the CD player.

SET name AUDIO status

name

  cdaudio or AliasName

This command controls the playback channels independently of the playback of an audio CD.

Status

  All/Left/Right on/off

This command lets you switch both playback channels, or only the left or right playback channels, on and off.

SET name DOOR status

name

  cdaudio or AliasName

This command opens and closes the door of the CD player. However, this works only with players that have an electronically controlled door that responds to MCI commands. If this isn't the case, you'll receive an error message when you execute this command.

Status

  Open/Closed This command opens or closes the access door of the CD player.

SET name TIME FORMAT units

name

  cdaudio or AliasName

This command specifies the units that the options FROM and TO use to locate positions within files.

Units

Milliseconds or Msf or Tmsf

> The specified units are used for the time format. The parameter Msf uses the time format minute/second/frame (MM:SS:FF); the parameter Tmsf, however, uses track/minute/second/frame (TT:MM:SS:FF).

STATUS name object

name

cdaudio or AliasName

> Returns certain information or conditions about the specified object. If an object isn't specified, the command will return the starting position of the first track in the specified time format.

Current track   Returns the number of the current track.

Objects

Length

> Returns the complete length of the CD in the specified time format.

Length track number

> Returns the length of the track number specified by the number parameter.

Media present   Returns the value True when a CD is in the player; otherwise False is returned.

Mode

> Returns the current CD player status. Possible values include stopped, playing, not ready, seeking and paused.

Number of tracks

> Returns the total number of tracks on the CD.

Position

> Returns the current position in the specified time format.

Ready

> Returns True if the specified device is ready; otherwise False is returned.

TimeFormat   Returns the active time format.

Appendix A

Glossary

A

Access Time
Amount of time it takes the hard drive or CD-ROM drive to locate requested information. This value is measured milliseconds.

ADC
Analog to Digital Converter. Device that converts analog sound to binary code form (digital information).

Animation
Moving graphic images. Several frames show a progression of movement, and thereby simulate movement.

Application
A program designed for a specific purpose. Word processors, spreadsheets and databases are applications.

ASCII
Acronym for American Standard Code for Information Interchange. ASCII is the standard for keyboard character codes, which applies to some extent to keyboards and printers. The ASCII standard covers key codes 0 to 127; individual computer manufacturers assign their own characters to codes 128 to 255. See also *Byte*.

Aspect ratio
Refers to the ratio of the horizontal to vertical size of the screen. Some monitors display rectangular pixels which can make the picture or image appear stretched.

Authoring software

Software used to develop tutorials and Computer Based Training (CBT) programs. Interactive links are used to connect related information.

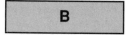

Board

A component that fits into the expansion slot of the system unit and expands the capabilities of the computer. A board can enable the computer to communicate with an external hardware device, such as a CD-ROM. See also *Interface card*.

Bookmark

Feature that enables the user to return to the previous screen or starting point after accessing related information.

bps

Bits per second. Used to measure the speed of modems.

Bus

A collection of communication lines transmitting signals between components on a circuit board or between the circuit board and expansion or other cards.

Byte

A group of eight bits. While a bit can assume only two states, 0 and 1, a byte can store from 0 up to 255 conditions. Most of the time a character is stored in a byte. Therefore, a byte can store up to 255 different characters. The standard ASCII character set consists of 128 characters; the additional characters generally used in PC software brings the total number of characters up to 255.

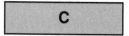

Cache

A special area of RAM to store the most frequently accessed information in RAM. You can greatly improve the speed of your system by using cache memory because it "optimizes" the cooperation among the different components of your system.

Camera

An external device that captures video images.

CD-ROM disk drive

A storage device that uses compact discs (CDs) to store data. Although a large amount of data can be stored on these disks, they're "Read Only Memory" disk drives. So data cannot be saved on the disc; it can only be read.

The advantage of using a CD-ROM include extremely high data density, storage capacity of approximately 680 Meg per diskette, and its excellence in multimedia applications.

CD-WORM disk drive

A storage device based on further development of CD-ROM disk drives. It's an acronym for "Write Once Read Many". These disk drives can write on the CD only once but can read it as often as required.

The advantages of these disk drives include data security, acceptable access times (50-80 ms) and the fact that it's impossible to overwrite or accidentally delete data since the data cannot be removed from the diskette.

Channel

A transmission line that can carry the sound of a separate instrument. Each MIDI port allows up to 16 separate channels for sending or receiving data. Each channel can function as a separate instrument in an ensemble, each using its own patch and responding independently to continuous controllers.

Clipboard

A temporary storage space that contains the most recent text or graphics that were cut or copied. You can then copy or paste the item into other documents.

Clock pulse

Smallest unit of time with which a sequencer can work. The accuracy with which a sequencer handles subtle rhythmic nuances depends on its timing resolution in clock pulses per quarter note. A quarter note is the default unit of time for one beat.

Clock speed

The speed of the processor is measured with the clock frequency. Unlike people, the processor consistently works internally at the same clock frequency. The IBM PC has a clock frequency of 4.77 MHz (Megahertz). Compatibles sometimes use higher frequencies, but higher speeds may create compatibility problems.

Compatible/Compatibility

Hardware and software that work together. A computer that is fully IBM compatible should be able to execute all programs that exist for the IBM PC.

Configuration

The collection of devices that comprise the complete computer system. In an extended sense, the word configuration may also refer to the software integration of the devices. For example, the software configuration for serial interface operation of a printer includes the preparation of software drivers that instruct the computer to use this configuration.

Controller card

A card (adapter) that connects the disk drive(s) to the computer.

Coprocessor

Name for electronic components that relieve the microprocessor of some important tasks. Increased performance can often be achieved through the use of coprocessors. For example, a math coprocessor often performs many of the math functions that can slow down the microprocessor during complicated graphic computations.

Databus

A line used to transmit data between the CPU and RAM or ROM memory.

Debugger

A utility that helps developers locate errors in a program. It may also provide suggestion for correcting errors.

Device driver

A subprogram to control communications between the computer and a peripheral.

Digital Analog Converter (DAC)

A device used to convert digital numbers to continuous analog signals.

Digitizing tablets

An input device that converts graphic and pictorial data into binary inputs.

DIP switch

Dual In-Line Package switch. A series of small switches used by computers and peripherals to configure the equipment.

Expansion slots

Slots or spaces inside the case for connecting cards to the motherboard. Most PCs contain these slots so it is easy to upgrade the system.

External hard drive

A hard drive that's located outside the PC case and connected by cables.

F

Field
An object that holds text entered by either the author or the user.

FM Synthesis
The least-expensive method for producing synthesized sound. FM synthesis uses one sine wave to control the frequency of another. Most synthesizers built into PC audio boards and sound modules use more sophisticated synthesis techniques for greater accuracy in reproducing the sounds of different instruments.

G

Graphical User Interface (GUI)
A graphics-based interface as found in Windows and on the Macintosh. This environment uses easy to understand icons and pull-down menus.

Graphics
Images created, managed and displayed using a computer. These images may be still or full-motion video.

Graphics card
Hardware device that allows the computer to display graphic images. The type of graphics card (EGA, VGA, Super VGA) determines the resolution of the images.

Graphics memory
Memory that's attached to a video graphics card that increases the display speed and the number of colors that can be displayed.

Ground
To make an electrical current connection to the earth or a conductor of equivalent effect.

H

Headphones
Allows you to listen to sound via connection to the CD-ROM drive or the sound card.

Hertz (Hz)
A unit of measure that equals a frequency of one cycle per second.

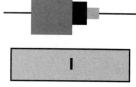

Icon

Graphical representation of a object, such as files, drives, directories, applications, etc.

Install

A process of attaching cards or other devices to the appropriate connectors or sockets.

Interactive links

Connections that let the user jump from one topic to another in a nonlinear way.

Interface

Connection between a PC, various peripherals, and the user. Allows data to be exchanged between the PC and peripherals, such as printers. If a device should be attached to the PC and a suitable interface isn't available, circuit boards, which contain an interface, can be obtained. Synonymous with port.

Interface card

A component that fits into the expansion slot of the system unit and expands the capabilities of the computer. A card can enable the computer to communicate with an external hardware device, such as a CD-ROM.

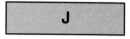

Joystick

Used to control object movements. Frequently used with games.

Joystick port

Port that accommodates the joystick. Usually part of the sound board and can be interchanged with the MIDI port.

Mathematical coprocessor

A microprocessor that increases the speed of the main processor by performing mathematical operations.

Megabyte (Meg)

1,024K; usually abbreviated simply as Meg (e.g., 20 Meg).

Megahertz (MHz)

A unit of measure that equals a frequency of 1 million cycles per second.

Memory (RAM)

Temporary storage in the computer. When the computer is switched off, the contents of this memory are lost.

MIDI

Musical Instrument Digital Interface. This is an international standard developed for digital music. The MIDI standard determines the cabling and hardware and communications protocol needed to transfer information, or music, between electronic musical instruments or recording equipment and a computer.

MPC Standard

Multimedia PC Standard. Popular standard developed to ensure that a computer system has all the necessary capabilities to run multimedia software. This standard was developed by Microsoft in cooperation with various hardware manufacturers. This standard refers specifically to PCs running under Windows with multimedia capabilities and also ensures that any separately sold hardware or software with the MPC logo will be compatible.

Multimedia

Any form of communication that uses more than one medium to present information. This also refers to a computer program that integrates text, graphics, animation and sound.

Multimedia PC

A computer that meets the MPC standard.

Multitasking

This the process of running multiple programs or tasks on the same computer at the same time. Therefore, you do not need to exit one application before starting a different applications.

The number of programs you can have open simultaneously depends on the operating system, amount of available memory, CPU speed, capacity and peripheral speed.

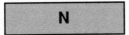

Navigation

Refers to a user's progress through a multimedia application.

NTSC

National Television Standards Committee. The TV standard used in the US. It is 525 lines of resolution transmitted at 60 half frames (interlaced) per second.

OCR software

Optical Character Recognition. Software used to interpret scanned characters as text information rather than as meaningless shapes.

Operating system

The program that enables the computer to perform basic memory and diskette management tasks, and permits the user to communicate with the computer through the keyboard. The operating system can be loaded from a diskette (MS-DOS) or can be stored permanently in the computer (e.g., the Tandy 1000 HX has MS-DOS built into a chip in the computer).

Optical storage device

A storage device that uses a laser beam to read information from the disk. A CD-ROM is an example of an optical storage device.

PAL

Phase Alternate Line. This is the standard signal output by televisions in most countries outside of North America and Japan.

Panning

Positions sounds to the left or right in a stereo sound field, creating the effect of different instruments playing in different parts of the room. You must be able to control panning in order to take advantage of the stereo capabilities of high-end synthesizers and some MPC boards.

Patch

Set of tone-generating parameters that determines one of the instrument sounds (such as flute or jazz guitar) that's produced by a synthesizer.

Pitch bend

Gradual change in a tone's frequency (highness or lowness). For example, this can be used to create effects like vibrato or to produce more natural note attacks on some instruments.

Pixels

An abbreviation of picture elements. These are the individual dots on your screen. The more pixels a computer can display, the better the resolution. The resolution defines the maximum number of dots into which a screen is divided. The picture quality improves and becomes more reliable with higher resolutions.

Ports

Found on synthesizers and PC MIDI interface cards. MIDI In and Out ports receive and transmit musical data from other MIDI devices via MIDI cables. A MIDI Through port retransmits data exactly as it is received via the MIDI In port.

Resolution

A measurement expressed in horizontal and vertical dots for printers and pixels for monitors. The larger the resolution the sharper and better the image.

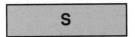

Sampling rate

This is the frequency with which samples are taken and converted in digitizing operations. This is measured in kilohertz (KHz). The MPC standard requires a sound card with a recording sampling rate of at least 11 KHz and an output rate of 11 and 22 KHz.

Scanner

A device that digitizes photographs and drawings so that they can be displayed on the computer.

SCSI interface

Small Computer System Interface. Interface that allows several hardware devices to be connected in a daisy chain configuration.

Slot

Name for a connector inside the PC where additional circuit cards can be inserted to enhance the capabilities of the computer. Lately some PCs on the market do not have these slots, and therefore cannot be enhanced easily.

Sound card

Hardware device that records and plays sound used in multimedia applications.

Speakers

Hardware used to amplify sound from the sound card or CD-ROM.

Stereo

Sound recorded on two channels.

TIFF

An acronym for Tagged Image File Format. Standard file format used to capture graphic images. These images are stored in a bitmapped format.

On hardware that supports grays scales (Macintosh II), the pixels of a TIFF image display different shades of gray. The pixels are black/white on other hardware.

Touch screen

Device that allows user to input information by touching the screen.

Transfer rate

The rate at which CD-ROM drive can transfer located information to the computer. Measured as kilobytes per second.

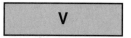

Virtual reality

Computer generated reality that can interact with all the senses. Usually a glove and goggles are used so that the user can experience three-dimensional interaction with the computer.

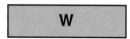

Wave file

Format used by Microsoft Windows with Multimedia Extensions for storing digitized audio on disk. These files are saved with a .WAV extension.

Waveform

The pattern of a sound wave or other electronic signal in analog form.

Appendix B

Overview of Multimedia Products

If you're looking for additional information on the products and titles we discuss in this book, please contact your favorite dealer. You can also contact the manufacturers directly at the addresses listed.

It's important to note that the world of multimedia is constantly changing. Therefore, the products and manufacturers are also changing. The names, addresses, products and information in this section is subject to change.

Animation Software

You can use animation software for not only fun but to create sophisticated presentations. Although many animation software titles are desgined strictly for the creative user, others are available which let you create powerful business presentations.

If you're looking for 3-D software, make certain to define the type of work you want to do first. Rendering levels, lighting options and texture mapping features are very important.

Other important considerations for animation purposes include timeline- and keyframe-based animation interfaces, alpha channel support and fast preview. Ask your local dealer for more support.

3D Studio
Animator / Animator Pro
Multimedia Explorer
Autodesk, Inc.
2320 Marinship Way
Sausalito, CA 94965
(800) 525-2763

Deluxe Paint Animation
Electronic Arts Inc.
1450 Fashion Island Blvd
San Mateo, CA 94404
(800) 245-4525

Animation Works Interactive
Gold Disk Inc.
5155 Spectrum Way
Mississauga, Ontario l4W 5A1
(416) 602-4000

Action!
Macromedia, Inc.
600 Townsend St.
San Francisco, CA 94103
(415) 442-0200

PowerPoint 3.0
Microsoft Corporation
1 Microsoft Way
Redmond, WA 98052

Movie
LANTERN Corporation
63 Ridgemoor Drive
Clayton, MO 63105
(314) 725-6125

PC Animate Plus
Presidio Software Inc.
2215 Chestnut Street
San Francisco, CA 94123
(415) 474-6437

Authoring Systems

If you want to create multimedia presentations or programs, you must muse an authoring systems.

A good authoring system should be able to integrate text, still graphics, animation, and video. Also, sound is very important. An authoring system should be able to use MIDI or CD-Audio and digitized sound.

Other considerations include support for interactivity, ability to generate run-time files and the ability to add new features or extensions.

Authoring systems are now used in kiosks, sales and software presentations and other animated entertainment.

IconAuthor for Windows
AimTech Corporation
20 Trafalgar Square
Nashua, NH 03063
(603) 883-0220

Animator
Animator Pro
Multimedia Explorer
Autodesk, Inc.
2320 Marinship Way
Sausalito, CA 94965
(800) 525-2763

MediaBlitz
Mulitmedia Make Your Point
Toolbook
Asymetrix Corporation
110 110th Avenue NE Suite 717
Bellevue, WA 98004
(206) 462-0501

Authorware Professional
Authorware, Inc.
275 Shoreline Dr. Suite 535
Redwood City, CA 94065
(800) 288-4797

Hyperties
Cognetics Corporation
55 Princeton Heightstown Rd
Princeton Junction, NJ 08550
(609) 799-5005

HSC InterActive
HSC Software
1661 Lincoln Blvd
Suite 101
Santa Monica, CA 90404
(310) 392-8441

Multimedia Development Kit
Microsoft Corporation
1 Microsoft Way
Redmond, WA 98052
(800) 227-4679

Passport Producer
Passport Designs, Inc.
100 Stone Pine Road
Half Moon Bay, CA 94019
(415) 726-0280

Q/Media for Windows
Q/Media Software Corporation
312 East 5th Avenue
Vancouver, B.C. V5T 1H4
(604) 879-1190/(800) 444-9356

AuthorWare Professional
Macromedia Inc.
600 Townsend Street
San Francisco, CA 94103
(415) 442-0200

Image Editors

Image editors are used to imitate a darkroom. You can choose from many image editors to scale images, change resolutions or add special effects (colors, designs or patterns). Image editors can also be used to crop, sharpen or blur images.

PhotoFinish
Publisher's Paintbrush
ZSoft Corporation
450 Franklin Rd
Suite 100
Marietta, GA 30067
(404) 428-0028

Halo Desktop Imager
Media Cybernetics
5201 Great America Pkwy Suite 3102
Santa Clara, CA 95054
(408) 562-6076

PixoFoto 1.1
PixoArts Corp.
4600 Bohannon Drive Suite 220
Menlo Park, CA 94025
(415) 323-6592

WinRix
Rix SoftWorks, Inc.
18552 MacArthur Blvd Suite 200
Irvine, CA 92715
(213) 685-5141

PhotoStyler
Aldus Corporation
411 First Ave. S.
Suite 200
Seattle, WA 98104
(206) 622-5500

Picture Publisher
Micrografx, Inc.
1303 E. Arapaho Road
Richardson, TX 75081
(800) 733-3729

MIDI Sequencers

These programs let you modify or create music in the MIDI format. They record and store music sequences from a MIDI device (instrument or sampler). A MIDI sequencer should offer the basic editing functions: Cut, copy, paste, merge, insert, transposition, inversion, retrograde, and tempo changes.

Ask your dealer for additional features.

MusicCad
Alla Breve Music Software, Inc.
1105 Chicago Ave Suite 111
Oak Park, IL 60302
(708) 524-9441

Cadenza
Big Noise Software, Inc.
PO Box 23740
Jacksonville, FL 32241
(904) 730-0754

Ballade
Dynaware USA, Inc.
950 Tower Lane Suite 1150
Foster City, CA 94404
(415) 349-5700

Audio Trax
Pro-4 Version 4.6 / Pro-5
Trax-Windows
Passport Designs, Inc.
100 Stone Pine Road
Half Moon Bay, CA 94019
(415) 726-0280

Cakewalk 4.0
Cakewalk Pro
Twelve Tone Systems
44 Pleasant Street
Watertown, MA 02172
(617) 926-2480

Midisoft Studio
Midisoft Corporation
15513 N.E. 52nd. St.
Redmond, WA 98502
(206) 881-7176

Prism
Dr. T's Music Software Inc.
100 Crescent Road
Needham, MA 02194
(617) 455-1454

Sequencer Plus
Voyetra Technologies
333 Fifth Avenue
Pelham, NY 10803
(800) 233-9377

MPC Upgrade Kits

The least expensive method of upgrading your present system may be to purchase a multimedia upgrade kit. Since the upgrade kits may vary in contents, features and price, make certain you know what you need before shopping. At the very least, purchase an upgrade kit which has a CD-ROM drive and a sound card. Other upgrade kits may also include software, speakers, microphone and other equipment you may not need.

One important consideration is to make certain that the MPC upgrade kit is compatible with your components and peripherals.

MKB-01 or MKA-01
Media Resources
640 Peunte St
Brea, CA 92621
(714) 256-5048

MPC Upgrade Kit Plus
Pro16 Multimedia System
Media Vision, Inc.
3185 Laurelview Court
Fremont, CA 94538
(510) 770-8600

Multimedia CD Station
Procom, Technology
2181 Dupont Ave.
Irvrine, CA 92715
(800) 800-8600

MultiSound MPC Upgrade Kit
Turtle Beach Systems, Inc.
Cyber Center, Unit 33
1600 Pennsylvania Ave.
York, PA 17404

Sound Blaster Multimedia Upgrade Kit
Creative Labs, Inc.
1901 McCarthy Blvd.
Milpitas, CA 94035
(408) 428-6600

Tandy MPC Upgrade Kit
Tandy Corporation
700 One Tandy Center
Fort Worth, TX 76102
(817) 878-4969

PC Sound Cards

The sound card is one of the most important components in an MPC system. A good PC sound card should be able to generate and play back MIDI arrangements (synthesizers). Most sound cards also feature a MIDI interface with one input and one output port.

An important consideration when purchasing sound cards is the sampling rate. This is the frequency with which samples are taken and converted in digitizing operations. The MPC standard requires a sound card with a recording sampling rate of at least 11 KHz and an output rate of 11 and 22 KHz.

Although 8-bit sound boards meet the MPC standard, you should consider a 16-bit board. The improvement in sound quality is usually worth the additional cost.

Stereo F/X
ATI Technologies
3761 Victoria Park Avenue
Scarborough, Ontario, M1W 3S2
(416) 756-0718

Sound Blaster
Sound Blaster 16
Sound Blaster Pro
Creative Labs, Inc.
1901 McCarthy Blvd.
Milpitas, CA 94035
(408) 428-6600

AdLib Gold
AdLib, Inc.
50 Stanford St.
Suite 800
Boston, MA 02114
(800) 463-2686

Audio Master
Omni Labs
13177 Ramona Blvd Suite F
Irwindale, CA 91706
(800) 736-8439

AudioCanvas
ProMedia Technologies
1540 Market Street Suite 425
San Francisco, CA 94102
(415) 621-1399

Audioport
Pro AudioSpectrum 16
Pro AudioSpectrum Plus
Media Vision, Inc.
3185 Laurelview Court
Fremont, CA 94538
(510) 770-8600

Sound Editors

One disadvantage of working with MIDI files is that they are difficult to edit. Therefore, many users prefer using sound editors to edit digital audio instead of MIDI files.

The features in sound editors let you record, edit, rearrange, mix, process and play back sound files in several formats.

More powerful sound editors have the ability of crossfading, removing or boosting specific frequencies, time compression and expansion and pitch shifting.

Alchemy
Passport Designs, Inc.
100 Stone Pine Road
Half Moon Bay, CA 94019
(415) 726-0280

AudioView
Voyetra Technologies
333 Fifth Avenue
Pelham, NY 10803
(800) 233-9377

Wave for Windows
Sample Vision
Turtle Beach Systems, Inc.
Cyber Center, Unit 33
1600 Pennsylvania Ave.
York, PA 17404
(717) 843-6916

Video Editing Systems

Although you don't yet have the editing power of a Hollywood studio, today's video editing systems are becoming quite powerful.

Lower-end systems mainly provide control and status information. More advance systems have digital editing features. This lets you store video on a hard drive and then quickly clip, log or edit the video.

Video Machine
Fast Electronics U.S., Inc.
5 Commonwealth Road
Natick, MA 01760
(508) 655-3278

Personal Producer
Matrox Electronic Systems Ltd.
1055 St. Regis Blvd.
Dorval, Quebec H9P 2T4
(514) 685-2630

Amilink/Windows
RGB Computer and Video Inc.
4152 Blue Heron Blvd. W.
Suite 118
Riviera Beach, FL 33404
(407) 844-3348

D/Vision-Pro
Touchvision Systems Inc.
1800 West Winnemac
Chicago, IL 60640
(312) 989-2160

Virtual Reality

DataGlove
VPL Research Inc.
656 Bair Island Rd. Suite 304
Redwood City, CA 94063

WorldToolKit
Sense8 Corporation
4000 Bridgeway
Suite 101
Sauasalito, CA 94965

CD-ROM Magazines

Nautilus
Metatic Corporation
7001 Discovery Blvd.
Dublin, OH 43017
(614) 761-2000

Appendix C

CD-ROM Demos, Samplers and Programs

Demos and Samplers

The following demonstration programs are included on the companion CD-ROM. Since these programs demonstrate the basic features of the products, they aren't fully operational. If you would like to purchase these programs or need more information, contact your dealer or the manufacturer listed.

HSC Interactive

This is an authoring program. Although the demo displays the features of the program, you cannot save files.

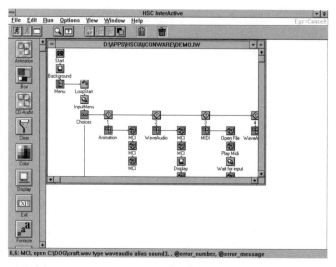

For more information: **HSC Software 1661**
Lincoln Boulevard Suite 101
Santa Monica, CA 90404   **(310) 392-8441**

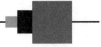

Master Tracks Pro 4 for Windows

This program lets you record, edit, and play musical compositions on your PC and MIDI instruments. It contains a clear, easy-to-use graphical user interface. This interface provides several views of a musical piece, allowing you to visualize and accurately control your music. You can easily synchronize music to film, video, multimedia presentations, or multitrack audio tape.

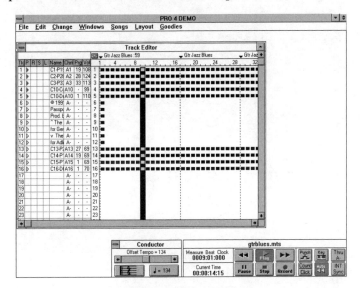

For more information: **Passport Designs, Incorporated**
                               100 Stone Pine Road
                               Half Moon Bay, CA 94019   (415) 726-0280

Slide Show/Sequencer Plus Gold

Slide Show is a VGA multimedia slide show containing information on Voyetra PC sound products for DOS and Windows. The Sequencer Plus Gold demo program is a full-featured working version of the program except you cannot save files.

With this program, you can record, edit, and arrange songs piece-by-piece. You can also play back the song by transmitting the MIDI data to external synthesizers connected to the PC's MIDI port or to the built-in FM Synthesizer on most PC sound cards.

For more information: **Voyetra Technologies**
                               333 Fifth Avenue
                               Pelham, NY 10803   (914) 738-4500

OZ-WIN

This is a video editing program for Windows 3.1. It's used to perform professional-level video editing on the PC. This program must be used with 100% V-LAN compatible hardware for editing and animation control and the ability to display video from source or record decks on the PC.

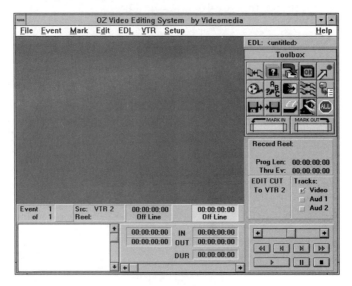

For more information: Videomedia
                               175 Lewis Road
                               Pelham, NY 10803   (408) 227-9977

Q/Media for Windows

Q/Media for Windows by Quorum Computer Corporation is a complete authoring system which lets you create multimedia shows with video, animation, graphics, and audio. The uses for Q/Media are limited only by your imagination. Q/Media imports presentations from Windows presentation packages like Microsoft PowerPoint, Aldus Persuasion, Harvard Graphics for Windows, and Lotus Freelance for Windows.

For more information: Q/Media Software Corporation
                         312 East 5th Avenue
                         Vancouver, B.C. V5T 1H4(604) 879-1190/(800) 444-9356

Wave For Windows

This program edits wave audio on the hard disk of any MPC compatible computer. You can record, edit, and play back digital sound with this program.

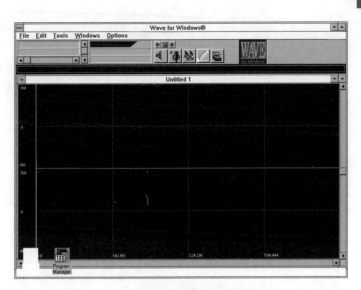

For more information: Turtle Beach Systems
                                     P.O. Box 5074
                                     York, PA 17405   (717) 843-6916

The Companion CD-ROM

The Multimedia Mania companion CD-ROM contains hundreds of megabytes of
data. This data includes DOS programs, Microsoft Windows applications, and tools
for processing graphics and sounds.

CDSTART.EXE

The CDSTART.EXE program in the root directory of the companion CD-ROM is a
Windows application written in Microsoft Visual Basic. CDSTART.EXE lets you
access many of the files on the companion CD-ROM.

NOTE

If CDSTART.EXE cannot read or open a file, it will display a dialog box (and, in
some cases, play a message in WAV file format over your sound card). If this
happens, just exit the CDSTART.EXE application, and run the application you need
to view the file. For example, use the Media Player to play back MIDI and Wave
files; or use Paintbrush to view most BMP and PCX files.

Running CDSTART.EXE

Run Microsoft Windows. Select **File/Run...** from the Program Manager. When the
"Run" dialog box appears, enter the drive letter for your CD-ROM drive and the
name CDSTART.EXE. In the following illustration, we entered drive G:

Click [OK]. The following window appears:

This window has a menu bar with four menu titles (**File**, **Bonus**, **Sampler**, and **Abacus**), and six icons which you can click to access sound files, samples, video files, animations, graphics, and shareware.

Let's look at the menus first, then the icons.

The **File** menu items access the same information as the buttons (**Sound...**, **Samples...**, **Video...**, **Animation...**, **Graphics...**, and **Shareware...**). The **File** menu also provides the traditional **Exit** item for exiting the CDSTART.EXE application.

The **Bonus** menu's **CD-ROM Catalog...** item opens a MultiMedia ToolBook application describing hundreds of available CD-ROMs.

The **Sampler** menu accesses the demo and sampler programs described earlier in this Appendix.

The **Abacus** menu contains a single item (**About Abacus**), which displays a dialog box describing how you can contact Abacus.

Icons

The six icons let you access or install components found on the Multimedia Mania companion CD-ROM.

The "Sound" icon lets you install a PC speaker driver (install this driver only if you have no sound card), view directories of MIDI and WAV files which you can play back using Media Player, and run an Excel worksheet containing sound notes (run this only if you have Microsoft Excel).

The "Sample Files" icon lets you run a stand-alone Authorware Star application, run an Excel worksheet acting as a slide show (run this only if you have Microsoft Excel), view a series of Multimedia ToolBook application files, run a PictureBook application or a Visual Basic application, play a demo round of Dr. T's Composer Quest or Moraff's World.

The "Video" icon lets you view the available Multimedia ToolBook applications for video animation. Some of these applications will only run if you have Screen Machine installed on your system—VIDEOPUR.TBK will run without Screen Machine.

The "Animation" icon opens a dialog box from which you can view animation files created using Autodesk Animator, Autodesk 3D Studio and Multimedia ToolBook.

The "Graphics" icon lets you access Kodak Photo CD samples (warning—each of these two samples is 18 Meg in length), photos by European photographer Von Buelow, and some fine art rendered in BMP format.

The "Shareware" icon lets you access DOS and Windows tools for sound, graphics and general maintenance.

The Companion CD-ROM In Brief

Here's a general listing of the contents of the companion CD-ROM. You'll find DIR.TXT and README.TXT files in most of the subdirectories, which provide brief descriptions of the contents of each directory.

The root directory contains the CDSTART.EXE application run from Microsoft Windows, and two companion files which CDSTART.EXE needs to run (THREED.VBX and VBRUN200.DLL).

Note: Any changes which were made to the CD-ROM are explained in the README.TXT file.

You can use the CDSTART.EXE application from within Windows to view most files, and run some of them. However, not all files are executable. Some files may require installation on your system. If this is the case, follow the instructions displayed on the screen.

The companion CD-ROM contains the following directories. We've included general descriptions of each directory's contents:

```
.SHAREWR  Shareware collection
.....WIN  Windows shareware
.........GFXTOOLS: Graphics tools, including animations, screen savers,
.........AUDIO     Windows audio applications, including CD audio
                   players, WAV file tools, percussion synthesizers and
                   a MIDI sequencer
.........UTIL:     Windows utilities, including file archiver
                   interfaces, VGA drivers, batch macro language, check
                   printers, text editor, font editors, file deleters
                   and CRT tools
.........FUN:      Windows game - FACEMAKER
.....DOS: DOS programs
.........AUDIO:    DOS audio tools, including a talking clock, FM music
                   player, MOD file players, Sputter sound players,
                   MIDI software and VOC editing software
.........GFXTOOLS: DOS graphics tools, including the IMPROCES image
                   processor, virtual reality, kaleidoscopes and more
.........UTIL: DOS based utilities, featuring two screen savers
.........FUN:      Moraff's World demo version
.....COMP: Compression utilities, for ARJ, LHA and PKZIP compression,
           as well as a compression manager
.LEARNER: Tutorials and other learning programs
.....ASW: Authorware Star examples
.....VIEWER: Examples using Microsoft viewer
.........MUS_DICT: Music dictionary example using Viewer
.WINDOWS: Windows apps
.....ICONVERT: Screen Machine SM Camera
.....SPEAKER: PC speaker driver for sound
.....ANIMATE:Autodesk Animator examples
.....TOOLBOOK: Multimedia Toolbook runtime version
.DEMOS: Demo software
.....TOOLBOOK:Multimedia ToolBook MM tools
.........MULTIMED
.........MUSIC: Multimedia ToolBook music catalog
.....CQUEST: Dr. T's Composer Quest demo
.ANIMATE: Animations
.....3DS: Autodesk 3D Studio
```

```
.....PLAYER -Autodesk Animator Player
.....PARROT - SB Talking Parrot conversion files
.....TOOLBOOK - Video animations with ToolBook
.....ANIWIN  Windows and Autodesk Animations
.....MERLIN - Animated wizard
.....ANI  Autodesk Animator files of a business logo
.EXCEL -Excel application data
.....SLIDES
.....SNDNOTES - Excel database with embedded sound notes
.PRESENT - Presentation
.....PICTURE - European PictureBook Professional demo
.....ASW - Authorware Star examples
.....MMPLAY DOS Multimedia Player
.....TSHOW  MM demo using Tempra Show
.....EXCEL - Excel slide show demo
.MIDI: MIDI files and WAV implementations
.....MAPPER
.KODAK  Photo CD photographs
.....PICTURES: Miscellaneous graphics
.SND_REC: Sound examples
.BUELOW: Graphics of photographs
.CDROMDIR: Multimedia ToolBook example of a CD-ROM catalog
.PROGDEV: Multimedia programming using Visual Basic
.SAMPLER:CONTAINS DEMOS FROM ARIS; HARVARD SYSTEMS; VOYETRA; and MORE
.....ARIS: BEST OF MEDIACLIPS
.....R_SOFT: READYSOFT DEMOS (Space Ace, etc.)
.....WAVE: Wave for Windows demo edition
.....M_TRACKS: Demo version of Master Tracks Pro sequencer
.....VOYETRA:  Voyetra sound & visual demo
.....QMEDIA:   Demo version of Q/Media for Windows
.....HSC       HSC Interactive authoring system
.....PGC:      Pacific Gold Coast's WINspiration media player
.....BOB:      Best of the Bureau - text at a glance
.....OZ  OZ Video system
.EMM  Animation and sound demo from EMM Studios, Basel Switzerland
```

Multimedia Mania

Index

F

G

H

I

Abacus pc catalog

Order Toll Free 1-800-451-4319

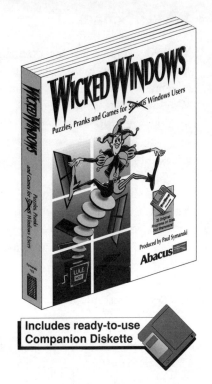

Wicked Sounds

Wicked Sounds and its companion diskette let Windows users take full advantage of the sound capabilities of Windows. The companion diskette includes over 40 great sound effects including traffic noise, sounds from the animal kingdom and musical excerpts.

Wicked Sounds includes a sound database to keep track of all sound files so users can find a sound quickly and easily by specifying its name, comment or the date.

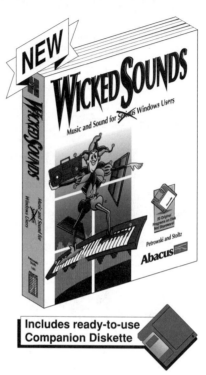

Includes ready-to-use Companion Diskette

Wicked Sounds includes:

- Over 40 new sounds in WAV format
- New Event Manager manages 12 different events
- Sound database with diverse sound functions
- Integrate comments in wave files
- Play back several sounds in any sequence

Wicked Sounds ISBN 1-55755-168-5. Item: #B168. Suggested retail price $29.95 with companion disk. $39.95 Canadian. System requirements: IBM PC or 100% compatible 286, 386 or 486; hard drive; Windows 3.1 and above. Sound card with digital sound channel highly recommended (Windows compatible).

Q·MEDIA

Yes, RUSH ME

Q/Media for Windows

AT THE SPECIAL OFFER PRICE OF $79.00*

Q/Media for Windows puts the power of multimedia tools at your finger-tips. It's so easy to use, **you'll never make an ordinary presentation again!** In no time at all you'll **drag and drop** video, animation, audio or graphic files onto your screen. You'll add slides from Microsoft Powerpoint™, Harvard Graphics™, Lotus Freelance™, CorelDraw™ or other Windows applications. Q/Media for Windows makes it **WYSIWYG-easy.** And you can do it all without special training and without expensive hardware. Over 10MB of clip media is included.

Call To Order
800-444-9356
or
Fax or Mail Today!

Please ship me Q/Media for Windows immediately at the special offer price of **$79.00** (plus $12.00 for shipping and handling).

Name:_____

Organization:_____

Address:_____

City: _____ Telephone: _____

State: _____ Zip: _____

_____ I enclose my check for $79.00 ,plus $12.00 shipping and handling

_____ Bill my VISA Card

_____ Bill my Mastercard

_____ Bill my American Express

Card # _____

Expiry Date: _____

Card Holder Name _____

FAX TODAY (604) 879-0214
or
Mail To:
Q/Media Software Corporation
312 East 5th Avenue
Vancouver, B.C.   V5T 1H4
Phone: (604) 879-1190

* Limit one per customer. Special Offer may be discontinued without notice.

NOW'S YOUR CHANCE TO PURCHASE THE QUEST MULTIMEDIA AUTHORING SYSTEM AT A SPECIAL PRICE

• Since its release in 1985, the Quest Multimedia Authoring System has become one of the premier authoring systems on the market today. Thousands of users in government, education, industry, and the military have discovered how Quest can help them meet their training needs.

• Now, Allen Communication is offering the Quest Multimedia Authoring System at **10% off** its regular price. That's a discount of almost $400.

• Allen Communication also offers a working model package for only **$45.00** that will allow you to quickly become familiar with Quest. This package includes documentation to guide you through the production of a short multimedia course, and allows you to create your own course of up to 25 frames.

QUEST MULTIMEDIA AUTHORING SYSTEM ORDER FORM

Ship to: _____

Company Name: _____

Street Address: _____

City: _____ State: _____ Zip: _____

Daytime Phone: _____